❖

The Virtues
Contemporary Essays on Moral Character

ROBERT B. KRUSCHWITZ
Georgetown College

ROBERT C. ROBERTS
Wheaton College

Wadsworth Publishing Company
Belmont, California
A Division of Wadsworth, Inc.

Philosophy Editor: Kenneth King
Editorial Associate: Debbie Fox
Production Editor: Lisa Danchi
Print Buyer: Barbara Britton
Designer: Andrew H. Ogus
Copy Editor: Jonas Weisel
Cover: Andrew H. Ogus

Printed in the United States of America   49

1 2 3 4 5 6 7 8 9 10—91 90 89 88 87

ISBN 0-534-06720-4

Library of Congress Cataloging-in-Publication Data

The Virtues : contemporary essays on moral character.

Bibliography: p.
1. Virtues.   I. Kruschwitz, Robert B.   II. Roberts, Robert Campbell, 1942–
BJ1521.V58   1986   179'.9   86-11137
ISBN 0-534-06720-4

For our parents,
Verlin and Ruth Kruschwitz
and Verne and Betty Roberts

❖
Contents

CONTENTS

Preface

In compiling this book, our purpose has been twofold. The book is an anthology for use as a virtues supplement in an otherwise standard introductory ethics course populated by bright students. To this end, we have applied a criterion of readability in our selection of the essays. We eliminated a number of excellent pieces because they required reading skills beyond those of smart undergraduates. Even after sifting for readability, however, we realized that some of the essays are challenging, so we have provided a summary/ introduction to each essay to guide the student through the dialectic.

We have also sought to create a handbook of the recent philosophical work on the virtues; thus we have selected from the best recent essays in the field. Moreover, we have included a bibliography more extensive than one would ordinarily expect in an under-graduate textbook. Indeed this is the most complete and up-to-date bibliography now available. These features make the book a resource for a concentrated upper-division seminar in the virtues.

We thank Ken King, of Wadsworth Publishing Company, along with the reviewers of the manuscript, Dennis Rohatyn of University of San Diego and Joseph R. Des Jardins of Villanova University, for suggestions that substantially shaped the book. Thanks go also to Wheaton College for a summer grant that facilitated the last stages of the editing process. And for their forbearance and many other virtues, we thank our wives, Vicki and Elizabeth.

Robert B. Kruschwitz
Robert C. Roberts

Introduction

In the past fifteen years an ever-increasing number of Anglo-American philosophers of ethics have started afresh by taking a very old approach. Faced with the seeming dead ends of debating the classic modern positions on "normative ethics,"[1] and the aridity of "metaethics,"[2] they have turned back to something like the approach of Aristotle and Plato and Saint Thomas Aquinas – to a study of the virtues and vices. Increasingly, professional philosophy journals publish articles with titles like "Talents, Abilities, and Virtues," "Traits of Character: A Conceptual Analysis," "Freedom and Virtue," "Character, Virtue, and Freedom," "Integrity," "Forgiveness," "Prudence," "Generosity," "Wisdom," "Moral Sensitivity," "On Sympathy," and so forth. (See the bibliography at the end of this volume.) In other words, a number of moral philosophers are turning decidedly "psychological" or "anthropological" in their ethical theorizing. They are asking less about the nature and foundations of moral *rules* and *language*, and more about the nature and traits of the moral *person*.

To be sure, moral philosophers are still asking questions like What reason can anybody have for *being* moral, rather than just giving the *appearance* of being moral when that serves one's purposes?, What rationale is there for adopting this or that set of ethical standards?, and How do we avoid the conclusion that ethical standards are just a matter of cultural conditioning or individual opinion? But more and more, these questions are approached by looking at what the *traits* amount to – virtues like autonomy, truthfulness, compassion, courage, justice, generosity; or, alternatively, vices like heteronomy, indifference toward suffering, cowardice, injustice, and stinginess. When we see what some trait or traits amount to in an individual life – how that life is shaped at some fairly deep level by virtues or vices, and how these correspond to or fail to correspond to their bearer's human nature – then we may have a way of answering the preceding questions.

Another line of inquiry is the investigation of a range of concepts that are not themselves virtue or vice concepts but that are necessary background for any psychology of the moral life. Such concepts include pleasure, emotion, intention, choosing, wanting, will power, attention, rule-following, imagination, and taking-as-a-paradigm. An understanding of these phenomena is necessary to answer the questions, What kind of trait is a virtue (or a vice)? and What are the processes by which virtues and vices are acquired?

Until recently, oddly, Anglo-American philosophers of ethics typically tried to adopt a posture of neutrality with regard to moral issues. They thought they could (and should!) discuss ethics without revealing whether they thought ethics was a good thing – whether, for example, anybody "ought" to be just, compassionate, and truthful rather than unjust, cruel, and mendacious. W. D. Hudson spoke for the tradition when he began a book of ethics with these words: "This book is not about what people ought to do. It is about what they are doing when they *talk* about what they ought to do. Moral philosophy, as I understand it, must not be confused with moralizing. A moralist is someone who . . .

engages in reflection, argument, or discussion about what is morally right or wrong, good or evil. . . . [A] moral philosopher . . . thinks and speaks about the ways in which moral terms, like 'right' or 'good,' are used by moralists when they are delivering their moral judgments."[3]

Returning to the classical concerns about the nature of the good life and of human fulfillment in both its individual and social dimensions, the contributors to the present volume tend not to believe in any clean break between philosophical thinking about ethics and "moralizing" — if moralizing is taken to mean thinking about how human beings ought to live their lives. The two seminal philosophers in the contemporary discussion of the virtues, Elizabeth Anscombe and Alasdair MacIntyre, are both quite self-aware of being, *in their role as philosophers*, moral reformers. The bulk of this introduction will be an exposition of their central contributions.

Elizabeth Anscombe's "Modern Moral Philosophy"

The recent turn to the virtues by mainline British and American philosophers was marked historically by the appearance, in 1958, of Elizabeth Anscombe's provocative and wide-ranging essay "Modern Moral Philosophy."[4] According to Anscombe, the terms 'morally right,' 'morally wrong,' and 'moral obligation,' as used by modern philosophers, lack content in two ways. First, they do not rule out any particular actions. As modern philosophers use the term 'morally wrong,' even a court's knowingly condemning an innocent person need not be morally wrong: Where condemning an innocent person to death would, say, prevent a civil war, it might be the right thing to do. In modern philosophical usage, to call an action "morally wrong" always leaves open the possibility that in other circumstances the same action might *not* be morally wrong; and this suggests to Anscombe that the expression 'morally wrong' lacks content.

Second, the notions of right, wrong, and obligation are *legal* notions, thus implying the existence of some legal authority. Modern moral philosophers have wanted to speak of moral obligations and duties without tying these to any plausible notion of the *giver* of the law. But if you have an obligation, notes Anscombe, it must surely be with respect to some obliging *authority*, a person or group of persons who lays down the law and is justified by position, power, or nature in thus laying it down.

The natural and traditional way of grounding the moral law is by taking God to be its giver. He is the agent who creates obligations by His acts of legislation. But modern philosophers are disinclined to allow God this role. Even when they admit that God exists and gives laws, they tend to think that being *moral* requires that a person "have a judgment that he ought (morally ought) to obey the divine law."[5] Thus, while God perhaps tells us what we ought to do (just as a parent may tell us this), it is not His saying so that makes it obligatory; it is obligatory because and only because it is *moral*. So God Himself must be "obedient" to the moral law, and unless He is, you are under no moral obligation to take Him seriously. And here one has to say "moral" in a certain tone of voice and with a certain look in one's eye and a certain feeling in one's heart. But, according to Anscombe, the look in one's eye and the feeling in one's heart don't succeed in covering up the incoherency of the concept of a legislation without any legislator.

Modern philosophers have tried to find a source of moral legislation in society, conscience, nature, or some sort of contract, says Anscombe. But each of these theories has problems that render it unconvincing.[6] If we do not believe in God, there is only one way to have ethical "norms": "It might remain to look for 'norms' in human virtues: just as *man* has so many teeth, which is certainly not the average number of teeth men have, but is the number of teeth for the species, so perhaps the species *man*, regarded not just biologically, but from the point of view of the activity of thought and choice in regard to the various departments of life — powers and faculties and use of things needed — 'has' such-and-such virtues: and this 'man' with the complete set of virtues is the 'norm,' as 'man' with, e.g., a complete set of teeth is a norm."[7]

Anscombe goes on, however, to say that this way of securing "norms" for ethics does not quite secure "law" in the sought-for sense. The "obligation" expressed in such sentences as "a man ought to be at peace with himself" or "a human is fully functioning only if she is courageous," is not the same as that expressed when we say, "it is a person's duty to keep his promises." So, although the virtues approach provides a substitute rationale for moral norms, it does not justify us in speaking of moral obligations. Unless we take God to be the authority, we ought to give up talk about moral obligations, and just talk, as Aristotle does, about the virtues—about, that is, the kinds of actions characteristic of a fully developed specimen of humanity.

Presumably there is nothing impossible about an ethical view in which God is postulated as the authority behind the moral law *and* action- and character-norms are buttressed with Aristotelian-like insights into what is "normal" or "natural" for a human being.[8] The norms that God legislates are presumably consistent, on the whole, with the "demands" that can be read off human nature, even though the latter may be supplemented by the former and it will be in principle God's prerogative to override human wisdom on occasion. Indeed, the form that virtue ethics has taken during most of its history is theological: Since the nature that is to be realized is conceived of as the condition that God intended, it is possible to adjust one's understanding of human nature by considering what God has commanded human beings to do and be. But at the same time it is possible to let philosophical analysis of human nature set parameters for the interpretation of scriptural materials about ethics and the good life. If a virtue-based ethics is compatible with a concept of divine law, it would seem to follow from Anscombe's view that a person drawing on both of these resources would be in a better initial position than anybody else to give a full account of ethics.

What would philosophical ethics consist of if we took Anscombe's advice? Basically it would be a kind of normative psychology, whose purpose would be to determine what it is to be a human being, in the sense of a fully developed or "flourishing" one. The virtues would be the various forms of this well-being or flourishing that the philosophical inquiry would bring to light, and the theory would function by "locating" these virtues in the resulting larger depiction of human life.

The argument behind this psychological inquiry would run something like this:

Since justice is a virtue, and injustice a vice, and virtues and vices are built up by the performances of the action in which they are instanced, an act of injustice will tend to make a man bad; and essentially the flourishing of a man *qua* man consists in his being good (e.g., in virtues); but for any X to which such terms apply, X needs what makes it flourish, so a man needs, or ought to perform, only virtuous actions; and even if, as it must be admitted may happen, he flourishes less, or not at all, in inessentials, by avoiding injustice, his life is spoiled in essentials by not avoiding injustice—so he still needs to perform only just actions.[9]

The fundamental concept here is that of human flourishing. The virtues are aspects of a fully human life, and are fostered by certain actions; therefore, these actions are *normative* for human beings—not in the sense of demanded or commanded, but in the sense of prescribed, on condition that one wants to flourish rather than live a spoiled life. (And, of course, anybody who thinks he or she doesn't want to flourish is just confused.)

But how do we know what human flourishing consists in? For matters beyond the trivial such as the "normal" number of teeth, the "normal" blood pressure and temperature, and, moving farther out, the "need" for some kind of positive self-regard, this question can be answered only by a philosophical-psychological investigation of what it is to be human. Anscombe recommends that we start way back, far prior to ethics, and then work ourselves up to a philosophical psychology that includes analysis of virtue concepts: "But meanwhile—is it not clear that there are several concepts that need investigating simply as part of the philosophy of psychology and,—as I should recommend—*banishing ethics totally* from our minds? Namely, to begin with: 'action,' 'intention,' 'pleasure,' 'wanting.' More will probably turn up if we start with these. Eventually it might be possible to advance to considering the concept 'virtue'; with which, I suppose, we should be beginning some sort of a study of ethics."[10] Concerning this enterprise, Anscombe goes on a little later in the essay: "It can be seen that philosophically there is a huge gap, at present unfillable as far as we are concerned, which needs to be filled by an account of human nature, human action, the type of characteristic a virtue is, and above all of human 'flourishing.' And it is the last concept that appears the most doubtful."[11]

Anscombe's well-known book *Intention*,[12] as well as her numerous essays on philosophical psychology, can be seen as contributions to this project. But other thinkers in increasing numbers have taken up the challenge to provide "an adequate philosophy of psychology, in which we are conspicuously lacking."[13] Most of the essays in the present collection are examples of the continuing effort to meet this challenge.

Alasdair MacIntyre's *After Virtue*

Our Predicament According to MacIntyre

Twenty-three years after Anscombe's essay, Alasdair MacIntyre published *After Virtue*,[14] the other focal point in the contemporary renascence of interest in the virtues. We will spend a large portion of the rest of this introduction expounding MacIntyre's argument, in part because of its intrinsic importance and pivotal character, and in part because, as an historical argument, it will take us through a lot of territory that ought to be touched upon in an introduction like the present one. MacIntyre's book is, however, exceedingly rich and subtle, and no short summary can do it justice.

MacIntyre's point of departure, like Anscombe's, is the bankruptcy of modern moral philosophy, and indeed of the moral consciousness of most of recent Western civilization (which is dominated by what he often refers to as "modern liberal individualism"). In our world, moral debate about central issues tends to go on endlessly, neither side winning by rational argument. Some say that justice is served by forcing richer people, through taxation, to share their wealth with poorer ones, because everyone has a right to basic necessities of life. Others argue this is not just, because it unduly restricts the freedom of the wealthy (and of the poor, to the extent that they may become wealthy) to do as they please with the fruits of their labor, ingenuity, or good fortune. Some say abortion at an early stage of pregnancy is every woman's right, since every person has a right to determine what happens in his or her own body, and an embryo at that stage is a part of its mother's body. Others say that such abortions are almost always wrong, because an embryo, even at that stage, is an innocent, identifiable human individual, and knowingly to kill such an individual is immoral. Valid arguments can be constructed for each of the preceding four positions; the disagreement comes from the different *premises*, or starting points, of the arguments. (Philosophers, just like ordinary people, divide up into such camps as these; the chief difference is that the philosophers' arguments are more careful and detailed.)

Why can't people agree on their moral starting points? The reason, MacIntyre argues, is that we do not belong to any consistent, shared moral tradition. Instead we are the inheritors of fragments, often mutually inconsistent, of moral traditions and philosophies.

For the most part we are unaware of where these parts of traditions came from and indeed of the fact that they are leftover fragments, isolated from the whole systems of moral thought and life to which they originally belonged. Rather we vaguely believe there is something called "morality," a single body of concepts on which all decent people draw when they make moral decisions. And so we are frustrated that we can't terminate our moral debates rationally. Thus our moral mind-set comes to have two sides—one coming from our recognition that our contemporary moral debates are fundamentally unsettle-able, the other from the residue of the moral traditions from which we have inherited our fragments, in which moral debates *were* settleable.

On the one side, because there is no way of securing rational agreement in moral debate, we tend to think morality is not a rational affair at all. We see it as a matter of commitments, feeling, individual interpretation, and individual choice. If you can't *rationally* decide whether to make the right to necessities more basic than the right to free disposal of property, then you just "hunker down" over one side or the other, just make a "decision of principle" or consult your feelings. And you realize that the arguments you use in moral debate are ultimately just *rhetoric*. Their purpose is not to find or express truth or enlighten your opponent, but to give expression to your feelings and manipulate your opponent into seeing things your way, like the ads for soft drinks or an arms manufacturer lobbying for a government contract.

Related to the loss of rationality in ethics is the loss of the moral self. MacIntyre sketches contemporary "characters"—that is, personality types that function for us as moral paradigms: the Bureaucratic Manager, the Rich Playperson, and the Therapist. These "characters" have in common that they are all manipulators of other persons, and tend to seek goods external to practices. (Money is a good external to the practice of medicine, while the well-being of one's patients is a good internal to that practice. Fame is a good external to the practice of philosophy, while wisdom is a good internal to it.) This tendency toward the failure of moral rationality and the deterioration of individual moral substance MacIntyre calls "emotivism," naming it after the twentieth-century movement in metaethics that articulates it philosophically.

But, on the other side, we are never completely at ease with emotivism. Even if we often find ourselves taking refuge in "decisions of principle," this remains a desperate move. It is not how things ought to be! We sense that as long as we are only expressing our feelings and manipulating our interlocutors, our stance cannot be called "morality." Candor about emotivist theory is incompatible with emotivist practice: even if we are crass enough to manipulate others in argument, still, we can't let our interlocutor know we are only subjecting him or her to nonrational rhetoric. The rhetoric won't work unless the listener believes we are offering an argument!

We are unhappy emotivists, and our predicament is the result of a long and bumpy history that MacIntyre chronicles in *After Virtue*. His construal of this history is also an argument that a version of a recurring moment in that history—the Aristotelian tradition of the virtues—contains a path out of our predicament. If we can become Aristotelians in a certain sense, we will find ways to settle our moral debates rationally, while at the same time rescuing our moral selfhood from the formlessness and emptiness characteristic of the twentieth-century "characters."

A History of the Virtues

Heroic Societies. The history begins with "heroic societies," the most prominent example being the one in Homer's *Iliad*. In that society the actions required of a person were determined by fixed social roles, which in turn were determined by the person's social status: "Every individual has a given role and status within a well-defined and highly determinate system of roles and statuses. The key structures are those of kinship and of the household. In such a society a man knows who he is by knowing his role in these structures; and in knowing this he knows also what he owes and what is owed to him by the occupant of every other role and status."[15] To fulfill the role of head of household was to protect it in battle, and for this one must be fitted by courage. Such a person would also be bound by ties of kinship and friendship with other households and their heads; these ties would also demand entering into battle, with a consequent need for fidelity and courage. Duties in heroic society were not separable from social roles. To be a friend or brother meant to endeavor to take the life of anyone who took the life of your friend or brother. This meant that a certain storyline, of which the final episode was the violent death of the hero, characterized virtually every inhabiter of the role. Membership in a heroic society ensured the impossibility of moral doubt on the central issues, and ensured that the occupant of the role had a firm personal identity and undoubting sense of his or her identity. According to MacIntyre, the heroic poetry has two things to teach us about ethics: "First that all morality is always to some degree tied to the socially local and particular and that the aspirations of the morality of modernity to a universality freed from all particularity is an illusion; and secondly that there is no way to possess the virtues except as part of a tradition in which we inherit them and our understanding of them from a series of predecessors in which series heroic societies hold first place."[16]

The Sophists and Plato. By contrast with the society of Homer's poems, the Athens of Socrates (469–399 B.C.) and Plato (427–347 B.C.) showed what we would call moral "pluralism." The Athenians agreed with heroic society that virtues are conditions for personal success within a social fabric, but because of intercourse with the "outside world," the Athenians were vividly aware, as the heroes were not, of the *variety* of customs and of virtue concepts. Furthermore, the social matrix supporting and giving sense to the virtues had shifted from the Homeric family to the city-state. The result was a far less clear and consistent use of the moral vocabulary. For example, it was agreed that *dikaiosune* (justice) is a virtue and that it, like other virtues, is intimately linked with the pursuit of happiness and the fulfillment of desire; but there was much disagreement about what this virtue means.

The sophists concluded from this failure of agreement that there was no such thing as *dikaiosune* in itself, but only *dikaiosune*-as-practiced-in-a-given-city. This extreme "cultural relativism" was difficult to maintain and made some sophists easy prey of Socrates' efforts to trap them in inconsistency. If they claimed there is no *dikaiosune*-in-itself, while nevertheless assuming their own concept of *dikaiosune* in criticizing other conceptions, they seemed to say that there both is, and is not, *dikaiosune*-in-itself. This inconsistency could be avoided, as Callicles did (see Plato's *Gorgias*), by claiming without wavering that the "virtuous" person is one who uses his cunning to dominate others "and who uses his domination to satisfy his desires without limit."[17]

Plato's theory of the virtues tries to avoid both relativism and the ruthless, antisocial character of Callicles' conception of "virtue." His strategy is to present a universal philosophical psychology that entails an idea of happiness and satisfaction of human desire radically different from that of Callicles. The human soul is composed of three parts: the desiring part (bodily appetites), the high spirited part (certain emotions), and the reasoning part. Virtue is the proper functioning and harmonious interaction of these parts. A person has *sophia* ("wisdom") when the reasoning part is in touch with reality and above all with the Form of the Good. This enables it to legislate humanly appropriate behavior. *Sophrosune* ("temperance") occurs when the desiring part is restrained according to what reason declares to be humanly appropriate behavior. *Andreia* ("courage") is a preservative of knowledge of what is good, which functions where fear and pleasure threaten to diminish that knowledge. As the virtue of the high spirited part, courage would seem also to include those emotional dispositions implementing the dictates of reason—for example, feeling repugnance for wrongdoing and joy in good conduct. Finally, *dikaiosune* ("justice") is the presence of the other three virtues, each part of the soul functioning according to its nature and thus appropriately interacting with the other parts. The soul flourishes when it thus realizes its true nature. It is this, argues Plato, that human beings really desire, even though they may think they desire, as Callicles claims, to dominate others and enjoy the fruits of such domination.

The social matrix fitting such a person of virtue is a city-state with a structure analogous to that of a perfected human personality. The guardians (reasoning part) will legislate with wisdom, the warriors (high spirited part) will execute the will of the guardians, and the workers (desiring part) will provide the economic energy in the city. And each part will exemplify *dikaiosune* as it performs its own, and only its own, function with excellence, thus fitting into an organic harmony with the whole. MacIntyre notes that while Plato believed there was no existing political order that supported virtue as he conceived it, "nonetheless the concept of virtue remains a political concept; for Plato's account of the virtuous man is inseparable from his account of the virtuous citizen."[18]

Several points can be made about Plato's conception of the virtues. First, it is in acquiring the virtues that a person achieves the well-being characteristic of humans. Second, what this well-being amounts to is dictated by a culture-transcendent human nature, reflected in Plato's philosophical psychology. But, third, Plato believes that the realization of that nature is tied to a political order or social matrix. Fourth, since no political order adequate to human nature exists on earth, the political order in which Plato embeds the virtuous person is itself transcendent (ideal). This raises the question whether having the virtues is a real possibility. Fifth, Plato does not believe in tragedy, if we mean by tragedy a situation in which a perfectly virtuous person is caught in a ruining conflict. Virtue = harmony = success = happiness; so, if a seemingly virtuous person is caught in a "tragic" situation, he must have a hidden personal flaw. There are no essentially tragic situations. Plato's disbelief in tragedy is tied to his belief in the unity of the virtues. Two virtues cannot conflict because to have any virtue is to have all the virtues. It is not possible, as the tragedian Sophocles believed it was, that exercising "the virtue of doing what is required of a sister (Antigone) or a friend (Odysseus) be at odds with the exercise of the virtues of justice (Creon) or of compassion and truthfulness (Neoptolemus)."[19]

Aristotle. On these points Plato's pupil Aristotle agreed with him on all but the fourth. Aristotle was more optimistic than Plato about the constitution of his own city-state, Athens, as providing a context for the actualization of human nature in the virtues. Thus Aristotle's "sociology" is less idealized and more empirical than Plato's. Indeed his ethics is equally an ethics of the Athenian citizen and a universally human ethics. On the second point, Aristotle agreed that there is a human nature independent of cultures, and that it is the job of the ethical theorist to explicate this nature and thus to show what its full realization in the virtues would look like. But in its details Aristotle's philosophical psychology is much richer than, and in some ways divergent from, Plato's.

As we remarked earlier, Aristotle is the hero in MacIntyre's story. It is the "Aristotelian tradition" in its various forms from which we must learn if we are to extricate ourselves from the confusions and characterlessness of "modern liberal individualism." This tradition includes such predecessors of Aristotle as Sophocles and Plato, and such successors as the Christian theologian Thomas Aquinas (1224–74) and the English novelist Jane Austen (1775–1817); but Aristotle himself is the greatest representative of the tradition.[20] Four aspects of Aristotle's moral philosophy stand out as essential, in MacIntyre's view, to the project of restoring ethical rationality and substance.

First, Aristotle's ethical thought is *teleological*. The basic idea here is that human nature is not just whatever people happen, on the average, to be. It is a built-in *goal*, and one that perhaps few individuals ever reach. There is almost always a difference between the way humans are, and the way they would be if they achieved, or actualized, their nature. (It is conceivable, indeed, that *no* individuals ever achieve their human nature.) The virtues are features of self-actualization, characteristics of the human being who has become what his nature dictates that he should be. Furthermore, this achievement is something that people must themselves undertake. A beet seed contains within it the tendency to become a fully realized beet; and if it is placed in appropriate conditions of soil, moisture, temperature, and the passage of time, it will become the best beet it can, something with all the beet virtues. However, it is no part of beet nature to *undertake* to become a fully actualized beet; it is enough that it be placed in a fitting environment. But an aspect of the human virtues, dictated by human nature, is that the individual become a responsible initiator of the actions characteristic of justice, courage, temperance, and wisdom.

Second, the concept of *pleasure* has a central place in Aristotle's ethical thought. He points out that pleasure naturally accompanies unimpeded excellent activity. When you are doing something well (let us say, building a deck on the back of your house), in conditions that do not hinder you, then you "enjoy yourself" in the activity. But the virtues are capacities for humanly excellent activities. So given unhindering external conditions, the virtues are capacities for pleasure, for leading a life of enjoyment. As the virtuous person enjoys being who he or she is and performing actions characteristic of himself or herself, the individual is directly aware of the goodness of his or her life.

MacIntyre points out how Aristotle differs from the utilitarians in his treatment of pleasure. For them pleasure (some call it happiness) is the good, the goal of all action, while for Aristotle it is a natural accompaniment of the humanly excellent life. For them the amount of pleasure an action produces is what determines the moral goodness or badness of it. For Aristotle the criterion is the much more complex matter of what human nature is, and pleasures are judged good or bad according to what activities they accompany. For the utilitarians pleasure is some single mental state that can in principle be measured and added up. For Aristotle pleasure is activity- and excellence-relative; there are as many different pleasures as there are "faculties" and activities of faculties.

Third, Aristotle gives a central place to the virtue of *friendship*. Indeed he devotes a larger proportion of his *Nicomachean Ethics* to this than to any other single topic. Friendship is important because it is the human bond necessary to the kind of community in which people can flourish (develop the virtues). What is friendship? It is not just liking one another, or enjoying some common hobby or professional pursuit, but sharing with others the aim of realizing the common, or "political" good (that is, the good of the *polis*). Thus friendship is at the same time patriotism.

From our modern individualist perspective, it is hard to conceive of people genuinely bound together by ties of affection in the pursuit of the well-being of their society. Instead we think of "politics" as a factional enterprise engaged in by persons seeking their own individual "political" advancement. MacIntyre states that "from an Aristotelian point of view, a modern liberal political society can appear only as a collection of citizens of nowhere, who have banded together for their common protection. They possess at best that inferior form of friendship that is founded on mutual advantage."[21] Thus we have no real sense of political community and, consequently, lack the social context that, according to Aristotle, is necessary if we are to become human.

Fourth is Aristotle's conception of *practical reasoning*, or reasoning leading to action. Aristotle's picture includes four elements: a want, a major premise, a minor premise, and an action. Anytime a person reasons practically, he or she must want something. Let us say you want to sharpen a pencil neatly and with minimum effort. You believe (major premise) that anyone who wants to sharpen a pencil neatly and easily is well advised to use a pencil sharpener. Through inquiry you learn that (minor premise) there is a pencil sharpener in the next room. Finally (action) you go to that room and sharpen your pencil.

Moral reasoning is a species of practical reasoning. If an agent is to reason about justice to any practical effect, he or she must be the sort of person who wants just states of affairs. In general, the virtues all contain or presuppose a concern about the well-being of the agent and the community. Second, the agent must believe (major premise) propositions of the following sort: job discrimination against persons on the basis of their ethnic background is unjust, taking away a person's property without his or her permission is unjust, and so on. Third, the agent must be able to recognize (minor premise) truths of the following sort: This is a case of ethnic discrimination, this is a case of taking property without permission, and so on. Practical circumstances, of course, are much more complicated than being just a matter of a single major and a single minor premise presenting themselves in splendid isolation. Consequently, these premises must be ranked in weight relative to other morally (and perhaps nonmorally) relevant beliefs; in other words, the agent must have refined judgment, or what Aristotle calls *phronesis* ("practical wisdom"). Practical wisdom is a virtue pervading all the other virtues, since actions will not properly exemplify the virtues if they are not intelligent. In this connection MacIntyre observes also how Aristotle's conception of the moral life differs from that of most modern philosophers, for whom moral rules are basic. For Aristotle, it is the virtues that are basic; the rules are, necessarily and at their best, embodied in the intelligence of the morally mature individual. As MacIntyre notes, "Knowing how to apply the law is itself possible only for someone who possesses the virtue of justice."[22]

Stoicism and the Middle Ages. The next stage in our history is that of Stoicism (Zeno, fourth century B.C.; Chrysippus, third century B.C.; Epictetus, first century A.D.; Marcus Aurelius, second century A.D.), which arose when the city-state ceased to be the main form of political life and was replaced, first by the Macedonian kingdom and later by the Roman empire. Stoicism, anticipating modern morality, is a philosophy of individualism, a symptom of the individual's being cut off from a close-knit community committed to a social goal of human flourishing. To be a citizen, in Stoic terms, can only mean to be a citizen of the world at large. Stoicism is a morality of law, but not of the positive laws of a political community. Instead the laws are of nature — such as that all humans will die, that pain is a consequence of desire, or that people are in control of nothing that happens but only of their attitudes toward happenings. Virtue is central for the Stoics, but it is virtue in the singular rather than, as in the Aristotelian tradition, the multiple virtues of the good citizen. The one virtue is the submission of one's will to nature, the willing acceptance of the harsh ways reality is. And so virtue is interiorized; it is no longer embodied, as it was in heroic society, in action contributions to the communal welfare. Virtue is practiced, not as a way of securing a healthy social order, but as an end in itself. MacIntyre points out that elements of Stoicism recur regularly in the history of ethics: "whenever the virtues begin to lose their central place, Stoic patterns of thought and action at once reappear"[23] — for example, in the twelfth century in Abelard and in the eighteenth century in Kant.

MacIntyre makes almost no mention of the Christian church fathers, and gives only a sketchy account of the medieval period. The latter was characterized by philosophical conflict and only partially successful efforts to synthesize diverse traditions, which included elements of Stoicism and of course Christianity, as well as Aristotelianism. Saint Thomas Aquinas, as a strict Aristotelian, is "an unexpectedly marginal figure to the history which I am writing."[24] With his theistic framework Aquinas complicates and adds to Aristotle, without essentially altering the scheme: "The table of virtues and vices has to be amended and added to and a concept of sin is added to the Aristotelian concept of error. The law of God requires a new kind of respect and awe. The true end of man can no longer be completely achieved in this world, but only in another. Yet the threefold structure of untutored human-nature-as-it-happens-to-be, human-nature-as-it-could-be-if-it-realized-its-telos and the precepts of rational ethics as means for the transition from one to the other remains central to the theistic understanding of evaluative thought and judgment."[25] Aquinas, then, combines the notion that morality is obedience to the decrees of God with the notion that morality's function is to specify what it will take for humans to actualize their human nature or essence.

The Enlightenment. By the late seventeenth and eighteenth centuries, says MacIntyre, secularization was rooting out the belief that moral precepts could be traced to the will of God, and a new concept of rationality excluded thinking of human nature as something not actual and observable, but as a potentiality to be actualized. This new concept of rationality had roots both in Protestant theology, which claimed that sin had corrupted the mind's capacity to discern true human nature, and in the rising new science, which tended to think of rationality as methodical observation and generalization, and as deductive logic. At the same time, however, the *content* of morality was derived largely from classical Christianity. David Hume (1711–76), for example, believed in the chastity of women, and Immanuel Kant (1724–1804) believed in the absolute prohibition of lying. "Marriage and the family are *au fond* as unquestioned by Diderot's rationalist *philosophe* as they are by Kierkegaard's Judge Wilhelm; promise-keeping and justice are as inviolable for Hume as they are for Kant. Whence did they inherit these shared beliefs? Obviously from their shared Christian past."[26] This combination of retaining belief in morality while undercutting its traditional rational supports posed an urgent challenge to philosophers, namely the challenge to find an alternative foundation for morality. The philosophers' response to this challenge MacIntyre calls "the Enlightenment project of finding a rational justification for morality."

All the participants in the Enlightenment project looked to actual, observable human nature for a justification of traditional moral norms. Hume tried to find it in such supposedly universal feelings as the "sentiment of humanity"—a feeling of sympathy for one another that all human beings supposedly share. The difficulty with this view is that apart from a particular culture and training that inculcates such sentiments, people just don't seem to have these feelings.

Kant argued that morality is founded on "pure practical reason," a kind of rationality essential to human nature. The ultimate principle of this rationality is the Categorical Imperative: So act that you can will the maxim of your action as a universal law. Kant supposed that you could take any immoral maxim, such as "When there's no other way out of a tough situation, lie" or "When your spouse is away for more than a week, you may adulterize with a friendly person." If you then imagine its being made into a principle that holds universally for all human beings, then you will be imagining a contradictory state of affairs. Thus violating the rules of morality has a result similar to that of violating the laws of logic: you do so at the price of logical incoherence. The chief difficulty with Kant's proposal is that it is false: universalizing an immoral maxim almost never yields a contradiction.

According to MacIntyre, the Danish thinker Søren Kierkegaard (1813–55) was addressing the same problem as Hume and Kant. But he looked for the foundation (not quite the justification) of morality neither in the sentiments nor in the rationality characteristic of human nature, but in "the characteristics of fundamental decision-making."[27] Looking back on the earlier, Humean and Kantian versions of the Enlightenment project, Kierkegaard sees clearly that *there is no rational foundation for morality*. Morality belongs to a different order than things that can be decided through reasoned investigation; it is something the individual must simply choose for himself or herself out of the vigor of his or her own will, without reasons. Thus Kierkegaard, in MacIntyre's view, anticipates the emotivism and existentialism of the twentieth century. But Kierkegaard's effort, too, is a failure, since it involves saying at the same time that traditional morality can have authority over us (otherwise it wouldn't be morality), *and* that each individual is the sole and ultimate source of the principles of morality. MacIntyre remarks, "The contradiction in Kierkegaard's doctrine is plain."[28]

It remains for Friedrich Nietzsche (1844–1900) to draw the radical conclusion from the failure of the Enlightenment project: the individual must "raze to the ground the structures of inherited moral belief and argument,"[29] with their communal conceptions of justice, respect for others, and compassion, and rebuild upon the naked ground the honestly self-absorbed, self-glorifying, noncommunicating "great man" whose final authority is his own will to power.

In the last chapter of *After Virtue*, MacIntyre poses the alternatives: Nietzsche *or* Aristotle? The historical argument of the entire book has been that a broadly Aristotelian approach to ethics—which is to say, an ethics of the virtues—is the *only* rational way to avoid the Nietzschean conclusion, which in so many ways (though always half-heartedly) our contemporary culture has drawn. Let us conclude this very sketchy summary of *After Virtue* with a brief account of MacIntyre's own proposed version of Aristotelianism—his account of the nature of the virtues.

MacIntyre's Account of the Virtues

MacIntyre presents his concept of a virtue in terms of three conceptual "stages": the concepts of a *practice*, the *narrative order of a single human life*, and a *moral tradition*.

"Practices," in MacIntyre's sense, are complex and demanding activities with standards of excellence and goods "internal" to them. A few examples are chess, architecture, physics, baseball, historiography, farming, portrait painting, running a household or a city, and playing the violin. All the practices just listed can lead to such *external* goods as money, prestige, and the pleasures of the palate. But, in addition, they all have goods *internal* to them: in physics, say, insight into the relations between physical phenomena, in architecture the design of a beautiful and functional space, in violin playing a near-perfect performance of the Mendelssohn concerto, or in running a household the rearing of healthy and virtuous children. Attaining the goods internal to a practice requires the practitioner to submit to the rules of the practice (for example, the canons of scholarship, the techniques of farming, the rules of baseball), and this, in turn, places the practitioner in a social context. In some practices the immediate social context is very evident: a baseball player cannot play alone, a scholar is necessarily dependent on the work of other scholars, the violinist who plays the Mendelssohn concerto must work with the members of the orchestra, and so on. But every practice has the social dimension of the historical tradition that has given rise to its rules and canons of excellence. Even if the violinist plays only solo performances, he or she can begin to realize the goods internal to violin playing only by aligning himself or herself to the tradition by taking lessons from a teacher, studying the classical violin works, imitating some great violinists, and so forth.

Now MacIntyre argues that a virtue is a learned human quality necessary to attain any goods internal to a practice. "We have to learn to recognize what is due to whom [justice]; we have to be prepared to take whatever self-endangering risks are demanded along the way [courage]; and we have to listen carefully to what we are told about our own inadequacies and to reply with the same carefulness for the facts [truthfulness]."[30] While there are certainly dishonest violinists, cowardly farmers, and cheating baseball players, still, without these virtues the kinds of social involvement that are the necessary background of these practices would not be possible. Furthermore, unless at least some practitioners along the way practice with the virtues, the tradition sustaining the practice is in jeopardy of decaying. If portrait painters began to care only about making money and being interviewed on talk shows, and consequently ceased to listen honestly to the tradition of portrait painting and its judgments upon their work, the practice would be in danger of dying out. One can see how MacIntyre's theory so far is broadly Aristotelian. Without practices, the characteristically human form of life would not exist; without certain virtues, practices could not be learned, carried on, and sustained; so these virtues are essential to any distinctly human form of life.

The second stage in MacIntyre's account of the virtues is "the narrative concept of selfhood."[31] Throughout *After Virtue*, MacIntyre is on the prowl against a particular concept of the human self, with roots in the Enlightenment, which is incompatible with the Aristotelian virtues. The emotivist or existentialist self is a being who has a past and a future only incidentally; its "character" (if you want to glorify it with that name) is determined by what it happens at the moment to be choosing or by the role that it happens at the moment to be playing. "Authenticity" is procured by forthrightly owning up to one's choices and to the fluidity with which the self moves from role to role. Authenticity so understood is the only human virtue.

Against this radically disjointed and nonhistorical concept of selfhood, MacIntyre contrasts "a concept of a self whose unity resides in the unity of a narrative which links birth to life to death as narrative beginning to middle to end."[32] This, then, is the concept of a self with continuity, with personal identity—a self that can be "characterized" not just by its present role or decision, or even by the chronological listing of its life-episodes, its decisions and its evolution through roles, but by the unity that is its biography, both retrospective and prospective. MacIntyre invites us to notice that biographical narrative is what makes sense of the individual episodes—the actions and decisions—of a human life. Without their setting-in-the-story, these actions and decisions do not present themselves as intelligible.

The individual person must be a self whose actions make sense as parts of a narrative whole stretching back into his or her past and forward into the future. The details of this story are largely determined by factors other than the individual's decisions—that is, the persons the individual finds himself or herself related to, the nation and culture he or she is born into, and the individual's status within these. By virtue of being placed, and taking one's place, in such a setting, the individual has a personal identity and comes to know what that identity is.

But not just any narrative form shapes a self capable of possessing justice, truthfulness, courage, and friendship; not all narratives are such that the protagonist needs the *virtues* for successful pursuit of the story line. What, then, is the required narrative form? It is the form of a quest for *the human good*. An individual life must be the story of a search to know and achieve his or her human well-being or flourishing. But where shall we seek a conception of the human good? We start, says MacIntyre, with our knowledge of the goods internal to human practices and with the recognition that these goods need to be *ordered*. The goods internal to chess are surely on a different plane of importance than the goods internal to structuring a society. In the process of seeking to rank things that we already know to be good, and to order our lives with respect to this ranking, we will come to a clearer understanding both of what the human good is, and of ourselves. And the virtues will be qualities required of us in this quest for the human good: "The virtues therefore are to be understood as those dispositions which will not only sustain practices and enable us to achieve the goods internal to practices, but which will also sustain us in the relevant kind of quest for the good, by enabling us to overcome the harms, dangers, temptations and distractions which we encounter and which will furnish us with increasing self-knowledge and increasing knowledge of the good."[33]

The third stage in MacIntyre's account of the nature of the virtues is the concept of a moral tradition. There is no such thing as abstract, universal morality. Each of us must launch the quest for our human good from the vantage point of some *particular* moral tradition, indeed from our own particular place within that tradition. If you are an American, your moral tradition unavoidably includes certain democratic ideals, an individualistic conception of political freedom, and, in its history, the institution of black slavery and the bombing of Hiroshima. Even if you stand in rebellion against certain elements of this tradition, the terms and issues of your rebellion are set by the tradition. The values to which you appeal in your rebellion must initially be found in the tradition. Furthermore, the particular dimensions of your quest for the human good are determined by such things as the period in that history in which you were born, the moral and political persuasions and powers of your family, and your race. Your moral tradition is neither a straitjacket nor a dispensable outer garment: "Without those moral particularities to begin from there would never be anywhere to begin; but it is in moving forward from such particularity that the search for the good, for the universal, consists. Yet particularity can never be simply left behind or obliterated. The notion of escaping from it into a realm of entirely universal maxims which belong to man as such, whether in its eighteenth-century Kantian form or in the presentation of some modern analytical moral philosophies, is an illusion."[34]

If a moral tradition is a necessary background for an individual's life to have the narrative form of a pursuit of the good amid the goods internal to human practices, a moral tradition itself requires the historical background of courageous, truthful, and just individuals who inhabit it. Moral traditions are subject to decay, disintegration, and disappearance, and they are sustained, ultimately, only if there are persons who practice them with integrity. This is the third way in which the virtues are necessary for the prosecution of a fully human life. MacIntyre nicely summarizes: "The virtues find their point and purpose not only in sustaining those relationships necessary if the variety of goods internal to practices are to be achieved and not only in sustaining the form of an individual life in which that individual may seek out his or her good as the good of his or her whole life, but also in sustaining those traditions which provide both practices and individual lives with their necessary historical context."[35]

The Virtues and Contemporary Moral Debate

How can reckoning with these very general truths about the nature of the virtues help us to resolve the interminable moral debates of our day and to escape the emotivist self that we are all threatening to become? Obviously MacIntyre's theory of the virtues is not directly a solution to the question of whether early abortions are permissible, or whether building weapons capable of destroying the earth is an acceptable strategy in international politics, or whether it is just for government to tax the rich to support the poor. It is not a formula for resolving moral debates. Rather, it is an invitation to adopt a different conception of the nature of morality, and thus of moral debate, than the one presupposed by the parties to the previously mentioned debates.

MacIntyre's book is an argument that our incapacity to resolve such moral debates is the result of a mind-set that has evolved historically from abandoning the Aristotelian perspective in ethics. If we recognize that morality is always bound to a social tradition, we will not expect conclusive resolutions of moral debates unless these are carried on within a sufficiently rich and coherent tradition. And if we reckon that moral thinking requires a notion of human nature not just as it is, but as it would be if it realized its *telos*, or ultimate end, then we shall seek to recapture a tradition in which inquiry into our *telos* is a basic and legitimate exercise of human rationality. The questions these debates raise cannot be answered rationally in our secular and "pluralistic" situation ("modern liberal individualism"), which is one of a moral noncommunity not focused on human-nature-as-*telos* but seeking instead, with only confused fragmented remnants of traditions, abstract community- and tradition-free moral principles. But the questions can be answered rationally within a concrete moral community in which the human *telos* is concertedly sought.

MacIntyre's optimism about finding rational answers to the moral questions besetting us is due in large part to his rejection of the Enlightenment belief in rationality with a big *R*. Part of the restoration of morality in our day must be a liberation from this false and constricting picture. Rationality is far more faceted, historical, community-centered, and infused with human needs and yearnings than the Enlightenment would have us believe. And because rationality is good for more than just figuring out how things "tick," there is a place in it for Aristotle's project of debating and envisioning the human good.

The Nature and Structure of This Anthology

The present collection of essays is divided into three parts, characterized by increasing specificity. The first part contains an essay on the social importance of the virtues and essays on moral theorizing and the relevance of the virtues to this enterprise. The second part has papers on general features of moral psychology: the nature of the moral self, the connection between desires and ethical reasoning, the character and place of will power in the moral life, and the nature, significance, and conditions of perfection of character ("sainthood"). The essays of the third part are about individual vices and virtues: envy, servility, and sentimentality; justice, autonomy, generosity, and compassion. These are, of course, but a tiny sampling of human virtues and vices, and in this volume the papers serve as illustrations of the kind of detail-work that is being done and needs to be done.

If an ethics of virtue is to be built upon the ruins of moral philosophy, it needs to include both close-ups and aerial photographs of the terrain. To MacIntyre's historical argument and broad theory of the virtues must be added the detailed philosophical work in moral psychology that Anscombe has urged us to do. If well done, this work will put meat on the bones of virtues reflection in the coming years. If MacIntyre is right, philosophy is not, or at any rate need not be, a side-issue of culture—an ineffectual, if fascinating, concern of the folks at the university. In the past it has significantly shaped our moral consciousness. It can and probably will be a shaper of our cultural and individual lives in the new century that is dawning. Often quietly and behind the scenes, no doubt, it will shape our self-concepts, our science, our education, our theology and church life, and our politics. The essays in Parts Two and Three are but a number of beginnings in the direction of that detailed philosophical work to which Anscombe has challenged us and of which MacIntyre's history suggests the need.

Notes

1. Normative ethics is the enterprise of justifying ethical precepts in the sense of establishing (1) that the precept is ethical as opposed to *non*ethical, thus showing, for example, why "Speak the truth" is an ethical precept while "Trim your toenails on alternate Tuesdays" is not, and (2) that the

precept is ethical as opposed to *un*ethical, thus showing, for example, why "Share your goods with those in need" is an ethical precept while "Disregard those in need" is an unethical one. The two chief competing normative ethical schools in modern moral philosophy are the utilitarian and the deontological. Utilitarianism justifies ethical precepts by reference to the Greatest Happiness Principle ("Always so act [or choose your rules] that your action [or rule choice] results in the greatest possible balance of happiness for the greatest possible number of people"). Immanuel Kant, the greatest of the deontologists, justifies ethical precepts by reference to the Categorical Imperative ("Always so act that you can consistently will that the precept enjoining your action be a universal law").

2. The metaethicist, unlike the normative ethicist, tries not to *advocate* any morality, but only to engage in the morally neutral activity of *describing the meaning of ethical terms*. Thus when G. E. Moore says that 'good' stands for an intuitable nonnatural property, and C. L. Stevenson says ethical utterances are expressions of feeling and efforts to get others to share your feelings, and R. M. Hare says that ethical utterances are universal prescriptions, they are all "doing metaethics." See the quote from Hudson in this section.

3. *Modern Moral Philosophy* (Garden City, N.Y.: Doubleday, 1970), 1.

4. Elizabeth Anscombe, "Modern Moral Philosophy," *Philosophy* 33 (1958): 1–19.

5. Ibid., 8.

6. Ibid., 13–14.

7. Ibid., 14.

8. See Alasdair MacIntyre, *After Virtue*, 2d ed., 53.

9. Anscombe, 18.

10. Ibid., 15.

11. Ibid., 18.

12. Basil Blackwell, publisher, 1963 (2d ed.).

13. Anscombe, 1.

14. Notre Dame University Press, 1981; 2d ed., 1984. Page references are to the pages in the first edition, followed by the pages in the second edition in square brackets.

15. *After Virtue*, 115 [122].

16. Ibid., 119 [126–27].

17. Ibid., 131 [140].

18. Ibid., 132 [141].

19. Ibid., 133 [142].

20. For comments on the relations Aristotle bears to this tradition, see 154 [165].

21. Ibid., 147 [157].

22. Ibid., 143 [152].

23. Ibid., 158 [170].

24. Ibid., 166 [178].

25. Ibid., 51 [53].

26. Ibid., 49 [51].

27. Ibid., 50 [52].

28. Ibid., 41. MacIntyre's interpretation of Kierkegaard is more plausible as an account of how Kierkegaard has been *read* in the twentieth century, than as a reading of Kierkegaard himself. As MacIntyre admits, his reading goes against both Kierkegaard's self-interpretation and that of "the best Kierkegaard scholars of our own time, such as Louis Mackey and Gregor Malantschuk" (40). The editors believe that Kierkegaard's thought about the human condition has far more in common with Aristotle's than with that of C. L. Stevenson, R. M. Hare, and J.-P. Sartre. He should be read as in some respects like Aquinas—as a relatively lonely figure trying to restore the tradition of the virtues in his own day.

29. Ibid., 238 [256].

30. Ibid., 178 [191].

31. Ibid., 202 [217].

32. Ibid., 191 [205].
33. Ibid., 204 [219].
34. Ibid., 205f [221]. MacIntyre is referring in this last line to such philosophers as Alan Gewirth, whose work he discusses on 64–65 [66–67].
35. Ibid., 207 [223].

Part One

Ethical Theory and the Virtues

This book is divided into three groups of papers, and the groups reflect a progress from generality to specificity. The first group contains general essays about the project of focusing our ethical reflection on the virtues and vices. The second deals with what we might call the psychological foundations of the virtues. And the third gets down to the business of discussing specific virtues and vices.

The recent renewal of interest in the virtues and vices constitutes a shift of *substance* and of *method* in thinking about ethics. The shift is away from discussion of rules, policies, principles, and goods, approached primarily through the analysis of problem-cases in ethical action, to a discussion of traits, approached through reflection on characters, their stories, psychological makeup, and the conditions of their thriving.

The essays in this first section bear on the justification for that shift. Those by Phillips, Stocker, and Alderman commend the shift, while the one by Louden voices some cautions about abandoning the older modern approach to ethics. Phillips argues that widespread exemplification of the virtues is essential to decent social life; Stocker and Alderman, on the other hand, propose that modern ethical theories are deficient in various ways because of their abstraction from persons.

Reading Introduction

Authenticity or Morality?
Derek L. Phillips

Phillips distinguishes two outlooks on self and society. The first is the *therapeutic sensibility*, of which the ideal is to be true to one's own "needs," to be "authentic," and to be "in touch with one's feelings." The second is *morality*, the belief that one should limit the fulfillment of one's private desires when not limiting them would infringe other people's rights. We cannot, says Phillips, tolerate life in a society where many in the population are "authentic" and thus giving free reign to their undisciplined urges and "needs." We can to some extent limit the disruptive acts of "authentic" individuals by police-state methods, but the price is too high, both in money and liberties lost. So the best way to secure a decent life for everybody is widespread morality. Morality, however, is not just assent to the principles of justice, but the *internalization* of those principles by individuals who thus exemplify the trait or virtue of justice. Being moral is a matter of moral emotions, such as guilt and shame at one's own wrongdoing. And it is also a matter of the "complementary" virtues such as wisdom, temperance, courage, and sincerity. To the extent that the principles of morality are integrated into human personalities, the tactics of external control become unnecessary.

Authenticity or Morality?

DEREK L. PHILLIPS

It is very curious that many people today who pride themselves on their willingness to talk openly about their sexual life and other personal matters, should seem almost embarrassed by references to morality. Not only does the use of such words as *evil* and *wicked* make people uneasy, but even talk about right and wrong, good and bad, blame and responsibility, seems to be avoided among those who are quite ready to speak of their own fears, hang-ups, desires, wants, aggressions, and uncertainties. Rarely nowadays do we hear anyone characterized with reference to such old-fashioned virtues as wisdom, courage, temperance, or justice. Instead of being evaluated on the basis of their goodness, responsibility, wisdom, or sense of justice, people today are more often judged in terms of their being open, frank, flexible, spontaneous, outgoing, and the like. As I have noted elsewhere, "authenticity" has replaced morality as the standard of human adequacy.[1]

    For many people in the contemporary age, authenticity is viewed as the chief "virtue" to which they should aspire. In a very limited sense, authenticity resembles the old Greek doctrine of living according to one's nature, of "knowing thyself" and "becoming what you

Derek L. Phillips, "Authenticiteit or Moraliteit?" *Wijsgerig Perspectief op Maatschappij en Wetenschap* 22 (1982). Reprinted by permission of the publisher.

are." But for the Greeks, man was regarded essentially as a rational being who was susceptible to moral education and improvement in terms of the development of his own ideal possibility. Every person was required to discover and know this ideal possibility (or "daimon"). Today, by contrast, many persons no longer view man as essentially a rational being whose reason is the master of his soul. Thus, authenticity is now pursued in the absence of any ideal about what reason or rationality requires. That is, the present emphasis on authenticity requires man to follow his own nature without his being told what that nature is.

With the new authenticity, people are encouraged to fulfill their own emotional requirements and to seek immediate gratification of their impulses. The concern is not with one's moral life, but rather with one's inner emotional life. The self is to be judged not by adherence to moral standards or by the possession of moral virtues, but by the degree of allegiance to one's internal feelings and impulses. Authenticity nowadays requires people to "get in touch with their feelings" and to act "naturally" on the basis of those feelings, free from artificial constraints imposed by society. Frankness about one's own needs and desires and about what one thinks of other people, expressed in a sincere manner, is supposed to show that one has indeed come into intimate contact with his or her "real self." But, as we know, all sorts of immoral, criminal, and just plain rude behavior is paraded under the banner of being truly authentic.

In this essay, attention will be devoted to three general, but interrelated, topics. First, I will briefly discuss the disappearance of authority and the appearance of the therapeutic sensibility as factors responsible for the replacement of morality by authenticity as the present standard of human adequacy. Then, I will consider how (what sociologists call) "social order" can be assured either (1) through community sanctions and pressures or (2) through the actions of individuals. With regard to the latter, I will compare the effectiveness of individual actions guided by a commitment to authenticity with those guided by a commitment to morality. My exploration of morality will emphasize the importance of moral principles, the moral emotions, and the virtues. Finally, I will try to make clear why, for both moral and sociological reasons, we must reject authenticity and embrace morality as the proper standard of human adequacy.

I

The Disappearance of Authority

The most important factor relating to the general disappearance of morality is undoubtedly the shattering of authority. At one time it was widely assumed that there existed a *pre-established order* (concerning, for example, God, and the laws of nature) outside and independent of human beings, and it was further assumed that men could *discover* this pre-established order through the use of their cognitive abilities. According to this view, discoveries made by the methods of philosophy, theology, and science constituted faithful and accurate reflections or representations of an order completely independent of the discoverers. Thus with the right methods and concepts, human observers could be brought into contact with the sources of order outside themselves.

For a variety of reasons that I can only touch on here, this older view of knowledge and truth has just about disappeared. Among other things, it is now obvious that the quality and nature of what is known is strongly influenced by those doing the asking, i.e., by human beings themselves.[2] As a consequence of the death of the older view, the authoritative position of those who once claimed a right to pronounce on the true nature of things has been seriously called into question. First, religion lost its authority in moral matters for most of mankind. Although it was once widely accepted that moral rules were the rules given to us by God, this no longer holds true. As people gained more knowledge of the extent to which different religions offered different sets of moral rules, the problem arose as to which of these various rules "really" reflected what God demanded. And, of course, there inevitably arose the problem of how atheists, or deists, could be expected to act morally if they rejected the idea that God gives men and women moral rules to live by.

Related to the disappearance of religious authority is the failure of modern science to discover the moral standards necessary for organized social life. For example, Emile Durkheim, one of the founding fathers of sociology, recognized that morality is a means for preserving society, for holding it together, for cementing human relationships. He wanted to take morality out of the hands of speculative philosophers and make sociology a scientific foundation for verified knowledge about the moral values and standards necessary for social solidarity and the integration of individuals into society.[3] But, of course, neither Durkheim nor succeeding generations has provided the sort of scientific foundation for morality that Durkheim wanted. Nor has any other science been able to provide such a foundation.

In fact, comparative sociology and anthropology have done much to encourage the view that moral values and principles are completely "relative," i.e., that what is right or wrong, good or bad, depends entirely on what is considered right or wrong, good or bad, within one's own society. Taken a step further, many have concluded from the study of sociology and anthropology that right and wrong, good and bad, and the like, do not depend even on the widely-held societal norms but are fully determined by the social norms within one's own particular group. And taken still further, some persons today conclude that each individual makes his or her own morality, i.e., that there is no source of morality external to oneself.

Whatever the reasons, it is clear that the old moralities of custom and religion are husks and shells. Numerous commentators have also pointed to the collapse of authority within the family, the traditional source of much moral teaching and guidance.[4] Unsure themselves as to what is right and wrong, anxious not to thwart the child's need to "get in touch" with his or her true feelings, a large number of parents today are reluctant or unable to advocate and help implement moral standards and principles in their children. Many, for example, seem to accept the view that people should be ruled by their desires and believe that one can throw over one's own moral rearing without emotional consequences. But such persons often also experience a conflict between their present desires and their earlier moral training. This conflict is frequently expressed in their inability to consistently stand behind any coherent set of "dos and don'ts" for their children's behavior. Given their own uncertainty about morality and their need to adequately prepare their children for life outside the home, they silently acquiesce in accepting whatever behavioral norms are deemed appropriate (i.e., fashionable) for people like themselves.

Very much like their children, many parents today live without collective moral ideals and discipline, and thus without reliance upon and obedience to recognized authorities who embody and defend those moral ideals. Many among us, and especially the young, presume that an individual can live freely and fully with no counsel or dictates other than his or her desires. When no authority is recognized in moral matters, the result is inevitable: old notions of good and bad, right and wrong, just and unjust, collapse and die.

In fact, however, most people are apparently not able to live fully and freely without some commitment to principles and ideals, though these obviously need not be moral in character. For the most part, I believe, they indeed are not. While some persons do have a need to know what morality demands, many others want merely to know what will bring them happiness, satisfaction, or gratification. Large numbers of people today are anxiously busy trying to find the key to their own life and self-fulfillment.

The Therapeutic Sensibility

As many observers have noted, the contemporary age is therapeutic, not religious.[5] People nowadays, in the words of Christopher Lasch, hunger not for personal salvation but "for the feeling, the momentary illusion, of personal well-being, health, and psychic security."[6] With the loss of authority, especially that of religion and, more recently, the family, the individual—in a very real sense—stands alone: uncertain, insecure, and lacking any inner sense of standards and direction. Whatever problems he or she may have are defined as arising not from weaknesses of character or lack of inner-control, but increasingly as "psychic" difficulties. For many today, evil and morally wrong actions are dissolved into sickness and social maladjustment.

It is this new personality type with new problems who is referred to as "psychological man" by Rieff, as "protean man" by Hendin, and who is described in terms of "narcissism" by Sennet and Lasch.[7] Lacking the forms of authority formerly represented by parents, teachers, and the clergy, this new personality type lacks an internalized ego-ideal concerning a code of moral conduct. In place of the internalized standards which once helped to guide an individual's actions, it is today the therapists—of one or another stripe—who help achieve the modern equivalent of salvation: "authenticity" or mental health.

With the new therapies, all restrictions and inhibitions are to be eliminated, all in the name of realizing authenticity. In essence, as Alt points out, the therapeutic ideal "deems individuals incapable of guiding their own relationships and seeks to replace their judgment with behavioral canons derived from psychiatric and social sciences."[8] Older ideas of moral limits and personal responsibility are replaced by an emphasis on acquiring the correct techniques for emotional and relational management. Whereas the moral life begins with renunciation ("Thou shalt not . . ."), the therapeutic life begins with the renunciation of renunciation ("Thou shalt not commit a 'shalt not'").

Although it is a successor to religious and moral thinking, the therapeutic sensibility is clearly not itself concerned with morality. As Lasch observes: "Even when therapists speak of the need for 'meaning' and 'love,' they define love and meaning simply as fulfillment of the patient's emotional requirements. . . . 'Love' as self-sacrifice as self-abasement, 'meaning' as submission to a higher loyalty—these submissions strike the therapeutic sensibility as intolerably oppressive, offensive to common sense and injurious to personal health and well-being."[9]

But for some persons today, even one or another type of therapy—Freudian, Reichian, gestalt, sex, Silva Mind Control, Esalen, or whatever—is not enough. The authenticity which they demand is sought in a wide variety of religious groups, in mysticism, meditation, scientology, astrology, drugs, the occult, the superstitions, and even madness. These, too, reflect the therapeutic ideal of finding one's self through commitment to one or another method or movement that promises comfort and psychic relief.

Plagued by uncertainty, anxiety, and an inner emptiness, those in search of authenticity, having rejected the possibility of there being any rationally justifiable rules of moral conduct, embrace the therapeutic sensibility. Hence, what was once thought to be within the control of the individual is now to be regulated by technology. The acceptance of moral principles and the virtues of character which are to accompany them has often been replaced by psychological and social engineering. Many of their advocates, in fact, look with happy anticipation toward the day when moral character will be superceded by psychological and sociological know-how. Yet, despite the self-professed need of many today to establish their own unique, personal identity, those in search of authenticity all too often surrender themselves to whatever causes appear to promise comfort and psychic relief. In their pursuit of authenticity, such persons find themselves more and more dependent on one or another mode of therapeutic thought and practice. The result, of course, is to remove the individual from critical judgment and relieve him of responsibility for his actions. Without such responsibility, i.e., without the possibility of acting otherwise than one does, there is no morality.

II

Whether the standards that guide human conduct are to come from morality, from the therapeutic sensibility, or elsewhere, it is obvious that people's relations with one another have to be governed by some set of standards of human conduct. Sociologists, in this connection, frequently speak of the need for "social order."[10] Because different individuals and groups can never stand in complete isolation from all other individuals and groups, they require a stable and coherent social environment in which they are enabled to plan securely, engage in social relationships, carry on transactions, and work to attain their purposes. Regularities of human behavior and uniformities of social relationship allow people to anticipate and rely upon a settled course of events. These regularities and uniformities of conduct provide the order that is the necessary matrix of social life.

Among multitudes of persons living together, a general context of social order serves to protect and extend the well-being of both individual human beings and the wider society in which they find themselves. It assures that irregularities of behavior, inconstancies of relationship, and unresolvable conflicts of interest are the exception rather than the rule. What this means is that a society can remain sound and stable only through the existence of widespread regularities and uniformities of conduct among those disparate individuals and groups who constitute the society.

How, then, is such social order to be assured? Simplifying somewhat, it can be said that there are two general ways of helping to assure that social order which human beings require: (1) the community can exercise effective social control over the actions of individual members, or (2) individuals themselves can exercise responsibility over their own actions. In reality, of course, both of these methods are found—in varying combinations—in all societies.

We all know that human beings can be kind, sympathetic, and loving, that they can help those in distress, that they can suffer hardship and inconvenience for the sake of others. But we also know that human beings can be extremely cruel, selfish, and act in the most extraordinarily inhumane ways toward others. Lying, stealing, cheating, killing, assault, and rape are familiar to all of us. So are a variety of other actions which reflect man's inhumanity to man: the causing of pain, the violation of the freedom and opportunities of others, the interference with their well-being.

Many of us today live amid crime, violence, terrorism, racial and sexual discrimination, widespread dishonesty, immorality by public officials, verbal assaults in the streets, lurid and offensive advertisements, and among numerous persons who view us, at best, as potential partners to be manipulated and controlled to their advantage. All of these things can be described with the now old-fashioned word "evil"; they are all things, some would say, that we should avoid whenever possible.

But I will refrain for now from characterizing such behaviors with one or another term of moral discourse (evil, bad, wrong), and will simply assume that, under normal circumstances, such actions as the following are prima facie "disruptive" of the regularities of social relationships which every society and all human beings require: lying, stealing, rape, killing, and assault. Under certain circumstances, of course, some of these actions might be seen as required to preserve order and stability. In a situation of war, for example, killing might sometimes be accepted as justifiable—most especially when one is defending one's country against foreign attack or invasion.

Obviously, the main burden of preventing such actions as the above can be seen as falling on those who are tempted to engage in such actions; they usually have the choice of avoiding such conduct if they so choose. But because these acts are threatening and disruptive for other persons as well, the burden of preventing such conduct also falls to a large extent on the rest of the community. The community or society has a vested interest in discouraging and preventing disruptive actions. To the extent that these actions do not occur, this will be largely the result of some combination of the influences of individual control and community sanctions and pressure.

Control by the Community

Let me begin by considering how the community can help to discourage such conduct. For one thing, the community could utilize *fear* as a means of preventing disruptive and threatening actions. People could be obliged to inform on other persons who engage, or are thought to be planning to engage, in certain actions. Parents, children, friends, and acquaintances could be reported to the central authorities in such circumstances. And there might be, literally, a policeman on every street corner, in every factory, in every classroom, and even in every home. Under such conditions, the community could help assure that many disruptive actions were discouraged or eliminated. But, obviously, such conditions and such a climate of fear would also help constitute the worst sort of repressive and closed society.

In fact, even in contemporary non-totalitarian societies, there is much today that evidences the community's attempt to discourage disruptive and threatening actions. In many large American cities, for example, there are policemen in schools, in apartment complexes, on subway cars, and in public buildings. In many stores in the United States, and here in Holland as well, customers are required to check their bags upon entering; this is, of course, to discourage stealing. And in some large department stores, certain expensive goods are chained so as to prevent their unauthorized removal. Cameras are an increasingly common feature in stores, schools, public buildings, and on the streets so as to monitor people's activities. All of these various measures are intended to discourage certain kinds of conduct that threaten social order.

One way to minimize disruptive actions, then, is through various sanctions and controls from others in the community. But this means of assuring social control is enormously costly. It is costly not only in financial terms but, more importantly, it is costly in terms of infringements on our liberties, invasions of our privacy, and losses of our human dignity. Unfortunately, many persons today are unable to even recognize the costs we pay in terms of losses of liberty, privacy, and dignity. For them, surveillance cameras, police personnel, and body searches (in the case of air travel) are accepted as "normal" features of the human environment.

Let me now consider the alternative means of assuring social order and minimizing disruptive actions: the control of their actions by individuals themselves. Such control can arise in two different ways: (1) on the basis of individual actions which people think will best assure that their own desires will be satisfied, or (2) on the basis of individual actions which people think are good or right for their own sake. The first direction is that taken by those in pursuit of authenticity; the second is taken by individuals who emphasize moral thinking and the moral point of view.

The Authentic

For those persons whose actions are guided by a search for authenticity, it is assumed that "ego-satisfaction" is the final aim of all action and that the "pleasure principle" is the basic "drive" which underlies the actions of all persons. This means, of course, that while some actions may be considered "bad" because of their results for the individual actor, they cannot be bad in themselves. Human nature is such, they claim, that everyone aims at the fulfillment of his or her own desires. According to those who accept the dictates of the therapeutic sensibility, everyone is governed by the pursuit of self-interest, and human relations are based on a calculation of gains and losses which will arise from one or another form of action.

Whenever one can realize one's own desires without interference from others, one should do so. When this isn't possible, one should be ready to sell or present oneself in such a way that others can be manipulated so as to secure one's own advantage. Should this require getting along with others (no matter whom the "others" may be or what they might believe) or fitting in with the supposed needs of society or one or another organization or group, then one should act accordingly. Deep down, we are told, even the most intimate relationships are guided by the desire of all participants to exploit the other(s).

Guided by that assumption, some today turn to "assertiveness therapy" which seeks to rid the individual of all "feelings of anxiety, ignorance, and guilt that . . . are used efficiently by other people to get us to do what they want."[11] Other persons attempt to learn to exert control, to exercise power, and to extend their influence over the actions of other people. Since everyone else is also presumed to be guided by a concern with control, power, and influence, one must master the techniques of manipulation to avoid being a victim of the desires of the rest. This sort of therapeutic sensibility is based on the view, as Lasch remarks, "that success depends on psychological manipulation and that all of life . . . centers on the struggle for interpersonal advantage, the deadly game of intimidating friends and seducing people."[12]

The important sociological question here, of course, is whether individuals whose actions are regulated by a concern with the authenticity of their own desires and impulses, and by an emphasis on impression-management and negotiations, can be expected to act in such a way as to help avoid "disruptive" behaviors and assure social order.

Given the unbounded self-interest of such persons, the answer is clearly *no*. Since the therapeutic sensibility assumes that individuals are guided almost entirely by considerations of self-interest and, so far as possible, act to choose the least costly means (for themselves) of achieving their own private ends or aims, conflict seems inevitable. Because people are viewed as wanting different things (to satisfy their differing desires and impulses) and because they are seen as competing for scarce goods (money, fame, attention, power), conflict and disruption seems unavoidable. After all, such persons cannot be expected to voluntarily comply with the expectations of others, including the expectations of the law, unless such compliance better serves the realization of their own desires than does non-compliance. Thus they will refrain from lying, cheating, stealing, killing, and the like, only when it appears to be prudent to do so.

People whose actions are regulated by prudence, reject the idea that there are moral virtues, obligations, or other requirements which are independent of prudence. Living by the doctrines of authenticity and prudence is, then, not a kind of morality. Since such persons view social relationships as reducible to individual desires or to a calculation of means and ends, *moral discourse* does not even exist for them. Moral judgments, they believe, are reducible to questions of the most subjective personal taste. ("If it feels good, do it.") They do not accept that it is possible to establish the things that are in principle right or wrong for themselves as well as for others. Because there is no moral foundation for their actions, they cannot be expected to act on the basis of something other than their own desires and impulses. And in so far as they do refrain from "disruptive" actions, this is the result of their being guided by prudence, and by techniques of emotional and relational management—not by principles of morality.

The Moral

In contrast to those whose allegiance is to authenticity and self-interest, there are some (although, I believe, many fewer than even in the recent past) who want to distinguish what they *ought* to do from what they *want* to do. The actions of these persons are guided by considerations of morality. Whereas authenticity involves a concern with what one wants for oneself, morality is primarily concerned with interpersonal relations, i.e., with actions that affect persons other than oneself. In order for actions or discourse to be moral, there must be reference to the important interests of at least one person other than the agent.[13] Morality has the function of checking what would be the result of prudence alone.

Morality concerns the good and the right way of our being in the world as human beings. It includes insight and action: insight into the nature and likely consequences of our actions in order to recognize right and wrong, good and evil; and action to help assure the right and secure the good, while avoiding the wrong and diminishing evil. But morality also includes standards and principles that specify what we may and may not do. These standards and principles are necessary for structuring and guiding our social relationships. They function, ideally at least, to assure the greatest possible freedom for everyone compatible with the restraints necessary for organized social life. Such standards and principles must, of course, be rationally justifiable.

Although I do not intend to pursue the matter very far here, it is clear that such rational justification is indeed possible. The work of scholars like Rawls, Nozick, Gewirth, and Habermas makes it apparent that moral preferences and moral judgments are not just personal, not just a function of what an individual happens to value.[14] Nor, contrary to the views of various "relativists," are they completely a function of what is believed in and accepted in the wider society in which one lives. To the contrary, evaluative questions about what is morally right and wrong are no less objective and decidable than many empirical questions.

There is an important difference between a proposition like "I don't like fish" and a proposition like "Killing is wrong." In the first case one expresses only one's most subjective personal taste, and there is no implication that one's taste ought to be shared by other people. There is no suggestion that people who take another view of the matter ought to be condemned, and still less is there any sense that a foundation has been laid in the statement for committing other people to it. But in the proposition about the moral wrongness of killing, the logic would be notably different. In asserting that "Killing is wrong," one would be conveying more than a mere personal view. One would be saying, rather, that killing ought to be regarded as wrong by others as well as oneself, and that the grounds on which it is wrong would not depend for their validity on whether they are accepted by anyone in particular, or even by a majority of those who have a viewpoint on the matter.

Such actions as killing, theft, lying, rape, and the other disruptive actions mentioned earlier are not, then, merely "disruptive." They are also *morally wrong*; they represent a failure to respect certain moral principles. Therefore, it would simply be inconsistent with the logic of the terms to say that "people should be left free to kill or not to kill, to steal or not to steal, etc. as it suits their desires or impulses." If certain actions can be shown to be wrong, they may properly be removed from the domain of personal choice and forbidden to people generally.

Someone who understands and accepts the moral wrongness of killing, stealing, and engaging in similar acts, is less likely – other things being equal – to commit such acts than is someone whose behavior is guided simply by his or her personal desires and preferences. When such a person is tempted to engage in wrongful conduct, he or she is likely to be deterred from doing so by anticipatory *guilt*; the capacity to react with anticipatory guilt may motivate resistance to morally wrong actions. Because guilt is a painful feeling that individuals are motivated to avoid, feelings of true guilt will serve to discourage wrongful conduct. In cases where such people do engage in wrongful conduct, they will experience guilt feelings and will seek to atone for their wrongdoings. True guilt, then, has both preventive and remedial consequences.[15]

It seems clear, therefore, that mere assent to one or another moral principle is not enough for the moral life. In addition, there must be a tendency for individuals to observe the principle and a tendency to feel guilty (or, when appropriate, ashamed) when disobeying its dictates.

Further, of course, morality also includes those *virtues* which are admirable both in themselves and because they facilitate morally right action.[16] But such virtues as prudence, temperance, courage, sympathy, kindness, honesty, and trustworthiness are not innate traits in human beings; they must be acquired by teaching and practice. These are dispositions not just to think or to feel in certain ways, but they are also dispositions to *act* in certain ways in certain kinds of situations.[17]

Plato and Aristotle seemed to conceive of morality almost entirely in terms of the virtues and the virtuous, rather than in terms of what is right or obligatory. The Greeks gave primary attention to the four cardinal virtues of wisdom, courage, temperance, and justice. Although I agree that these are all among the excellences of free persons and are usually admirable in themselves, the possession of such qualities is not a sufficient condition for morality. With the exception of justice, which is a true moral virtue, these virtues – as well as such virtues as sincerity and kindness – are not moral virtues. Ordinarily they are to be encouraged and desired, but they are not necessarily associated with the moral point of view.

An individual can, for example, serve an evil cause with tremendous courage, and complete sincerity, and can show unusual kindness and sympathy towards others who support the same cause. What this means is that the display of these virtues may be associated with widespread cruelty, torture, killing, and a general inhumanity toward those who oppose the cause. Hitler and Stalin are only two among the many tyrants of our time who have possessed these virtues to a high degree.

Thus, none of the above virtues is unqualifiedly good, since someone who acts according to them may act for immoral purposes or in immoral ways. In my view, one cannot construct a moral view from these virtues alone. But if they are joined to the appropriate moral viewpoint, they can have considerable importance for morality. In order for courage, wisdom, and the like, to be moral virtues, they must be guided by the supreme moral virtue: *justice*. The moral virtue of justice consists of the recognition that there are moral principles which specify what is right and wrong, and the disposition to act in accord with these principles.

While someone could be courageous and sincere and a Nazi or a Stalinist, no one whose actions were guided by a concern with justice could have accepted Hitler's and Stalin's views. Similarly today; a thief or a kidnapper may show considerable courage in his actions, and an expert at impression-management may exhibit great sincerity in manipulating others to achieve his own selfish ends. But someone whose actions are guided by a recognition of the moral wrongness of stealing, kidnapping, and the like, will either refrain from such conduct or will experience feelings of true guilt when he or she acts wrongly.

Hence, the moral virtue of justice, guided by moral principles, is primary; other virtues are secondary. Nevertheless, the morality of principle and the morality of virtue are complementary. The virtues, as I have noted, are virtues of form only. They do not become moral virtues until they are guided by moral principles. But, similarly, principles without the appropriate virtues are impotent. Only if people have the disposition to *act* on the basis of moral principles can those principles come to influence our relations with one another. For the moral life, then, moral principles, moral emotions, and the virtues are all required to help assure that people act in the ways that morality requires.

In a society where everyone accepted and acted in accordance with moral principles concerning the wrongness of various acts, and experienced guilt feelings when they did not do so, there would be a very limited need for community pressures and sanctions to discourage wrongful conduct: a large police force, various safeguards against theft and other crimes, cameras filming our activities in public places, and a wide variety of other mechanisms designed to discourage and control wrongful conduct. In such a society, we would no longer have to bear the financial costs of a large and expensive legal system, and we would be better able to exercise our liberties, enjoy our privacy, and cherish our human dignity.

III

If people are to be enabled to live together in peace and harmony, then, individuals must act on the basis of what they *ought* to do and not on the basis of what they *want* to do. But in today's world, where the emphasis is on authenticity and where it is widely assumed that people can (and should) live entirely by the dictates of their own desires, even those persons whose actions *are* guided by moral considerations must—as a matter of prudence and personal safety—take account of the many among us who ignore and reject the dictates of morality.

We live in a world today where more and more people appear to be pursuing their desires and indulging their tastes without regard for the well-being or moral status of those around them. They reject the idea that there can be a measure of the difference between decent and indecent desires or between the kinds of tastes that are morally acceptable and unacceptable for people living in the midst of other human beings. In short, we are experiencing the apparent disintegration of any standards that might claim to govern our actions according to some understanding of civility and moral decency.

What is missing is a sense of a people who are joined together by a perception of common principles concerning what is morally permissible and impermissible, and who share an understanding of what morality entails and justice demands. It has been traditionally thought that someone who can restrain himself or herself out of respect for some interests other than his or her own, someone who cultivates the virtues of character and the moral emotions, is a far better person, a far more praiseworthy individual, than someone who respects nothing beyond his or her own desires and self-interest. With the emergence of the cult of authenticity and the therapeutic sensibility in the contemporary world, however, the fulfillment of one's own desires and impulses has come to replace morality as the standard of human adequacy.

If we aspire to a society where our actions are to be governed by *internal* rather than *external* mechanisms, we must reject the pursuit of authenticity and embrace morality as the timeless and universal standard of human adequacy. Unless our actions are guided by the acceptance of moral principles, the operation of the moral emotions, and the functioning of the virtues, life will become more and more like a jungle and the barbarians in our midst will devour the rest of us.[18]

Notes

1. Derek L. Phillips, "In Praise of Guilt: Morality and Guilt in the Modern Age," *de gids*, vol. 3, no. 4 (1982). At different points in this essay I draw freely on that article.

2. See, for example, Thomas S. Kuhn, *The Structure of Scientific Revolutions*, 2d ed. (Chicago: University of Chicago Press, 1972); Derek L. Phillips, *Wittgenstein and Scientific Knowledge* (London: Macmillan, 1977); Richard Rorty, *Philosophy and the Mirror of Nature* (Princeton: Princeton University Press, 1980).

3. Emile Durkheim, *Essays on Morals and Education*, edited with an introduction by W.S.F. Pickering (London: Routledge & Kegan Paul, 1979).

4. See, for example, Christopher Lasch, *Haven in a Heartless World* (New York: Basic Books, 1977); Jacques Donzelot, *The Policing of Families* (New York: Pantheon, 1979).

5. Philip Rieff, *The Triumph of the Therapeutic* (New York: Harper and Row, 1966); Philip Rieff, *Fellow Teachers* (New York: Harper and Row, 1973); Christopher Lasch, *The Culture of Narcissism* (New York: Norton, 1979).

6. Lasch, *Culture of Narcissism*, 7.

7. Rieff, *Triumph of the Therapeutic*; Herbert Hendin, *The Age of Sensation* (New York: McGraw-Hill, 1975); Richard Sennett, *The Fall of Public Man* (New York: Random House, 1978); Lasch, *Culture of Narcissism*.

8. John Alt, "Authority, Reason, and the Civilizing Process," *Theory and Society* 10 (May 1981), 393.

9. Lasch, *Culture of Narcissism*, 13.

10. This is discussed in Derek L. Phillips, *Equality, Justice, and Rectification* (London: Academic Press, 1979).

11. Lasch, *Culture of Narcissism*, 65–66.

12. Ibid., 66.

13. This is made especially clear in Alan Gewirth, *Reason and Morality* (Chicago: University of Chicago Press, 1978).

14. John Rawls, *A Theory of Justice* (Cambridge, Mass.: Harvard University Press, 1971); Robert Nozick, *Anarchy, State, and Utopia* (New York: Basic Books, 1971); Gewirth, *Reason and*

Morality; Jürgen Habermas, *Legitimation Crisis*, trans. Thomas McCarthy (Boston: Beacon Press, 1975).

15. I discuss the difference between "true guilt," that is, rational and appropriate guilt, and "neurotic guilt" in Phillips, "In Praise of Guilt."

16. For excellent discussions of the virtues, see Lawrence C. Becker, "The Neglect of Virtue," *Ethics* 85 (1975), 110–22; Philippa Foot, *Virtues and Vices and Other Essays in Moral Philosophy* (Berkeley: University of California Press, 1978); James D. Wallace, *Virtues and Vices* (Ithaca, N.Y.: Cornell University Press, 1978).

17. See Rawls, *Theory of Justice*; Gewirth, *Reason and Morality*.

18. I would like to thank Klaske Muizelaar for her many helpful suggestions on an earlier version of this essay.

Reading Introduction

The Schizophrenia of Modern Ethical Theories
Michael Stocker

This essay is an attack on modern ethical theories. According to Stocker, if a
moral theory cannot be *lived* by, it is a bad theory. By this standard most modern
moral theories are bad. Stocker argues that moral theories provide reasons for
ethical action. Egoism, for example, says that self-interest is a good reason;
utilitarianism says that the well-being of the greatest number is a good reason;
hedonism says that pleasure is a good reason; Kant tells us that the call of duty is
a good reason; and so on. But if any such reason is to be integrated into the moral
life, it must become a motive for action. That is, the moral agent needs to be
moved by the consideration of self-interest, social well-being, pleasure, duty, or
whatever. But if we succeed in making any of these fundamental theory-begotten
reasons into the basic motives of our actions, we lose something essential in the
ethical life. We lose the person-relatedness of ethical actions and attitudes,
because full-blooded love, friendship, affection, fellow feeling, and community are
inconsistent with our being moved by the considerations that modern ethical
theories would enjoin. The effort, for example, to be a friend of someone out of a
desire to promote the well-being of society or out of duty will prevent a person
from achieving full-blooded friendship.

Another possibility exists, however, and it is perhaps this alternative that we
see most often among persons influenced by ethical theory. A person goes ahead
and enters into healthy relationships with friends and family, while nevertheless
holding the values recommended by some modern theory. In this case the individual exhibits a split between what he or she affirms theoretically and what
actually motivates him or her. Thus the "schizophrenia" of modern ethical
theories.

The Schizophrenia of Modern Ethical Theories

MICHAEL STOCKER

Modern ethical theories, with perhaps a few honorable exceptions, deal only with reasons,
with values, with what justifies. They fail to examine motives and the motivational
structures and constraints of ethical life. They not only fail to do this, they fail as ethical
theories by not doing this—as I shall argue in this paper. I shall also attempt two correlative
tasks: to exhibit some constraints that motivation imposes on ethical theory and life; and
to advance our understanding of the relations between reason and motive.

From *Journal of Philosophy* 73, 14 (August 12, 1976): 453–66. Reprinted by permission of the author and
the publisher, *Journal of Philosophy*.

One mark of a good life is a harmony between one's motives and one's reasons, values, justifications. Not to be moved by what one values—what one believes good, nice, right, beautiful, and so on—bespeaks a malady of the spirit. Not to value what moves one also bespeaks a malady of the spirit. Such a malady, or such maladies, can properly be called *moral schizophrenia*—for they are a split between one's motives and one's reasons. (Here and elsewhere, 'reasons' will stand also for 'values' and 'justifications.')

An extreme form of such schizophrenia is characterized, on the one hand, by being moved to do what one believes bad, harmful, ugly, abasing; on the other, by being disgusted, horrified, dismayed by what one wants to do. Perhaps such cases are rare. But a more modest schizophrenia between reason and motive is not, as can be seen in many examples of weakness of the will, indecisiveness, guilt, shame, self-deception, rationalization, and annoyance with oneself.

At the very least, we should be moved by our major values and we should value what our major motives seek. Should, that is, if we are to lead a good life. To repeat, such harmony is a mark of a good life. Indeed, one might wonder whether human life—good or bad—is possible without some such integration.

This is not, however, to say that in all cases it is better to have such harmony. It is better for us if self-seeking authoritarians feel fettered by their moral upbringing; better, that is, than if they adopt the reason of their motives. It would have been far better for the world and his victims had Eichmann not wanted to do what he thought he should do.[1]

Nor is this to say that in all areas of endeavor such harmony is necessary or even especially conducive to achieving what is valued. In many cases, it is not. For example, one's motives in fixing a flat tire are largely irrelevant to getting under way again. (In many such cases, one need not even value the intended outcome.)

Nor is this even to say that in all "morally significant" areas such harmony is necessary or especially conducive to achieving what is valued. Many morally significant jobs, such as feeding the sick, can be done equally well pretty much irrespective of motive. And, as Ross, at times joined by Mill, argues, for a large part of ethics, there simply is no philosophical question of harmony or disharmony between value and motive: you can do what is right, obligatory, your duty no matter what your motive for so acting. If it is your duty to keep a promise, you fulfill that duty no matter whether you keep the promise out of respect for duty, fear of losing your reputation, or whatever. What motivates is irrelevant so far as rightness, obligatoriness, duty are concerned.

Notwithstanding the very questionable correctness of this view so far as rightness, obligatoriness, duty are concerned,[2] there remain at least two problems. The first is that even here there is still a question of harmony. What sort of life would people have who did their duties but never or rarely wanted to? Second, duty, obligation, and rightness are only one part—indeed, only a small part, a dry and minimal part—of ethics. There is the whole other area of the values of personal and interpersonal relations and activities; and also the area of moral goodness, merit, virtue. In both, motive is an essential part of what is valuable; in both, motive and reason must be in harmony for the values to be realized.

For this reason and for the reason that such harmony is a mark of a good life, any theory that ignores such harmony does so at great peril. Any theory that makes difficult, or precludes, such harmony stands, if not convicted, then in need of much and powerful defense. What I shall now argue is that modern ethical theories—those theories prominent in the English-speaking philosophical world—make such harmony impossible.

Criticism of Modern Ethics

Reflection on the complexity and vastness of our moral life, on what has value, shows that recent ethical theories have by far overconcentrated on duty, rightness, and obligation.[3] This failure—of overconcentrating—could not have been tolerated but for the failure of not dealing with motives or with the relations of motives to values. (So too, the first failure supports and explains the second.) In this second failure, we find a far more serious defect of modern ethical theories than such overconcentration: they necessitate a schizophrenia between reason and motive in vitally important and pervasive areas of value, or alternatively they allow us the harmony of a morally impoverished life, a life deeply deficient in what is valuable. It is not possible for moral people, that is, people who would achieve what is valuable, to act on these ethical theories, to let them comprise their motives. People who do let them comprise their motives will, for that reason, have a life seriously lacking in what is valuable.

These theories are, thus, doubly defective. As ethical theories, they fail by making it impossible for a person to achieve the good in an integrated way. As theories of the mind, of reasons and motives, of human life and activity, they fail, not only by putting us in a position that is psychologically uncomfortable, difficult, or even untenable, but also by making us and our lives essentially fragmented and incoherent.

The sort of disharmony I have in mind can be brought out by considering a problem for egoists, typified by hedonistic egoists. Love, friendship, affection, fellow feeling, and community are important sources of personal pleasure. But can such egoists get these pleasures? I think not—not so long as they adhere to the motive of pleasure-for-self.

The reason for this is not that egoists cannot get together and decide, as it were, to enter into a love relationship. Surely they can (leaving aside the irrelevant problems about deciding to do such a thing). And they can do the various things calculated to bring about such pleasure: have absorbing talks, make love, eat delicious meals, see interesting films, and so on, and so on.

Nonetheless, there is something necessarily lacking in such a life: love. For it is essential to the very concept of love that one care for the beloved, that one be prepared to act for the sake of the beloved. More strongly, one must care for the beloved and act for that person's sake as a final goal; the beloved, or the beloved's welfare or interest, must be a final goal of one's concern and action.

To the extent that my consideration for you—or even my trying to make you happy— comes from my desire to lead an untroubled life, a life that is personally pleasing for me, I do not act for your sake. In short, to the extent that I act in various ways toward you with the final goal of getting pleasure—or, more generally, good—for myself, I do not act for your sake.

When we think about it this way, we may get some idea of why egoism is often claimed to be essentially lonely. For it is essentially concerned with external relations with others, where, except for their effects on us, one person is no different from, nor more important, valuable, or special than any other person or even any other thing. The individuals as such are not important, only their effects on us are; they are essentially replaceable, anything else with the same effects would do as well. And this, I suggest, is intolerable personally. To think of yourself this way, or to believe that a person you love thinks of you this way, is intolerable. And for conceptual, as well as psychological, reasons it is incompatible with love.

It might be suggested that it is rather unimportant to have love of this sort. But this would be a serious error. The love here is not merely modern-romantic or sexual. It is also the love among members of a family, the love we have for our closest friends, and so on. Just what sort of life would people have who never "cared" for anyone else, except as a means to their own interests? And what sort of life would people have who took it that no one loved them for their own sake, but only for the way they served the other's interest?

Just as the notion of doing something for the sake of another, or of caring for the person for that person's sake, is essential for love, so too is it essential for friendship and all affectionate relations. Without this, at best we could have good relations, friendly relations. And similarly, such caring and respect is essential for fellow feeling and community.

Before proceeding, let us contrast this criticism of egoism with a more standard one. My criticism runs as follows: Hedonistic egoists take their own pleasure to be the sole justification of acts, activities, ways of life; they should recognize that love, friendship, affection, fellow feeling, and community are among the greatest (sources of) personal pleasures. Thus, they have good reason, on their own grounds, to enter such relations. But they cannot act in the ways required to get those pleasures, those great goods, if they act on their motive of pleasure-for-self. They cannot act for the sake of the intended beloved, friend, and so on; thus, they cannot love, be or have a friend, and so on. To achieve these great personal goods, they have to abandon that egoistical motive. They cannot embody their reason in their motive. Their reasons and motives make their moral lives schizophrenic.

The standard criticism of egoists is that they simply cannot achieve such nonegoistical goods, that their course of action will, as a matter of principle, keep them from involving themselves with others in the relevant ways, and so on. This criticism is not clearly correct. For there may be nothing inconsistent in egoists' adopting a policy that will allow them to forget, as it were, that they are egoists, a policy that will allow and even encourage them to develop such final goals and motives as caring for another for that person's own sake. Indeed, as has often been argued, the wise egoist would do just this.

Several questions should be asked of this response: would the transformed person still be an egoist? Is it important, for the defense of egoism, that the person remain an egoist? Or is it important only that the person live in a way that would be approved of by an egoist? It is, of course, essential to the transformation of the person from egoistical motivation to caring for others that the person-as-egoist lose conscious control of him/herself. This raises the question of whether such people will be able to check up and see how their transformed selves are getting on in achieving egoistically approved goals. Will they have a mental alarm clock which wakes them up from their nonegoistical transforms every once in a while, to allow them to reshape these transforms if they are not getting enough personal pleasure—or, more generally, enough good? I suppose that this would not be impossible. But it hardly seems an ideal, or even a very satisfactory, life. It is bad enough to have a private personality, which you must hide from others; but imagine having a personality that you must hide from (the other parts of) yourself. Still, perhaps this is possible. If it is, then it seems that egoists may be able to meet this second criticism. But this does not touch my criticism: that they will not be able to embody their reason in their motives; that they will have to lead a bifurcated, schizophrenic life to achieve what is good.

This might be thought a defect of only such ethical theories as egoism. But consider those utilitarianisms which hold that an act is right, obligatory, or whatever if and only if it is optimific in regard to pleasure and pain (or weighted expectations of them). Such a view has it that the only good reason for acting is pleasure vs. pain, and thus should highly value love, friendship, affection, fellow feeling, and community. Suppose, now, you embody this utilitarian reason as your motive in your actions and thoughts toward someone. Whatever your relation to that person, it is necessarily not love (nor is it friendship, affection, fellow feeling, or community). The person you supposedly love engages your thought and action not for him/herself, but rather as a source of pleasure. . . .

Just as egoism and the above sorts of utilitarianisms necessitate a schizophrenia between reason and motive—and just as they cannot allow for love, friendship, affection, fellow feeling, and community—so do current rule utilitarianisms. And so do current deontologies.

What is lacking in these theories is simply—or not so simply—the person. For, love, friendship, affection, fellow feeling, and community all require that the other person be an essential part of what is valued. The person—not merely the person's general values nor even the person-qua-producer-or-possessor-of-general-values—must be valued. The defect of these theories in regard to love, to take one case, is not that they do not value love (which, often, they do not) but that they do not value the beloved. Indeed, a person who values and aims at simply love, that is, love-in-general or even love-in-general-exemplified-by-this-person "misses" the intended beloved as surely as does an adherent of the theories I have criticized.

The problem with these theories is not, however, with *other*-people-as-valuable. It is simply—or not so simply—with *people*-as-valuable. Just as they would do *vis-à-vis* other people, modern ethical theories would prevent each of us from loving, caring for, and valuing ourself—as opposed to loving, caring for, and valuing our general values or ourself-qua-producer-or-possessor-of-general-values. In these externality-ridden theories, there is as much a disappearance or nonappearance of the self as of other people. Their externality-ridden universes of what is intrinsically valuable are not solipsistic; rather, they are devoid of all people.

It is a truism that it is difficult to deal with people as such. It is difficult really to care for them for their own sake. It is psychically wearing and exhausting. It puts us in too open, too vulnerable a position. But what must also be looked at is what it does to us—taken individually and in groups as small as a couple and as large as society—to view and treat others externally, as essentially replaceable, as mere instruments or repositories of general and nonspecific value; and what it does to us to be treated, or believe we are treated, in these ways.

At the very least, these ways are dehumanizing. To say much more than this would require a full-scale philosophical anthropology showing how such personal relations as love and friendship are possible, how they relate to larger ways and structures of human life, and how they—and perhaps only they—allow for the development of those relations which are constitutive of a human life worth living: how, in short, they work together to produce the fullness of a good life, a life of eudaimonia.

Having said this, it must be acknowledged that there are many unclarities and difficulties in the notion of valuing a person, in the notion of a person-as-valuable. When we think about this—e.g., what and why we value—we seem driven either to omitting the person and ending up with a person-qua-producer-or-possessor-of-general-values or with a person's general values, or to omitting them and ending up with a bare particular ego.

In all of this, perhaps we could learn from the egoists. Their instincts, at least, must be to admit themselves, each for self, into their values. At the risk of absurdity—indeed, at the risk of complete loss of appeal of their view—what they find attractive and good about good-for-self must be, not only the good, but also and preeminently the for-self.

At this point, it might help to restate some of the things I have tried to do and some I have not. Throughout I have been concerned with what sort of motives people can have if they are to be able to realize the great goods of love, friendship, affection, fellow feeling, and community. And I have argued that, if we take as motives, embody in our motives, those various things which recent ethical theories hold to be ultimately good or right, we will, of necessity, be unable to have those motives. Love, friendship, affection, fellow feeling, and community, like many other states and activities, essentially contain certain motives and essentially preclude certain others; among those precluded we find motives comprising the justifications, the goals, the goods of those ethical theories most prominent today. To embody in one's motives the values of current ethical theories is to treat people externally and to preclude love, friendship, affection, fellow feeling, and community—both with others and with oneself. To get these great goods while holding those current ethical theories requires a schizophrenia between reason and motive.

I have not argued that if you have a successful love relationship, friendship, . . . then you will be unable to achieve the justifications, goals, goods posited by those theories. You can achieve them, but not by trying to live the theory directly. Or, more exactly, to the extent that you live the theory directly, to that extent you will fail to achieve its goods. . . .

It might be expected that, in those areas explicitly concerned with motives and their evaluation, ethical theories would not lead us into this disharmony or the corresponding morally defective life. And to some extent this expectation is met. But even in regard to moral merit and demerit, moral praise- and blameworthiness, the moral virtues and vices, the situation is not wholly dissimilar. Again, the problem of externality and impersonality, and the connected disharmony, arises.

The standard view has it that a morally good intention is an essential constituent of a morally good act. This seems correct enough. On that view, further, a morally good intention is an intention to do an act for the sake of its goodness or rightness. But now, suppose you are in a hospital, recovering from a long illness. You are very bored and restless and at loose ends when Smith comes in once again. You are now convinced more than ever that he is a fine fellow and a real friend—taking so much time to cheer you up, traveling all the way across town, and so on. You are so effusive with your praise and thanks that he protests that he always tries to do what he thinks is his duty, what he thinks will be best. You at first think he is engaging in a polite form of self-deprecation, relieving the moral burden. But the more you two speak, the more clear it becomes that he was telling the literal truth: that it is not essentially because of you that he came to see you, not because you are friends, but because he thought it his duty, perhaps as a fellow Christian or Communist or whatever, or simply because he knows of no one more in need of cheering up and no one easier to cheer up.

Surely there is something lacking here—and lacking in moral merit or value. The lack can be sheeted home to two related points: again, the wrong sort of thing is said to be the proper motive; and, in this case at least, the wrong sort of thing is, again, essentially external.[4]

Some Questions and Concluding Remarks

I have assumed that the reasons, values, justifications of ethical theories should be such as to allow us to embody them in our motives and still act morally and achieve the good. But why assume this? Perhaps we should take ethical theories as encouraging indirection—getting what we want by seeking something else: e.g., some say the economic well-being of all is realized, not by everyone's seeking it but by everyone's seeking his/her own well-being. Or perhaps we should take ethical theories as giving only indices, not determinants, of what is right and good.

Theories of indirection have their own special problems. There is always a great risk that we will get the something else, not what we really want. There are, also, these two related problems. A theory advocating indirection needs to be augmented by another theory of motivation, telling us which motives are suitable for which acts. Such a theory would also have to explain the connections, the indirect connections, between motive and real goal.

Second, it may not be very troubling to talk about indirection in such large-scale and multi-person matters as the economics of society. But in regard to something of such personal concern, so close to and so internal to a person as ethics, talk of indirection is both implausible and baffling. Implausible in that we do not seem to act by indirection, at least not in such areas as love, friendship, affection, fellow feeling, and community. In these cases, our motive has to do directly with the loved one, the friend, . . . , as does our reason. In doing something for a loved child or parent, there is no need to appeal to, or even think of, the reasons found in contemporary ethical theories. Talk of indirection is baffling, in an action- and understanding-defeating sense, since, once we begin to believe that there is something beyond such activities as love which is necessary to justify them, it is only by something akin to self-deception that we are able to continue them.

One partial defense of these ethical theories would be that they are not intended to supply what can serve as both reasons and motives; that they are intended only to supply indices of goodness and rightness, not determinants. Formally, there may be no problems in taking ethical theories this way. But several questions do arise. Why should we be concerned with such theories, theories that cannot be acted on? Why not simply have a theory that allows for harmony between reason and motive? A theory that gives determinants? And indeed, will we not need to have such a theory? True, our pre-analytic views might be sufficient to judge among index theories; we may not need a determinant theory to pick out a correct index theory. But will we not need a determinant theory to know why the index is correct, why it works, to know what is good about what is so indexed?[5]

Another partial defense of recent theories would be that, first, they are concerned almost entirely with rightness, obligation, and duty, and not with the whole of ethics; and, second, that within this restricted area, they do not suffer from disharmony or schizophrenia. To some extent this defense, especially its second point, has been dealt with earlier. But more should be said. It is perhaps clear enough by now that recent ethicists have ignored large and extremely important areas of morality—e.g., that of personal relations and that of merit. To this extent, the first point of the defense is correct. What is far from clear, however, is whether these theories were advanced only as partial theories, or whether it was believed by their proponents that duty and so on were really the whole, or at least the only important part, of ethics.

We might be advised to forget past motivation and belief, and simply look at these theories and see what use can be made of them. Perhaps they were mistaken about the scope and importance of duty and so on. Nonetheless they could be correct about the concepts involved. In reply, several points should be made. First, they were mistaken about these concepts, as even a brief study of supererogation and self-regarding notions would indicate. Second, these theories are dangerously misleading; for they can all too readily be taken as suggesting that all of ethics can be treated in an external, legislation-model, index way. (On 'legislation-model' see below.) Third, the acceptance of such theories as partial theories would pose severe difficulties of integration within ethical theory. Since these theories are so different from those concerning, e.g., personal relations, how are they all to be integrated? Of course, this third point may not be a criticism of these theories of duty, but only a recognition of the great diversity and complexity of our moral life.[6]

In conclusion, it might be asked how contemporary ethical theories come to require either a stunted moral life or disharmony, schizophrenia. One cluster of (somewhat speculative) answers surrounds the preeminence of duty, rightness, and obligation in these theories. This preeminence fits naturally with theories developed in a time of diminishing personal relations; of a time when the ties holding people together and easing the frictions of their various enterprises were less and less affection; of a time when commercial relations superseded family (or family-like) relations; of a time of growing individualism. It also fits naturally with a major concern of those philosophers: legislation. When concerned with legislation, they were concerned with duty, rightness, obligation. (Of course, the question then is, Why were they interested in legislation, especially of this sort? To some small extent this has been answered, but no more will be said on this score.) When viewing morality from such a legislator's point of view, taking such legislation to be the model, motivation too easily becomes irrelevant. The legislator wants various things done or not done; it is not important why they are done or not done; one can count on and know the actions, but not the motives. (This is also tied up with a general devaluing of our emotions and emotional possibilities—taking emotions to be mere feelings or urges, without rational or cognitive content or constraint; and taking us to be pleasure-seekers and pain-avoiders—forgetting or denying that love, friendship, affection, fellow feeling, and desire for virtue are extremely strong movers of people.) Connected with this is the legislative or simply the third-person's-eye view, which assures us that others are getting on well if they are happy, if they are doing what gives them pleasure, and the like. The effect guarantees the cause—in the epistemic sense. (One might wonder whether the general empiricist confusion of *ratio cognoscendi* and *ratio essendi* is at work here.)

These various factors, then, may help explain this rather remarkable inversion (to use Marx's notion): of taking the "effect," pleasure and the like, for the "cause," good activity.

The traditional views of morally good action also suffer from something like an inversion. Here, however, it is not causal, but philosophical. It is as if these philosophers have taken it that, because these various good things can all be classified as good, their goodness consists in this, rather than conversely. The most general classification seems to have been reified and itself taken as the morally relevant goal.

These inversions may help answer a question which afflicts this paper: Why have I said that contemporary ethics suffers from schizophrenia, bifurcation, disharmony? Why have I not claimed simply that these theories are mistaken in their denomination of what is good and bad, right- and wrong-making? For it is clear enough that, if we aim for the wrong goal, then (in all likelihood) we will not achieve what we really want, what is good, and the like. My reason for claiming more than a mere mistake is that the mistake is well reasoned; it is closely related to the truth, it bears many of the features of the truth. To take only two examples (barring bad fortune and bad circumstances), good activity does bring about pleasure; love clearly benefits the lover. There is, thus, great plausibility in taking as good what these theories advance as good. But when we try to act on the theories, try to embody their reasons in our motives—as opposed to simply seeing whether our or others' lives would be approved of by the theories—then in a quite mad way, things start going wrong. The personalities of loved ones get passed over for their effects, moral action becomes self-stultifying and self-defeating. And perhaps the greatest madnesses of all are— and they stand in a vicious interrelation—first, the world is increasingly made such as to make these theories correct; and, second, we take these theories to be correct and thus come to see love, friendship, and the like only as possible, and not very certain, sources of pleasure or whatever. We mistake the effect for the cause and when the cause-seen-as-effect fails to result from the effect-seen-as-cause, we devalue the former, relegating it, at best, to good as a means and embrace the latter, wondering why our chosen goods are so hollow, bitter, and inhumane.[7]

Notes

1. It might be asked what is better for such people, to have or lack this harmony, given their evil motives or values; in which way they would be morally better. Such questions may not be answerable.

2. See my "Act and Agent Evaluations," *Review of Metaphysics* 27, 1, 105 (September 1973): 42–61.

3. See ibid. and my "Rightness and Goodness: Is There a Difference?" *American Philosophical Quarterly* 10, 2 (April 1973): 87–98.

4. For a way to evade this problem, see my "Morally Good Intentions," *The Monist* 54, 1 (January 1970): 124–41, where it is argued that goodness and rightness need not be the object of a morally good intention, but rather that serious goods or right acts can be.

5. Taking contemporary theories to be index theories would help settle one of the longest-standing disputes in ethical philosophy—a dispute which finds Aristotle and Marx on the winning side and many if not most contemporary ethicists on the other. The dispute concerns the relative explan-atory roles of pleasure and good activity and good life. Put crudely, many utilitarians and others have held that an activity is good only because and insofar as it is productive of pleasure; Aristotle and Marx hold of at least many pleasures that if they are good this is because they are produced by good activity. The problem of immoral pleasures has seemed to many the most important test case for this dispute. To the extent that my paper is correct, we have another way to settle the dispute. For, if I am correct, pleasure cannot be what makes all good activity good, even prescinding from immoral pleasures. It must be activity, such as love and friendship, which makes some pleasures good.

6. Part of this complexity can be seen as follows: Duty seems relevant in our relations with our loved ones and friends, only when our love, friendship, and affection lapse. If a family is "going well," its members "naturally" help each other; that is, their love, affection, and deep friendship are sufficient for them to care for and help one another (to put it a bit coolly). Such "feelings" are at times worn thin. At these times, duty may have to be looked to or called upon (by the agent or by others) to get done at least a modicum of those things which love would normally provide. To some rough extent, the frequency with which a family member acts out of duty, instead of love, toward another in the family is a measure of the lack of love the first has for the other. But this is not to deny that there are duties of love, friendship, and the like.

7. I wish to thank all those who have heard or read various versions of this paper and whose comments have greatly encouraged and helped me. These topics are discussed further in "Values and Purposes: The Limits of Teleology and the Ends of Friendship," *Journal of Philosophy* 77 (December 1981):747–65.

Reading Introduction

By Virtue of a Virtue
Harold Alderman

Harold Alderman addresses the question, What is the best starting point for an ethical theory? and answers that the *character* of some outstandingly ethical individual such as Socrates, the Buddha, or Confucius is the best starting point. Alderman's answer is at odds with all of mainline modern moral philosophy, which has for the most part taken as theoretical starting point either some *rule*, such as "always act so as to treat persons not as means only, but as ends in themselves," or some *good*, such as pleasure or the greatest happiness of the greatest number of people. According to Alderman, a moral theory, to be adequate, must do two things. First, it must account for the *objectivity* of moral truths; that is, it must explain how moral insights or claims can be right, not just for an individual or within a culture, but for all human beings. Second, it must account for certain features of moral *subjectivity*; that is, it must fit the psychological processes by which people assimilate moral truths and the procedures by which they make moral decisions. Rule- and good-based theories, says Alderman, succeed in the first task but fail at the second; a character-based theory is superior in that it succeeds at both.

In the first stage of his argument Alderman establishes the power of a character-based theory to account for the objectivity of moral truths. Essentially the reason is that the character of a Socrates, for example, is every bit as obviously *correct* as any rule or good that might be proposed as foundational. The paradigmatic moral individuals are transculturally recognizable as such, and thus silently demonstrate the objectivity of moral perception.

The second stage of the argument is devoted to showing the weakness of good- and rule-based theories both when it comes to explaining how people assimilate morality and when it comes to actually justifying moral decisions. We do not become moral people just by projecting good goals for ourselves and then devising ways to achieve them, as a utilitarian theory would seem to suggest. Nor do we do this by learning a set of rules and then bringing our will into conformity with them, as a theorist like Kant would seem to suggest. We become moral by living in a community of people whose behaviors we imitate—behaviors that, ideally at least, illuminate important truths about the possibility of being human.

As to the psychology of moral decision-making, Alderman argues particularly against rule-based theories. Rules are no doubt useful here and there in the moral life, but they are "conceptually secondary." The crucial mechanism by which people make moral decisions, claims Alderman, is *the decision procedure of envisionment*, which involves using imagination to decide what a paradigmatic individual might do in some morally problematic situation. This decision procedure can be enhanced through study of literary, religious, and philosophical texts in which paradigmatic character is depicted.

By Virtue of a Virtue

HAROLD ALDERMAN

I

Beginning with G.E.M. Anscombe's "Modern Moral Philosophy" in 1958, various critics—e.g., Frankena, Foot, MacIntyre, and Murdoch—have, to one extent or another, expressed dissatisfaction with the condition of modern moral philosophy.[1] Prior to this round of critiques, H. A. Prichard in 1912 asked the question "Is Moral Philosophy Based on a Mistake?" in an essay of that title in *Mind*.[2] One finds precedent for these expressions of discontent with the ground rules of moral philosophy in both Aristotle and Kant, two thinkers whose reformulations of the questions and procedures of ethics proved seminal for the discipline. Even neglecting other important developments in contemporary moral philosophy (such as those in natural law theory), the diversity and rigor of these critiques alone suggest that the prognosis for the discipline of ethics is quite favorable. Philosophy in at least one of its dimensions has recovered that self-reflective attentiveness that marks its most productive phases.

So it is that several of these contemporary critiques raise the suspicion that what is wrong with moral philosophy is that it operates outside of a context in terms of which talk about moral laws or moral goods would be intelligible. Our contemporary situation can thus be contrasted with, for example, that of Aristotle for whom a discussion of "magnificence" was firmly rooted in an Athenian context in terms of which an argument over the merits of that particular virtue might be resolved. Alasdair MacIntyre's *After Virtue* brings this line of reflection into sharp new focus with a series of illuminating discussions concerning the role of the virtues both in the history of moral practices and in the logic of moral argument. In general, MacIntyre tries to show that "contemporary moral debate is interminable" (70); that is, he tries to show *why*, given the nature of contemporary moral philosophy, there is "no rational way of securing moral agreement" (6). Because I believe MacIntyre is successful in his demonstration, I shall, in this paper, take that demonstration for granted and try to construct a set of arguments designed to show how, in terms of a universally accessible paradigmatic character, we have at hand a way of avoiding the "interminable" regress of moral debate. Thus although my argument is derivative to MacIntyre's diagnosis and dependent, in part, upon his treatment of the concept of virtue, the proposal I develop here for the resolution of moral arguments is, sadly to say, somewhat at odds with his own.

Thus, in effect, I shall be arguing that no rules or goodness theories can provide an adequate foundation for the important theoretical needs which the discipline of ethics is expected to meet. In elaborating this argument, in addition to MacIntyre I shall be indebted primarily to the work of Lawrence Becker, A. S. Cua, and Stanley Hauerwas,

Originally published in the *Review of Metaphysics* 36 (September 1982): 127–53. Reprinted with permission.

each of whom, in very different ways that will not often be directly addressed here, has made it easier once again to begin taking seriously the idea of virtue and its related family of concepts.[3]

Before going on with my argument, I want to call attention to what I take to be the conceptual power of goodness or law theories, a power which I see as lying in their ability to give unity to the phenomena of moral experience. In saying things like "all men ought to pursue good X" or "all men ought to do their duty Y," both axiological and deontological moral theorists take for granted that we share a common human situation, a situation demanding moral response. Further, in defending such notions as common goods and common obligations, axiological and deontological moral philosophies argue for an objectivity of goods and rules which yields a presumption against subjectivism or relativism. It is in these two regards that such theories primarily are to be commended. However, in their preoccupation with the objectivity of rules or goods, such theories conceal a crucial feature of morality: the efforts of disparate moral agents to make moral sense of their experience. Such theories also fail to notice important features of the decision procedures actually employed by moral agents in those times of moral quandary when clarity about moral matters is most desperately needed. Their very preoccupation with the objectivity of goods or rules thus obscures for both axiological and deontological theories the *context* of moral agency, a context in which rules and notions of the good have—as I shall argue—only a secondary role.

With these reflections in mind, in Section II, I want to show *why* character is the appropriate, most adequate, and necessary terminus of moral argument. There is, as I shall argue, a transcultural dimension of character, one most clearly manifest in the paradigmatic individuals, which constitutes its moral dimension. In Section III, I continue my defense of the central role of paradigmatic character in moral philosophy by considering the following things: the relation between character and goods, the relation between character and rules, the concept of narrative argument, and the notion of a decision procedure based on the logic of imitation. The task of re-thinking moral philosophy as I see it, then, requires retrieving the concept of paradigmatic character, the concept whose elucidation describes the human context of moral practice. It is only in this context that it is possible to have something like a rational and non-provincial resolution of moral arguments.

II

If one is to avoid infinite regress in any sort of argument it must be possible at some point simply to say something like, "Look, that's just the way things are" or something like, "*Now*, do you see?" When a philosopher reaches such a point in argument all he can do— since he does not have recourse to rhetoric or intimidation—is go through the argument again, perhaps emphasizing certain key points, perhaps inventing analogies, or perhaps paraphrasing what he has already said. But he must always get back to some such terminal point, some such grounding appeal, and he must also be able to make clear that he *has* reached such a point and that—argument exhausted—there is nothing else he can do.

As a class, moral claims are traditionally grounded in metaphysical claims; that is, it is recognized that it makes sense to say "one ought to do so and so" only because the injunction presupposes that "reality is of such and such a nature." Thus one sort of ultimate appeal for the resolution of disagreement in moral argument involves showing that someone has gotten his reality ascriptions wrong. Much contemporary debate over the morality of abortion, for example, involves arguments of this sort. But there is one class of moral disagreement that cannot be resolved in this way and that is when the disputants share a metaphysics and when it can be shown that they do not disagree in this regard in any significant way. How is this sort of moral dispute to be resolved? That is, what is the bottom line of appeal when, for example, two naturalists *disagree* on the morality of abortion? There is, I think, still another interesting moral situation which does not admit of resolution by appeal to metaphysics, and that is when two moralists who adopt different metaphysical schemata come to the same moral conclusions: for example, when a naturalist and a super-naturalist both condemn the practice of abortion. Upon what do two moralists who adopt divergent metaphysics base their *agreement*? Generally, the answer to these sorts of questions has been that there are certain ultimate and obvious rights, goods or rules, which must be taken for granted—however arduously the moral philosopher has labored to discover their obviousness. This style of final appeal keeps arguments within the explicitly moral domain; it says, in effect, "look, morally speaking that's just the way things are." Given these remarks, it is obvious that for rights, rule, or goodness moralities, the rights, the rules, or the goods are taken as ultimate and as giving final warrant to the moral philosophies for which they constitute the court of final appeal.

It is G. E. Moore's intuitionism, in modern moral philosophy, that most clearly recognizes that moral appeals are *ultimately* tied to some kind of direct apprehension. Historically, things would have gone better for moral philosophy if Moore's insight had been taken more seriously, and it seems to me that this insight *can* be taken seriously, however amusing it may be to recall that Moore's early disciples went around trying to intuit non-natural properties.[4] The problem with Moore's analysis was that it substituted the *ultimate* appeal to paradigmatic cases for too much of the preliminary work of justification. If we avoid the difficulty of collapsing the distinction between ultimate and penultimate maneuvers in moral reasoning, we remain safe in taking seriously what Moore has to teach us about the terminus of moral argument.

Two recent authors (Gass and Pincoffs) have tried to reinstate something like Moore's insight by arguing that what is wrong with modern moral philosophy is that it is preoccupied with extreme or ambiguous cases.[5] The merit of their somewhat different arguments is that they try to begin the work of moral philosophy with an appeal to obvious (though not ultimate) cases. Thus Gass, for example, observes that there is something obviously wrong with baking an "obliging stranger" who agrees to let you use him in an experiment. Aristotelian moral philosophy involved a different sort of appeal to obvious cases insofar as it argued that in order to be a responsible Athenian one had merely to imitate the behavior of the obviously good Athenian citizen. By showing the citizen what he was *for the most part* to do, Aristotle's ethics prepared individuals for action *in extremis*—though such was not its primary intent—by giving them confidence that they knew the right thing to do. The wisdom of Aristotle's approach—however provincial some of its specific recommendations—lies in that it clearly understands that one learns how to act by acting and that one first learns how to undertake *appropriate action* in the quotidian of one's experience simply by observing how things are done.

I take it that Moore's recognition that we must appeal to something *ultimately* obvious and Gass and Pincoffs's injunction to begin with *initial obvious cases* are both salutary for moral philosophy. Taken together these recommendations show us a way beyond moral philosophy's pre-occupation with the appeal to the putative obviousness of certain rights, goods, or rules; and they do this by making overt the necessity of an appeal to some sort of obvious case. The point is that it is not obvious that the only type of entity to which one might make a final moral appeal is either a right, a rule, or a good. And the further point is that it *is* obvious that in appealing to some final court of rights, goods, or rules, moral philosophy is employing the criterion of obviousness. Thus this paper offers as another possibility of ultimate moral appeal the moral obviousness of the character of the paradigmatic individual. In that character the obviousness of the initial obvious cases is exemplified and we have at hand a way to retain both the objectivity of moral philosophy and the primacy of the moral agent.

The appeal to the character of paradigmatic individuals is itself, in some ways, a radically traditional sort of appeal. Underlying Plato's moral philosophy, for example, is his certainty that Socrates is the moral paradigm. All of Plato's dialogues may be read as an attempt to set out the character of Socrates in such a way that the reader will be led to imitate him. It is perhaps equally obvious that for Aristotle, Aristotle himself is the moral paradigm. Thus if we want to be virtuous citizens of the Aristotelian *polis*, we must act like Aristotle—or at least like an Aristotle with a sense of humor. Nietzsche in the 19th century portrays the character of Zarathustra as the paradigmatic philosophical individual and enjoins us, in part IV of *Thus Spoke Zarathustra*, to imitate that character. For each of these philosophers, then, it is character that in some important senses is the bottom line of moral appeal. The appeal to character is, of course, even more central in the arguments and practices of the great religious traditions.

Nevertheless, however central the appeal to character has been in moral argument or however central I argue it ought to be, a first obligation of any argument such as this is to suggest some prima facie reasons as to why character is a more adequate final court of appeal in moral philosophy than either rights, goods, or rules. Let me begin this argument with a discussion of Karl Jaspers's list of paradigmatic individuals in his book, *The Great Philosophers*.[6] Jaspers singles out Socrates, Buddha, Confucius, and Christ as paradigmatic individuals, acknowledging that he might well have chosen Moses, Mohammed, and Lao Tsu, among others. Jaspers's acknowledgement of a certain imprecision in his list seems to raise doubts about the possibility of any clear specification as to who counts as a paradigmatic individual. Would not, for instance, philosophers, poets, and novelists, as well as ordinary and extraordinary individuals, all come up with different lists of paradigmatic individuals? And if they did, would this not itself count as a telling objection? By way of a first general attempt to deflect such a line of argument, I want to say that it is *not* at all obvious that differences in class, profession, and talent would affect who gets named as a paradigmatic individual any more than they would affect what rights, rules, or goods get named as obvious and fundamental on lists compiled for natural law theorists, deontologists, and teleologists. In the second place, it *is* obvious that if class and professional differences *do* affect the compilation of rights, goods, rules, or paradigmatic individuals, this itself would not yield an effective objection to the possibility of compiling non-provincial lists of goods, rights, rules, or paradigmatic individuals. All it would do is show that such lists would initially have to cope with the biases reflected in class, profession, and so forth. The third and telling point, of course, is that from the fact that a group of people approve of a good, a right, a rule, or a paradigmatic individual, it does not follow that they should be given approval. Jaspers's list of paradigmatic individuals thus merely provides us with a reasonable set of clues – the initial obvious cases – we need to get on with the argument.

Given these general remarks, I do have to argue that it is logically necessary to specify a common set of character traits which will be shared by all paradigmatic individuals, and I want to make this argument even while acknowledging that no such set of traits is to be found in this paper. In arguing for the possible common set of character traits I thus reject Jaspers's and Cua's assumptions that no such set can be described. My argument is itself, I think, not one whit more tenuous than the presumption in favor of the possibility of universal rights, goods, or duties, a presumption made by every natural law theorist and deontologist and by many axiologists. Indeed, the skeptical presumption against the very possibility of such a specification of paradigmatic character traits seems to me little more than an ad ignorantium of modern relativism.

From a longer list of Jaspers, then, I have culled the following family of identifying characteristics. In terms of these characteristics we can identify the paradigmatic individuals whose character provides us with the best clue for the description and ordering of those elusive dispositional traits, the virtues themselves.

1. They set norms by their attitudes and actions.
2. They *indicate* what is to be done and their demands are never fully expressed in instructions.
3. They possess great empathy.
4. All stress silence, speak in parables, and emphasize that their highest teaching can be expressed only indirectly.
5. They do not write.
6. They are preoccupied with overcoming death and suffering, and they themselves exemplify this overcoming.
7. They believe human love is universal and unlimited.

The most obvious result of this list of characteristics is that it clearly places the paradigmatic individual in the domain of praxis rather than in the domain of theory. The paradigmatic individuals thus exemplify a style of life that emphasizes the Aristotelian insight that moral philosophy is a practical science, one to be learned by practicing what certain key individuals *do* rather than by analyzing what they *say*. This feature of the list itself yields one presumption in favor of taking the character of paradigmatic individuals as the final line of appeal in moral argument, and it does this because it helps make sense of the common charge made against philosophy that it is nothing but a matter of "words,

words, words." Thus, in this regard at least, the world's objection to the "impracticality" of philosophy might prove justified.

At no point in his own discussion of the paradigmatic individuals does Jaspers raise doubts about the possibility of *recognizing* them as such: the cases of Buddha, Christ, and Confucius make it overwhelmingly obvious that character is the final line of moral appeal in diverse moral traditions. This historical fact itself further indicates the prima facie cogency of taking the concept of paradigmatic character more seriously in moral philosophy, and it does this on the grounds that the task of philosophy is to clarify the practices of the everyday world and not to legislate them out of existence. The assumption that either goods or rules are logically prior to character in moral argument thus runs counter to the shared wisdom of the Buddhist, Christian, and other moral traditions. To make somewhat different use of this same point, the institutional and intellectual traditions derived from the four paradigmatic individuals constitute a rather rigorous test of their status as moral paradigms, however modern it may be to remember P. T. Barnum's observation on the possibilities of belief. Thus to ignore these tests and to begin with the skeptical question "but how do we know they are moral paradigms?" is to eschew what is obvious; such skepticism begs the question against the very possibility of the moral life, a possibility demonstrated in the lives of the paradigmatic individuals. The point here is that one can begin neither moral nor mathematical arguments with critics who doubt the possibility of such arguments. The further point is that this sort of access to the domain of moral argument yields the possibility of understanding the canons diverse human traditions actually invoke as the bottom line of moral argument.

In addition to its positive gains, Jaspers's discussion also raises two difficulties with the concept of the paradigmatic individual which are important for different reasons. In the first place, we must acknowledge that the traditional practices established by the paradigmatic individuals differ in major respects, and this seems to raise the problem of Babel: should we try to imitate Buddha, Christ, Lao Tsu, or Socrates? But this is a specious problem, for what is most obvious about the paradigmatic individuals—as with the great moral theories—is that there is a common core of obvious behaviors endorsed by all of them. And it is with these obvious cases of obviously moral behavior that we must begin our discussion, otherwise we merely—once again—accede to an unsubstantiated skepticism which seems utterly to relativize the domain of moral practice.

The "obvious differences" in the Buddhist, Christian, and other *traditions*, then, seem to me to stand to the *character of their founders* in the same way the reasons of traditional moral theory stand to their conclusions (i.e., rights, rules, or goods): they are different kinds of support for the same "conclusions." The differences in the moral philosophies of, for example, Kant, Aristotle, and Mill, lie primarily in the reasons they give for their conclusions and not primarily in the conclusions themselves. So it is also with the differences in the paradigmatic individuals. Of course—and this is the key point—the kinds of "reasons" (i.e., the traditions and practices) which support the characters of the paradigmatic individuals are of a different logical type than those which support the *conclusions* of traditional moral philosophy. And this means that the structures holding together a moral stance that takes the character of paradigmatic individuals as fundamental will be different from those of contemporary moral philosophy: they will be narrative, literary, and historical rather than evidential, logical, and scientific. This is a point to which I shall return in the next section of my paper.

The second difficulty which Jaspers raises is that of deciding if a paradigmatic individual is being appropriately imitated. This I take it is an empirical and not a logical problem, and I also take it that this is a particularly modern problem when so many Westerners are trying to be Buddhists. This difficulty seems to me to be interesting in the following ways. In the first place, the problem of appropriate imitation is an intra-traditional problem; it is, for example, the problem of how a Westerner appropriately imitates Christ, a problem addressed by Thomas à Kempis and resolved, however imperfectly, by the monastic tradition of Christianity. One knows that one appropriately *imitates* Christ if one lives as a viable member of a community whose task it is to know what 'appropriate' means in a tradition which takes such imitation as its *raison d'être*. The test is, of course, the same for the Buddhist, Confucian, and Socratic traditions; and in all cases it is true that one never knows if the test of "appropriateness" is perfectly met. But this sort of objection also holds for rights, rule, or goodness theories: Do I *really* know the good? Have I *really* understood the categorical imperative? The odd result of this observation is that it becomes evident that moral philosophies which assume the character of paradigmatic individuals as the bottom line of argument are in a stronger position than contemporary moral philosophies on this point, for they have both traditions and institutions, as well as arguments, to employ in the tests of appropriateness, whereas, contemporary moral philosophy has only the books of philosophers. Each of the monastic orders, churches, and sects, is then a mechanism for making the test of appropriate imitation, and it is no telling objection to this line of argument to say, "Well, which one of them has got Christ right?" The point, of course, is that we never know for sure. But more importantly it is the very dialogue between varying interpretations of Christ's character which keeps the question of "appropriate imitation" open and rescues it from mere dogmatism.

The second focus of the problem of appropriate imitation is extra-traditional and may seem logical rather than empirical: *Can*, for example, a Westerner be a Buddhist? Of course he can if he knows the texts, traditions, and institutions of Buddhism. But can he know those? And the answer is: of course he can if he knows the appropriate languages or if translations are commensurate with the original texts (and I think they can be). Now saying these things is not meant to minimize difficulties; for it is difficult enough merely to learn a language and to get to know a different culture. How much more difficult it must be to get to understand the peak spiritual achievements of an alien tradition.

Having acknowledged the extra-traditional problem of appropriate imitation, I want, nonetheless, to argue that it is the attempt at such imitation and not the difficulties that accompany it which is interesting, for in an odd way the attempt is both supportive of the idea of the universality of the paradigmatic individuals and at the same time, logically superfluous. That is, in the first place, if an alien paradigmatic individual can be recognized as such, it must be because he illuminates certain features of the seeker's own experience. Otherwise why—assuming no mere preoccupation with the exotic—would he be sought? The ability to recognize alien paradigmatic individuals as such thus supports two important conclusions: there is such a thing as *human* experience and the paradigmatic individuals manifest universally *human* character traits. But this is the point at which the argument gets interesting, for if the alien paradigmatic individual can be recognized as such (e.g., Buddha), it is only because he is analogous to some other paradigmatic individual (e.g., Christ); but in this situation it is (for Westerners) Christ who is the explanatory term of the analogy and Buddha who is the unknown. Thus a Westerner can recognize an "alien" paradigmatic individual only to the extent he knows the paradigmatic individual of his own tradition, but since paradigmatic individuals express fundamentally *human* truths, there is no reason to seek to know an alien paradigmatic individual. A Westerner *can* be a Buddhist, but why should he? Now I take it that there may be serious answers to this last question. For example, one might want to argue that in this epoch Buddhism and Christianity emphasize different aspects of the human predicament that need to be attended to, and therefore Westerners ought to learn those other aspects by becoming Buddhists. But this is not the sort of answer it seems to be, for what the answer really says is that no tradition is perfect and that traditions learn from each other. Thus what we are left with is an injunction to explore another tradition in order to "perfect" our own, so that we may more perfectly imitate our own traditional paradigmatic individual. The key part of all of this, however, is that insofar as traditions, institutions, practices, etc., are "reasons" supporting the character of a paradigmatic individual, one will always be able to give better reasons for the imitation of an indigenous paradigmatic individual than one will for an alien; that is, one always has a better understanding of one's native tradition. The imitation of alien paradigmatic individuals thus carries with it the greater risk of dogmatism and is therefore to that extent, at least, to be abjured.

This line of argument establishes a presumption in favor of the idea that paradigmatic individuals are universally accessible and that their character has transcultural significance. This does not, however, mean that I have shown that in all respects all paradigmatic individuals endorse the very same range of appropriate behaviors, so that all questions about conflict between paradigmatic individuals are eliminated. Nevertheless, my argument does make plausible the conclusion that the appeal to the character of paradigmatic individuals involves something more than a mere appeal to the contingencies of cultural practices. More strongly than this, I think that close attention to a comparative study of the paradigmatic individuals will show that there are no irresolvable conflicts between them. Those conflicts that do exist will prove to be resolvable in terms of some account of being human that is neither merely provincial nor merely formal.[7]

Since the necessity of some universally human dimension of character is a central element of my argument I want to garner additional support for the possible existence of such a dimension from two other sources. First, it seems to me that this dimension is much more than hinted at in those great works of literature which can be read across major historical, linguistic, and cultural divides. The access that all readers have to the quintessentially human experiences of, for example, Oedipus, Quixote, Ishmael, or Beowulf yields such a strong presumption in favor of a human dimension of character that probably only we analytically minded philosophers might ignore it in favor of the tidier, theoretical domains of rights, rules, and goods. Indeed, the preoccupation of great dramatists, poets, and novelists to re-tell these or similar tales is an effort to re-new in the writer's own appropriate idiom the hero's quintessentially human struggle with the matters ideally resolved by the paradigmatic individuals. The great works of both Western and Eastern literature, then seem to me to provide a second obvious—perhaps banally so—set of clues to the *human* domain of experience which the paradigmatic individuals most perfectly exemplify. Having said these things, it is not my intention to pursue either of these sets of clues toward anything like an adequate philosophical description of the dimensions whose existence I think they support. Rather, I mean to take seriously the very style of philosophical argument which this paper suggests has been somewhat neglected in moral philosophy—the presentation of clear and important cases—and, for the time being, to rest content with the promise made by my presentations.[8] Nonetheless, remembering Moore's failure, I would acknowledge the need to complete the presentations with further philosophical defense. Yet the presentations themselves have their own autonomy and it is with this in mind that I end this section of my paper with yet a third presentation.

Sir Richard Francis Burton, the 19th century scholar, geographer, soldier, anthropologist, and linguist, provides an historical case that further supports the conclusion that there is a cross cultural dimension of human character. Since Burton himself exemplifies the experience of the multitude of travelers who have been able to recognize character in individuals with whom they do not share primary cultural membership, his case is particularly decisive. In general, Burton, as many sources make clear, had the uncanny knack of being not only a virtuous Victorian (who always knew the right Victorian thing to do, though he did not always do it) but of also knowing in disparate, alien cultures what counted as appropriate behavior. Given this knack, Burton was always recognized as a man of virtue; that is to say, he was able either to imitate appropriately the "right" behavior of worlds radically different from his own or, when failing this, he, nonetheless, was able to act in such a way as to be recognized as a man of character. Thus, Burton, for example, successfully lived as an Indian native while spying for the British Army and, more dramatically, while disguised as an Arab-speaking Persian he was one of the first Europeans to visit Mecca. By contrast, when Burton enters Dahomey for the first time, knowing neither the language nor the standard behaviors, he is, at a crucial juncture, nonetheless perceived by King Gelele as a man of character.[9] Both Burton, the alien, and Gelele, the King, step outside their cultures to meet in the quintessentially human dimension.

Burton's arrival in Dahomey became an occasion for Gelele to order the performance of the brutal "Ku To Man" ceremony. This ceremony had as its dramatic climax the ritual execution of a number of slaves, the number being determined by the importance of the event which occasioned it. Burton is appalled by the executions that take place, and he has the audacity to demand that the King release some of the prisoners and to insist that he, himself, be absent from all the killings. The King accepts Burton's admonitions, although he nonetheless executes twenty-three slaves in Burton's honor. Burton gives a careful description of the grisly scene: the resigned and terrified victims, the execution platform, the mute testimony of the fresh corpses, and the bleached skulls of earlier "messengers."

The point of these remarks is that King Gelele tolerates Burton's violations of well-established Dahomean customs and does so in such a way that rather than being offended he recognizes that Burton is a man of character, who in some sense has done the right thing. But in what regard does Burton do the right thing? Surely no one would draw from this case a rule to the effect that one ought to rebuff the King's hospitality by correcting his kingly etiquette, for it is clear that Burton's achievement lies in his *violation* of standard behavior. Thus what is communicated in this event is character and not a sensitivity to the rules of an alien etiquette. Burton *shows* Gelele that there is a dimension in which they can meet which is neither English nor Dahomean. With his typically dramatic sense of his own presence, Burton reveals that he is a brave and decisive man who will not easily abandon the moral demands of his own culture. To all of these roles the King responds with friendliness: he and Burton can meet outside of the host-guest relationship because the king acknowledges a set of virtues which can be recognized across the boundaries of their cultures. The triumphant moment of this meeting takes place when the King invites Burton to dance with him in a ritual dance, and there in the African bush two strangers share a common and human meeting place. As a gleeful but somewhat awed Dahomean populace looks on, the King dances with an alien. This experience of Richard Burton – but one of many – thus shows in a decisive way that there is a transcultural dimension of character which can be recognized without argument. It is this dimension that constitutes the human dimension of character, a dimension that is manifest in the heroes of literature and, in an ideal way, in the paradigmatic individuals. It is to this dimension that moral philosophy must make its final appeal.

III

In this part of my argument I want to indicate what a moral philosophy, re-thought in the way I have argued is necessary, would look like. That is, I want to give a first indication of its conceptual terrain and thus also to develop a further set of arguments in its defense. In order to begin this discussion I want to separate my previous critique of goodness theories from my critique of law theories. I have to do this because I now must acknowledge that my earlier, apparently parallel, opposition to rules and goods theories seems to break down insofar as it is appropriate to deem this virtue theory itself a species of goodness theory. I am willing to so deem it with the proviso – as I argued in the preceding section – that there is a convincing prima facie warrant for taking the character of the paradigmatic individual as the summum bonum; no such warrant is available for any other conception of the good. Thus it seems to me to be utterly absurd to argue that there are ever circumstances under which paradigmatic character is morally undesirable. By contrast, it is not absurd to argue that under some circumstances neither pleasure nor the greatest happiness of the greatest number is morally desirable. The example of the indulgent libertine – for which the aristocratic drug addict is the paradigm – establishes the case against the hedonist, and the example of the tyranny of a majority over a minority – for which the ante bellum South is but one of all too many paradigms – makes the case against the utilitarian. Now, I realize that both the hedonist and the utilitarian have what they take to be forceful responses to these not altogether original objections, but it is not my goal here to try to rebuff their responses. My goal is rather more direct and I think more devastating for both the hedonistic and the utilitarian positions: if – as I have argued – no similar, intuitively damning objections can even be formulated against the conclusion that in *all* circumstances paradigmatic character is a moral desideratum, then this impossibility alone places all other goods in a secondary, provincial relationship to the universal good of paradigmatic character.

Given my argument that the good of character is logically fundamental, it follows that in several important senses rules, although at least heuristically helpful, are also conceptually secondary. It is to these various senses and to their ramifications that I now must attend. Let me begin this way: In being with a moral paradigm one learns to be virtuous the same way one learns to cook, dance, write, play football, and so forth, and that is by imitating persons who are good at those sorts of things. Since being moral means learning how to do the right thing, it seems to me not at all logically odd to argue that learning how to be moral is strictly analogous to all other cases of *learning how to*. Rules, then, are secondary in the first place in the sense that they are not necessary to learn how to be moral. And this is true in the sense that an anthropologist would never learn how to behave appropriately in an alien community simply by asking for the rules of right behavior. Rather he would do so by observing what people do and, in particular, by observing what the people do who are approved of by the culture. For neither the moral agent nor the anthropologist can rules give an adequate orientation to all the nuances and contingencies of appropriate behavior. What they both require is a certain character. Like children and anthropologists, then, moral agents are appropriately taught by exemplification. The difficulties of modern moral philosophy, given this remark, can be seen as analogous to the difficulties of the "new math" insofar as it substitutes the rules of set theory for the praxis of ordinary arithmetical behavior. The traditional teacher *shows* her pupils that you always write "$1 + 1 = 2$," and the pupils practice writing it; and they do so successfully to the extent that the teacher manifests the sort of character traits that motivate children to imitate her behavior. Or, to introduce one more telling case, if it is impossible to teach a seven-year old how to ride a bicycle by giving him the right set of rules, is it not absurd to think that a set of moral rules is sufficient to teach a person how to live a life?

The secondary role of rules can be emphasized from another direction by calling attention to the shared conception that people who, for example, paint or dance by the rules are somehow missing the point of what they do. In these sorts of rule following behavior, the essence of the praxis which is to be learned is somehow missed and the behavior is criticized as "just going through the moves." In the same sense, a sociopath who followed the rules of appropriate behavior would be missing the point of the moral life. Kant, in drawing the distinction between "acting in accordance with" and "acting because of," shows that following the rules is not a sufficient condition of morality, although his own conception of "acting because of" is itself misleading to the extent that it allows many contemporary theorists to divorce rule following behavior from the development of desirable character traits.

Now although my interpretation holds that the concept of being moral is to be explicated in terms of the logic of *acting like* rather than in terms of the logic of rule following, it is nonetheless true that one can formulate rules for what one is doing when one imitates either a craftsman or a moral paradigm. But when someone (e.g., the craftsman) is in a position to formulate adequate rules, he no longer needs them. Thus, rules are superfluous for *becoming like* a craftsman (after all, he did it without them) and are unnecessary when one *is* a craftsman. Rules, as Collingwood observed, are late developments in the moral life.[10] Perhaps they are autobiographical footnotes which we have mistaken for the life itself.

Another limitation of rules is indicated from a different direction by Lawrence Becker when he calls attention to the problems rule theories have with the analysis of excuses or exceptions.[11] We are all familiar with the phenomenon of saying such things as "even though he broke the rule he is still a good man." Becker takes such occurrences as indicating the need to *supplement* rule theories by reference to the character of moral agents. From my point of view, such occurrences indicate more fundamental problems in that they show that character is logically prior to the obligation to follow some rule. It is, after all, always in the context of a justifying prior judgment that someone is of good character that we are willing to make exceptions, the point being that we recognize that for some persons breaking the rules does not affect any judgment made about them. It would be conceptually odd to make exceptions if rules were logically fundamental. The point I want to make here is the one Nietzsche made in *The Genealogy of Morals*: it is the character of certain persons which provides the warrant for following or not following rules and not the obviousness of some rules which justifies approving of the character of the persons who follow those rules. Becker wants to say that the character of the moral agent has "significant" impact on how we regard the morality of actions. I want to say that it is morally decisive. It is because of this decisiveness that we are willing to say that when, for example, two teachers strike a pupil under exactly the same circumstances that in one case the action is morally warranted (or at least acceptable) and in the other it is not. This sort of judging behavior thus indicates not a provincial and inconsistent application of rules but rather an incisive perception of what is fundamental in moral arguments.

But, of course, there are rules and then there are rules, and the categorical imperative, as Kant made quite clear, is a rule unlike any other. What relationship does this most austere of all rules hold to paradigmatic character? The answer, it seems to me, is quite straightforward: the ability to meet the challenge of the categorical imperative is the ultimate test of paradigmatic character. That is, in the domain of moral praxis, adherence to the standards of the categorical imperative is independent evidence that the character of a moral agent is paradigmatic. Thus for all cases where the claim can be made that "so and so is a paradigmatic individual," the claim must also be made that "so and so never— ideally—violates the standards of behavior mandated by the categorical imperative." Thus to return to a theme of the previous section, one essential attribute of all paradigmatic individuals is this strict adherence to the canons of the categorical imperative. The reason this strict adherence *is* an essential attribute of all paradigmatic individuals is suggested by Kant: by regarding all moral agents as ends-in-themselves, the paradigmatic individual creates the very possibility of a universality of paradigmatic character. Thus the practice of adhering strictly to the categorical imperative establishes the seriousness with which the paradigmatic individual regards character as the universal good. Such adherence thus becomes a leading clue in that further investigation of the concept of paradigmatic character, for which this paper calls.[12] It also becomes the litmus test we must employ in anything like a revision of Jaspers's list.

Given the fundamental role of character in this re-visioned portrait of moral philosophy, the standards of formal completeness that hold for a Kantian rule theory cannot be applied to an ethics of virtue. The sorts of connections that hold between rules (deductive) are not those that hold between virtues or states of character. To put the point negatively, let me paraphrase Gödel and say that if a moral philosophy is deductively complete (a rule theory) it is substantively inadequate, and if it is substantively adequate (a virtue theory) it will necessarily be formally unsatisfactory. The point here is that although any virtue theory must be deductively incomplete, the canon of deductive completeness is simply inappropriate. Rather, the canon of completeness appropriate to this conception of an ethics of virtue is that of narrative completeness, and thus the appropriate structure of any possible substantively adequate moral philosophy must be more like the structure of a story than like the structure of a formal system. A narrative structure is, of course, complete only when it has told the story it means to tell.

The fundamental stories to be told in a virtue theory such as that envisioned here are about paradigmatic individuals; they are depictions of character which will be complete only to the extent that they reveal what is morally essential in the praxis of some paradigmatic individual. It is thus from such character itself that we must derive the canon of narrative completeness. It is precisely because the virtues in the character of a paradigmatic individual are not themselves deductively related that the parts of an adequate moral narrative are not to be deductively ordered. The problem of the unity of the virtues, which generally has been posed as a logical problem and which troubled scholastic philosophy, is instead a dramatic, human, and characterological problem, and there is as much unity of the virtues as the character of some paradigmatic individual reveals — and no more and no less. It is for these reasons that only literary portrayal can remain faithful to the standard of completeness that is manifest in the character of the paradigmatic individual.

This proposal for an appeal to the standards of literary depiction in moral argument seems to me neither logically odd nor historically unusual. Beginning in our own age, Wittgenstein, in the *Philosophical Investigations*, undertakes an essentially narrative depiction of philosophy and does so in such a way that although his depiction may be reconstructed deductively, it by no means depends on such a reconstruction for its cogency. Indeed, it seems to me quite clear that if so reconstructed the force of Wittgenstein's depiction would be diminished. As with a virtue theory such as I am proposing here, I want to argue that Wittgenstein's depiction of philosophy depends for its substantive adequacy on the form of its presentation, a point apparently overlooked by so many philosophers who claim to take Wittgenstein seriously while nonetheless constructing their arguments in a formal attire that is inimical to his own work.

In the 19th century, both Kierkegaard and Nietzsche pay considerable attention to the literary depiction of character. In the 20th century, Sartre in a major dimension of his *philosophical* activity portrays character so vividly that he has won a Nobel prize in literature. Plato, of course, in the beginning of our tradition, and in spite of himself, depends in great measure on the devices of literature. And this dependency is not just didactic, since it is only in terms of literary expression that a number of Plato's most essential insights can even be formulated. It is, of course, not only within the tradition of philosophy itself that the appeal to literary depiction achieves a sort of historical warrant. All the major religious traditions are *primarily* concerned to portray the character of paradigmatic individuals: thus we have the Gospels in which Christ himself, at crucial moments, is portrayed as a teller of stories. And thus we also have the Sutras of Buddhism and the narrative accounts of Mohammed's life in the Koran, which show them both to be essentially tellers of stories that are intended to portray their own character. Although the very fact that such appeals have been taken seriously is a presumption in their favor, the epistemological force of the appeal to narrative depiction is, nonetheless, something that must be isolated for philosophical analysis.[13] This force, it seems to me, as Aesop recognized, derives from the fact that telling a story is a more adequate way of getting through a moral crisis (or of expressing a moral point) than is citing a rule or specifying a good.[14]

The reconstruction of moral argument as the narrative depiction of character forces the conclusion that the major texts of traditional moral philosophy are either wrong-headed (Kant and Mill) or that in important ways they have been wrongly responded to (Aristotle). Such reconstruction also forces the conclusion that, to the extent that these texts *cannot* be read as narrative portraits, we must look elsewhere for the more fundamental texts of moral philosophy, the texts which reveal the central forum of moral argument. This forum I suggest, in addition to Aristotle, would necessarily include Thomas à Kempis's *On the Imitation of Christ*, Nietzsche's *Thus Spoke Zarathustra*, and Thoreau's *Walden Pond*, to name but the most important. And the fundamental moral question would then be seen to be: which of these narratives tells the human tale most fully? Which of them – if any – gives something like a genuine portrait of the moral life? The problem, then, is that of choosing between alternative characterizations of paradigmatic individuals. It is the problem of deciding when a true tale is well told. This problem raises anew the need for an adequate philosophy of literature. But the absence of such a philosophy does not inhibit us from making the obvious sort of judgments that would exclude Hitler's *Mein Kampf* or Huysmans's *La Bas* from the arena of serious moral claims, anymore than the absence of an adequate criterion for choosing between rules or goods inhibits us from recognizing that some putative "goods" (e.g., the masochist's pain) and rules (e.g., "Children ought not to read until they have all their permanent teeth") are prima facie absurd. How does one choose between possible, alternative characterizations of paradigmatic character? One does so in exactly the same way that one chooses between rules or goods – very carefully.

To say that the characterization of paradigmatic individuals is the point of moral philosophy is thus not to say that such characterizations are to be done willy-nilly. As with the mandating of rules or the specification of goods or rights, characterizations of paradigmatic individuals require support from the rest of philosophy; and thus we are led back to metaphysics and epistemology. It is just such support that precludes our taking seriously as moral paradigms such obvious moral absurdities as the character of Charles Manson or the Nuremberg laws. Virtue theories, like axiological, deontological, and rights theories are in need of good reasons. This view of moral philosophy, then, stresses its dependence on the rest of philosophy as, I would argue, would any close scrutiny of rights, rule, or goodness theories. And it should be obvious that the point of my argument is not that with the turn toward the characterization of paradigmatic individuals things become philosophically easier, but that they become morally and philosophically adequate.

A crucial feature of this relative adequacy is the decision procedure that derives from construing moral philosophy in the way I have argued is necessary. In this view of things, determining what one ought to do involves neither knowing and applying a rule nor specifying a good and predicting which course of action will most efficiently yield access to it. Rather one resolves moral ambiguity and makes choices by envisioning what some paradigmatic individual would do in the same situation; and knowing what he would do requires an imaginative experiment of envisioning him doing it (a *Gedanken* experiment). One might prepare for these imaginative experiments by, for example, living with the paradigmatic individual, by reading characterizations of his life, or by having personal contact with one of his disciples. In either case what one would try to do is to exemplify a certain character. Aristotle, as I have noted, recognized that one acquired virtuous character by *acting like* the person who has such character.

Additional support for the cogency of this decision procedure of envisionment derives from the common moral experience of asking a trusted friend what he would do in some problematic situation. Such appeals, of course, might be justified by saying that we trust the friend to know the right rules or goods. Undoubtedly such explanations cover a large number of the cases, but they do not cover what I take to be the crucial feature of such appeals. In the first place, we would not ask the advice of someone—even thinking he knew the right rules or appropriate goods—if we doubted his character. For persons of bad character (perhaps lacking the virtue of empathy) cannot be trusted to hear one's intimate moral problems or to give good advice. A person of bad character might well know the right thing to do but deliberately give inappropriate advice. More decisively, the advice of a friend is most important exactly under those conditions when, not being sure we see the point of his advice, we do what he recommends *because* he recommends it. The point of these remarks becomes particularly clear, I think, when we consider the sorts of moral quandary in which, having no one to consult, we conduct imaginative interior dialogues with absent friends or counselors, asking ourselves what they might do in a difficulty like ours. In such cases we take up a line of action or judgment exactly because we think we can identify what some seeming moral exemplar would do (or would advise us to do) if he were only in our situation (or if he were available to advise us). In all such cases it is the character of the imagined friend or counselor that provides the moral warrant for the decisions we make.

The difficulties that are endemic to this sort of decision procedure do not, at least, place it at any disadvantage with respect to the decision procedures of moral philosophies whose final appeal is to rules or other goods. Each of the decision procedures is apparently biased with respect to the possession of certain skills. As Alasdair MacIntyre has argued, for example, Kant's moral philosophy can be most advantageously used by persons who are ingenious in describing cases and in generalizing the maxims to be tested by the categorical imperative.[15] Logical and analytical skills permit a more subtle access to the highly formal decision procedure of the categorical imperative, and thus permit persons of great analytical skills to be more sophisticated Kantians. Such a decision procedure is clearly biased against poets and painters. By contrast, the ability to use something like the hedonic calculus depends upon synthetic and predictive skills which are not uniformly distributed through the population of moral agents. So also the ability to envision the activity of a paradigmatic individual derives from the possession of the sorts of mimetic skills that would make one a great actor, the sorts of skills dependent upon the virtue of empathy. This decision procedure would thus seem to deny easy access to, for example, football coaches and social scientists.

But in this case, as in so many others, things are not quite what they seem to be. For if, as I take to be obviously true, we all learn our first lessons through imitating the practices of family or friends, then it follows that we *all* have something like an initial privileged access to the realm of skill required to utilize the decision procedure of envisionment, a decision procedure based explicitly on our abilities to imitate the behavior of others. This realm of skill is one that belongs equally to each of us, regardless of whether we are initially members of privileged or underprivileged, moral or immoral communities, and each of us in our own communities is equally dependent upon the exercise of this skill. Thus it seems that this skill is of a different sort than the predictive skills of the hedonic calculus or the analytic skills involved in the use of the categorical imperative. For if as mature moral agents there seems to be an inequality in its distribution, this inequality would be the result not of non-acquisition of a specialized technique but of a failure to exercise a common and human *techne* that we all necessarily possess as members of some community or other. Although the reasons for such failures are themselves important and interesting, it is enough for my current purposes to note that the imitative skills of the decision procedure of envisionment are, in fact, sui generis and that they seem to define the very minimal conditions of a community of moral agents.[16] Thus a moral philosophy that takes as its primitive notion the idea of a universally accessible realm of paradigmatic character yields a decision procedure that not only provides us with an explicit mechanism for judging the morality of actions—as must any adequate moral philosophy—but that also calls attention to the way in which the mechanism itself is clearly rooted in the original learning practices of all moral agents. Such a decision procedure thus bridges the seeming gap between moral agents and is a constant reminder of that ideal and original democracy of moral agency that achieves its fullest expression in the lives of the paradigmatic individuals.

IV

In conclusion, I have argued that virtue (i.e., the character of paradigmatic individuals) is the primary moral category and that it is neither reducible to nor dependent upon either some rule or some other notion of the good. Rules and other notions of the good are, at best, either analytic clarifications of what we mean by virtuous character or maps which indicate how it might be acquired. Indeed, it seems to me quite obvious that if paradigmatic character is so reducible or so dependent, then there can be no virtue theory since any such theory would simply be either an incomplete rule theory or a sub-set within some other goodness theory. An incomplete theory is, of course, an inadequate theory; and it is the point of this paper to have argued that a virtue theory of the sort defended here is not, in principle, inadequate. More strongly it is the point of this paper to have argued that the appropriate canons of adequacy in moral theory can first be glimpsed only in the context of an approach such as that argued here, an approach which clearly ties all moral discourse to the domain of moral agency, a domain ideally manifest in the praxis of the paradigmatic individuals. Without such a tie, moral discourse becomes *merely* formal and *necessarily* without significant reference to the domain of praxis it is meant to illuminate.

Having said these things, what is now needed—and it is a difficult set of needs to meet—is more complete analyses of the family of concepts that clusters around the concepts of character and paradigmatic individual, as well as more thorough analyses of the relationship between this family of concepts and those of rights, goods, and law theories. I here have had to limit myself to a first sketch of these analyses and to arguing that such analyses are necessary in order to rescue moral philosophy from its mostly technical pre-occupations, pre-occupations which do not reflect the actual practices of moral agents or important domains of moral tradition and reasoning. Such pre-occupations cannot provide anything like an appropriate, rational terminus for moral arguments, a terminus which at one and the same time must be both objective (i.e., non-provincial) and personal (i.e., focused on the moral agent). Given the self-imposed limitations of this paper I want nonetheless, without hubris, to claim that I at least know where to look for the adequate moral philosophy which awaits such analyses, and that is toward a further philosophical examination of the classical portraits of the paradigmatic individuals. In this claim, as well as in others advanced in this essay, my argument, I hope, is not without virtue.[17]

Notes

1. G.E.M. Anscombe, "Modern Moral Philosophy," *Philosophy* 33, 124 (January 1958): 1–19. See also William Frankena, "Prichard and the Ethics of Virtue: Notes on a Footnote," *Monist* 54, 1 (January 1970): 1–17, and "The Ethics of Love Conceived as an Ethics of Virtue," *Journal of Religious Ethics* 1, 1 (1973): 21–36. Also in this connection see Philippa Foot, "Moral Beliefs," *Proceedings of the Aristotelian Society* 59 (1958–59): 83–104; Alasdair MacIntyre, *After Virtue* (Notre Dame, Ind.: University of Notre Dame Press, 1981); Iris Murdoch, "The Sovereignty of Good Over Other Concepts," reprinted in this volume, and also "Vision and Choice in Morality," *Christian Ethics and Contemporary Philosophy*, ed. Ian Ramsey (New York: Macmillan, 1966). This latter paper is an extended commentary on R. W. Hepburn's paper cited below (footnote 14).

2. H. A. Prichard, "Is Moral Philosophy Based on a Mistake?" *Mind* (1912): 21–37. This is the first essay in the twentieth century to raise the discussion of virtue theories.

3. Aristotle's moral philosophy is *properly* to be construed as the first important virtue theory. However, insofar as the virtue of justice has generally been taken in isolation from the other virtues and regarded solely as a *formal* mechanism for deciding the proper distribution of goods, Aristotle's moral philosophy has been distorted and its character as a virtue theory thereby neglected. See Lawrence Becker, "Axiology, Deontology and Agent Morality: The Need for Coordination," *The Journal of Value Inquiry* 6, 3 (Fall 1972): 213–20, and *On Justifying Moral Judgments* (Atlantic Highlands, N.J.: Humanities Press, 1973), and "The Neglect of Virtue," *Ethics* 85, 2 (January 1975): 110–22. See also A. S. Cua, *Dimensions of Moral Creativity* (University Park: Pennsylvania State University Press, 1978); Stanley Hauerwas, *Character and the Christian Life: A Study in Theological Ethics* (San Antonio: Trinity University Press, 1975), and *Vision and Virtue, Essays in Christian Ethical Reflections* (Notre Dame, Ind.: Fides Publishers, Inc., 1974); Alasdair MacIntyre, *After Virtue*.

4. See J. M. Keynes's memoir published in *The Bloomsbury Circle*, ed. S. P. Rosenbaum (Toronto: University of Toronto Press, 1975).

5. William H. Gass, "The Case of the Obliging Stranger," *Philosophical Review* 66 (1957): 193–204. See also Edmund Pincoffs, "Quandary Ethics," *Mind* 80, 320 (October 1971): 552–71.

6. Karl Jaspers, *The Great Philosophers* (New York: Harcourt, Brace & World, 1962), especially 97–106. Cf. A. S. Cua, "Morality and the Paradigmatic Individuals," in *Dimensions of Moral Creativity*.

7. Such an account is, I think, available in terms of Heidegger's description of being-in-the-world in *Sein und Zeit*. There we get a global portrayal of the human situation that yields criteria in terms of which we can identify different styles of moral agency without being overwhelmed by the apparently irreducible differences in cultures. Heidegger's work, in my view, thus supplies the basis for something like that "philosophical psychology" which Anscombe ("Modern Moral Philosophy") has argued is needed to make sense of virtue theories. Such a "philosophical psychology" will have to take account of the theory of natural rights which is undergoing a sort of renaissance in contemporary moral philosophy. The relationship between natural rights and paradigmatic character is rooted in the assumption of a universally shared human condition, as an assumption to which both rights theories and virtue theories such as this are committed. Cf. A. S. Cua, *Dimensions of Moral Creativity*, 77–78.

8. Most philosophers from Socrates on have been aware of the usefulness of presenting clear examples in complex arguments. My point is that such presentations are the *focus* of philosophical argument and not mere supporting devices. In contemporary philosophy, the essays of Judith Jarvis Thomson exemplify the focal role of such presentations. Cf., for example, her "The Right to Privacy," *Philosophy and Public Affairs* 4 (Summer 1975): 295–314 and "A Defense of Abortion," *Philosophy and Public Affairs* 1 (Fall 1971): 47–66 among others.

9. Richard Francis Burton, *A Mission to Gelele, King of Dahome* (London: Routledge and Kegan Paul, 1966).

10. Robin George Collingwood, *An Autobiography* (London: Oxford University Press, 1939), especially 100–106.

11. Lawrence C. Becker, "The Neglect of Virtue."

12. A. S. Cua's careful description of "Confucian Paradigmatic Individuals" in *Dimensions of Moral Creativity* is an important move in such an investigation. Alasdair MacIntyre's descriptions of the virtues in heroic societies, etc., and his linkage of the concept of virtue with the concept of a practice make further important contributions to such an investigation. See his chapters 10–15 in *After Virtue*.

13. This presumption is supported by the rather plausible belief that people keep doing something only if, in some sense or other, it works. Cf. Lawrence Sklar's treatment of this theme in his "Methodological Conservatism," *Philosophical Review* 84, 3 (July 1975): 374–400.

14. Cf. Alasdair MacIntyre, "Epistemological Crises, Dramatic Narrative and the Philosophy of Science," *The Monist* 60 (October 1977): 453–72. See also MacIntyre's comments on narrative and story telling in *After Virtue*, especially 135, 191–94 and 201–202. See also R. W. Hepburn's "Vision and Choice in Morality," in *Christian Ethics and Contemporary Philosophy*, ed. Ian Ramsey (New York: Macmillan, 1966). Cf. Stanley Hauerwas, *Truthfulness and Tragedy* (Notre Dame, Ind.: University of Notre Dame Press, 1977). See also my *Nietzsche's Gift* (Athens, Ohio: Ohio University Press, 1977).

15. Alasdair MacIntyre, *A Short History of Ethics* (New York: Macmillan, 1976), 197–98.

16. Imitative skills atrophy because of the nature of the communities in which those skills must be exercised. Thus, for example, in underprivileged communities where children are used as professional beggars, the children's imitation of their given role models necessarily truncates the development of the very imitative skills that permit them to become economically valuable members of their communities; for in all such situations what is lacking is the very sort of role model in which the notion of moral autonomy is central. The failure of the exercise of original imitative skills is thus a failure of moral community. It is a failure of some group of moral agents to move from the idea of their community of interest to the idea of the human community of autonomous moral agents. Or to put this discussion in terms of the virtue of empathy, the

children's original disposition to identify with their role models ceases because the very agents with whom the children identify use them as objects rather than teach them to be agents.

17. I am indebted to Lawrence Becker for early discussions of some of these themes and to both him and Roger Pilon for criticisms of an early draft of this essay. I would also like to acknowledge the support of N.E.H. during the summer of 1978 when a very different first draft of this paper was written. This final version was completed with the support of an N.E.H. Fellowship for College Teachers (1981–82).

Reading Introduction

On Some Vices of Virtue Ethics
Robert B. Louden

Louden argues that "virtue ethics" cannot meet some of the needs that traditional ethical theories have met. "Virtue ethics" differs from the other theories, says Louden, in two ways. First, it provides for evaluating, not acts, but agents. And second, it says that the appropriate motivation for acts is neither a sense of duty nor a desire to foster happiness, but the virtues themselves, such as love, friendship, and justice.

If we limit ourselves to evaluating agents rather than acts, says Louden, our theory will fail:

1. To provide guidance for finding our way out of practical moral quandaries, such as whether to abort mentally retarded fetuses
2. To make sense of cases (like those depicted in tragedies) in which good people do harmful actions
3. To allow us to make lists of specific acts that for social reasons must be absolutely prohibited
4. To provide any way for us to notice when good persons have gone bad, since we have nothing but the person's actual character to go on
5. To discourage moral "backsliding," since the theory will provide no constant motivation to be vigilant for the goodness of our *acts*

Louden discusses three more vices of virtue ethics:

1. It is generally agreed that a person's being virtuous (let us say, being kind) is not to be understood simply in terms of outwardly observable actions. For example, that a person goes about doing acts of kindness is not enough to qualify him or her as kind; he or she must also do these acts in the "spirit" of kindness. But this fact about virtue implies that we have no way of knowing which people are virtuous since a person's "spirit" cannot be observed. But since virtue ethics relies so heavily on paradigmatic individuals, it must presuppose that we *can* recognize a virtuous person when we see one.
2. Virtue ethics asserts not only a gulf between virtue and actions, but also a gulf between virtue and the *results* of actions. Thus the virtue ethicist would think that a word of kindness spoken to a grief-stricken person may exemplify the virtue of kindness, and thus be morally praiseworthy, even if the word had the effect of plunging the mourner even deeper into grief. This means that virtue ethics cannot provide for criticizing actions on the basis of their consequences. But this is something any adequate moral theory ought to provide for.
3. For a final vice, Louden argues that virtue ethicists are overly optimistic about the power of virtues to stem social evils. Because modern society is so complex, and there is so little basis for moral agreement, we need more rules

and regulations than we needed in earlier times. Thus the virtue ethicist's hope that we can do without rules is "utopian."

Louden ends with an appeal for a study of the virtues that does not, as "virtue ethics" does, make the virtues the sole basis of ethical theory.

On Some Vices of Virtue Ethics

ROBERT B. LOUDEN

It is common knowledge by now that recent philosophical and theological writing about ethics reveals a marked revival of interest in the virtues. But what exactly are the distinctive features of a so-called virtue ethics? Does it have a special contribution to make to our understanding of moral experience? Is there a price to be paid for its different perspective, and if so, is the price worth paying?

Contemporary textbook typologies of ethics still tend to divide the terrain of normative ethical theory into the teleological and deontological. Both types of theory, despite their well-defined differences, have a common focus on acts as opposed to qualities of agents. The fundamental question that both types of theory are designed to answer is: What ought I to do? What is the correct analysis and resolution of morally problematic situations? A second feature shared by teleological and deontological theories is conceptual reductionism. Both types of theory start with a primary irreducible element and then proceed to introduce secondary derivative concepts which are defined in terms of their relations to the beginning element. Modern teleologists (the majority of whom are utilitarians) begin with a concept of the good—here defined with reference to states of affairs rather than persons. After this criterion of the good is established, the remaining ethical categories are defined in terms of this starting point. Thus, according to the classic maxim, one ought always to promote the greatest good for the greatest number. Duty, in other words, is defined in terms of the element of ends—one ought always to maximize utility. The concepts of virtue and rights are also treated as derivative categories of secondary importance, definable in terms of utility. For the classic utilitarian, a right is upheld "so long as it is upon the whole advantageous to the society that it should be maintained," while virtue is construed as a "tendency to give a net increase to the aggregate quantity of happiness in all its shapes taken together."[1]

For the deontologist, on the other hand, the concept of duty is the irreducible starting point, and any attempt to define this root notion of being morally bound to do something in terms of the good to be achieved is rejected from the start. The deontologist is committed to the notion that certain acts are simply inherently right. Here the notion of the good is only a derivative category, definable in terms of the right. The good that we are to promote is right action for its own sake—duty for duty's sake. Similarly, the virtues tend

American Philosophical Quarterly 21 (July 1984):227–36. Reprinted by permission of the publisher.

to be defined in terms of pro-attitudes towards one's duties. Virtue is important, but only because it helps us do our duty.

But what about virtue ethics? What are the hallmarks of this approach to normative ethics? One problem confronting anyone who sets out to analyze the new virtue ethics in any detail is that we presently lack fully developed examples of it in the contemporary literature. Most of the work done in this genre has a negative rather than positive thrust— its primary aim is more to criticize the traditions and research programs to which it is opposed rather than to state positively and precisely what its own alternative is. A second hindrance is that the literature often has a somewhat misty antiquarian air. It is frequently said, for instance, that the Greeks advocated a virtue ethics, though what precisely it is that they were advocating is not always spelled out. In describing contemporary virtue ethics, it is therefore necessary, in my opinion, to do some detective work concerning its conceptual shape, making inferences based on the unfortunately small number of remarks that are available.

For purposes of illustration, I propose to briefly examine and expand on some key remarks made by two contemporary philosophers—Elizabeth Anscombe and Philippa Foot—whose names have often been associated with the revival of virtue movement. Anscombe, in her frequently cited article, "Modern Moral Philosophy," writes: "you can do ethics without it [viz., the notion of 'obligation' or 'morally ought'], as is shown by the example of Aristotle. It would be a great improvement if, instead of 'morally wrong,' one always named a genus such as 'untruthful,' 'unchaste,' 'unjust.'"[2] Here we find an early rallying cry for an ethics of virtue program, to be based on contemporary efforts in philosophical psychology and action theory. On the Anscombe model, strong, irreducible duty and obligation notions drop out of the picture, and are to be replaced by vices such as unchasteness and untruthfulness. But are we to take the assertion literally, and actually attempt to do moral theory without any concept of duty whatsoever? On my reading, Anscombe is not really proposing that we entirely dispose of moral oughts. Suppose one follows her advice, and replaces "morally wrong" with "untruthful," "unchaste," etc. Isn't this merely shorthand for saying that agents *ought* to be truthful and chaste, and that untruthful and unchaste acts are *morally wrong* because good agents don't perform such acts? The concept of the moral ought, in other words, seems now to be explicated in terms of what the good person would do.[3]

A similar strategy is at work in some of Foot's articles. In the Introduction to her recent collection of essays, *Virtues and Vices and Other Essays in Moral Philosophy*, she announces that one of the two major themes running throughout her work is "the thought that a sound moral philosophy should start from a theory of virtues and vices."[4] When this thought is considered in conjunction with the central argument in her article, "Morality as a System of Hypothetical Imperatives," the indication is that another virtue-based moral theory is in the making. For in this essay Foot envisions a moral community composed of an "army of volunteers," composed, that is, of agents who voluntarily commit themselves to such moral ideals as truth, justice, generosity, and kindness.[5] In a moral community of this sort, all moral imperatives become hypothetical rather than categorical: there are things an agent morally ought to do if he or she wants truth, justice, generosity, or kindness, but no things an agent morally ought to do if he or she isn't first committed to these (or other) moral ideals. On the Foot model (as presented in "Morality as a System"), what distinguishes an ethics of virtue from its competitors is that it construes the ideal moral agent as acting from a direct desire, without first believing that he or she morally ought to perform that action or have that desire. However, in a more recent paper, Foot has expressed doubts about her earlier attempts to articulate the relationship between oughts and desires. In "William Frankena's Carus Lectures" (1981), she states that "*thoughts* [my emphasis] about what is despicable or contemptible, or low, or again admirable, glorious or honorable may give us the key to the problem of rational moral action."[6] But regardless of whether she begins with desires or with thoughts, it seems clear her strategy too is not to dispense with oughts entirely, but rather to employ softer, derivative oughts.

In other words, conceptual reductionism is at work in virtue ethics too. Just as its utilitarian and deontological competitors begin with primitive concepts of the good state of affairs and the intrinsically right action respectively and then derive secondary concepts out of their starting points, so virtue ethics, beginning with a root conception of the morally good person, proceeds to introduce a different set of secondary concepts which are defined in terms of their relationship to the primitive element. Though the ordering of primitive and derivatives differs in each case, the overall strategy remains the same. Viewed from this perspective, virtue ethics is not unique at all. It has adopted the traditional mononomic strategy of normative ethics. What sets it apart from other approaches, again, is its strong agent orientation.

So for virtue ethics, the primary object of moral evaluation is not the act or its consequences, but rather the agent. And the respective conceptual starting points of agent and act-centered ethics result in other basic differences as well, which may be briefly summarized as follows. First of all, the two camps are likely to employ different models of practical reasoning. Act theorists, because they focus on discrete acts and moral quandaries, are naturally very interested in formulating decision procedures for making practical choices. The agent, in their conceptual scheme, needs a guide—hopefully a determinate decision procedure—for finding a way out of the quandary. Agent-centered ethics, on the other hand, focuses on long-term characteristic patterns of action, intentionally downplaying atomic acts and particular choice situations in the process. They are not as concerned with portraying practical reason as a rule-governed enterprise which can be applied on a case-by-case basis.

Secondly, their views on moral motivation differ. For the deontological act theorist, the preferred motive for moral action is the concept of duty itself; for the utilitarian act theorist, it is the disposition to seek the happiness of all sentient creatures. But for the virtue theorist, the preferred motivation factor is the virtues themselves (here understood non-reductionistically). The agent who correctly acts from the disposition of charity does so (according to the virtue theorist) not because it maximizes utility or because it is one's duty to do so, but rather out of a commitment to the value of charity for its own sake.

While I am sympathetic to recent efforts to recover virtue from its longstanding neglect, my purpose in this essay is not to contribute further to the campaign for virtue. Instead, I wish to take a more critical look at the phenomenon, and to ask whether there are certain important features of morality which a virtue-based ethics either handles poorly or ignores entirely. In the remainder of this essay, I shall sketch some objections which (I believe) point to genuine shortcomings of the virtue approach to ethics. My object here is not to offer an exhaustive or even thoroughly systematic critique of virtue ethics, but rather to look at certain mundane regions of the moral field and to ask first what an ethics of virtue might say about them, and second whether what it says about them seems satisfactory.

Agents vs. Acts

As noted earlier, it is a commonplace that virtue theorists focus on good and bad agents rather than on right and wrong acts. In focusing on good and bad agents, virtue theorists are thus forced to deemphasize discrete acts in favor of long-term, characteristic patterns of behavior. Several related problems arise for virtue ethics as a result of this particular conceptual commitment.

Casuistry and Applied Ethics

It has often been said that for virtue ethics the central question is not "What ought I to *do*?" but rather "What sort of person ought I to *be*?"[7] However, people have always expected ethical theory to tell them something about what they ought to do, and it seems to me that virtue ethics is structurally unable to say much of anything about this issue. If I'm right, one consequence of this is that a virtue-based ethics will be particularly weak in the areas of casuistry and applied ethics. A recent reviewer of Foot's *Virtues and Vices*, for instance, notes that "one must do some shifting to gather her view on the virtues." "Surprisingly," he adds, "the studies of abortion and euthanasia are not of much use."[8] And this is odd, when one considers Foot's demonstrated interest in applied ethics in conjunction with her earlier cited prefatory remark that a "sound moral theory should start from a theory of virtues and vices." But what can a virtues and vices approach say about specific moral dilemmas? As virtue theorists from Aristotle onward have rightly emphasized, virtues are not simply dispositions to behave in specified ways, for which rules and principles can always be cited. In addition, they involve skills of perception and articulation, situation-specific "know-how," all of which are developed only through recognizing and acting on what is relevant in concrete moral contexts as they arise. These skills of moral perception and practical reason are not completely routinizable, and so cannot be transferred from agent to agent as any sort of decision procedure "package deal." Due to the very nature of the moral virtues, there is thus a very limited amount of advice on moral quandaries that one can reasonably expect from the virtue-oriented approach. We ought, of course, to do what the virtuous person would do, but it is not always easy to fathom what the hypothetical moral exemplar would do were he in our shoes, and sometimes even he will act out of character. Furthermore, if one asks him why he did what he did, or how he knew what to do, the answer—if one is offered—might not be very enlightening. One would not necessarily expect him to appeal to any rules or principles which might be of use to others.

We can say, à la Aristotle, that the virtuous agent acts for the sake of the noble (*tou kalou heneka*), that he will not do what is base or depraved, etc. But it seems to me that we cannot intelligently say things like: "The virtuous person (who acts for the sake of the noble) is also one who recognizes that all mentally deficient eight-month-old fetuses should (or should not) be aborted, that the doctor/patient principle of confidentiality must always (or not always) be respected." The latter simply sound too strange, and their strangeness stems from the fact that motives of virtue and honor cannot be fully routinized.

Virtue theory is not a problem-oriented or quandary approach to ethics: it speaks of rules and principles of action only in a derivative manner. And its derivative oughts are frequently too vague and unhelpful for persons who have not yet acquired the requisite moral insight and sensitivity. Consequently, we cannot expect it to be of great use in applied ethics and casuistry. The increasing importance of these two subfields of ethics in contemporary society is thus a strike against the move to revive virtue ethics.

Tragic Humans

Another reason for making sure that our ethical theory allows us to talk about features of acts and their results in abstraction from the agent and his conception of what he is doing is that sometimes even the best person can make the wrong choices. There are cases in which a man's choice is grounded in the best possible information, his motives honorable and his action not at all out of character. And yet his best laid plans may go sour. Aristotle, in his *Poetics*, suggests that here lies the source of tragedy: we are confronted with an eminent and respected man, "whose misfortune, however, is brought upon him not by vice (*kakia*) and depravity (*moktheira*) but by some error of judgment (*hamartia*)" (1453a8–9). But every human being is morally fallible, for there is a little Oedipus in each of us. So Aristotle's point is that *regardless of character*, anyone can fall into the sort of mistake of which tragedies are made. Virtue ethics, however, since its conceptual scheme is rooted in the notion of the good person, is unable to assess correctly the occasional (inevitable) tragic outcomes of human action.

Lawrence Becker, in his article, "The Neglect of Virtue," seems at first to draw an opposite conclusion from similar reflections about virtue theory and tragedy, for it is his view that virtue ethics makes an indispensable contribution to our understanding of tragedy. According to him, "there are times when the issue is not how much harm has been done, or the value to excusing the wrongdoer, or the voluntary nature of the offending behavior, but rather whether the sort of character indicated by the behavior is 'acceptable' or not—perhaps even ideal—so that the 'wrongful' conduct must be seen simply as an unavoidable defect of it."[9] As Becker sees it, Oedipus merely comes off as a fool who asked too many questions when viewed from the perspective of act theories. Only a virtue ethics, with its agent perspective, allows us to differentiate tragic heroes from fools, and to view the acts that flow from each character type in their proper light. And the proper light in the case of tragic heroes is that there are unavoidable defects in this character type, even though it represents a human ideal. Becker's point is well taken, but its truth does not cancel out my criticism. My point is that virtue ethics is in danger of blinding itself to the wrongful conduct in Oedipal acts, simply because it views the Oedipuses of the world as honorable persons *and* because its focus is on long term character manifestations rather than discrete acts. To recognize the wrong in Oedipal behavior, a theory with the conceptual tools enabling one to focus on discrete acts is needed. (Notice, incidentally, that Becker's own description does just this.)

Intolerable Actions

A third reason for insisting that our moral theory enable us to assess acts in abstraction from agents is that we need to be able to identify certain types of action which produce harms of such magnitude that they destroy the bonds of community and render (at least temporarily) the achievement of moral goods impossible. In every traditional moral community one encounters prohibitions or "barriers to action" which mark off clear boundaries in such areas as the taking of innocent life, sexual relations, and the administration of justice according to local laws and customs.[10] Such rules are needed to teach citizens what kinds of actions are to be regarded not simply as bad (a table of vices can handle this) but as intolerable.[11] Theorists must resort to specific lists of offenses to emphasize the fact that there are some acts which are absolutely prohibited. We cannot articulate this sense of absolute prohibition by referring merely to characteristic patterns of behavior.

In rebuttal here, the virtue theorist may reply by saying: "Virtue ethics does not need to articulate these prohibitions—let the law do it, with its list of do's and don't's." But the sense of requirement and prohibition referred to above seems to me to be at bottom inescapably moral rather than legal. Morality can (and frequently does) invoke the aid of law in such cases, but when we ask *why* there is a law against, e.g., rape or murder, the proper answer is that it is morally intolerable. To point merely to a legal convention when asked why an act is prohibited or intolerable raises more questions than it answers.

Character Change

A fourth reason for insisting that a moral theory be able to assess acts in abstraction from agents and their conception of what they're doing is that peoples' moral characters may sometimes change. Xenophon, toward the beginning of his *Memorabilia* (I.II.21), cites an unknown poet who says: "Ah, but a good man is at one time noble (*esthlos*), at another wicked (*kakos*)." Xenophon himself agrees with the poet: ". . . many alleged (*phaskonton*) philosophers may say: A just (*dikaios*) man can never become unjust; a self-controlled (*sophron*) man can never become wanton (*hubristes*); in fact no one having learned any kind of knowledge (*mathesis*) can become ignorant of it. I do not hold this view. . . . For I see that, just as poetry is forgotten unless it is often repeated, so instruction, when no longer heeded, fades from the mind."[12]

Xenophon was a practical man who was not often given to speculation, but he arrived at his position on character change in the course of his defense of Socrates. One of the reasons Socrates got into trouble, Xenophon believed, was due to his contact with Critias and Alcibiades during their youth. For of all Athenians, "none wrought so many evils to the *polis*." However, Xenophon reached the conclusion that Socrates should not be blamed for the disappearance of his good influence once these two had ceased their close contact with him.

If skills can become rusty, it seems to me that virtues can too. Unless we stay in practice we run the risk of losing relative proficiency. We probably can't forget them completely (in part because the opportunities for exercising virtues are so pervasive in everyday life), but we can lose a certain sensitivity. People do become morally insensitive, relatively speaking—missing opportunities they once would have noticed, although perhaps when confronted with a failure they might recognize that they had failed, showing at least that they hadn't literally "forgotten the difference between right and wrong." If the moral virtues are acquired habits rather than innate gifts, it is always possible that one can lose relative proficiency in these habits. Also, just as one's interests and skills sometimes change over the course of a life as new perceptions and influences take hold, it seems too that aspects of our moral characters can likewise alter. (Consider religious conversion experiences.) Once we grant the possibility of such changes in moral character, the need for a more "character free" way of assessing action becomes evident. Character is not a permanent fixture, but rather plastic. A more reliable yardstick is sometimes needed.[13]

Moral Backsliding

Finally, the focus on good and bad agents rather than on right and wrong actions may lead to a peculiar sort of moral backsliding. Because the emphasis in agent ethics is on long-term, characteristic patterns of behavior, its advocates run the risk of overlooking occasional lies or acts of selfishness on the ground that such performances are mere temporary aberrations—acts out of character. Even the just man may on occasion act unjustly, so why haggle over specifics? It is unbecoming to a virtue theorist to engage in such pharisaic calculations. But once he commits himself to the view that assessments of moral worth are not simply a matter of whether we have done the right thing, backsliding may result: "No matter how many successes some people have, they still feel they 'are' failures; no matter how many lies some people tell, they still feel they 'are' fundamentally honest."[14] At some point, such backsliding is bound to lead to self-deception.

I have argued that there is a common source behind each of these vices. The virtue theorist is committed to the claim that the primary object of moral evaluation is not the act or its consequences but rather the agent—specifically, those character traits of the agent which are judged morally relevant. This is not to say that virtue ethics does not ever address the issue of right and wrong actions, but rather that it can only do so in a derivative manner. Sometimes, however, it is clearly acts rather than agents which ought to be the primary focus of moral evaluation.

Who Is Virtuous?

There is also an epistemological issue which becomes troublesome when one focuses on qualities of persons rather than on qualities of acts. Baldly put, the difficulty is that we do not seem to be able to know with any degree of certainty who really is virtuous and who vicious. For how is one to go about establishing an agent's true moral character? The standard strategy is what might be called the "externalist" one: we try to infer character by observing conduct. While not denying the existence of some connection between character and conduct, I believe that the connection between the two is not nearly as tight as externalists have assumed. The relationship is not a necessary one, but merely contingent. Virtue theorists themselves are committed to this claim, though they have not always realized it. For one central issue behind the "Being vs. Doing" debate is the virtue theorist's contention that the moral value of Being is not reducible to or dependent on Doing; that the measure of an agent's character is not exhausted by or even dependent on the values of the actions which he may perform. On this view, the most important moral traits are what may be called "spiritual" rather than "actional."[15]

Perhaps the most famous example of a spiritual virtue would be Plato's definition of justice (*dikaiosunē*). Plato, it will be remembered, argued that attempts to characterize *dikaiosunē* in terms of an agent's conduct are misguided and place the emphasis in the wrong place. *Dikaiosunē* for Plato is rather a matter of the correct harmonious relationship between the three parts of the soul: "It does not lie in a man's external actions, but in the way he acts within himself (*tēn entos*), really concerned with himself and his inner parts (*peri eauton kai ta eautou*)" (*Rep.* 443d). Other spiritual virtues would include such attitudes as self-respect and integrity. These are traits which do have a significant impact on what we do, but whose moral value is not wholly derivable from the actions to which they may give rise.

If there are such spiritual virtues, and if they rank among the most important of moral virtues, then the externalist strategy is in trouble. For those who accept spiritual virtues, the Inner is not reducible to or dependent on the Outer. We cannot always know the moral value of a person's character by assessing his or her actions.

But suppose we reject the externalist approach and take instead the allegedly direct internalist route. Suppose, that is, that we could literally "see inside" agents and somehow observe their character traits first-hand. (The easiest way to envision this is to assume that some sort of identity thesis with respect to moral psychology and neurophysiology is in principle correct. Lest the reader object that this is only a modern materialist's silly pipe dream, I might add that at least one commentator has argued that Aristotle's considered view was that the presence of the virtues and vices depends on modifications of the brain and nervous system; and that the relevant mental processes in ethics have accompanying bodily states.)[16] Here the goal will be to match specific virtues with specific chemicals, much in the manner that identity theorists have sought to match other types of mental events with other specific neurophysiological events. However, even on this materialistic reading of the internalist strategy, nothing could be settled about virtues by analyzing chemicals without first deciding who has what virtue. For we would first need to know who possessed and exhibited which virtue, and then look for specific physical traces in him that were missing in other agents. But as indicated earlier in my discussion of the externalist strategy, this is precisely what we don't know. An analogy might be the attempt to determine which objects have which colors. Regardless of how much we know about the physical make-up of the objects in question, we must first make color judgments. However, at this point the analogy breaks down, for the epistemological problems involved in making color judgments are not nearly as troublesome as are those involved in making virtue judgments.[17]

To raise doubts about our ability to know who is virtuous is to bring skepticism into the center of virtue ethics, for it is to call into question our ability to identify the very object of our inquiry. This is not the same skepticism which has concerned recent writers such as Bernard Williams and Thomas Nagel, when they reflect on the fact that "the natural objects of moral assessment are disturbingly subject to luck."[18] Theirs is more a skepticism *about* morality, while mine is a skepticism *within* morality. The sort of skepticism to which I am drawing attention occurs after one has convinced oneself that there are genuine moral agents who really do things rather than have things happen to them. As such, my skepticism is narrower but also more morality-specific: it concerns not so much queries about causality and free will as doubts about our ability to know the motives of our own behavior. As Kant wrote, "the real morality of actions, their merit or guilt, even that of our own conduct, . . . remains entirely hidden from us."[19] Aquinas too subscribed to a similar skepticism: "Man is not competent to judge of interior movements, that are hidden, but only of exterior acts which are observable; and yet for the perfection of virtue it is necessary for man to conduct himself rightly in both kinds of acts."[20]

Now it may be objected here that I am making too much of this epistemological error, that no one actually "lives it" or contests the fact that it is an error. But I think not. To advocate an ethics of virtue is, among other things, to presuppose that we can clearly differentiate the virtuous from the vicious. Otherwise, the project lacks applicability.

Consider for a moment the Aristotelian notion of the *spoudaios* (good man) or *phronimos* (man of practical wisdom)—two essentially synonymous terms which together have often been called the touchstone of Aristotle's ethics. Again and again in the *Nicomachean Ethics* the *spoudaios/phronimos* is pointed to as the solution to a number of unanswered problems in Aristotle's ethical theory. For instance, we are told to turn to the *spoudaios* in order to learn what really is pleasurable (1113a26–28). And we must turn to an actual *phronimos* in order to find out what the abstract and mysterious *orthos logos* really is (right reason or rational principle—a notion which plays a key role in the definition of virtue) (1107a2, 1144b24). Even in discussing the intellectual virtue of *phronēsis* or practical wisdom, Aristotle begins by announcing that "we shall get at the truth by considering who are the persons we credit with it" (1140a24). But who are the *phronimoi*, and how do we know one when we see one? Aristotle does say that Pericles "and men like him" are *phronimoi*, "because they can see what is good for themselves and what is good for men in general" (1140b8–10). However, beyond this rather casual remark he does not give the reader any hints on how to track down a *phronimos*. Indeed, he does not even see it as a problem worth discussing.

The reasons for this strange lacuna, I suggest, are two. First, Aristotle is dealing with a small face to face community, where the pool of potential *phronimoi* generally come from certain well established families who are well known throughout the *polis*. Within a small face to face community of this sort, one would naturally expect to find wide agreement about judgments of character. Second, Aristotle's own methodology is itself designed to fit this sort of moral community. He is not advocating a Platonic ethics of universal categories.

Within the context of a *polis* and an ethical theory intended to accompany it, the strategy of pointing to a *phronimos* makes a certain sense. However, to divorce this strategy from its social and economic roots and to then apply it to a very different sort of community—one where people really do not know each other all that well, and where there is wide disagreement on values—does not. And this, I fear, is what contemporary virtue ethicists have tried to do.[21]

Style Over Substance

In emphasizing Being over Doing, the Inner over the Outer, virtue theorists also lay themselves open to the charge that they are more concerned with style than with substance. For as I argued earlier, virtue theorists are committed to the view that the moral value of certain key character traits is not exhausted by or even dependent on the value of the actions to which they may give rise. When this gulf between character and conduct is asserted, and joined with the claim that it is agents rather than actions which count morally, the conclusion is that it is not the substance of an agent's actions which is the focus of moral appraisal. The implication here seems to be that if you have style, i.e., the style of the virtuous person, as defined in the context of a concrete moral tradition, it doesn't so much matter what the results are. ("It's not whether you win or lose, but how you play the game that counts.") As Frankena remarks, in a passage which underscores an alleged basic difference between ancient and contemporary virtue ethics:

> The Greeks held . . . that being virtuous entails not just having good motives or intentions but also doing the right thing. Modern views typically differ from Greek views here; perhaps because of the changed ways of thinking introduced by the Judeo-Christian tradition, we tend to believe that being morally good does not entail doing what is actually right . . . even if we believe (as I do) that doing what is actually right involves more than only having a good motive or intention. Today many people go so far as to think that in morality it does not matter much *what* you do; all that matters, they say, is *how* you do it. To parody a late cigarette advertisement; for them it's not how wrong you make it, it's how you make it wrong.[22]

But it is sophistry to claim that the consequences of the lies of gentlemen or Aristotelian *kaloikagathoi* aren't very important, or that the implications of their rudeness are somehow tempered by the fact that they are who they are. This line of thought flies in the face of our basic conviction that moral assessment must strive toward impartiality and the bracketing of morally irrelevant social and economic data.

It seems to me that this particular vice of virtue ethics is analogous to the Hegelian "duty for duty's sake" critique of formalist deontologies. Virtue-based and duty-based theories are both subject to the "style over substance" charge because their notion of ends is too weak. Both types of theory speak of ends only in a derivative sense. For the duty-based theorist, the good is an inherent feature of dutiful action, so that the only proclaimed end is right action itself. For the virtue-based theorist, the good is defined in terms of the virtuous agent. ("Virtue is its own reward.") Aristotle, as noted earlier, in distinguishing the true from the apparent good, remarks that "that which is in truth an object of wish is an object of wish to the good man (*spoudaios*), while any chance thing may be so to the bad man" (*EN* 1113a26–28).

While no one (except the most obstinate utilitarian) would deny these two respective ends their place in a list of moral goods, it appears that there is another important type of end which is left completely unaccounted for. This second type of end is what may be called a *product-end*, a result or outcome of action which is distinct from the activity that produces it. (An example would be a catastrophe or its opposite.) Virtue-based and duty-based theories, on the other hand, can account only for *activity-ends*, ends which are inherent features of (virtuous or dutiful) action. Virtue-based theories then, like their duty-based competitors, reveal a structural defect in their lack of attention to product-ends.[23]

Now it might be said that the "style over substance" charge is more appropriately directed at those who emphasize Doing over Being, since one can do the right things just to conform or for praise. One can cultivate the externalities, but be inwardly wretched or shallow. I grant that this is a problem for act theorists, but it is a slightly different criticism than mine, using different senses of the words "style" and "substance." "Style," as used in my criticism, means roughly: "morally irrelevant mannerisms and behavior," while "substance," as I used it, means something like: "morally relevant results of action." The "substance" in this new criticism refers to good moral character and the acts which flow from it, while "style" here means more "doing the right thing, but without the proper fixed trait behind it." However, granted that both "style over substance" criticisms have some validity, I would also argue that mine points to a greater vice. It is one thing to do what is right without the best disposition, it is another not to do what is right at all.

Utopianism

The last vice I shall mention has a more socio-historical character. It seems to me that there is a bit of utopianism behind the virtue theorist's complaints about the ethics of rules. Surely, one reason there is more emphasis on rules and regulations in modern society is that things have gotten more complex. Our moral community (insofar as it makes sense to speak of "community" in these narcissistic times) contains more ethnic, religious, and class groups than did the moral community which Aristotle theorized about. Unfortunately, each segment of society has not only its own interests but its own set of virtues as well. There is no general agreed upon and significant expression of desirable moral character in such a world. Indeed, our pluralist culture prides itself on and defines itself in terms of its alleged value neutrality and its lack of allegiance to any one moral tradition. This absence of agreement regarding human purposes and moral ideals seems to drive us (partly out of lack of alternatives) to a more legalistic form of morality. To suppose that academic theorists can alter the situation simply by re-emphasizing certain concepts is illusory. Our world lacks the sort of moral cohesiveness and value unity which traditional virtue theorists saw as prerequisites of a viable moral community.[24]

The table of vices sketched above is not intended to be exhaustive, but even in its incomplete state I believe it spells trouble for virtue-based moral theories. For the shortcomings described are not esoteric—they concern mundane features of moral experience which any minimally adequate moral theory should be expected to account for. While I do think that contemporary virtue theorists are correct in asserting that any adequate moral theory must account for the fact of character, and that no ethics of rules, pure and unsupplemented, is up to this job, the above analysis also suggests that no ethics of virtue, pure and unsupplemented, can be satisfactory.

My own view (which can only be stated summarily here) is that we need to begin efforts to coordinate irreducible or strong notions of virtue along with irreducible or strong conceptions of the various act notions into our conceptual scheme of morality. This appeal for coordination will not satisfy those theorists who continue to think in the single-element or mononomic tradition (a tradition which contemporary virtue-based theorists have inherited from their duty-based and goal-based ancestors), but I do believe that it will result in a more realistic account of our moral experience. The moral field is not unitary, and the values we employ in making moral judgments sometimes have fundamentally different sources. No single reductive method can offer a realistic means of prioritizing these different values. There exists no single scale by means of which disparate moral considerations can always be measured, added, and balanced.[25] The theoretician's quest for conceptual economy and elegance has been won at too great a price, for the resulting reductionist definitions of the moral concepts are not true to the facts of moral experience. It is important now to see the ethics of virtue and the ethics of rules as adding up, rather than as cancelling each other out.[26]

Notes

1. The rights definition is from Bentham's "Anarchical Fallacies," reprinted in A. I. Melden, ed., *Human Rights* (Belmont, Calif.: Wadsworth, 1970), 32. The virtue definition is from Bentham's "The Nature of Virtue," reprinted in Bhiku Parekh, ed., *Bentham's Political Thought* (New York: Barnes and Noble, 1973), 89.

2. G. E. M. Anscombe, "Modern Moral Philosophy," *Philosophy* 33 (1958): 1–19; reprinted in J. J. Thomson and G. Dworkin, eds., *Ethics* (New York: Harper & Row, 1968), 196.

3. Anscombe appears to believe also that moral oughts and obligations only make sense in a divine law context, which would mean that only divine command theories of ethics employ valid concepts of obligation. I see no reason to accept such a narrow definition of duty. See pp. 192, 202 of "Modern Moral Philosophy." For one argument against her restrictive divine law approach to moral obligation, see Alan Donagan, *The Theory of Morality* (Chicago: University of Chicago Press, 1977), 3.

4. Philippa Foot, *Virtues and Vices and Other Essays in Moral Philosophy* (Berkeley and Los Angeles: University of California Press, 1978), xi.

5. Foot, "Morality as a System of Hypothetical Imperatives," *The Philosophical Review* 81 (1972): 305–16; reprinted in *Virtues and Vices*, 157–73. See especially the long concluding footnote, added in 1977.

6. Foot, "William Frankena's Carus Lectures," *The Monist* 64 (1981): 311.

7. For background on this "Being vs. Doing" debate, see Bernard Mayo, *Ethics and the Moral Life* (London: Macmillan & Co., Ltd., 1958), 211–14, and William K. Frankena, *Ethics*, 2d ed. (Englewood Cliffs, N.J.: Prentice Hall, 1973), 65–66.

8. Arthur Flemming, "Reviving the Virtues." Review of Foot's *Virtues and Vices* and James Wallace's *Virtues and Vices. Ethics* 90 (1980): 588.

9. Lawrence Becker, "The Neglect of Virtue," *Ethics* 85 (1975): 111.

10. Stuart Hampshire, ed., *Private and Public Morality* (New York: Cambridge University Press, 1978), 7.

11. Alasdair MacIntyre, *After Virtue* (Notre Dame: University of Notre Dame Press, 1981), 142.

12. It is curious to note that contemporary philosophers as different as Gilbert Ryle and H. G. Gadamer have argued, against Xenophon and myself, that character cannot change. See H. G. Gadamer, "The Problem of Historical Consciousness," p. 140 in P. Rabinow and W. M. Sullivan, eds., *Interpretive Social Science* (Berkeley and Los Angeles: University of California Press, 1979), and Gilbert Ryle, "On Forgetting the Difference Between Right and Wrong" in A. I. Melden, ed., *Essays in Moral Philosophy* (Seattle: University of Washington Press, 1958).

13. One possibility here might be to isolate specific traits and then add that the virtuous agent ought to *retain* such traits throughout any character changes. (E.g.: "The good man will not do what is base, regardless of whether he be Christian, Jew, or atheist.") However, it is my view that very few if any moral traits have such a "transcharacter" status. The very notion of what counts as a virtue or vice itself changes radically when one looks at different traditions. (Compare Aristotle's praise for *megalopsuchia* or pride as the "crown of the virtues" with the New Testament emphasis on humility.) Also, one would expect basic notions about what is base or noble to themselves undergo shifts of meaning as they move across traditions.

14. Becker, "The Neglect of Virtue," 112.

15. I have borrowed this terminology from G. W. Trianosky-Stillwell, *Should We Be Good? The Place of Virtue in Our Morality* (Doctoral Dissertation, University of Michigan, 1980).

16. W. F. R. Hardie, *Aristotle's Ethical Theory*, 2d ed. (Oxford: Clarendon Press, 1980), ch. 6, esp. 111–13.

17. I am indebted to Bill Robinson for help on this criticism of the internalist strategy.

18. Thomas Nagel, "Moral Luck," in *Mortal Questions* (New York: Cambridge University Press, 1979), 28. See also Bernard Williams, "Moral Luck," in *Moral Luck: Philosophical Papers 1973–1980* (New York: Cambridge University Press, 1981).

19. Kant, *Critique of Pure Reason*, A552 = B580, n. 1.

20. Thomas Aquinas, Saint. *Summa Theologica*, I-II Q. 91, a. 4.

21. I would like to thank Arthur Adkins for discussion on these points.

22. William K. Frankena, *Thinking About Morality* (Ann Arbor: University of Michigan Press, 1980), 52–53.

23. My own position on this topic is contra that of utilitarianism. I believe that activity-ends are clearly the more important of the two, and that most product-ends ultimately derive their moral value from more fundamental activity-ends. (The importance of saving lives, for instance, borrows its value from the quality of life it makes possible. "Life at any price" is nonsense.) But I also believe, contra deontology and virtue ethics, that any adequate moral theory must find room for both types of ends.

24. For similar criticism, see Mayo, *Ethics and the Moral Life*, 217; and MacIntyre, *After Virtue*.

25. See Thomas Nagel, "The Fragmentation of Value," 131–32, 135 in *Mortal Questions* (New York: Cambridge University Press, 1979). A similar position is defended by Charles Taylor in his recent essay, "The Diversity of Goods," in A. Sen and B. Williams, eds., *Utilitarianism and Beyond* (New York: Cambridge University Press, 1982).

26. Earlier versions of this essay were read at the 1982 American Philosophical Association Pacific Division Meetings, and at the 1981 Iowa Philosophical Society Meeting at Grinnell College. I am very grateful for useful criticisms and suggestions offered on these occasions. I would also like to thank Marcia Baron, Lawrence Becker, James Gustafson, W. D. Hamlyn, Bob Hollinger, Joe Kupfer, and Warner Wick for criticisms of earlier drafts. Portions of the present version are taken from my doctoral dissertation, *The Elements of Ethics: Toward a Topography of the Moral Field* (University of Chicago, 1981).

❖

Part Two

Moral Psychology

Humans are the only animals within our immediate purview that are capable of acquiring traits such as stinginess, greed, envy, deceitfulness, sloth, cruelty, cowardice, vanity, grudge-bearing, sentimentality, contempt, and treachery, or such other traits as generosity, temperance, loyalty, magnanimity, ethical discernment, courage, fairness, truthfulness, industry, gratitude, self-control, perseverance, patience, gentleness, and compassion. The expression "moral psychology" as we use it here denotes a philosophical inquiry into the nature of persons, bearing on their capacity to become morally *characterized* — which is to say, to have either virtues or vices. In other words, moral psychology treats the age-old philosophical question What is it to be a human being after all?, but it asks this question with respect to the particular issues of moral character.

A sampling of questions falling in the category of moral psychology are discussed in the essays in this section: Is a human being primarily a creator of values, or a perceiver of them? (Murdoch) To what extent can a person's moral character transcend his or her culture? (Murdoch, Slote) What kind of thing is "will power" and how is it developed? (Roberts) Are there different *kinds* of virtues, and if so how do they interact with one another in the ethical personality? (Roberts) Can a person transcend his or her desires — that is, choose to do something that he does not *want* to do, because it is the *appropriate* thing to do? And if so, how is this possible? (Dent) In addition to moral excellences, there are nonmoral excellences, such as musical and athletic and philosophical skills, and capacities for esthetic enjoyment; what would their relative weight and interrelation be in the constitution of the most perfect personality? (Wolf, Adams) What connections are there between religious beliefs and the possession of moral virtues? (Adams) It is obvious that the inquiry of moral psychology is basic to any discussion of the virtues, and is a sort of preliminary to sketching the contours of individual virtues.

Reading Introduction

The Sovereignty of Good Over Other Concepts
Iris Murdoch

Murdoch believes that the concept of a *person* suggested by moral philosophy since Kant has been both psychologically unrealistic and morally degrading. The neo-Kantian self does not consult a standard outside itself, but is "autonomous," creating its own "values." He or she is not a "seer" of ethical truth, but a maker of it, not a character with certain virtues, but a thin, abstract will that produces behaviors. In this essay Murdoch offers, with help from Plato, an alternative conception of the moral person.

Though she does not believe in God, her idea of the virtuous life bears a formal similarity to Christianity. She does not use the words *obedience*, *submission*, and *authority*, yet something like these concepts is central to her moral psychology. Just as, in Christianity, a person grows spiritually through focusing in obedient submission on the authoritative will of God and by turning away from self, so here one becomes virtuous through forgetfulness of self and focusing on something like Plato's idea of the Good. One becomes excellent through learning to see the excellence in objects or by submitting to the disciplines necessary to achieve excellence in some task. Examples that Murdoch mentions are the contemplation of birds, flowers, and great art and the discipline of learning a language. In all these cases an objective reality places demands on the person; by submitting to the "authority" of these realities, one becomes a better person. Similarly, what is needed to make hard moral decisions is not the "radical choice" of the existentialists, nor "soul-searching," but a kind of unselfish willingness to see the situation fairly, an obedient submission to reality. Most of our moral decisions are shabby not because we do not "know enough ethics," but because our fat, relentless ego distorts our vision. Because virtue is a matter of eschewing self-absorption, the ruthlessly truthful contemplation of one's own death is a very great tutor in the virtues. Murdoch ends her essay by considering two characteristics of the Platonic concept of the Good: on the one hand, its power to unify other concepts such as courage, freedom, truth, and humility by being "sovereign" over them; and, on the other, its indefinability.

The Sovereignty of Good
Over Other Concepts

IRIS MURDOCH

The development of consciousness in human beings is inseparably connected with the use of metaphor. Metaphors are not merely peripheral decorations or even useful models, they are fundamental forms of our awareness of our condition: metaphors of space, metaphors of movement, metaphors of vision. Philosophy in general, and moral philosophy in particular, has in the past often concerned itself with what it took to be our most important images, clarifying existing ones and developing new ones. Philosophical argument which consists of such image-play, I mean the great metaphysical systems, is usually inconclusive, and is regarded by many contemporary thinkers as valueless. The status and merit of this type of argument raises, of course, many problems. However, it seems to me impossible to discuss certain kinds of concepts without resort to metaphor, since the concepts are themselves deeply metaphorical and cannot be analyzed into non-metaphorical components without a loss of substance. Modern behavioristic philosophy attempts such an analysis in the case of certain moral concepts, it seems to me without success. One of the motives of the attempt is a wish to 'neutralize' moral philosophy, to produce a philosophical discussion of morality which does not take sides. Metaphors often carry a moral charge, which analysis in simpler and plainer terms is designed to remove. This too seems to me to be misguided. Moral philosophy cannot avoid taking sides, and would-be neutral philosophers merely take sides surreptitiously. Moral philosophy is the examination of the most important of all human activities, and I think that two things are required of it. The examination should be realistic. Human nature, as opposed to the natures of other hypothetical spiritual beings, has certain discoverable attributes, and these should be suitably considered in any discussion of morality. Secondly, since an ethical system cannot but commend an ideal, it should commend a worthy ideal. Ethics should not be merely an analysis of ordinary mediocre conduct, it should be a hypothesis about good conduct and about how this can be achieved. How can we make ourselves better? is a question moral philosophers should attempt to answer. And if I am right the answer will come partly at least in the form of explanatory and persuasive metaphors. The metaphors which I myself favor and the philosopher under whose banner I am fighting I will make clear shortly.

First, however, I wish to mention very briefly two fundamental assumptions of my argument. If either of these is denied what follows will be less convincing. I assume that human beings are naturally selfish and that human life has no external point or $\tau\epsilon\lambda\sigma\varsigma$. That human beings are naturally selfish seems true on the evidence, whenever and wherever we look at them, in spite of a very small number of apparent exceptions. About the quality of this selfishness modern psychology has had something to tell us. The psyche is a

The Sovereignty of Good Over Other Concepts by Iris Murdoch, Leslie Stephen Lecture 1967, Cambridge University Press, 1967. Reprinted by permission of the publisher.

historically determined individual relentlessly looking after itself. In some ways it resembles a machine; in order to operate it needs sources of energy, and it is predisposed to certain patterns of activity. The area of its vaunted freedom of choice is not usually very great. One of its main pastimes is daydreaming. It is reluctant to face unpleasant realities. Its consciousness is not normally a transparent glass through which it views the world, but a cloud of more or less fantastic reverie designed to protect the psyche from pain. It constantly seeks consolation, either through imagined inflation of self or through fictions of a theological nature. Even its loving is more often than not an assertion of self. I think we can probably recognize ourselves in this rather depressing description.

That human life has no external point or τέλος is a view as difficult to argue as its opposite, and I shall simply assert it. I can see no evidence to suggest that human life is not something self-contained. There are properly many patterns and purposes within life, but there is no general and as it were externally guaranteed pattern or purpose of the kind for which philosophers and theologians used to search. We are what we seem to be, transient mortal creatures subject to necessity and chance. This is to say that there is, in my view, no God in the traditional sense of that term; and the traditional sense is perhaps the only sense. When Bonhoeffer says that God wants us to live as if there were no God I suspect he is misusing words. Equally the various metaphysical substitutes for God—Reason, Science, History—are false deities. Our destiny can be examined but it cannot be justified or totally explained. We are simply here. And if there is any kind of sense or unity in human life, and the dream of this does not cease to haunt us, it is of some other kind and must be sought within a human experience which has nothing outside it.

The idea of life as self-enclosed and purposeless is of course not simply a product of the despair of our own age. It is the natural product of the advance of science and has developed over a long period. It has already in fact occasioned a whole era in the history of philosophy, beginning with Kant and leading on to the existentialism and the analytic philosophy of the present day. The chief characteristic of this phase of philosophy can be briefly stated: Kant abolished God and made man God in His stead. We are still living in the age of the Kantian man, or Kantian man-god. Kant's conclusive exposure of the so-called proofs of the existence of God, his analysis of the limitations of speculative reason, together with his eloquent portrayal of the dignity of rational man, has had results which might possibly dismay him. How recognizable, how familiar to us, is the man so beautifully portrayed in the *Grundlegung*, who confronted even with Christ turns away to consider the judgment of his own conscience and to hear the voice of his own reason. Stripped of the exiguous metaphysical background which Kant was prepared to allow him, this man is with us still, free, independent, lonely, powerful, rational, responsible, brave, the hero of so many novels and books of moral philosophy. The *raison d'être* of this attractive but misleading creature is not far to seek. He is the offspring of the age of science, confidently rational and yet increasingly aware of his alienation from the material universe which his discoveries reveal; and since he is not a Hegelian (Kant, not Hegel, has provided Western ethics with its dominating image) his alienation is without cure. He is the ideal citizen of the liberal state, a warning held up to tyrants. He has the virtue which the age requires and admires, courage. It is not such a very long step from Kant to Nietzsche, and from Nietzsche to existentialism and the Anglo-Saxon ethical doctrines which in some ways closely resemble it. In fact Kant's man had already received a glorious incarnation nearly a century earlier in the work of Milton: his proper name is Lucifer.

The center of this type of post-Kantian moral philosophy is the notion of the will as the creator of value. Values which were previously in some sense inscribed in the heavens and guaranteed by God collapse into the human will. There is no transcendent reality. The idea of the good remains indefinable and empty so that human choice may fill it. The sovereign moral concept is freedom, or possibly courage in a sense which identifies it with freedom, will, power. This concept inhabits a quite separate top level of human activity since it is the guarantor of the secondary values created by choice. Act, choice, decision, responsibility, independence are emphasized in this philosophy of puritanical origin and apparent austerity. It must be said in its favor that this image of human nature has been the inspiration of political liberalism. However, as Hume once wisely observed, good political philosophy is not necessarily good moral philosophy.

This impression is indeed an austere one, but there is something still to be added to it. What place, one might ask, is left in this stern picture of solitary all-responsible man for the life of the emotions? In fact the emotions have a rather significant place. They enter through a back door left open by Kant and the whole romantic movement has followed after. Puritanism and romanticism are natural partners and we are still living with their partnership. Kant held a very interesting theory about the relation of the emotions to the reason. He did not officially recognize the emotions as part of the structure of morality. When he speaks of love he tells us to distinguish between practical love which is a matter of rational actions, and pathological love which is a mere matter of feeling. He wants to segregate the messy warm empirical psyche from the clean operations of the reason. However, in a footnote in the *Grundlegung* he allows a subordinate place to a particular emotion, that of *Achtung*, or respect for the moral law. This emotion is a kind of suffering pride which accompanies, though it does not motivate, the recognition of duty. It is an actual experience of freedom (akin to the existentialist *Angst*), the realization that although swayed by passions we are also capable of rational conduct. A close relation of this concept is Kant's handsome conception of the Sublime. We experience the Sublime when we confront the awful contingency of nature or of human fate and return into ourselves with a proud shudder of rational power. How abject we are, and yet our consciousness is of an infinite value. Here it is Belial, not Satan, who speaks.

> *For who would lose,*
> *Though full of pain, this intellectual being,*
> *Those thoughts that wander through eternity . . .*

The emotions are allowed to return to the scene as a kind of allowable, rather painful, thrill which is a by-product of our status as dignified rational beings.

What appears in Kant as a footnote and a side-issue takes, however, a central place in the development which his philosophy underwent in the romantic movement. I would sum this up by saying that romanticism tended to transform the idea of death into the idea of suffering. To do this is of course an age-old human temptation. Few ideas invented by humanity have more power to console than the idea of purgatory. To buy back evil by suffering in the embrace of good: what could be more satisfying, or as a romantic might say, more thrilling? Indeed the central image of Christianity lends itself just this illegitimate transformation. The *Imitatio Christi* in the later work of Kierkegaard is a distinguished instance of romantic self-indulgence on this theme, though it may seem unkind to say this of a great and most endearing writer who really did suffer for telling his society some truths. The idea of a rather exciting suffering freedom soon began to enliven the austerity of the puritan half of the Kantian picture, and with this went a taming and beautifying of the idea of death, a cult of pseudo-death and pseudo-transience. Death becomes *Liebestod*, painful and exhilarating, or at worst charming and sweetly tearful. I speak here of course, not of the great romantic artists and thinkers at their best, but of the general beaten track which leads from Kant to the popular philosophies of the present day. When the neo-Kantian Lucifer gets a glimpse of real death and real chance he takes refuge in sublime emotions and veils with an image of tortured freedom that which has been rightly said to be the proper study of philosophers.

When Kant wanted to find something clean and pure outside the mess of the selfish empirical psyche he followed a sound instinct but, in my view, looked in the wrong place. His inquiry led him back again into the self, now pictured as angelic, and inside this angel-self his followers have tended to remain. I want now to return to the beginning and look again at the powerful energy system of the self-defensive psyche in the light of the question, How can we make ourselves better? With such an opponent to deal with one may doubt whether the idea of the proud, naked will directed towards right action is a realistic and sufficient formula. I think that the ordinary man, with the simple religious conceptions which make sense for him, has usually held a more just view of the matter than the voluntaristic philosopher, and a view incidentally which is in better accord with the findings of modern psychology. Religion normally emphasizes states of mind as well as actions, and regards states of mind as the genetic background of action: pureness of heart, meekness of spirit. Religion provides devices for the purification of states of mind. The believer feels that he needs, and can receive, extra help. 'Not I, but Christ.' The real existence of such help is often used as an argument for the truth of religious doctrines. Of course prayer and sacraments may be 'misused' by the believer as mere instruments of consolation. But, whatever one thinks of its theological context, it does seem that prayer can actually induce a better quality of consciousness and provide an energy for good action which would not otherwise be available. Modern psychology here supports the ordinary person's, or ordinary believer's, instinctive sense of the importance of his states of mind and the availability of supplementary energy. Psychology might indeed prompt contemporary behavioristic philosophers to re-examine their discarded concepts of 'experience' and 'consciousness.' By opening our eyes we do not necessarily see what confronts us. We are anxiety-ridden animals. Our minds are continually active, fabricating an anxious, usually self-preoccupied, often falsifying *veil* which partially conceals the world. Our states of consciousness differ in quality, our fantasies and reveries are not trivial and unimportant, they are profoundly connected with our energies and our ability to choose and act. And if quality of consciousness matters, then anything which alters consciousness in the direction of unselfishness, objectivity and realism is to be connected with virtue.

Following a hint in Plato (*Phaedrus*, 250) I shall start by speaking of what is perhaps the most obvious thing in our surroundings which is an occasion for 'unselfing,' and that is what is popularly called beauty. Recent philosophers tend to avoid this term because they prefer to talk of reasons rather than of experiences. But the implication of experience with beauty seems to me to be something of great importance which should not be by-passed in favor of analysis of critical vocabularies. Beauty is the convenient and traditional name of something which art and nature share, and which gives a fairly clear sense to the idea of quality of experience and change of consciousness. I am looking out of my window in an anxious and resentful state of mind, oblivious of my surroundings, brooding perhaps on some damage done to my prestige. Then suddenly I observe a hovering kestrel. In a moment everything is altered. The brooding self with its hurt vanity has disappeared. There is nothing now but kestrel. And when I return to thinking of the other matter it seems less important. And of course this is something which we may also do deliberately: give attention to nature in order to clear our minds of selfish care. It may seem odd to start the argument against what I have roughly labelled as 'romanticism' by using the case of attention to nature. In fact I do not think that any of the great romantics really believed that we receive but what we give and in our life alone does nature live, although the lesser ones tended to follow Kant's lead and use nature as an occasion for exalted self-feeling. The great romantics, including the one I have just quoted, transcended 'romanticism.' A self-directed enjoyment of nature seems to me to be something forced. More naturally, as well as more properly, we take a self-forgetful pleasure in the sheer alien pointless independent existence of animals, birds, stones and trees. 'Not how the world is, but that it is, is the mystical.'

I take this starting-point, not because I think it is the most important place of moral change, but because I think it is the most accessible one. It is so patently a good thing to take delight in flowers and animals that people who bring home potted plants and watch kestrels might even be surprised at the notion that these things have anything to do with virtue. The surprise is a product of the fact that, as Plato pointed out, beauty is the only spiritual thing which we love by instinct. When we move from beauty in nature to beauty in art we are already in a more difficult region. The experience of art is more easily degraded than the experience of nature. A great deal of art, perhaps most art, actually is self-consoling fantasy, and even great art cannot guarantee the quality of its consumer's consciousness. However, great art exists and is sometimes properly experienced and even a shallow experience of what is great can have its effect. Art, and by 'art' from now on I mean good art, not fantasy art, affords us a pure delight in the independent existence of what is excellent. Both in its genesis and its enjoyment it is a thing totally opposed to selfish obsession. It invigorates our best faculties and, to use Platonic language, inspires love in the highest part of the soul. It is able to do this partly by virtue of something which it shares with nature: a perfection of form which invites unpossessive contemplation and resists absorption into the selfish dream life of the consciousness.

Art however, considered as a sacrament or a source of good energy, possesses an extra dimension. Art is less accessible than nature but also more edifying since it is actually a human product, and certain arts are actually 'about' human affairs in a direct sense. Art is a human product and virtues as well as talents are required of the artist. The good artist, in relation to his art, is brave, truthful, patient, humble; and even in non-representational art we may receive intuitions of these qualities. One may also suggest, more cautiously, that non-representational art does seem to express more positively something which is to do with virtue. The spiritual role of music has often been acknowledged, though theorists have been chary of analyzing it. However that may be, the representational arts, which more evidently hold the mirror up to nature, seem to be concerned with morality in a way which is not simply an effect of our intuition of the artist's discipline.

These arts, especially literature and painting, show us the peculiar sense in which the concept of virtue is tied on to the human condition. They show us the absolute pointlessness of virtue while exhibiting its supreme importance; the enjoyment of art is a training in the love of virtue. The pointlessness of art is not the pointlessness of a game; it is the pointlessness of human life itself, and form in art is properly the simulation of the self-contained aimlessness of the universe. Good art reveals what we are usually too selfish and too timid to recognize, the minute and absolutely random detail of the world, and reveals it together with a sense of unity and form. This form often seems to us mysterious because it resists the easy patterns of the fantasy, whereas there is nothing mysterious about the forms of bad art since they are the recognizable and familiar rat-runs of selfish day-dream. Good art shows us how difficult it is to be objective by showing us how differently the world looks to an objective vision. We are presented with a truthful image of the human condition in a form which can be steadily contemplated; and indeed this is the only context in which many of us are capable of contemplating it at all. Art transcends selfish and obsessive limitations of personality and can enlarge the sensibility of its consumer. It is a kind of goodness by proxy. Most of all it exhibits to us the connection, in *human* beings, of clear realistic vision with compassion. The realism of a great artist is not a photographic realism, it is essentially both pity and justice.

Herein we find a remarkable redemption of our tendency to conceal death and chance by the invention of forms. Any story which we tell about ourselves consoles us since it imposes pattern upon something which might otherwise seem intolerably chancy and incomplete. However, human life is chancy and incomplete. It is the role of tragedy, and also of comedy, and of painting to show us suffering without a thrill and death without a consolation. Or if there is any consolation it is the austere consolation of a beauty which teaches that nothing in life is of any value except the attempt to be virtuous. Masochism is the artist's greatest and most subtle enemy. It is not easy to portray death, real death, not fake prettified death. Even Tolstoy did not really manage it in *Ivan Ilyich*, although he did elsewhere. The great deaths of literature are few, but they show us with an exemplary clarity the way in which art invigorates us by a juxtaposition, almost an identification, of pointlessness and value. The death of Patroclus, the death of Cordelia, the death of Petya Rostov. All is vanity. The only thing which is of real importance is the ability to see it all clearly and respond to it justly which is inseparable from virtue. Perhaps one of the greatest achievements of all is to join this sense of absolute mortality not to the tragic but to the comic. Shallow and Silence. Stefan Trofimovich Verhovensky.

Art then is not a diversion or a side-issue, it is the most educational of all human activities and a place in which the nature of morality can be *seen*. Art gives a clear sense to many ideas which seem more puzzling when we meet with them elsewhere, and it is a clue to what happens elsewhere. An understanding of any art involves a recognition of hierarchy and authority. There are very evident degrees of merit, there are heights and distances; even Shakespeare is not perfect. Good art, unlike bad art, unlike 'happenings,' is something pre-eminently outside us and resistant to our consciousness. We surrender ourselves to its *authority* with a love which is unpossessive and unselfish. Art shows us the only sense in which the permanent and incorruptible is compatible with the transient; and whether representational or not it reveals to us aspects of our world which our ordinary dull dream-consciousness is unable to see. Art pierces the veil and gives sense to the notion of a reality which lies beyond appearance; it exhibits virtue in its true guise in the context of death and chance.

Plato held that beauty could be a starting-point of the good life, but he came to mistrust art and we can see played out in that great spirit the peculiarly distressing struggle between the artist and the saint. Plato allowed to the beauty of the lovely boy an awakening power which he denied to the beauty of nature or of art. He seems to have come to believe that all art is bad art, a mere fiction and consolation which distorts reality. About nature he seems, in the context of the theory of forms, to have been at least once in doubt. Are there forms of mud, hair and dirt? If there are then nature is redeemed into the area of truthful vision. (My previous argument assumes of course, in Platonic terms, that there are.) Another starting-point, or road, which Plato speaks of more often however is the way of the τέχναι, the sciences, crafts, and intellectual disciplines excluding the arts. I think there is a way of the intellect, a sense in which intellectual disciplines are moral disciplines, and this is not too difficult to discern. There are important bridge ideas between morality and other at first sight different human activities, and these ideas are perhaps most clearly seen in the context of the τέχναι. And as when we use the nature of art as a clue, we may be able to learn more about the central area of morality if we examine what are essentially the same concepts more simply on display elsewhere. I mean such concepts as justice, accuracy, truthfulness, realism, humility, courage as the ability to sustain clear vision, love as attachment or even passion without sentiment or self.

The τέχνη which Plato thought was most important was mathematics, because it was most rigorous and abstract. I shall take an example of a τέχνη more congenial to myself: learning a language. If I am learning, for instance, Russian, I am confronted by an authoritative structure which commands my respect. The task is difficult and the goal is distant and perhaps never entirely attainable. My work is a progressive revelation of something which exists independently of me. Attention is rewarded by a knowledge of reality. Love of Russian leads me away from myself towards something alien to me, something which my consciousness cannot take over, swallow up, deny or make unreal. The honesty and humility required of the student – not to pretend to know what one does not know – is the preparation for the honesty and humility of the scholar who does not even feel tempted to suppress the fact which damns his theory. Of course a τέχνη can be misused; a scientist might feel he ought to give up a certain branch of study if he knew that his discoveries would be used wickedly. But apart from special contexts, studying is normally an exercise of virtue as well as of talent, and shows us a fundamental way in which virtue is related to the real world.

I suggested that we could see most clearly in the case of the τέχναι the nature of concepts very central to morality such as justice, truthfulness or humility. We can see too the growth and the inter-connection of these concepts, as when what looks like mere accuracy at one end looks more like justice or courage, or even love at the other. Developing a *Sprachgefühl* is developing a judicious respectful sensibility to something which is very like another organism. An intellectual discipline can play the same kind of role as that which I have attributed to art, it can stretch the imagination, enlarge the vision and strengthen the judgment. When Plato made mathematics the king τέχνη he was regarding mathematical thought as leading the mind away from the material world and enabling it to perceive a reality of a new kind, very unlike ordinary appearances. And one might regard other disciplines, history, philology, chemistry, as presenting us with a new kind of subject-matter and showing us a new reality behind appearance. These studies are not only an exercise in virtue, they might be thought of as introductory images of the spiritual life. But they are not the spiritual life itself and the mind which has ascended no farther has not achieved the whole of virtue.

I want now to make a closer approach to the central subject of my argument, the Good. Beauty and the τέχναι are, to use Plato's image, the text written in large letters. The concept Good itself is the much harder to discern but essentially similar text written in small letters. In intellectual disciplines and in the enjoyment of art and nature we discover value in our ability to forget self, to be realistic, to perceive justly. We use our imagination not to escape the world but to join it, and this exhilarates us because of the distance between our ordinary dulled consciousness and an apprehension of the real. The value concepts are here patently tied on to the world, they are stretched as it were between the truth-seeking mind and the world, they are not moving about on their own as adjuncts of the personal will. The authority of morals is the authority of truth, that is of reality. We can see the length, the extension, of these concepts as patient attention transforms accuracy without interval into just discernment. Here too we can see it as natural to the particular kind of creatures that we are that love should be inseparable from justice, and clear vision from respect for the real.

That virtue operates in exactly the same kind of way in the central area of morality is less easy to perceive. Human beings are far more complicated and enigmatic and ambiguous than languages or mathematical concepts, and selfishness operates in a much more devious and frenzied manner in our relations with them. Ignorance, muddle, fear, wishful thinking, lack of tests often make us feel that moral choice is something arbitrary, a matter for personal will rather than for attentive study. Our attachments tend to be selfish and strong, and the transformation of our loves from selfishness to unselfishness is sometimes hard even to conceive of. Yet is the situation really so different? Should a retarded child be kept at home or sent to an institution? Should an elderly relation who is a trouble-maker be cared for or asked to go away? Should an unhappy marriage be continued for the sake of the children? Should I leave my family in order to do political work? Should I neglect them in order to practice my art? The love which brings the right answer is an exercise of justice and realism and really *looking*. The difficulty is to keep the attention fixed upon the real situation and to prevent it from returning surreptitiously to the self with consolations of self-pity, resentment, fantasy and despair. The refusal to attend may even induce a fictitious sense of freedom: I may as well toss a coin. Of course virtue is good habit and dutiful action. But the background condition of such habit and such action, in human beings, is a just mode of vision and a good quality of consciousness.

It is a *task* to come to see the world as it is. A philosophy which leaves duty without a context and exalts the idea of freedom and power as a separate top level value ignores this task and obscures the relation between virtue and reality. We act rightly 'when the time comes' not out of strength of will but out of the quality of our usual attachments and with the kind of energy and discernment which we have available. And to this the whole activity of our consciousness is relevant.

The central explanatory image which joins together the different aspects of the picture which I have been trying to exhibit is the concept of Good. It is a concept which is not easy to understand partly because it has so many false doubles, jumped-up intermediaries invented by human selfishness to make the difficult task of virtue look easier and more attractive: History, God, Lucifer, Ideas of power, freedom, purpose, reward, even judgment are irrelevant. Mystics of all kinds have usually known this and have attempted by extremities of language to portray the nakedness and aloneness of Good, its absolute for-nothingness. One might say that true morality is a sort of unesoteric mysticism, having its source in an austere and unconsoled love of the Good. When Plato wants to explain Good he uses the image of the sun. The moral pilgrim emerges from the cave and begins to see the real world in the light of the sun, and last of all is able to look at the sun itself. I want now to comment on various aspects of this extremely rich metaphor.

The sun is seen at the end of a long quest which involves a reorientation (the prisoners have to turn round) and an ascent. It is real, it is out there, but very distant. It gives light and energy and enables us to know truth. In its light we see the things of the world in their true relationships. Looking at it itself is supremely difficult and is unlike looking at things in its light. It is a different kind of thing from what it illuminates. Note the metaphor of 'thing' here. Good is a concept about which, and not only in philosophical language, we naturally use a Platonic terminology, when we speak about seeking the Good, or loving the Good. We may also speak seriously of ordinary things, people, works of art, as being good, although we are also well aware of their imperfections. Good lives as it were on both sides of the barrier and we can combine the aspiration to complete goodness with a realistic sense of achievement within our limitations. For all our frailty the command 'be perfect' has sense for us. The concept Good resists collapse into the selfish empirical consciousness. It is not a mere value tag of the choosing will, and functional and casual uses of 'good' (a good knife, a good fellow) are not, as some philosophers have wished to argue, clues to the structure of the concept. The proper and serious use of the term refers us to a perfection which is perhaps never exemplified in the world we know ('There is no good in us') and which carries with it the ideas of hierarchy and transcendence. How do we know that the very great are not the perfect? We see differences, we sense directions, and we know that the Good is still somewhere beyond. The self, the place where we live, is a place of illusion. Goodness is connected with the attempt to see the unself, to see and to respond to the real world in the light of a virtuous consciousness. This is the non-metaphysical meaning of the idea of transcendence to which philosophers have so constantly resorted in their explanations of goodness. 'Good is a transcendent reality' means that virtue is the attempt to pierce the veil of selfish consciousness and join the world as it really is. It is an empirical fact about human nature that this attempt cannot be entirely successful.

Of course we are dealing with a metaphor, but with a very important metaphor and one which is not just a property of philosophy and not just a model. As I said at the beginning, we are creatures who use irreplaceable metaphors in many of our most important activities. And the decent man has probably always, if uncertainly and inexplicably, been able to distinguish between the real Good and its false double. In most ideological contexts virtue can be loved for its own sake. The fundamental metaphors as it were carry this love through and beyond what is false. Metaphors can be a mode of understanding, and so of acting upon, our condition. Philosophers merely do explicitly and systematically and often with art what the ordinary person does by instinct. Plato, who understood this situation better than most of the metaphysical philosophers, referred to many of his theories as 'myths,' and tells us that the *Republic* is to be thought of as an allegory of the soul. 'Perhaps it is a pattern laid up in heaven where he who wishes can see it and become its citizen. But it doesn't matter whether it exists or ever will exist; it is the only city in whose politics [the good man] can take part' (*Republic*, 592).

I want now to continue to explain the concept of the Good and its peculiar relation to other concepts by speaking first of the unifying power of this idea, and secondly of its indefinability. I said earlier that as far as I could see there was no metaphysical unity in human life: all was subject to mortality and chance. And yet we continue to dream of unity. Art is our most ardent dream. In fact morality does actually display to us a sort of unity, though of a peculiar kind and quite unlike the closed theoretical unity of the ideologies. Plato pictures the journeying soul as ascending through four stages of en-lightenment, progressively discovering at each stage that what it was treating as realities were only shadows or images of something more real still. At the end of its quest it reaches a non-hypothetical first principle which is the form or idea of the Good, which enables it then to descend and retrace its path, but moving only through the forms or true conception of that which it previously understood only in part (*Republic*, 510–11). This passage in the *Republic* has aroused a great deal of discussion but it seems to me that its general application to morality is fairly clear. The mind which has ascended to the vision of the Good can subsequently see the concepts through which it has ascended (art, work, nature, people, ideas, institutions, situations, etc., etc.) in their true nature and in their proper relationships to each other. The good man knows whether and when art or politics is more important than family. The good man sees the way in which the virtues are related to each other. Plato never in fact anywhere expounds a systematic and unitary view of the world of the forms, though he implies that there is a hierarchy of forms. (Truth and Knowledge, for instance, come fairly closely underneath Good, *Republic*, 509A). What he does suggest is that we work with the idea of such a hierarchy in so far as we introduce order into our conceptions of the world through our apprehension of Good.

This seems to me to be true. Plato's image implies that complete unity is not seen until one has reached the summit, but moral advance carries with it intuitions of unity which are increasingly less misleading. As we deepen our notions of the virtues we introduce relationship and hierarchy. Courage, which seemed at first to be something on its own, a sort of specialized daring of the spirit, is now seen to be a particular operation of wisdom and love. We come to distinguish a self-assertive ferocity from the kind of courage which would enable a man coolly to choose the labor camp rather than the easy compromise with the tyrant. It would be impossible to have only one virtue unless it were a very trivial

one such as thrift. Such transformations as these are cases of seeing the order of the world
in the light of the Good and revisiting the true, or more true, conceptions of that which we
formerly misconceived. Freedom, we find out, is not an inconsequential chucking of one's
weight about, it is the disciplined overcoming of self. Humility is not a peculiar habit of
self-effacement, rather like having an inaudible voice, it is selfless respect for reality and one
of the most difficult and central of all virtues.

Because of his ambiguous attitude to the sensible world, of which I have already
spoken, and because of his confidence in the revolutionary power of mathematics, Plato
sometimes seems to imply that the road towards the Good leads away from the world of
particularity and detail. However, he speaks of a descending as well as an ascending
dialectic and he speaks of a return to the cave. In any case, in so far as goodness is for use in
politics and in the market place it must combine its increasing intuitions of unity with an
increasing grasp of complexity and detail. False conceptions are often generalized, stereo-
typed and unconnected. True conceptions combine just modes of judgment and ability to
connect with an increased perception of detail. The case of the mother who has to consider
each one of her family carefully as she decides whether or not to throw auntie out. This
double revelation of both random detail and intuited unity is what we receive in every
sphere of life if we seek for what is best. We can see this, once more, quite clearly in art and
intellectual work. The great artists reveal the detail of the world. At the same time their
greatness is not something peculiar and personal like a proper name. They are great in
ways which are to some extent similar, and increased understanding of an art reveals its
unity through its excellence. All serious criticism assumes this, though it might be wary of
expressing it in a theoretical manner. Art reveals reality and because there is a way in
which things are there is a fellowship of artists. Similarly with scholars. Honesty seems
much the same virtue in a chemist as in a historian and the evolution of the two could be
similar. And there is another similarity between the honesty required to tear up one's
theory and the honesty required to perceive the real state of one's marriage, though
doubtless the latter is much more difficult. Plato, who is sometimes accused of over-
valuing intellectual disciplines, is quite explicit in giving these, when considered on their
own, a high but second place. A serious scholar has great merits. But a serious scholar who
is also a good man knows not only his subject but the proper place of his subject in the
whole of his life. The understanding which leads the scientist to the right decision about
giving up a certain study, or leads the artist to the right decision about his family, is
superior to the understanding of art and science as such. (Is this not what καίτοι νοητῶν
ὄντων μετὰ ἀρχῆς means? *Republic*, 511D.) We are admittedly specialized creatures
where morality is concerned and merit in one area does not seem to guarantee merit in
another. The good artist is not necessarily wise at home, and the concentration camp
guard can be a kindly father. At least this can seem to be so, though I would feel that the
artist had at least got a starting-point and that on closer inspection the concentration camp
guard might prove to have his limitations as a family man. The scene remains disparate and
complex beyond the hopes of any system, yet at the same time the concept Good stretches
through the whole of it and gives it the only kind of shadowy unachieved unity which it
can possess. The area of morals, and ergo of moral philosophy, can now be seen, not as a

hole-and-corner matter of debts and promises, but as covering the whole of our mode of living and the quality of our relations with the world.

Good has often been said to be indefinable for reasons connected with freedom. Good is an empty space into which human choice may move. I want now to suggest that the indefinability of the good should be conceived of rather differently. On the kind of view which I have been offering it seems that we do really know a certain amount about Good and about the way in which it is connected with our condition. The ordinary person does not, unless corrupted by philosophy, believe that he creates values by his choices. He thinks that some things really are better than others and that he is capable of getting it wrong. We are not usually in doubt about the direction in which Good lies. Equally we recognize the real existence of evil: cynicism, cruelty, indifference to suffering. However, the concept of Good still remains obscure and mysterious. We see the world in the light of the Good, but what is the Good itself? The source of vision is not in the ordinary sense seen. Plato says of it 'It is that which every soul pursues and for the sake of which it does all that it does, with some intuition of its nature, and yet also baffled' (*Republic*, 505). And he also says that Good is the source of knowledge and truth and yet is something which surpasses them in splendor (*Republic*, 508–9).

There is a sort of logical, in the modern sense of the word, answer to the question but I think it is not the whole answer. Asking what Good is is not like asking what Truth is or what Courage is, since in explaining the latter the idea of Good must enter in, it is that in the light of which the explanation must proceed. 'True courage is. . . .' And if we try to define Good as X we have to add that we mean of course a good X. If we say that Good is Reason we have to talk about good judgment. If we say that Good is Love we have to explain that there are different kinds of love. Even the concept of Truth has its ambiguities and it is really only of Good that we can say 'it is the trial of itself and needs no other touch.' And with this I agree. It is also argued that all things which are capable of showing degrees of excellence show it in their own way. The idea of perfection can only be exemplified in particular cases in terms of the kind of perfection which is appropriate. So one could not say in general what perfection is, in the way in which one could talk about generosity or good painting. In any case, opinions differ and the truth of judgments of value cannot be demonstrated. This line of argument is sometimes used to support a view of Good as empty and almost trivial, a mere word, 'the most general adjective of commendation,' a flag used by the questing will, a term which could with greater clarity be replaced by 'I'm for this.' This argument and its conclusion seem to me to be wrong for reasons which I have already given: excellence has a kind of unity and there are facts about our condition from which lines converge in a definite direction; and also for other reasons which I will now suggest.

A genuine mysteriousness attaches to the idea of goodness and the Good. This is a mystery with several aspects. The indefinability of Good is connected with the un-systematic and inexhaustible variety of the world and the pointlessness of virtue. In this respect there is a special link between the concept of Good and the ideas of Death and Chance. (One might say that Chance is really a subdivision of Death. It is certainly our most effective *memento mori*.) A genuine sense of mortality enables us to see virtue as the only thing of worth; and it is impossible to limit and foresee the ways in which it will be required of us. That we cannot dominate the world may be put in a more positive way. Good is mysterious because of human frailty, because of the immense distance which is involved. If there were angels they might be able to define good but we would not understand the definition. We are largely mechanical creatures, the slaves of relentlessly strong selfish forces the nature of which we scarcely comprehend. At best, as decent persons, we are usually very specialized. We behave well in areas where this can be done fairly easily and let other areas of possible virtue remain undeveloped. There are perhaps in the case of every human being insuperable psychological barriers to goodness. The self is a divided thing and the whole of it cannot be redeemed any more than it can be known. And if we look outside the self what we see are scattered intimations of Good. There are few places where virtue plainly shines: great art, humble people who serve others. And can we, without improving ourselves, really see these things clearly? It is in the context of such limitations that we should picture our freedom. Freedom is, I think, a mixed concept. The true half of it is simply a name of an aspect of virtue concerned especially with the clarification of vision and the domination of selfish impulse. The false and more popular half is a name for the self-assertive movements of deluded selfish will which because of our ignorance we take to be something autonomous.

We cannot then sum up human excellence for these reasons: the world is aimless, chancy, and huge, and we are blinded by self. There is a third consideration which is a relation of the other two. It is *difficult* to look at the sun: it is not like looking at other things. We somehow retain the idea, and art both expresses and symbolizes it, that the lines really do converge. There is a magnetic center. But it is easier to look at the converging edges than to look at the center itself. We do not and probably cannot know, conceptualize, what it is like in the center. It may be said that since we cannot see anything there why try to look? And is there not a danger of damaging our ability to focus on the sides? I think there is a sense in trying to look, though the occupation is perilous for reasons connected with masochism and other obscure devices of the psyche. The impulse to worship is deep and ambiguous and old. There are false suns, easier to gaze upon and far more comforting than the true one.

Plato has given us the image of this deluded worship in his great allegory. The prisoners in the cave at first face the back wall. Behind them a fire is burning in the light of which they see upon the wall the shadows of puppets which are carried between them and the fire and they take these shadows to be the whole of reality. When they turn round they can see the fire, which they have to pass in order to get out of the cave. The fire, I take it, represents the self, the old unregenerate psyche, that great source of energy and warmth. The prisoners in the second stage of enlightenment have gained the kind of self-awareness which is nowadays a matter of so much interest to us. They can see in themselves the sources of what was formerly blind selfish instinct. They see the flames which threw the shadows which they used to think were real, and they can see the puppets, imitations of things in the real world, whose shadows they used to recognize. They do not yet dream that there is anything else to see. What is more likely than that they should settle down beside the fire, which though its form is flickering and unclear is quite easy to look at and cosy to sit by?

I think Kant was afraid of this when he went to such lengths to draw our attention away from the empirical psyche. This powerful thing is indeed an object of fascination, and those who study its power to cast shadows are studying something which is real. A recognition of its power may be a step towards escape from the cave; but it may equally be taken as an end-point. The fire may be mistaken for the sun, and self-scrutiny taken for goodness. (Of course not everyone who escapes from the cave need have spent much time by the fire. Perhaps the virtuous peasant has got out of the cave without even noticing the fire.) Any religion or ideology can be degraded by the substitution of self, usually in some disguise, for the true object of veneration. However, in spite of what Kant was so much afraid of I think there is a place both inside and outside religion for a sort of contemplation of the Good, not just by dedicated experts but by ordinary people: an attention which is not just the planning of particular good actions but an attempt to look right away from self towards a distant transcendent perfection, a source of uncontaminated energy, a source of *new* and quite undreamt-of virtue. This attempt, which is a turning of attention away from the particular, may be the thing that helps most when difficulties seem insoluble, and especially when feelings of guilt keep attracting the gaze back towards the self. This is the true mysticism which is morality, a kind of undogmatic prayer which is real and important, though perhaps also difficult and easily corrupted.

I have been speaking of the indefinability of the Good; but is there really nothing else that we can say about it? Even if we cannot find it another name, even if it must be thought of as above and alone, are there not other concepts, or another concept, with which it has some quite special relation? Philosophers have often tried to discern such a relationship: Freedom, Reason, Happiness, Courage, History have recently been tried in the role. I do not find any of these candidates convincing. They seem to represent in each case the philosopher's admiration for some specialized aspect of human conduct which is much less than the whole of excellence and sometimes dubious in itself. I have already mentioned a concept with a certain claim and I will return to that in conclusion. I want now to speak of what is perhaps the most obvious as well as the most ancient and traditional claimant, though one which is rarely mentioned by our contemporary philosophers, and that is Love. Of course Good is sovereign over Love, as it is sovereign over other concepts, because Love can name something bad. But is there not nevertheless something about the conception of a refined love which is practically identical with goodness? Will not 'Act lovingly' translate 'Act perfectly,' whereas 'Act rationally' will not? It is tempting to say so.

However I think that Good and Love should not be identified, and not only because human love is usually self-assertive. The concepts, even when the idea of love is purified, still play different roles. We are dealing here with very difficult metaphors. Good is the magnetic center towards which love naturally moves. False love moves to false good. False love embraces false death. When true good is loved, even impurely or by accident, the quality of the love is automatically refined, and when the soul is turned towards Good the highest part of the soul is enlivened. Love is the tension between the imperfect soul and the magnetic perfection which is conceived of as lying beyond it. (In the *Symposium* Plato pictures Love as being poor and needy.) And when we try perfectly to love what is imperfect our love goes to its object *via* the Good to be thus purified and made unselfish and just. The mother loving the retarded child or loving the tiresome elderly relation.

Love is the general name of the quality of attachment and it is capable of infinite degradation and is the source of our greatest errors; but when it is even partially refined it is the energy and passion of the soul in its search for Good, the force that joins us to Good and joins us to the world through Good. Its existence is the unmistakable sign that we are spiritual creatures, attracted by excellence and made for the Good. It is a reflection of the warmth and light of the sun.

Perhaps the finding of other names for Good or the establishing of special relationships cannot be more than a sort of personal game. However I want in conclusion to make just one more move. Goodness is connected with the acceptance of real death and real chance and real transience and only against the background of this acceptance, which is psychologically so difficult, can we understand the full extent of what virtue is like. The acceptance of death is an acceptance of our own nothingness which is an automatic spur to our concern with what is not ourselves. The good man is humble; he is very unlike the big neo-Kantian Lucifer. He is much more like Kierkegaard's tax collector. Humility is a rare virtue and an unfashionable one and one which is often hard to discern. Only rarely does one meet somebody in whom it positively shines, in whom one apprehends with amazement the absence of the anxious avaricious tentacles of the self. In fact any other name for Good must be a partial name; but names of virtues suggest directions of thought, and this direction seems to me a better one than that suggested by more popular concepts such as freedom and courage. The humble man, because he sees himself as nothing, can see other things as they are. He sees the pointlessness of virtue and its unique value and the endless extent of its demand. Simone Weil tells us that the exposure of the soul to God condemns the selfish part of it not to suffering but to death. The humble man perceives the distance between suffering and death. And although he is not by definition the good man perhaps he is the kind of man who is most likely of all to become good.

Reading Introduction

Is Virtue Possible?
Michael Slote

Murdoch faults the neo-Kantians for their unrealistic moral psychology, but Michael Slote argues in this essay that Murdoch's own psychology is guilty of a certain unrealism. According to Murdoch, when people lack virtue, it is due to their being too self-centered, either by natural inclination or through the pernicious influence of some theory like that of the neo-Kantians. What they need is to "die to self," to contemplate the Good with greater respect and objectivity.

But, Slote asks, what if a person's entire *society* lacks sensitivity to some moral issue? If somebody has been trained from earliest childhood to believe that cannibalism is morally acceptable, can she come to see that stewing people is bad, just by bringing herself to take a less self-centered outlook? Slote thinks a highly plausible answer is no. Self-centeredness is only *one* barrier to virtue; there are also *cultural* barriers. What seems beyond moral reproach in one era or culture may seem profoundly immoral in another era or culture.

From this observation Slote goes on to raise a much more far-reaching question than his query about Murdoch's philosophy—namely, Is virtue possible *at all*? There was a time when a slave-owner might have been thought to be a man of exemplary virtue, but we are quite certain that he was not. Since an examination of history gives us every reason to think we are in the same position as the slave-owner (namely, that someday increased moral knowledge will enable people to look back on us and see how vicious we were), we should doubt whether anybody in our culture can be virtuous, and indeed whether anybody in any culture can be virtuous.

Is Virtue Possible?

MICHAEL SLOTE

Much attention has recently been paid to the nature and interrelations of the moral virtues and to the psychology of their embodiment in particular individuals. Although it has typically been assumed that a virtuous individual knows what is right in different situations and acts accordingly, both Iris Murdoch in *The Sovereignty of Good* (London: Routledge and Kegan Paul, 1970) and John McDowell in "Virtue and Reason" (*The Monist* 62, 1979, 331–50) have laid particular stress on the (Aristotelian) idea of perception in their accounts of the epistemology of virtue. Murdoch and McDowell offer a marvellously subtle and complex treatment of virtue, and their ideas have rich reverberations for our understanding of Plato and Aristotle's ethical thought. But their account of moral virtue is also importantly incomplete. And in what follows I shall argue, in particular, that their exclusive focus on internal defects that prevent people from seeing and doing what is right makes them overestimate the general accessibility of moral virtue and ignore the historical dimension of our attempts to understand "moral reality."[1]

I

The virtuous individual is often said to be capable of knowing right from wrong in the wide variety of circumstances that might arise in his life. This knowledge may not be embodied in any (complex) ethical precept completely formulable by him or even in principle; indeed that is part of the reason for saying, with Aristotle, that overall virtue – or any particular virtue – involves (or is) a quasi-perceptual capacity for recognizing what in the various circumstances in which one may be called upon to act, is the right thing to do. But knowledge is nonetheless required if one is to be a virtuous person and not just someone who by benign accident or at the behest of others does what a virtuous individual is supposed to do from knowledge.

Most accounts of moral virtue treat it as a disposition to be acquired only through a proper upbringing and education. But McDowell and Murdoch place a special emphasis on another precondition of virtue. What prevents some people from being virtuous at a given time can be something about them at that time which, though it may to some extent be due to faulty training, has independent explanatory force in understanding their lack of virtue. A person can be too self-centered, too emotional, too proud to get things morally right, and because such individual defects are widespread and difficult to overcome, Murdoch and McDowell both speak of (overall) virtue as very difficult to attain.

Nonetheless, I am more struck by the possibilities of virtue McDowell and Murdoch do not rule out than by those they do. For by talking about what virtuous individuals do

Michael Slote, "Is Virtue Possible?" *Analysis* 42 (March 1982):70–76. Reprinted by permission of the author.

and are like, they both imply that there *have been* virtuous individuals, and Murdoch makes an explicit commitment to that assumption by claiming that moral virtue can be found not only in the likes of Socrates, but among peasants as well. Furthermore, Aristotle (see, e.g., *Nicomachean Ethics* 1143a 25–35; 1144b 30–1145a 6) appears to have believed in the existence of virtuous individuals in his own day, and McDowell not only says he wishes to defend an Aristotelian conception of the inculcation and practice of virtue, but mentions no factor that might have made it more difficult to acquire virtue in Aristotle's time than in our own.

Indeed, if the sorts of factors they mention were the sole impediments to the development and exercise of virtue, then the attainment of virtue, as traditionally conceived, might be no more problematic than McDowell and Murdoch suggest. But it seems to me that there are other, less individualistic factors that must be brought into an account of virtue, and in the light of these I think it doubtful that virtue existed in the ancient world or can ever be found among the uneducated. It even becomes questionable whether virtue is attainable today, but these difficulties are perhaps best formulated in terms of examples.

II

We now regard slavery as an unjust institution that offends the basic rights of the enslaved. But in the ancient world—in Greece, in Rome, among the Church Fathers—no one ever wrote, or is known to have spoken, against slavery as such.[2] There were occasional discussions of the abuses and justifications of slavery, but it was never held that owning slaves was simply wrong. Murdoch and McDowell say that the virtuous individual takes account of the rights of others and of what is just and fair, and they use such moral notions *tout court*, with all the objectivity that that implies. But if we agree that slavery offends the rights of slaves, can we plausibly avoid saying that the keeping, buying, and selling of slaves not only is but was wrong; and will not that in turn commit us to saying that those engaged in such practices were not morally virtuous individuals? But such criticism will then also naturally extend beyond those who actually possessed slaves to people too poor to own slaves, perhaps even to slaves themselves. Even those who could not afford slaves would presumably have been *disposed* to own slaves if good fortune had made it possible. For slavery was simply accepted, as a natural fact, in the ancient world. No other system was known or, perhaps, even thought possible. So with benefit of hindsight, the assumption that slavery is wrong can lead one to question Aristotle's assumption that there actually were virtuous individuals to be found in his society and McDowell's seemingly unqualified endorsement of Aristotle's views about the nature and realization of virtue.

McDowell and Murdoch say that egotism, wilfulness, laziness, and bad temper can render someone incapable of seeing all that the virtuous person must see. But such variable factors of individual psychology—and various deficiencies of training—are the only barriers to virtue they mention, and if nothing else could stand in the way of virtue, then there would perhaps be no reason why virtue should not have been present in the sorts of individuals Aristotle regarded as virtuous. When, however, we consider the example of slavery — and other examples to be mentioned shortly — it can begin to seem questionable whether the above factors represent the only bars to moral virtue. If virtue requires the disposition to act justly, do the right thing, with regard to important issues, can we sensibly suppose that the failure of the ancient world to attain and act upon a correct moral view of slavery merely reflects personal weaknesses or deficient methods of moral training that, unluckily, happened to be fairly universal in those days? Presumably not.

I have never heard anyone suggest that the Greeks, ancient Hebrews, or early Christians were less able to instil moral values into their children than we are today — there is reason, in fact, to believe the contrary. And to say that the ancients were blinded to the injustice of slavery (say) by their inordinate greed would not account for the fact that those too poor to own slaves (even, I suppose, the large majority of slaves themselves) never thought of questioning slavery. Nor was ancient belief in the naturalness and inevitability of slavery (and in the existence of "natural slaves") *merely* a widespread rationalization of individual avarice. Rather, that belief is at least partly to be explained by the fact that slavery was a universal phenomenon. Just as ignorance of the alternative terms used by other languages can make matters of linguistic convention seem to be inevitable facts of nature, so too can ignorance of alternatives to a given social arrangement instil the belief that that arrangement is natural and inevitable and thus beyond the possibility of radical moral criticism. So if the ancients were unable to see what virtue required in regard to slavery, that was not due to personal limitations (alone) but requires some explanation by social and historical forces, by cultural limitations, if you will.[3] And if we today can see the wrongness of slavery, that is in part because we have the benefit of knowledge that makes slavery seem less natural and inevitable. For unlike the ancients we know of "experiments" in living without slavery; we possess an historical record of societies, among them our own, where slavery has been absent and people have survived and flourished, nonetheless.

Similar points arise in connection with issues other than slavery. Murdoch insists (1f.) that an "unexamined life" can be virtuous and that there are and can be virtuous peasants. And I believe she makes such claims because she regards personal defects as the only barriers to correct moral vision, to virtue. But there is reason to wonder whether such factors are the only ones that affect whether a peasant does the right thing. Consider, for example, a peasant father or mother who refuses to help his/her daughter leave a husband who is clearly unloving and abusive. We believe, do we not, that a woman has the right to leave such a husband (though there may be wrong *ways* of doing so), but what if the woman's own parents refuse to help her in this, telling her to stay with her husband and even rendering it impossible for her to leave him (she needs a small amount of money from them, say, in order to get away)? Such actions presumably express a failure to acknowledge the rights of the unhappy wife, and most of us would say that they are a wrong way to act towards a daughter in distress and in need. But what prevents her parents from doing right by her? Need it be envy of the new life she hopes to lead and they never had or (in the case of the father) sexist antagonism towards women generally? Need it be self-righteous anger reflecting frustration at having chosen wrongly for her (we are talking about a peasant society) or selfish discontent at having her once more dependent upon them? Can it not simply be that, despite all their love and desire to help her, they believe in *a holy book* that commands all women to stay with their husbands through thick and thin? Murdoch herself (74, 101) says that traditional religion is no barrier—is even, indeed, a positive aid—to virtue and right action. But then what can be said about the case at hand? Unless we hold, implausibly and against Murdoch's own tendencies, that only a blind or selfish person would accept the holiness of the book in question, we shall have to grant that the peasant parents may do the wrong thing for reasons having to do with social and cultural influences (as reflected of course in them) rather than through the sorts of personal, individually variable, vision-preventing defects she so exclusively focuses upon. And there are many, many other such situations where tradition and milieu would put "enlightened" views of right and wrong beyond the reach of (devout) peasants. So if Murdoch is right to insist that right action is a criterion of virtue and if modern views of the rights of women are correct, then the existence of virtue in unexamined lives seems very dubious.[4]

Nor would it be very easy for Murdoch and McDowell to evade the above conclusions by claiming that slavery was *not* wrong in the special circumstances of the ancient world or that "women's rights" *do not exist* in peasant societies. For they are self-avowed moral realists who hold that moral beings are seeking to understand an independent moral reality and, where appropriate (e.g., Murdoch, 55, 59, 69; McDowell, 346ff.), they have sought to distinguish their views from any form of moral relativism. Since, in addition, Murdoch and McDowell both speak freely, and in the most objectivistic terms, of justice, fairness, and rights, I find it impossible to imagine either of them being happy with the view that slavery was fair in ancient Greece or with the view that (certain) peasant women have no right to leave their husbands.

III

In that case a very real question must arise about whether overall virtue is possible even for us. We have been speaking as if the wide-ranging capacity for right action that seems problematic in relation to the Greeks or peasant societies presented no particular problem for such modern individuals as can perceive the rights of slaves and women and with proper education overcome the individual-psychological barriers to virtue that McDowell and Murdoch describe. But in fact I have no intention of being thus smug about current values and conceptions of morality. I have, for example, harped on the wrongness of slavery and the unavailability of that moral fact, and others, to the ancients, but I too admire Greek moral philosophy, and that very admiration causes me to wonder whether virtue is any more accessible nowadays than it was in classical antiquity. I assume that we now see aspects of right and wrong that the ancient world missed; but may we not also fail to see things the Greeks were able to see, and, more significantly, may there not be other moral issues on which both the ancients and we ourselves are blind? Someday, our descendants may regard twentieth century morality and moral philosophy as having been as hopelessly wrongheaded on certain issues (vegetarianism? children's rights? patients' rights?) as were ancient views about slavery. And they may have as much reason to do so as we currently have to be critical of ancient attitudes to slavery.

A natural enough induction from the history of previous *scientific* theories tells us that today's theories are very likely to turn out to be mistaken in important ways. Is there any less reason to believe the same about current-day moral thinking? If not, then there is reason to believe that moral virtue as traditionally understood is not accessible even today, but rather, like various kinds of scientific truth, is to be attained, if at all, only at the historical limit of human cultural endeavor, in a long run that no individual may ever encompass. McDowell and Murdoch have underscored the individually understandable obstacles to virtue, but because moral virtue is subject to social/historical influences and limitations that they never mention, the very possibility of virtue comes into question.

I believe, however, that I can see one reason why Murdoch and McDowell limit themselves to individualistic factors in talking about virtue and neglect the larger cultural factors I have been emphasizing. Both are wary of the scientism that holds that science can tell us everything about reality and that what it doesn't speak of doesn't exist. And they deliberately stay clear of those analogies between moral philosophy and science that moral philosophers are often so eager to develop. One such attempted analogy can be found in the idea of moral philosophy as a progressive discipline that (occasionally) arrives at new and better moral knowledge (theories) through the historical accumulation of greater non-moral knowledge—and by building on the ideas of previous (moral) philosophers. In rejecting such analogies, Murdoch and McDowell limit themselves to focusing on ontogenetic impediments to moral knowledge (vision) and right action: such limits and impediments as are due to be overcome by means of the phylogenesis of moral knowledge could be acknowledged or featured only by admitting the sort of analogy between progressing science and moral philosophy that seems repugnant to Murdoch and McDowell. [Thus when Murdoch speaks (38) of the "historically conditioned" aspects of virtue, she is in fact speaking only of the history of a particular individual who is to become virtuous by overcoming his own passions and foibles. History in the usual sense remains out of the picture.]

It is clear that I am not altogether averse to the above analogy between moral philosophy (and moral ideas generally) and science. It is dangerous to speak of moral progress, but I have risked doing so with regard to certain specific issues like slavery and the right (in principle) of a woman to leave her husband. Nonetheless, the main focus of my acceptance of the analogy is not the idea of similar progress, but rather of similar historical character. There seems to be something historically *developmental* about moral philoso-phy, even if this does not amount to progress as science understands (and achieves) it. Such an analogy with science does not force us to the sort of scientism McDowell and Murdoch decry. For one could hold that there was (phylogenetic) historical progress in moral theory without assuming that that occurred through some sort of convergence with scientific inquiry; the progress, if it occurs, can be directed, if you like, to a moral reality of the sort Murdoch and McDowell envisage.

In rejecting the analogy with historically developing science, Murdoch (27, 76) and McDowell (346ff.) also imply that moral philosophers have no contribution to make to our understanding (knowledge) of right and wrong—they can clarify concepts and indicate the structures and processes of the moral life, but that is another matter. This, however, ignores, or perhaps rejects, some important aspects of the history of moral philosophy. When it was first discussed in the eighteenth century, Utilitarianism was an original moral idea. No one had seriously thought that right action consisted in just what Utilitarianism says it does. Similarly, to take a more recent example, Rawls's difference principle (as opposed to aspects of his argument for it) seems to be a totally new substantive moral conception. Now even if neither the principle of utility nor the difference principle is actually true (or thus represents the moral knowledge that the ancients lacked and needed for the attainment of virtue), they are ideas worth taking seriously, real contributions to the attempt to know what is right (think how much has been learned by attempts to *refute* Utilitarianism and Rawls). And if new and promising ideas not about moral concepts but about actual right and wrong can thus emerge through the individual insight or vision of particular moral philosophers (or others), does this not locate another reason why virtue may not be attainable in those too-often-neglected factors of historical development that make some sort of analogy between science and moral thinking entirely plausible?

By focusing on characteristics of virtuous individuals, McDowell seeks to give an account of morality, as he says, from the inside out (331). Moral principles become secondary or drop out altogether, because the tendencies to right action that virtue requires cannot, he thinks, be grasped or formulated in any statable general moral principle(s). But if, as I have suggested, the development of moral thought and the realization of virtue wait upon the thinking up and theoretical sifting of such moral principles as the Utilitarians and Rawls introduced, then there is a place for an independent "principles" approach to moral philosophy alongside efforts to conceive morality from the standpoint of the virtuous individual.[5]

Notes

1. I shall be responding to a composite (and partial) picture of what Murdoch and McDowell say, but shall note differences of emphasis where relevant. McDowell acknowledges a debt to Murdoch and at no point indicates any disagreement with her work. Note further that my criticism will not hinge on anything either of them says, or fails to say, about *akrasia* (weakness of will).

2. See M. I. Finley, *Ancient Slavery and Modern Ideology* (London: Chatto and Windus, 1980), 120ff. Finley mentions only Euripides as a possible exception to the above generalization.

3. On the distinction between individual-psychological and social/historical factors, cf. C. Ryan, "Beyond Beliefs," *American Philosophical Quarterly* 18 (1981): 33–41 and references therein. On the unavailability to the Greeks of "enlightened" moral views about slavery, see T. H. Green, *Prolegomena to Ethics* (Oxford: Oxford University Press, 1883): chap. 5.

4. Murdoch says that no one is morally perfect. But my assumption that a virtuous individual should be capable of right action with regard to such important issues as slavery is hardly an insistence on moral *perfection*.

5. I am indebted to John McDowell, Myles Burnyeat, John Dillon, and Edward Erwin for helpful suggestions.

Reading Introduction

Desires and Deliberation
N.J.H. Dent

In the first part of this selection, Dent distinguishes two kinds of motivation or causes of human action: being motivated by a *desire* for something (for example, lusting after a new Corvette), and being motivated by the consideration that something is a *worthy*, *reasonable*, or *appropriate* goal of action (for example, concluding after due reflection that a Corvette is the most practical car for you in your circumstances). We can want things without believing them to be worthy or reasonable to want, and we can believe that a certain goal is worthy and reasonable without feeling any desire for it on that account. Many philosophers and psychologists think that people are motivated only by desires, so that when we decide between two courses of action, our decision is simply the outcome of competing desires. One desire pulls us in one direction, another desire in another direction. Our action is just the result of the "strongest" pull. While this pull-pull mechanical picture of motivation may be accurate for small children and animals, it does not describe mature human beings. We can be motivated not only by desires, but also by "deliberation"—that is, considerations of appropriateness.

Considerations of appropriateness can motivate us without being desires. But this seems mysterious and calls for an explanation. How do considerations of appropriateness move us to action, if they are not desires? Dent seeks to answer this question in the second part of our selection.

Suppose you have a burning desire for that new Corvette, and you have almost enough in the bank to cover it. But you were hoping to get through your last two years of college without working, and your bank account was marked for that. So you have two desires, and you must choose. If asked which of these desires *feels* most intense, you would probably say that your desire for the beautiful car is more intense than your aversion to working twenty-five hours a week in the school cafeteria for the next two years. The latter desire has a gray cast; it is shy and retreating by comparison with the brash loud claims of the Corvette. But you are not a child or animal, nor any other kind of "wanton." You do not simply "go" with the more urgent desire, but *weigh* buying the Corvette against the free time to study. And the kind of question you ask yourself, says Dent, is how the respective courses of action fit into your larger conception of a worthwhile life. Your conception of a satisfactory life includes being an educated professional person. In this context it seems clearly better to save that time for study than to have constantly available the option of rodding around in a Corvette.

The dual fact that you *have* a conception of a worthwhile life and that you are *concerned* to realize it makes it possible for you not to be the mere slave of the urges of the moment. You evaluate the desires with some degree of objectivity and choose rationally between them. This concern for a life well-lived is not a desire of the kind associated with our senses (taste, touch, and so on) or our emotions (fear, jealousy, and so on), though it is one that can and should become embodied in our emotions.

Desires and Deliberation

N.J.H. DENT

Hobbes writes of deliberation thus:

> When in the mind of man, appetites, and aversions, hopes, and fears, concerning one and the same thing, arise alternatively; and divers good and evil consequences of the doing, or omitting the thing propounded, come successively into our thoughts; so that sometimes we have an appetite to it; sometimes an aversion from it; sometimes hope to be able to do it; sometimes despair, or fear to attempt it; the whole sum of desires, aversions, hopes and fears continued till the thing be either done, or thought impossible, is that we call DELIBERATION . . . In *deliberation*, the last appetite, or aversion, immediately adhering to the action, or to the omission thereof, is that we call the WILL; the act, not the faculty, of *willing*.[1]

And Schopenhauer describes the matter like this:

> By means of his capacity to think, man can present to himself the motives whose influence on his will he feels in any order, alternately and repeatedly, in order to hold them up to his will. This is called deliberation. . . . The ability to deliberate . . . yields in reality nothing but the very frequently distressing conflict of motives, which is dominated by indecision and has the whole soul and consciousness of man as its battlefield. This conflict makes the motives try out repeatedly, against one another, their effectiveness on the will. This puts the will in the same situation as that of the body on which different forces act in opposite directions, until finally the decidedly strongest motive drives the others from the field and determines the will. This outcome is called resolve, and it takes place with complete necessity as the result of the struggle. . . .[2]

Are these, as they present themselves as being, accounts of deliberation and of deliberatively undertaken action? It seems to me that they are not. What is signally absent from both of them is anything recognizable as the agent's giving any consideration to the merits or demerits of the objectives which attract or repel him, reflecting upon their importance or lack of importance to him, aside and apart from his desire and aversion being worked upon and aroused; and anything recognizable as his establishing some

From N.J.H. Dent, *The Moral Psychology of the Virtues* (Cambridge: Cambridge University Press, 1984), 96-119. Reprinted by permission.

purpose for himself as that which has the weight of reason to recommend his undertaking it, as he judges. . . .

Schopenhauer's revealing analogy of the will with a body 'on which different forces act in opposite directions' displays very well how distorted his account is if offered as an account of deliberation and deliberative determination of action. It presents the deliberating subject's will as entirely a passive 'object', solely acted upon by certain influences, inclining it to this or repelling it from that; as wholly devoid of any capability of initiating any response to these influences, of shaping or directing their impact in any way, as if the 'will' were entirely inert, not possessed of any active propensities of its own but only the plaything of forces to which it is subjected. We may notice that it is simply not true in mechanics that the 'decisively strongest' force 'drives the others from the field'. Rather the body subjected to these forces finally moves in a direction and with a speed which continues at every moment to depend upon the magnitude and direction of the opposing, but weaker, force(s). But what could be the corresponding feature of 'resolve'? That my will only becomes fixed upon something more slowly; or that when I finally move I do so being continually held back in some degree by opposing attractions or aversions, as if running with a ball and chain tied to my legs? Also, if a body is subjected to forces which do not pull it in directly opposite directions, but push or pull it from angles other than 180° apart, it finally moves in a direction which is proportional to the magnitude of the forces and their angles of application and not in the same direction as any of the original forces. Are we then to suppose that a person torn between desire for the swings and desire for the roundabouts will finally end up on the helter-skelter, this being the natural 'resolution' of the psychic forces he is subjected to? It is obvious that there is no point of real correspondence here; the analogy is deeply defective. What is distinctive in deliberation is that one ceases to be merely worked upon by certain objects arousing one's feelings; one does not allow oneself to remain in this situation, even if this is how one found oneself to be situated at first. Rather one attempts actively to reckon with the significance and import these matters which have affected one bear, to undertake an appraisal of their weight, their claim to concern, and not just to leave the weight they carry for one to be a matter of the force of the impact they happen to be making upon one's mind or feelings at that time. The 'will', one might say, is the source of this active reckoning and according intent; it is not a merely inert object of impulsions.

The terms from physical mechanics which are unreflectively employed in describing the phenomena of deliberation too easily deceive one into thinking that the deliberative resolution of mental conflict exhibits the same basic patterns and laws as the resolution of the conflict of physical forces. But the 'weight' of reason is not the mass of argument multiplied by the acceleration of desire; it is its cogency, its legitimacy, its fitness to serve as a basis and determinant of purpose and desire. A weighty reason does not, like a weighty brick, fall upon one and impart a certain push to one's body *via* the energy-transmitting medium of desire. It does not stun one into unconsciousness of any other reasons which may, perhaps, 'carry force' in the case. It is that on the basis of which one sees a good case for doing one thing rather than others even if there be yet something still to be said for them. In deliberation we try to 'distance' ourselves from the insistent press of desires to their gratification and endeavor to take the measure of their claim to be gratified and not just to have them claim our interest, command our involvement. We try not to be wholly absorbed by such desirous concerns, to have our place in our situation wholly structured by them, but to retain our self-possession, our power to order them and not they us, to command their direction and effect and not they command us.[3]

The descriptions Hobbes and Schopenhauer offer fit reasonably well the state of mind of . . . a child torn between desire for a chocolate and fear of a beating, or of a dog possessed by the desire for a piece of meat but fearful of attack from its present owner. (Hobbes says explicitly that 'beasts also deliberate';[4] and, on his conception of what deliberation is, this would obviously be true.) Finally, the child or the dog may grab and run; or else they slink away, cowed, overborne, by their fear. It would be absurd, surely, to present these cases as paradigmatic of what deliberative reflection upon and determination of what to do consists in. If the child were to deliberate he would, in however rudimentary, incomplete, unsystematic and short-sighted a way, consider for a moment the importance that having the sweet had for him if its cost were a beating, an importance which involves considering more than that it now seems such an urgent priority to him while the desire is upon him, while he is possessed by it and sees his life according to its dictates. And if he were to act upon his deliberation he would be guided by this assessment he makes, not just be spurred on by the urgent demandingness of his desire. To feel first desire, then fear, back and forth, until one predominates and is 'immediately adhering to the action' is not to deliberate and to act upon one's deliberations. It is only to be drawn and repelled, willy-nilly, as one or the other feeling flows and ebbs, fills consciousness or drains out of it.

Nor is this point affected if the desires to which the person is subject, by which he is possessed, are more subtle and diverse in their effects upon him than is evident in the play of temptation and fear, which can overtly modify posture and expression. A person is just as much under the domination of, for instance, a desire for power or for the acclaim of others if these desires order his objectives and actions without his making any considered assessment of the importance to him of enjoying these things and governing his conduct accordingly, even if we cannot discern in the overt play of his expression and movement the impact of these desires upon him. Someone is still in the grip of these desires and does not have command of their influence upon him, so long as it remains the case that their arousal prompts him to their fulfilment and it is not the judgement that their objectives are fit to be achieved that guides his conduct.

There is one further step the argument may take which needs to be considered at this point. It may be said that the accounts that Hobbes and Schopenhauer give are adequate as accounts of practical deliberation, because to think of something as having importance to one, to think of it as something which merits one's pursuit, just *is* for that thing to excite more or less of an interest in us, for it to engender more or less of a desirous concern in us. . . . The conceptions we have of things being good or evil, the notion of making a comparative judgement of the weight or significance of these to us; all of these, it will be said, are just 'projections in thought' of the desires and aversions we feel at any particular time in their various strengths.[5] I have been arguing for a contrast between the strength of desire for, and the judgement of the importance of, some objective; but, it will be objected, the supposition that there is a contrast here rests on the mistaken idea that the 'merit' or 'importance' of something as an object for concern and pursuit is an attribute or property of that object whereas, in reality, these 'attributes' are just attributions we make as an expression of our being desirously affected by the object, and they have no more foundation in the character of the object than that.[6] So 'deliberatively reflecting on the merits of the case' would be, in actual fact, nothing other than experiencing the oscillation of desire and aversion, this however being present to the subject in the form of his appearing to think over the excellences and defects of various possible objectives and courses of action.

Such-like accounts of the character of claims that something possesses a value, is good or evil in some respect and to some degree, are of course very familiar. It would be out of the question fully to examine and assess them here. But one point which comes from them should be made. If such accounts are correct, it does *not* follow that what Hobbes and Schopenhauer have given are descriptions of practical deliberation. What follows is that practical deliberation does not, and cannot, occur. For if 'reflecting on the merits of the case' *is* only a roundabout expression of the strengths of the desires and aversions we feel in relation to various items in our situation, then practical deliberation does not take place. . . .

We can gain further insight into the contrasts between deliberative and non-deliberative resolutions of conflicts of desire by considering some points of Frankfurt's, in a well-known paper. . . .[7] Frankfurt describes a kind of creature he calls a 'wanton', whose actions 'reflect the economy of his first-order desires, without his being concerned whether the desires that move him to act are desires by which he wants to be moved to act'.[8] (By a first-order desire is meant a desire whose object is something other than to have or to lack a desire.) Again, Frankfurt writes:

> There is only one issue in the struggle to which his first-order conflict may lead: whether the one or the other of his conflicting desires is the stronger. Since he is moved by both desires, he will not be altogether satisfied by what he does no matter which of them is effective. But it makes no difference *to him* whether his craving or aversion gets the upper hand.[9]

What these descriptions capture very well is the absence from the life of the 'wanton' of what might be called 'taking one's desires in hand' and controlling and determining the influence they shall have upon one's conduct. Frankfurt's notion that the actions of a wanton 'reflect the economy' of his desires presents clearly all that could be involved in the determination of the action of one who was possessed only of sense- and passional desires. For all that disposes a man to act upon them is the strength of the hold they happen to have upon him.

Frankfurt himself believes that a crucial difference is made to the case by the possession of second-order desires or second-order 'volitions', these latter being desires not merely to have or to be without certain first-order desires but desires that one or another of one's first-order desires should be effective, should actually order one's action. He locates the possession and efficacy of second-order volitions as being central to what it is to be a person. I am not convinced, however, that this notion will do all the work he requires of it. For a man's second-order volitions may, for all that Frankfurt says of them, simply 'reflect the economy' of the strength and range of his second-order desires. And just because someone's ultimate action may 'reflect the economy' of a combination of both second- and first-order desires this does not seem fundamentally to change the character it had when dependent upon first-order desires alone (similar queries about Frankfurt's views are raised by Watson[10]).... However, this doubt does not affect the perceptiveness of his descriptions as serving to identify what would be distorted in any account of the origination of human action out of a conflict of desires which made no reference to the evaluation and control of those desires that their subject makes. Such action could be nothing but a reflection of the magnitude of the influence of the several desires and subject possessed; and one whose action was of this character would be a 'wanton'.

In contrast, for one who deliberates there is more than 'one issue in the struggle to which his first-order conflict may lead: whether the one or the other of his conflicting desires is the stronger'. To the deliberating agent, so long as his deliberative inquiry continues without check or distortion, the strength that any of his desires happen to possess at any moment will either be of no significance to his decision about what to do, or will be at most one desideratum among many to be taken into account. He *may* decide that he would secure peace of mind and freedom from an insistent unsatisfied longing if he were to gratify an intense desire that he feels. But, even in this case, it would still not be the intensity of his desire that made his undertaking any other course of action impossible to him. (Compare Schopenhauer: 'the decidedly strongest motive drives the others from the field and determines the will. This outcome is called resolve, and it takes place with complete necessity as the result of the struggle'.) It would rather be that he elected, on grounds which he takes to be cogent, to gratify his longing, perhaps only with the thought that he may thereby rid himself of it and not at all because what he longs for seems to him particularly worth pursuing. Presumably, too, if what he longed for seemed to him actually undesirable, he might think it better to put up with his unsatisfied longing and not to gratify it, possibly seeking some other way of ridding himself of it by, for example, seeking distraction in some other concerns altogether. For a wanton, on the other hand, action is determined, and necessarily determined, by his strongest desire, the one that, in the circumstances, 'gets the upper hand'. . . .

I have been arguing that in practical deliberation we endeavor to reach a judgement upon what we should best do in the circumstances in which we find ourselves, and to direct our conduct according to our judgement. And I have claimed that reaching such a judgement, and acting upon the basis of it, cannot be equated with the emergence of a dominant desire out of a conflict of desires, and with being moved to act by the intensity of that preponderant desire: In reaching such a judgement we consider the merits and demerits of the possible alternative courses of action which are available, we consider the cogency and weight of the reasons for or against various possibilities; and, when we act upon our deliberations, we act upon those reasons which establish this act as the one we should best undertake, as we assess the situation. The crucial issue which emerges from this discussion is to explain just what it is to regard something as a reason for proposing or doing something such that we can understand how *so* regarding something gives it both a rôle in the direction of our lives, and a rôle which is different in character from that it would possess if it were simply something that worked upon or excited our desire or aversion, by which states of excitation we were then moved to act. We need, that is, to show in what way taking something to be a reason for purposing or doing something is an action-directing state, a conative state; and to show how so taking it is a different kind of state from that state we are in when we have a certain desire or aversion of a certain intensity engendered in us.

Most centrally and fundamentally, to think of oneself as having a reason for pursuing a certain end or for doing something is to see that pursuit or act as making a contribution of more or less significance to one's conducting one's affairs, living one's life, as one believes that it is best that they should be conducted, as one believes it satisfactory or fit that it should be lived. It is to see that pursuit or act as leading indirectly to, or contributing immediately and constitutively to,[11] the realization of a shape and order in one's life which one thinks appropriate should be realized. . . . [12]

My claim is that someone has such a thought about a certain matter if he has some conception of how his life should be lived in order to be satisfactorily lived, and of how that matter has a significant bearing upon the realization of that conception. And someone thinks a certain matter provides no reason for (or against) proposing or doing something if he thinks it has no bearing whatever on the possible or adequate realization of his conception of a satisfactory order in his life; and thinks of it as providing a reason against proposing or doing something if he thinks it would detract from the possible or adequate realization of this conception—or, what comes to the same thing, if he thinks it would contribute to the realization of an order in and shape to his life he thinks unsatisfactory and unfit.[13]

To think of oneself as having reason to do something is not yet to determine upon doing it. For it can very well be that there are alternative courses of action available which one takes oneself to have a better reason for doing, which have a greater claim upon one's concern, as one assesses the matter. The consideration of this is, as I have already pointed out, a primary concern in practical deliberation. It is not until one has concluded that there is overall a decisive case, or as good a case as is needful or possible, for one particular course of action that one forms the resolution of embarking upon it. By that resolution one endeavors to make one's life assume that shape one thinks it is best that it take. One proceeds as one does with the conception of one's action being of sufficient importance to the well conducting of one's life.

One's capability to be directed in one's desire and action by reasons depends, therefore, upon two principal points. First, upon one's possession of some conception of how one would do well to live one's life, of what shape and order one's conduct of the business of living would satisfactorily take; and of how doing this or that would contribute to the realization of that conception, to giving reality to it in the actual material of one's activity. And secondly, upon one's possessing a concern to make it the case that the conduct of one's life will materially realize this conception one has, as it applies in this or that situation one is in.

There are several questions about these two points which call for further explanation, quite aside from the issue of considering what might be a just conception of how one should do well to live one's life which, as I have said, I do not mean to explore further here. First, is it at all plausible to suppose that we do have conceptions of a satisfactory shape for our lives to take?[14] Secondly, is it at all plausible to suppose that we have a concern to realize such conceptions in the actual substantive course of our living, even if it can be argued that we do have these conceptions? Thirdly, if such a concern is involved here, how does its nature and rôle in determining conduct differ materially from the nature and rôle of sense- and passional desires in determining our purposes and actions? Is it not just another kind of desire which may or may not be aroused in relation to certain beliefs we have? I shall try to respond adequately to all these questions.

First, then: is it plausible to suppose we do have conceptions of how we should do well to live our lives, pictures of what would be a satisfactory way to dispose our conduct? Let it be noted that the claim is not that we have one permanent, immutable conception throughout all our lives; it may, for all sorts of reasons, change in some or perhaps very many respects during our lives. Also, it could be that someone has conflicting conceptions at some particular time, in some respects; though if the conflict is too extreme the possibility of effective deliberative decision is removed. So the question at issue is not whether we have an utterly complete, comprehensive, consistent, wholly reasoned-out and totally defended conception of the shape our lives should take; it is whether we have some conception, which embraces some set of considerations in some sort of order, which provides at least a partial picture of the proper way in which one should live, as one thinks. Not that having a more complete and comprehensive conception is ruled out; only that it would not show that a negative answer to the question posed should be returned just because few possess such conceptions. With this in mind, I do not think it can be denied that it is very generally the case indeed that humans past childhood do come to possess such conceptions of how best to conduct themselves. We can well understand why this should be by reflecting again upon what is involved when someone is possessed of a certain passional desire.

. . . One who comes to be possessed of a passional desire will also have his thoughts about that which is the objective of his desire modified.[15] The onset of an active passion involves not changes in inclinations to act alone, but also changes in one's judgement and assessment of one's situation. For example, one who is in the grip of fear will be apt to be caused to think that he must get away from where he is, that this is an imperatively necessary thing for him to do. Again, one tortured by jealousy may well think that life is just not worth living if he is displaced as the special object of someone's affection, that there is simply no point in his carrying on with anything. To have such-like thoughts is, for the time for which one continues to be subject to the passion, to be making an assessment of how one should act, or of how the circumstances of one's life should be, if one's life is to be satisfactory, tolerable, worthwhile or whatever. It is to make a judgement about what it is desirable or needful for one to do, or for how things should be, if the course of one's life is to be good. Thus, already carried in the onset of passions there are conceptions of the importance of our lives being a certain way, however fleetingly possessed these conceptions may be, however little considered, and however little informed by awareness of any other considerations. We naturally and inevitably entertain such conceptions, which structure our apprehension of the significance of certain matters to the well living of our lives, as part and parcel of our being possessed by certain active passions.

But does it not follow from this, given my account of what it is to take oneself to have a reason for aiming at or doing something, that the person who runs away in fear 'sees reason' to run away; and one who, oppressed by jealousy, wishes to end his life 'sees reason' for doing so? Thus such men have the purposes they have, do what they do, on the basis of practical reasons, and there is therefore no difference between the mode of agency involved in the arousal of active passions and that involved in determination by practical reasons. This conclusion does not, however, follow. For, although it is true that one who is possessed by fear, for example, will take himself to have every reason to run away, it does not follow that he forms the purpose of running away on the basis of his judgement that he has reason to do this. It is rather that in consequence of or alongside the arousal of the desire to run away we are caused to think of this as something that we have a strong or overwhelming reason to do. It is not that, judging we have such reason, we form the intention of running.[16] The opinion as to what we have reason to do is, in this case at any rate, only an accompaniment to our desire, our impulse, to run and is not the basis or foundation for that desire. I shall return to this point below. For the present, the point of considering such cases as these is only to show that we do have conceptions of how we think it appropriate or imperative that our lives should be. And this is amply shown by the undeniable fact that we do acquire such ideas, if only for a short time, as an element in the onset of particular active passions. This, for the moment, is all that needs to be taken from these cases.

But, clearly, if we only possessed such conceptions so long as we were moved by a certain passion, we should have advanced the case very little. For there would be little or no stability in our pictures of what was significant to us; one moment something would be all-in-all to us, which at the next was a matter which seemed to us of negligible significance. I do not mean by this to imply that all our passions are fleeting. Some persist, remain with us as long-term dispositions in our concern, and establish a relatively stable sense of the import of something to us. But even in this case, that sense will not always be uppermost in the subject's mind; it will be apt to be overlaid by other preoccupations as they come upon him with insistence in particular situations. Now it is, I think, barely conceivable that someone of adult years should not have 'taken stock' of the variety of concerns he has felt from time to time and with varying intensity and permanence. These concerns will establish first this, then that, as being for a time of cardinal or substantial importance to him in his life. But he will come to some sense of which of these things have a more enduring significance to him, a sense of their significance which will survive the occasional disappearance or overlaying of any passionally engendered sense of their importance. One could say that he will come to an appreciation of their value. This need not, as I have said, involve arriving at any fully systematic, comprehensive, everywhere thought-out system of values, scale of priorities. (Such 'systems' may indeed omit to register as important as many things as they do sufficiently register.) It is rather that his picture of what matters to him for the satisfactory content and direction of his life ceases to be the creature of his feelings of the time alone. It acquires instead a certain degree of independence of that, a certain consistency and fixity which provides the outline, at any rate, of some of the matters which have an abiding import to him, which carry weight for him. Cases where someone is subject to conflicting desires, discussed earlier, would seem to provide a central occasion for the gradual establishing of this more stable sense of significance. Particularly where someone was in feeling inclined to attribute equal and great importance to two exclusive courses of action, he could hardly not be caused to consider which was overall the more material to him. To allow the importance of the one relative to the other to be decided simply by how his feelings happened finally to settle would not be to do justice to his present sense of the importance of both of them. It is no matter to be so lightly decided.[17]

Through such consideration we can, in principle, come to have a view of our situation which incorporates an awareness, a mindfulness, of much that is not immediately concerning us through the arousal or present insistence of our passions. We can come to see our present attractions and aversions in the light of a more general awareness of the matters which hold significance for us in relation to the wider context and direction of our lives. We do not, or need not, simply move from circumstance to circumstance, being wholly absorbed in the influence each has upon us, living through a sequence of fragmented and unconnected experiences. We can come to see our present position, with the concerns it arouses in us, as one episode in a life which stretches before and after, to the well conducting of which matters other than those which presently exercise our feelings are significant and material.

It is not, then, at all implausible to suppose that we come, no doubt only slowly, falteringly and partially, to acquire some sense of what has importance for the satisfactory shape and order of our lives which goes beyond what seizes us as having such importance when affected by the arousal of passion. And in this way I maintain that someone can see reason to do something, in terms of this conception and the priorities and saliences it contains, even although what he now sees reason to do is not presently and immediately connected with a passionally aroused desire.

However, even if this line of thought is cogent, it establishes, as yet, only that we hold beliefs about what it would be needful, desirable or important for us to do beyond what we are in our present passions inclined to believe to be such. It says nothing about whether or how holding such beliefs will make any difference to how we act. It might be, for example, that such beliefs merely provide an idle accompaniment to a course of behavior entirely determined by the intensity of present passion, and that they are not actually effective in contributing to the order and direction of conduct – at least so far as what has been argued for up to now goes. It is necessary, therefore, to consider how and why we are disposed to realize this conception we have, in the actual substantive content of our life. This is to turn to the second of the questions I raised earlier: is it at all plausible to suppose that we have a concern to realize these conceptions we have of a satisfactory shape and order for our lives to possess?

It is neither necessary, nor correct, to argue that if we do have such a concern – the character of which remains still to be specified – it is by virtue of that *alone* that we would translate our ideas of what we should best do into reality. . . . We can, so to speak, 'harness' the dispositions to act we have in our passions so that, through these, we may achieve that course of life we think appropriate. This we can do by duly informing and rectifying those valuations which occasion our passional responses, and those which we are disposed to make as a result of their arousal. But it is clear that, if this is to be done, there must be originally some determination to realize our considered conception of what is valuable and important which is over and above the determination to act we have through our passional desires. For, were this not so, we could of course do nothing different from what they inclined us to do since, *ex hypothesi*, this conception is not (or is not necessarily) operative in our passions; and if these are to be rectified, this must be through some other disposition to act than they provide. So whilst, in the end, it is not alone out of a specific distinctive concern to realize our conception of how we should best live that we realize that conception, there must be, in the beginning, some such distinctive concern if that conception is not to be merely idle and incapable of finding any place in the actual direction of our conduct. The question then is: is there such a distinctive concern, and what is its nature?[18]

It should not be so hard to conceive of our being able to give our concern to something, to commit our interest to it, just because we think of it as something which is material to the well living of our lives and without it needing to evoke a passional response from us. It would be strange rather than natural if we had a capability of coming to a conception of how best to conduct our lives, which extended beyond the concerns which possess us in our present passions, but we had no capability of having regard to this in the actual directon of our conduct, in how we specifically choose and act. Just as we can, and do, come to recognize that certain ends or forms of conduct have significance to us, even although we do not presently 'feel' their significance in our passional responsiveness, so we can, and do, come to have a concern for them which makes us intent upon giving them that place in our lives which would duly answer to their significance, even although a present passional interest in them is lacking or, though present, is ineffective. I am not saying that we always are duly mindful of their significance to us and duly concerned to reckon in our decisions and actions with them, but this is not what is at issue. The issue is whether we can, *at all*, extend our interest to these matters when they do not presently excite an interest in us or do so insufficiently. And it is hard to see that this can reasonably be doubted. The awareness of ourselves as having a life which extends beyond the present moment, a life which involves matters of import to us beyond those presently exercising our feelings and engaging our passional desires and aversions, is an awareness which naturally involves a concern to shape the course of our lives to those matters.

We are not creatures who simply blunder from situation to situation wholly taken up in each of them, but we are interested in our life having a certain overall direction and shape, at least in respect of some of its features. We attribute such significance to certain factors or purposes that we cannot allow their effect upon our choices and actions to be dependent upon whether they simply *happen* to be uppermost in our minds or inclinations at some particular moment. Rather we govern and rule those passing inclinations with a view to making our life go (or not go) a certain way; we do not leave it to the adventitious economy of our present feelings to see whether or not we shall be prompted to act in this way or that. We *make* it our business to direct our lives so that they shall follow one path rather than another; the path of our activity is not merely the outcome of our uppermost aroused interest. It is as natural a propensity in human beings to have some concern to mold their lives to a certain image of how their lives should be spent, as it is for them to be worked upon, in feeling, by this or that as it happens to engage some desire or aversion.

Butler, discussing the 'authority' which attaches to conscience, writes thus:

And the conclusion is, that to allow no more to this superior principle or part of our nature, than to other parts; to let it govern and guide only occasionally in common with the rest, as its turn happens to come, from the temper and circumstances one happens to be in; this is not to act conformably to the constitution of man: neither can any human creature be said to act conformably to his constitution of nature, unless he allows to that superior principle the absolute authority which is due to it.[19]

Without intending to discuss all the implications Butler sees in his notion of a 'superior principle', we can take, none the less, some important points from this passage. First, that it is just as much a 'part of our nature' to possess a 'superior principle'—which, for present purposes we may say is a conception of how best that we should live our lives—as it is to possess what Butler would call 'particular passions'. Secondly, that it would entirely defeat the character of that principle as 'superior' if the governance it had over our lives was merely dependent upon whether or not it happened to catch our attention and engage our interest at any particular moment. That is, in my terms, it would entirely defeat the character of one's conception of how one should live one's life as a conception which could serve to rectify one's passion, or could serve to cause one to act where no passion was excited, if the only hold that conception had over one's choice and action was 'as its turn happens to come, from the temper and circumstances one happens to be in'. That would reduce it to having the same status as objectives established by passions, perhaps dominant over or perhaps subordinated to these. Rather, one must 'allow' to it a measure of concern which will ensure that it has governance and control over occasional impulses; one must *give* it precedence and not simply hope it will take precedence.

In relation to one's stabilized sense of significance to one of certain matters, one may recognize the importance that one's passional concerns give to some things is excessive or defective, deformed, distorted or illusory in some way and degree. Or it may, by a happy chance, be appropriate and fitting. Through one's intent to acknowledge this significance, one may over-ride the inclinations to action which come from one's passions, or the inertia which comes from the lack of them. It should not be so difficult to credit that we can and do so conduct ourselves; nor to acknowledge that our doing so cannot be the outcome of just a further, different, aroused passional concern. Were it such a thing, it could not have any distinctive place in relation to the effect of our other concerns; it would simply stand alongside them. But then our sense of the significance of certain matters would precisely 'govern and guide only occasionally in common with the rest'. It is a fundamental rôle of our resolved intent based upon our judgements of significance to enable us to give a place in our lives to matters which attract an inapposite or no passional concern. We *fix* or *lodge* our concern in them, and do not remain merely dependent upon their catching our interest for them to direct our conduct.

We could put the contrast between a passional elicitation of interest in something and the deliberate placing of interest in something in recognition of its import to us in the following way. When the passional elicitation of interest is at issue, it is in consequence of accidents of our temperament, upbringing, the circumstances of the time and so on that certain things exercise a hold over our feelings, engender a desirous or aversive responsiveness in us, and cause us to attribute importance to doing or avoiding something. . . . When the deliberate placing of interest is at issue, it is in virtue of our assessment of the significance of something as contributing to the achievement of a satisfactorily lived life that we make it an object of concern to us, out of our overall determination that we should actualize that conception of a well-conducted life that we have. It is a concern grounded in our belief about the importance of the matter, and will survive as long as that belief does. It is not, as is the case with passions, a concern and a belief which are drawn out from us and survive only so long as we continue to be worked upon. When we place our deliberate interest in something we *make* it material to our lives; we do not remain reliant upon its having some impact upon us for it to enter into the directing of our affairs.

By this we can see the answer to the third question I raised earlier, concerning the differences between the nature and rôle of the concern with the well-conducting of one's life and the nature and rôle of sense and passional desires. When our desire of this or that is a rational one, it comes out of our recognition of the significance of some matter to the proper conducting of our lives as we conceive of that. We form a desire to undertake that purpose or this action upon the basis of its importance or claim to be acknowledged, as we assess it. Our having such a desire is not dependent upon the arousal of some active passion, does not depend upon 'the temper and circumstances one happens to be in'. One might put the contrast in terms of a difference between active desires and reactive desires; desires which embody our active intent to make our lives take a certain shape and order, and desires which embody our reaction and responsiveness to circumstances which impinge upon us.

None of this is, of course, to claim that we shall always be appropriately mindful of the considered significances that we place upon various matters for our lives, as I remarked earlier. One may become wholly absorbed in the concerns of the present, dominated by a certain passion, and be unable to retain clear awareness and heedfulness of those other considerations of which, in less trying times, one recognizes the importance. . . . The present purpose has been to try to clarify what it is to take oneself to have a reason for action and how and why it is that so taking oneself is a state which can direct one's conduct. That we do not always retain full awareness of what we have reason to do, as we believe, and that we do not always act as we have reason to act, as we believe, are familiar problems. Clearly, however, to have any clear account of them we must understand what it is to be aware of and act on practical reasons. And I have been trying to offer such understanding at this point.

On the other hand, we are not always presented with a conflict and antagonism between our rational and our passional and sense-desirous concerns. As I mentioned above, it can well be that what, through one's passional arousal, one is led to think of as important one also recognizes, in reason, to be important. Indeed, one may seek to rectify and order one's passional concerns so that this is not by chance but by design so. Also, it is most likely that some, at any rate, of those matters to which one affords importance in one's conception of how best to live one's life will be ones which first assumed an importance to one because they engendered some passional concern. Benson emphasizes this.[20] One's coming to apprehend them as truly important will comprise principally only a stabilization and consolidation of an existing desirous interest, not something quite separate and distinct from this. Equally, however, it is not plausible to suppose that everything one comes to attach importance to is the object of a pre-existing concern. And even when it is, coming to be appreciative of the importance of this object of an initial concern changes the rôle that plays in one's choices and conduct. It ceases to be only something which happens to call out an interest, but becomes something to which one determinately gives one's concern.

I have been trying to explain the character of the state of taking oneself to have a practical reason for pursuing or doing something, the state of having a 'rational desire'. It is necessary to say a few further words on the relation between having a rational desire and acting upon that desire. In the case of passional desires, the onset of the desire is at one and the same time the onset of a prompting, an inclination, to act in a certain way.[21] It is, already, an incipient movement. But one's having a rational desire to do something is not a spontaneous prompting which impels one into movement in the same way. It would be absurd to think of having to check or suppress an 'impulse' to action if one was disposed to acting on the basis of reasons. Rational desires are not states of excited readiness or propensity to move. A rational desire involves a belief that something has importance to the conduct of our lives and the determination to give place to that in our activity. This is not to be subject to the 'prick of desire', in Anscombe's words;[22] it is a form of self-determination by which we embody in our conduct our conception of what it is appropriate that we should do. The reasons upon which one acts, when one acts upon the basis of reasons, are identical with the reasons upon which one forms the desire of so acting, when one desires upon the basis of reasons. There is no question of one's finding in the fact that one has a rational desire to do something a further reason for doing it over and above the reasons one had for forming that desire in the first place.[23] Whereas the fact that one has a passional desire to do something may feature as a further reason for doing it (i.e., precisely in order to gratify that desire) over and above the reasons for doing that thing as such (i.e., without regard to the fact that it has engendered a desire in you). And this alone is sufficient to show that having a rational desire is not at all like a state of aroused interest. To say that someone has a rational desire to do something is to say that, providing the reasons to do it make a sufficient case in his eyes, he will do it; it is to say that he will act in view of those reasons. It is not to say that he is in a state of excited propensity which expresses itself in a certain kind of movement.

Notes

1. Thomas Hobbes, *Leviathan*, 1651, ed. M. Oakeshott (Oxford: Basil Blackwell, n.d.), part 1, chapter 6, 37–38.

2. Arthur Schopenhauer, *Essay on the Freedom of the Will*, 1841, trans. K. Kolenda (Indianapolis: Library of Liberal Arts, 1960), 36–37.

3. Cf. J. Watkins, "Three Views Concerning Human Freedom," section 6, in R. S. Peters, ed., *Nature and Conduct* (New York: Macmillan, 1975).

4. *Leviathan*, part 1, chapter 6.

5. See *Leviathan*, part 1, chapter 6, 32: "Good, Evil."

6. Compare David Hume, *A Treatise of Human Nature*, 1739, ed. L. A. Selby-Bigge (Oxford: Oxford University Press, 1888), book 3, part 1, section 1, 469: "Vice and virtue, therefore, may

be compar'd to sounds, colours, heat and cold, which, according to modern philosophy, are not qualities in objects, but perceptions in the mind. . . ." Compare *Treatise*, book 2, part 2, section 6.

7. H. G. Frankfurt, "Freedom of the Will," *Journal of Philosophy* 68 (1971): 5–20.

8. Frankfurt, 12.

9. Frankfurt, 13.

10. Gary Watson, "Free Agency," *Journal of Philosophy* 72 (1975), 205–220.

11. For the notion of a "constitutive" means see L.H.G. Greenwood, *Aristotle: Nicomachean Ethics: Book Six* (Cambridge: Cambridge University Press, 1909), section II, 46 ff.; G.E.M. Anscombe, "Thought and Action in Aristotle," in R. Bambrough, ed., *New Essays on Plato and Aristotle* (London: Routledge and Kegan Paul, 1965); David Wiggins, "Deliberation and Practical Reasoning," *Proceedings of the Aristotelian Society* 76 (1976): 29–51; and J. L. Ackrill, "Introduction," *Aristotle's Ethics* (London: Faber and Faber, 1973), sections 4, 6.

12. See John McDowell, "Virtue and Reason," *The Monist* 62 (1979), 343–344, and *passim*, for an account of the nature and role of a "conception of how one should live." See also Wiggins; Anscombe. Anscombe writes (p. 155): "I suggest that the idea of rational wanting should be explained in terms of what is wanted being wanted *qua* conducive to or part of 'doing well,' or 'blessedness.'"

13. It is to be noted that I say "satisfactory" rather than "satisfying." If one achieves that life one believes to be satisfactory one may be (one may hope) satisfied (and not merely in that one has achieved it). But there need be no question of having an antecedent notion of what is satisfying to one, and making it the mark of a satisfactory life that it "maximizes satisfaction" (or some such thing) in those terms.

14. Cf. Anscombe, 144, 148–150.

15. Editor's note: Whenever you experience an emotion you construe your situation as desirable (or undesirable) in some way. Dent suggests that some emotions, "active passions" like friendly feeling, patriotism, fear, envy, or pity, also involve (1) a new, "passional desire" to act—to enhance the desirable (or modify the undesirable) aspects of your situation—and (2) a focusing of attention on the goal of enhancement (or modification) and how to achieve it. Dent's point in this section is that some rudimentary attention to and planning for the future accompanies every active passion.

16. Compare G.E.M. Anscombe, *Intention*, 2d ed. (Oxford: Basil Blackwell, 1963), section 35. She writes: ". . . Not everything. . . coming in the range of 'reasons for acting' can have a place as a premiss in a practical syllogism." See the surrounding examples which illustrate this point.

17. Cf. A.J.T.D. Wisdom, *Philosophy and Psychoanalysis* (Oxford: Basil Blackwell, 1964), 107–110 on "ethical effort"; also 163.

18. I take this "distinctive concern" to be what Aristotle intended in the notion of *boulesis*, and in the dependent notion of *prohaeresis*. See *Nicomachean Ethics*, book 3, chapters 2, 4; also N.J.H. Dent, "Varieties of Desire," *Proceedings of the Aristotelian Society, Supplementary Volume* 50 (1976): 153–175.

19. J. Butler, *Fifteen Sermons Preached at the Rolls Chapel*, 1729, preface, section 24; also Stuart N. Hampshire, *Freedom of the Individual* (London: Chatto and Windus, 1965), 44. Butler was clearly very anxious to distinguish the nature and role of "principles" from that of "particular passions," as not simply happening to be stronger or dominant at a time in their governance of a person's conduct. See also *Sermons*, sermon 1, section 8; sermon 2, section 3; section 8-11; and elsewhere. For a very interesting interpretation of "superior principle" see Mary Midgley, *Beast and Man* (Ithaca, N.Y.: Cornell University Press, 1978), chapter 11.

20. John Benson, "Varieties of Desire," *Proceedings of the Aristotelian Society, Supplementary Volume* 50 (1976): 183–184.

21. On "inclination" see Alan R. White, *Attention* (Oxford: Basil Blackwell, 1964), 93.

22. Anscombe, *Intention*, section 36.

23. See Thomas Nagel, *The Possibility of Altruism* (Oxford: Oxford University Press, 1970), 30; and Dent, N.J.H., "Varieties of Desire," *Proceedings of the Aristotelian Society, Supplementary Volume* 50, 153–175, esp. 167–170. Also see J. Raz, "Reasons for Action, Decisions and Norms" *Mind* 84 (1975), 481–499. The apparent counter-examples to the claim made here that come in Raz's argument are, I believe, only that. And, anyway, they are cases sufficiently abstruse as not to present a serious challenge to the claim.

Reading Introduction

Will Power and the Virtues
Robert C. Roberts

In this essay Roberts addresses the classical questions of the nature and interrelation of the virtues. What sort of trait is a virtue? There are, of course, many different virtues. But are all virtues one *kind* of trait? Or do they display some variety? And if there is variety among them, how do the different kinds of traits interact in the moral personality?

Roberts is silent about how many kinds of traits can be virtues. He concentrates on two kinds: the *virtues of will power* and the *substantive and motivational virtues*. The virtues of will power, he argues, are nonmotivating skill-like capacities for managing inclinations that threaten to disrupt our moral life and our higher self-interest. These virtues gain their *moral* significance in a number of ways. Since they do not embody moral rules or motives, they depend on their relation to the substantive and motivational virtues. They function as a kind of *preservative* of the motives and behavior characteristic of the substantive virtues. Further, acts of courage, patience, self-control, and so on become morally significant by being done from the motives characteristic of the other virtues. The virtues of will power also seem to play an important role in the *integration of the moral self*, the process by which the individual becomes in some sense the author of his or her own personality.

Roberts spends a good portion of the article considering objections to the thesis that any morally significant virtue could be a skill-like capacity. He ends by waging a positive argument by illustration for his thesis, and by mentioning two features necessary as background to the exercise of the virtues of will power: a passionate *concern* for something or other, and the individual's *belief in his or her power* to overcome adverse inclinations.

Will Power and the Virtues

ROBERT C. ROBERTS

I

A number of authors in the past twenty-five years have tried to answer the general question "What is a virtue?" or as G. H. von Wright says, to "shape a concept of a virtue." This project has thrown light on the nature of the virtues, but has sometimes tended to raise the expectation that they must all be the same kind of trait.[1] One proposition which has enjoyed general consent is the denial that virtues are skill-like dispositions or powers. I shall argue here that one group of virtues, which might be called the moral strengths or virtues of will power, are to a large extent skill-like.

Some theorists have proposed that moral virtues are all determinations of the good *will*. A broad-ranging list of traits having moral relevance will probably include some that are not easily corralled into this pen. For example, foresight and psychological insight are characteristics of an ideally moral person, yet it seems wrong to call them determinations of the will. And gentleness, politeness, and friendliness, in some people at least, are unwilled and nonwilling styles of behavioral demeanor. So probably not all morally relevant traits are matters of the will. Yet it is clear why philosophers might make this mistake, for many of the virtues most central to the moral life, such as honesty, courage, justice, compassion, and self-control, *are* determinations of the will.

But this observation is not very clarifying unless we know what will is. There are broadly two ways in which we employ 'will' or its cognates. In the first kind of case we designate inclinations and disinclinations, desires and aversions, motivations. If I go willingly to a horse race, I go gladly or at least with a minimum of distaste. A willful person is one who does just whatever he wants to, without regard for the rights or concerns of others. To lose the will to live is no longer to care much about living. In the second kind of case 'will' designates not motivations, but a family of capacities for *resisting* adverse inclinations. When we say someone has a "strong will" we are often referring to the presence in her of such virtues as perseverance, resoluteness, courage, patience, and self-control. When we speak of "efforts of will," we refer to the acts or activities which correspond to such virtues: fighting boredom, controlling one's emotions, resisting temptation, persevering in the face of discouragement, overcoming the impulse to flee, fighting anxiety, forcing oneself to the magnanimous gesture, and the like.[2] That this use of 'will' is distinct from its use to designate motivation is suggested by the oddity of the expression "an effort of wanting."

Where people make efforts, there exist human capacities. A person can make a muscular effort because in general he has muscular powers, and an effort to pay attention because in general he can pay attention. (Obviously, it doesn't follow that he has the power to do the particular act he tries to do; efforts can fail in many ways, and some of

The Philosophical Review 93 (April 1984):227–47. Reprinted by permission of the author and publisher.

these involve a failure to possess, or to possess enough of, the relevant capacity.) So if people do make efforts of will — that is, efforts to resist adverse inclinations — it follows that there exist human capacities by which to resist adverse inclinations. It will be my contention in this paper that the virtues of will power are indeed largely capacities, and that these are more like skills than like other kinds of capacities. But first it will be enlightening to discuss the relations between the virtues of will power and other virtues.

II

The most important distinction between kinds of virtues is that between the virtues of will power and those that are substantive and motivational. I call virtues like honesty, compassion, justice, generosity, promise-keeping, and kindness "substantive" because they are the psychological embodiment of ethical rules — the substance of the ethical patterns of behavior and judgment and emotion. To be honest is to be disposed to tell the truth in appropriate situations, to judge well which situations demand telling the truth, to be "alive" to dishonesty in oneself and others, and to feel uneasiness, guilt, indignation, sadness, and other emotions upon encountering dishonesty in oneself and others. Compassion is the disposition to help others who are suffering, to notice and recognize sufferers as sufferers, to judge them to be in some fundamental way similar to oneself, and to be sad to see suffering and glad to see it relieved.

By contrast, patience does not imply any characteristically ethical patterns of behavior, judgment, or emotion. Racists, cheats, sadists, and thieves may well be persevering, resolute, and self-controlled; and indeed they will be more likely to succeed in their chosen style of life if they are. Whether courage is equally lacking in moral substance has been questioned.[3] Philippa Foot has noted that we are disinclined to call particularly heinous acts, such as "a murder done for gain or to get an inconvenient person out of the way,"[4] courageous, even if they are done in circumstances which would require courage. But our disinclination here can be accounted for by the *associations* that 'courage' has for us: we do associate courage with the substantive moral virtues, and there are important anthropological reasons for this association, which in turn give courage its moral importance. And Foot admits that it is only the attribution of courage to the *act* that troubles us; we find no difficulty in calling a murderer courageous, nor in saying that his act "took courage."

By saying the substantive virtues are "motivational," I mean what I think Aristotle is talking about when he says

> We may even go so far as to state that the man who does not enjoy performing noble actions is not a good man at all. Nobody would call a man just who does not enjoy acting justly, nor generous who does not enjoy generous actions, and so on (*Nicomachean Ethics* 1099a).

To be just is to want just states of affairs to prevail and consequently, in the appropriate circumstances, to want to do what will bring about such states of affairs. Thus the just person takes satisfaction ("pleasure") in the performance and beholding of such actions, and feels frustration ("pain") at failure in them. But Aristotle seems to be less than lucid about the distinction between kinds of virtues that I am pointing out. For he says that "a man who endures danger with joy, or at least without pain, is courageous; if he endures it with pain, he is a coward (*Nicomachean Ethics* 1104b)."[5] But enjoying facing dangers is surely not a criterion of courage. There may be a psychological connection between a person's achieving self-mastery and his taking pleasure either in some aspects of the activity itself or in the fruits of it. But the quality of a person's self-mastery cannot be called into question on the account of his failing to enjoy it. Whereas the idea of a just person who nevertheless hates doing just actions, or is indifferent to their fruits, is a contradiction.

A person who enjoys enduring dangers is better called daredevilish than brave. A particularly bizarre illustration of what courage would be like if it were a motivational virtue has been collected by William James:[6]

> I believe, says General Skobeleff, that my bravery is simply the passion for and at the same time the contempt of danger. The risk of life fills me with an exaggerated rapture. The fewer there are to share it, the more I like it . . . a meeting of man to man, a duel, a danger into which I can throw myself head-foremost, attracts me, moves me, intoxicates me. I am crazy for it, I love it, I adore it. I run after danger as one runs after women . . . my entire nature runs to meet the peril with an impetus that my will would in vain try to resist.

If joy in enduring danger were a mark of courage, General Skobeleff would appear to be an exceptionally courageous man. And no doubt a casual observer of his exploits might call him courageous. But this peek at the General's interiority shows that his disposition is not courage. For whatever else courage may be, it is a virtue; but the disposition he describes is a vice. Even the courage of the thief elicits our admiration; for though his disregard for property rights is despicable, still he possesses a trait without which one leads a crippled life. But there is nothing admirable about the General's lust for dangers; and we can guess that people who possess it tend to be a menace both to society and to themselves. For positions of leadership we want courageous persons, but not daredevils. We do not want our generals to be enthusiasts for military exploits.

Unlike justice, compassion, generosity, and friendship, courage and self-control are not in themselves moral motives. A person can feed the poor out of compassion, struggle on behalf of the oppressed out of concern for justice (i.e., out of concern for people who are being treated unjustly), and perform sacrifices out of friendship. But actions exhibiting courage and self-control are not done *out of* courage and self-control.[7] Actions done out of moral motives may, however, be done *in virtue of* courage and self-control and patience, if the circumstances, psychological and environmental, demand such virtues.[8]

I think Plato is on the right track when he calls courage a "preservative."[9] A preservative is in the service of something other than itself that is cherished, and needed because this cherished thing is in some way threatened. Courage, self-control and patience are in the service of the moral and prudential life, and needed because this life is beset with trials. These trials, which are part of the everyday context in which we exercise the virtues, are functions of our desires and aversions. The virtues of will power are the capacities by which a person copes with these trials in the interests of the moral and prudential life.

Philippa Foot has noticed this "corrective" character of the virtues of will power:[10]

> As things are we often want to run away not only where that is the right thing to do but also where we should stand firm; and we want pleasure not only where we should seek pleasure but also where we should not. If human nature had been different there would have been no need of a corrective disposition in either place. . . .

But she mistakenly generalizes this characteristic to all the virtues:

> There is. . . a virtue of industriousness only because idleness is a temptation; and of humility only because men tend to think too well of themselves. Hope is a virtue because despair is a temptation. . . .

Her mistake is that of confusing the existence of something with the existence of its name or concept. If people were never led astray by fears and pleasures, it is plausible that courage and self-control themselves would not arise. For courage and self-control are (in large and basic part) the capacities to manage our inclinations, when they are wayward, to flee dangers and seek pleasures. But industriousness is needed not basically because people are prone to laziness, but because work is a good thing. Industriousness could exist in a world in which no one suffered from laziness, and hope in a world where no one ever despaired, and honesty in a world where no one lied—though it is likely that in such a world these virtues would not be named or much noticed. The substantive virtues are "corrective" in the trivial sense that there are vices which correspond to them; the virtues of will power are corrective in the significant sense that, in our present psychological condition but not in every imaginable one, they are needed to keep us on the path of virtue and our higher self-interest.

III

But this is not the whole story. In assessing the degree to which an action reflects moral credit on its agent, we often feel two contrary tendencies. On the one side, like Kant, we are inclined to give greater credit for actions (or character traits) which result from moral struggle. We might call this the hero assessment: just as running a mile in under four minutes is praised not as a speedy mode of transportation, but as an extraordinary feat for legs and lungs and spirit, so some acts are morally praised not just because they are good, but also because they are difficult. Why do we tend to think a moral achievement greater if more difficult? Not, I think, just because we have confused morality with athletics. One obvious reason is that morally difficult actions display some virtues—namely the virtues of will power. But I think a deeper basis for our feeling here is that the greater the moral obstacles (that is, contrary inclinations) a person has overcome in doing something, the more his action seems to be his own *achievement*, his own *choice*, and thus to reflect credit on him as an *agent*. It seems to show that his action is *his* in a special way.

But the moment we make the hero assessment we may have some doubts and think: the very fact that somebody *has* those fears and lusts and countermoral impulses which make right action difficult for him reflects discredit on him; an action is the more praiseworthy the more it is done purely out of moral inclinations and in the absence of contrary inclinations—that is, the more it is done *without* moral struggle. This we might call the purity of heart assessment. Here the emphasis is not on the agent as an achiever or chooser, but rather, I should almost say, as a personal *artifact*. Here we assess the individual not with respect to how he brought off the act or how he got to be the kind of person he is, but just with respect to what he *is* in the sense of the configuration of his cares and uncares. The ideally moral person is one who is concerned about important things and relatively unconcerned about relatively unimportant things, and so he does not have to struggle with himself to do what is right.

These kinds of assessments correspond to the kinds of virtues I have distinguished. When we make the hero assessment, we are demanding of an action or character trait that its accomplishment require one or more of the virtues of will power. If we make the purity of heart assessment, it is because we are laying emphasis on the motivational virtues. The virtues of will power are needed on the road to purity of heart because in most of us the moral inclinations are so weak and the road is so strewn with psychological obstacles. But unlike the motivational virtues, these are not the substance of the moral life and their "corrective" function is no longer needed when full sainthood has been attained.

But as I have suggested the virtues of will power are needed not only for their "corrective" function, but also because they are essential to the development of the agent's agenthood. Struggles are an important part of the way we become centers of initiation of actions and passions. They are the contexts in which the shape of our personality takes on that toughness and independence which we call "autonomy," and which seems to be a basic feature of mature personhood. Could a person gain autonomy without struggle, and thus without the capacities necessary to win in struggles? In a famous letter John Keats wrote,[11]

> The common cognomen of this world among the misguided and superstitious is 'a vale of tears' from which we are to be redeemed by a certain arbitrary interposition of God and taken to Heaven—What a little circumscribe [d] straightened notion! Call the world if you Please "'The vale of Soul-making" Then you will find out the use of the world. . . . I say *'Soul making'* Soul as distinguished from an Intelligence—There may be intelligences or sparks of the divinity in millions—but they are not Souls . . . till they acquire identities, till each one is personally itself. . . . Do you not see how necessary a World of Pains and troubles is to school an Intelligence and make it a soul?

We might generalize Keats's "World of Pains and troubles" to "a World of temptations" (psychological adversities). We can guess that it will never be possible to give a person a moral "identity"—a tough and abiding passion for justice or a stable and focused desire to relieve suffering—by injecting him with a drug or giving him a brain operation or fiddling with his genes. But the impossibility of giving somebody moral character in this way seems to be more than psychological. For even if we could in this way produce a being who was indistinguishable, in terms of his present dispositions, from a saint, still I think we would have no inclination whatsoever to canonize him. For the praise for his saintliness, and thus for his deeds, would not be due *him*. If it were due anyone, the pharmacologist or brain surgeon would seem more likely candidates. So the idea of somebody acquiring moral character without struggle seems not only psychologically, but logically amiss. Such a person does not have an appropriate moral *history*. Thus, if powers of will are those powers by which moral struggles are prosecuted, then they may be more than just "corrective." They may be a logically and psychologically necessary part of our development as persons.

The relation, then, between the virtues of will power and the substantive virtues is mutual need: neither kind can exist as moral virtues without the other kind. Without the virtues of will power, the moral motives would too often be sabotaged by counter-moral impulses and the relative weakness of the substantive virtues; nor would these latter be gained in a morally appropriate way. On the other hand, the character of a person who had only the virtues of will power would be empty of moral content.

IV

I want now to consider the view of the virtues of will power which I take to be the strongest alternative to my suggestion that they are capacities. In "Traits of Character: A Conceptual Analysis"[12] Richard Brandt argues that moral character traits are "the kind of dispositions that wants and aversions are" (27). They are inclinations which can be called into activity by features of a subject's environment or thoughts and which, when they have become active, issue in behavior of a type corresponding to the inclination. Thus a person with the trait of sympathy, if he sees a child in distress from falling off his bicycle, will go to the child and help or comfort him, if some other, competing and stronger, inclination is not presently active in him. For example, if what knocked the child from his bike is a bag of $100 bills falling off a truck, which are now floating up the street in the wind, the active trait of sympathy may start to be challenged by that of avarice. Assuming the sympathetic and avaricious individual judges the wind strong enough to render the fulfillment of the one desire incompatible with that of the other, then his behavior at that moment will be determined by the relative strength of these two inclinations. Brandt generalizes: the motivation theory of character traits

> holds that, under conditions not fully understood, they become active and generate "force vectors" in the psychological field of the person, their direction and degree depending partly on the person's beliefs; what the person actually does is a function of the force vectors in his psychological field at the moment of action (31).

This account, like Aristotle's, begins to fidget when virtues of will power are mentioned. Unlike Aristotle and Prichard, Brandt does not treat courage as though it is a passional virtue; but he does treat it as nothing but a function of passions, among which are to be found some moral ones. Such virtues, though not themselves tendencies of the desire/aversion sort, must be understood as the relative weakness of desires/aversions which stand in opposition to virtuous behavior. Thus the courage of the rat-phobic who crawls under the house after a child is simply the weakness, relative to his desire to free the child, of his desire to avoid the company of rats. On this analysis a *generally* courageous or self-controlled person is just one who has sufficiently intense moral and prudential desires and aversions that they override, generally, his morally and prudentially aversive passions.

Some cases of courage, etc., fit Brandt's analysis. We do sometimes ascribe courage to a person whose impulse to act virtuously is strong enough, by itself, to override his impulse to flee. Maybe this is typical of the courage of the saints: in them the passional virtues are so strong that in a sense they do not need courage. That is to say, in them courage is not a function of will power. But most of us would not have much courage or patience if we didn't have will power, so we are led, like James D. Wallace, to feel that Brandt's analysis has neglected something. These virtues are not just "privative states," but some kind of "positive capacity."[13]

V

If desires and aversions (duly shaped by our beliefs) were the only kind of element contributing to our psychological "force vectors," the virtues of will power would not be capacities or powers, but only patterns of relative strength among our desires and aversions. However, our desires and aversions are not the only psychological factors contributing to our actions and the course of our lives; for there is also such a thing as our *management* of our desires and aversions; and these capacities of self-management are an important aspect of the virtues of will power. People are capacitated in numerous ways. We have bodily powers like food and oxygen assimilation; physical strengths (muscles and bones); faculties (sight, hearing, smell); and aptitudes (mathematical, musical, linguistic). But the capacity to resist adverse inclinations seems to be learned. Since learned capacities are called skills, I propose that powers of will are skills of self-management.

Skills may be more or less completely mental, like the ability to focus attention at will, or motor, like riding a bicycle. But most skills have both motor and mental aspects. Riding a bike in traffic requires a combination of motor skill and knowledge of rules of the road, attentiveness to events occurring in the traffic, judgment about the speed of cars relative to their distance from oneself and one another and one's own speed or potential for speed, etc. It is characteristic of skills in both their mental and motor aspects that they become in large part "automatic" and unnoticed by their practitioners. Many skills combine procedures governed by rules which can be (though by no means always are) formulated, patterns of such "automatic" physical and mental behavior, and a certain element of creativity in the application of the rules and the "automatic" behaviors to new challenges. Most sports and games, and activities such as weaving, producing portrait photography, doing algebra, speaking a language, cooking, getting dressed, and cabinet building would be skills falling under this last description.

People can be more or less skilled in the management of their own inclinations, and these skills are an important part of the virtues of will power. We can be more and less "good at" breaking bad habits and forming new ones, at "deferring gratification," at resisting cravings and impulses; and we can be trained and/or train ourselves in the control of emotions like anxiety, fear, disappointment, anger, and hatred. I want to illustrate and partially analyze these truths in a moment. But before I do, let me consider four *a priori* objections to the proposal that virtues can be skills.

Three such arguments are found in James D. Wallace's book, *Virtues and Vices*, pp. 44–47. The first is this:

1. Courage and patience are capacities to overcome difficulties arising from inclinations contrary to right action.
2. Inclinations contrary to right action are not technical difficulties, but skills are always capacities to overcome technical difficulties.

So courage and patience are not skills.

The crux of the argument is the word 'technical'. It certainly sounds right to say that, of the various kinds of difficulties standing in the way of acting compassionately towards a rebellious and abusive teenage son, the difficulty of overcoming one's feelings of resentment towards him (which might be met by possessing the virtue of patience) is not a *technical* one. (We might say, "Not technical, but *moral!*") "Technical" difficulties in this situation might be questions of psychological strategy: What is in the son's best interest? To confront him and have it out? To assert some authority over him? To use benign neglect? To shower him with affection? Or some combination of these? To answer a "technical" question like this, one might consult a professional, thus perhaps increasing one's skill in handling rebellious sons. But one would not (so suggests Wallace's argument) seek such "technical" guidance as to, or training in, how to handle one's *own* feelings of resentment towards the son. *That* is a matter not of "technique," but of morality.

But why not seek such "technical" help in handling one's own emotions? One reason we are inclined to accept the "not technical, but moral" disjunction, is a failure to distinguish virtues like courage and patience from the substantive moral virtues like caring for one's children. But if somebody already has a moral motive, and then finds that bad habits and adverse emotions are getting in the way of acting lovingly, the psychologist has a potential role, and though we would not normally call this role "technical," what the psychologist may supply here is precisely information and training of a "how to" sort. I suggest that when this "how to" knowledge has become assimilated, the person will have gained in the virtue of patience.

Here is Wallace's second argument:

1. If any trait is a skill, then it can be inculcated through instruction in techniques and by practice that leads to proficiency.
2. But no virtue can be so inculcated.

So no virtue is a skill.

But the second premise is false. As Aristotle points out,

> By abstaining from pleasures we become self-controlled, and once we are self-controlled we are best able to abstain from pleasures. So also with courage: by becoming habituated to despise and endure terrors we become courageous, and once we have become courageous we will best be able to endure terror (*Nicomachean Ethics* 1104a–b).

In the next section I shall illustrate how the virtues of will power can be inculcated through instruction and practice.

In his third argument Wallace adapts an insight from Gilbert Ryle, namely that it is logically amiss to say someone has *forgotten* the difference between right and wrong. Wallace's argument is this:

1. If any trait is a skill, it can be forgotten.
2. But courage, self-control, and patience cannot be forgotten.
   So these traits are not skills.

Both premises are questionable. In general it is only more complicated skills that are forgettable, and even here it is unlikely that a skill, well-learned, will be completely forgotten. Someone who has played the piano well, and then lets twenty years elapse without practicing, will get rusty indeed. But that she has not lost all her skill will be evident from how quickly it comes back with practice. A total loss of the skill would require more than forgetting; it would take some kind of injury or illness or aging process resulting in neurological or muscular deterioration. But simpler skills are virtually unforgettable: one does not forget how to swim, or ride a bike, or walk. It is possible that courage and self-control are simple enough to be as unforgettable as bike-riding. (Though maybe, like biking, they are susceptible to considerable development and sophistication.)

It seems to me that courage, etc., cannot be flat forgotten; but if we allow that getting "rusty" is a sort of forgetting or partial forgetting, it is not so obvious that one cannot forget courage. See the autobiography of Gordon Liddy, who in prison felt it necessary to exercise himself in withstanding pain, to make sure that he hadn't gone "soft."

Unlike Wallace, Ryle nowhere claims it is logically amiss to say someone has forgotten a *virtue*, but only to say that someone has forgotten the difference between right and wrong.[14] Ryle explains this impossibility by the fact that to know the difference between right and wrong is a matter of *caring* about right and wrong, and ceasing to care is not a sort of forgetting. In my terms, Ryle is only claiming the impossibility of forgetting the substantive and motivational virtues—because only these "tell us," as it were, the difference between right and wrong.

Wallace is clear enough about the difference between the substantive virtues and the virtues of will power not to explain the supposed unforgettability of self-control and patience by the supposition that they are modes of caring.

> The reason is not that there is a motivational component to these things that cannot be lost by forgetting. The reason why one cannot forget how to be brave or honest is like the reason why one cannot forget how to see or how to be strong: there is no "how to" to these things (47).

But as we shall see in the next section, this supposition too is false.

A fourth argument that no virtue is a skill has been presented by Philippa Foot. Following Aristotle and Aquinas she notes that when a person's action bespeaks a lack of a skill (let us say he misspells a word), he can defend himself against the implication by saying "I did it intentionally." But when his action bespeaks a lack of virtue (let us say he tells a lie), he does not exculpate himself by saying "I did it intentionally." Thus no virtue is a skill.[15]

This argument overlooks that virtues relate in more than one way to morality. It is of course true that an action does not become any the less immoral by being intentional; and so where doing the moral thing (say, being compassionate) requires the exercise of a skill virtue (say, patience), the fact that one's failure of patience was intentional is no *moral* exculpation. But claiming that the failure to exercise patience was intentional *would* defend against the accusation of lacking patience. But patience is a virtue. So it is false that one cannot defend against the implication of failure to possess a virtue by claiming that failure to exercise it was intentional.

VI

I shall now indicate sketchily some ways people manage their adverse inclinations, and draw attention to the skill-likeness of these ways. Like other skills, some of these "ways" are strategic, like the duck hunter's knowledge of the precise moment when to rise in the blind, while others are more basic, like his ability to squeeze the trigger without disrupting his aim. My argument is not that because there are strategies for *developing* courage, courage must be a skill. (One might develop compassion by the strategy of meditating on the lives of compassionate people.) It is rather that being courageous is *in itself* (often subtlely and sub-consciously) in part strategic, and so is formally like those many skills that have strategic dimensions. Nor is my argument that merely because the exercise of these virtues can develop them, they must be skills. (Performing compassionate actions can perhaps cause a person to become more compassionate.) Instead, I shall try to describe the exercises leading to the acquisition of the virtues of will power in such a way as to highlight *specific* similarities between these exercises and ones which issue in skills. I shall speak first of the management of cravings and impulses, then of emotions.

Cravings and Impulses. Søren Kierkegaard depicts a gambler struggling against his compulsion:[16]

> Imagine that he . . . said to himself in the morning, "So I solemnly vow by all that is holy that I shall nevermore have anything to do with gambling, nevermore— tonight shall be the last time." Ah, my friend, he is lost! Strange as it may seem I should venture to bet rather on the opposite, supposing that there was a gambler who at such a moment said to himself, "Very well, thou shalt be allowed to gamble all the rest of thy life, every blessed day—but tonight thou shalt let it alone," and so he did. . . . For the resolution of the first man was a knavish trick of lust, but that of the other is a way of hoaxing lust. . . . Lust is strong merely in the instant. . . .

The more normal development of this aspect of self-control might occur as follows: parents teaching their children to defer gratification would begin with small stretches of time. They would say not "Here is your Easter basket, and you may eat your chocolate bunny the day after tomorrow," but instead, "after dinner, you may bite off his ear." (And, by the way, they will not set the temptation out of the child's reach until the appointed time, nor keep a nervous eagle eye out so as to slap the hand that reaches for the bunny, but will let the child develop her *own* ability to resist the impulses she may feel.) If the parents are wise in engineering settings for gratification-deferment which are manageable for the child, she may grow up with an unreflective tendency to pick for herself deferment goals that are realistic given her own powers of resistance, and thus put herself in for a minimum of discouragement. It is imaginable that this skill of self-management might develop without any explicit discussion of its rules or reflection on them, and might be as natural as speaking one's native language. A cabinet builder follows a dictum which might be expressed, "He who starts a project square and level has less need of compensating exercises in ensuing stages." When he was a novice his teacher perhaps had to voice the dictum a few times, but after he had built some cabinets himself the dictum became integrated into the practice, sinking to the status of a mentally unrehearsed policy or rule of skill founded on the ineluctible geometric properties of cabinets, floors and walls. The remark that "lust is strong merely in the instant" is an easily accessible piece of psychological wisdom, one which can become as integral a part of a person's dealings with himself as the carpenter's dictum is of his dealings with boards and nails. The more self-mastering person knows, either intuitively or perhaps expressly, such things as that committing oneself to long-term abstention from the fulfillment of a strong impulse is probably either self-deceptive or likely to overwhelm and discourage. Skill at the management of impulses and cravings must take this fact of human nature into consideration, just as carpentry must take geometric truths into consideration. (I am told that "one day at a time" is one of the basic rules of Alcoholics Anonymous.)

We can imagine that at first, upon hearing or formulating for himself this dictum, the weak-willed gambler might succeed in "hoaxing his lust" by explicitly telling himself that he is not promising to abstain for life, after all, but only for the next twenty-four hours. Then when the next day comes, he renews his commitment, assuring himself that it is only for the day, etc. But after the rule has been successfully applied a few times, the "hoaxing" may gradually change to a habit, a sub-conscious policy of choosing manageable time-parameters for one's choices of self-denial. When this happens, the individual is beginning to gain a stronger will.

The way of mastering impulses that I have just discussed is "strategic": In its more self-conscious (though not in its deeper and more usual) forms it involves considering what one is up against, and then in the light of this figuring out a way to meet the challenge. But there may also be an aspect of impulse-mastery that is more basic. Boyd Barrett[17] proposes a number of exercises by which a person can increase his ability to resist impulses. These involve doing such "useless" things as standing on a chair for ten consecutive minutes and trying to do so contentedly; listening to the ticking of a clock and making some definite movements at every fifth tick; and replacing in a box, slowly and deliberately, one hundred matches. In all these activities one is almost certain to get impulses to quit: boredom, physical discomfort, thoughts of things one would rather be doing. We might speculate that here one does not necessarily resist the impulse by some "method" such as hoaxing the lust or re-construing the impulse. Maybe one resists the impulse to discontinue the activity by simply continuing the activity. If this interpretation is correct, then there would seem to be a power to resist impulses which is a *basic* ability – basic not in the sense that it is unlearned, but in the sense that one does not exercise it by exercising some *other* ability. It would be like some people's ability to look cross-eyed or wiggle their ears.

Emotions. Some impulses are emotions, as when fear is the impulse to flee, or boredom the impulse to quit an activity. But others are not: for example, physical pain, and "lusts" for sex, money, gambling, and philosophic discussion. Conversely, not all adverse emotions are impulses: an impulse, it seems, has to be directed at *doing* something, and when I experience an adverse emotion such as malicious joy, I may not have an inclination to do anything at all. In such cases the emotion is "adverse" not because of what it may *lead* to, but because it is itself unfitting, morally or from the point of view of psychological health or happiness.

There are two senses in which we may "control" an emotion: if it is an impulse to some undesirable behavior such as fleeing a danger which should be faced, or emitting some angry behavior that will have untoward consequences, then "controlling" it may just mean resisting the impulse to act in such ways. But it may also mean the reshaping of the emotion itself: mitigating the anger or fear, or eliminating them altogether. For the sake of brevity I shall focus here on the control of emotions in the second sense.

Any of the virtues of will power may involve power over emotions. Self-control can be, among other things, a mastery of anger, resentment, malicious joy, scorn, hatred and envy. Where patience is directed to a task, the emotion with which it typically has to do is boredom. (A related virtue is tenaciousness or perseverance, whose emotional adversary seems to be primarily discouragement or some degree of hopelessness.) Where patience is used in dealing with people, emotions typically mastered are anger and resentment and boredom. The emotions that courage relates to are fear and anxiety.

In some cases anger diminishes with oblique behavioral "expression." Thus a man may diminish his anger at an oppressive boss by kicking pasteboard boxes around in the privacy of his garage and cursing loudly. It may help to imagine the boss's face or backside in the boxes and to go through the procedure in a somewhat ritualistic and comical manner. Similar activities may have the effect of increasing one's anger at the boss, so knowing when this sort of thing will work and prescribing to oneself and carrying out appropriate rituals is clearly a skill-like ability.

One can often alter an emotion by behaving in a way that conflicts with it. Thus if I am afraid of someone, one way to handle the fear is to stand up straight, look him in the eye, and speak clearly in an even, strong voice. The fear may not disappear entirely, but it will certainly be less than if I shrink back, speak in a weak mumble, and generally present myself to myself as one who is in an oppressive situation.[18] I think that courageous people are typically aware, intuitively, of the influence that their bodily dispositions and voice and speech have on their anxiety and fear, and practice this kind of self-management. It is far from obvious that courageous people typically feel fears and anxieties less intensely than cowardly people. But through practice in facing up to threatening situations, they have learned how to manage and mitigate their fears.

Skillful self-talk is another way of controlling emotion. I am becoming impatient with my four-year-old's bedtime delaying tactics, and so I talk to myself: "I did the same when I was four," or "Notice how ingenious his tactics are—bright little guy, huh?" or "Just relax and bear with it a moment longer; it *will* soon be over." Such self-talk often mitigates or even dispels the welling anger, along with the urges to be abrupt, to behave punishingly, and generally to lose my cool. Perseverance may also involve self-talk making use of "the power of positive thinking," as well as the tactics of reading "encouraging" literature (e.g., to help one persevere in a diet or a language-learning program) and associating with "encouraging" people. But self-talk and these more external self-management tactics are crude forms of this aspect of self-control: the experienced self-controller just flashes the strategic thoughts across her mind at the appropriate moments, the way a basketball player moves intelligently but without deliberation in the split-second of court action.

VII

Before I end, I must put the thesis of this paper in perspective. I have argued that the virtues of will power are in an important aspect skills or skill-like powers. But I have nowhere claimed that this is the whole story of these virtues.

There may be saints whose patience and courage do not involve any exercise of will power, in the form either of efforts of will or of an effortless mastery of adverse impulses and emotions. The reason their goodness involves no exercise of will power is what makes them saints: they don't *have* any adverse impulses or emotions to which will power might be directed. Whether there are any saints in this sense I don't know; but there are certainly particular acts of courage and perseverance that involve no exercise of will power. Some acts of heroic courage are performed so spontaneously that there can be no question of the individual overcoming his fears; he just doesn't have any fears at the moment.

But even when skills of self-mastery are still needed there are two other kinds of feature typical of people with the virtues of will power. First, they *care* intensely about something. I have argued that the virtues of will power, when they are moral, derive their moral import from the concerns in the interest of which they are exercised. But the virtues of will power are never exercised apart from any motivation whatsoever; and generally speaking, the more intense the concerns, the more likely that the skills of self-mastery will be exercised and their power increased. So where courage does have moral import, it will be generally true that the deeper the courage the more powerful the moral concerns of the individual. Not all passionate people are courageous, but it is typical of courageous people that they are passionate.

The second aspect of the virtues of will power is self-confidence. There is a correlation between people's ability to handle their adverse inclinations and the confidence of their belief in their ability to determine their own destiny. Of course it is typical of skilled people in general that they are confident of themselves in respect of the skill in question. And so, since self-mastery is so fundamental to the successful conduct of a human life, it might seem that self-confidence is a by-product of the virtues of will power rather than an element of them. But while self-mastering skills clearly cause self-confidence, it is equally true that self-confidence grounds the exercise of self-mastery skills. When an athlete loses his self-confidence, he loses some of his ability to exercise his skill, even though his skill *per se* (so to speak) is not at all diminished. Similarly in a situation of testing the individual who has ceased to believe that he can persevere will show himself as weak, even though he possesses all the necessary skills to see him through his difficulty. An athlete needs three things for success: the requisite skills, an enthusiasm for the game, and a belief in his own powers. And the virtues of will power are the athletic side of the moral life.

Notes

1. Important essays in which this tendency is evident are chapter 7 of von Wright's *The Varieties of Goodness* (London: Routledge, 1963); R. B. Brandt's "Traits of Character: A Conceptual Analysis," *American Philosophical Quarterly* 7 (1970): 23–37; Philippa Foot's "Virtues and Vices" in *Virtues and Vices* (Berkeley: University of California Press, 1978); and John McDowell's "Virtue and Reason," *Monist* 62 (1979): 331–50.

2. When I call a virtue a "virtue of will power" I do not suggest that every action exemplifying it is an exercise of will power. There are acts of courage and patience and perseverance (I am less sure about self-control) that do not require will power, much less an effort of will. I use this name to indicate a salient, but not necessary, feature of these virtues. Also, will power is probably, as a matter of psychological fact, always needed in the *acquisition* of these virtues.

3. Lester Hunt has argued that all virtues are dispositions to act on principles (see his "Character and Thought," *American Philosophical Quarterly* 15, 3 (1978): 177–86), and has thus sought the principle which courage is the disposition to act on. He comes up with the following: courageous acts "are the ones which are done from the principle that one's own safety, in general, has no more than a certain measure of importance." ("Courage and Principle," *Canadian Journal of Philosophy* 10, 2 (1980): 289). But this principle is clearly not a moral one.

4. Foot, "Virtues and Vices," 15.

5. But compare 1117b.

6. *The Varieties of Religious Experience* (Garden City, N.Y.: Doubleday, 1978), 266–67, note. H. A. Prichard finds another way of making courage a passional virtue: for him it is not an enjoyment of dangers, but "the desire to conquer one's feelings of terror arising from the sense of shame which they arouse." *Moral Obligation* (New York, N.Y.: Oxford University Press, 1950), 13. While some courageous actions are motivated by shame of fear, the most typical moral examples are motivated in other ways (see below). But the essential point is that there is *no* motive that always goes with courageous actions.

7. Though they are sometimes done for the sake of courage and self-control, as when you "do every day or two something for no other reason than that you would rather not do it, so that when the hour of dire need draws nigh, it may find you not unnerved and untrained to stand the test" [William James, *Principles of Psychology*, vol. 1 (Cambridge, Mass.: Harvard University Press, 1981), 126], or as when, like G. Gordon Liddy, you eat a rat as an exercise in mastering your fear of rats [*Will: The Autobiography of G. Gordon Liddy* (New York: St. Martin's Press, 1980), 24]. But this kind of case is untypical, the typical case being that of acting courageously or self-controlledly for the sake of some other end. If someone always acted courageously *only* to exhibit courage or to train herself in it, and never out of friendship, justice, compassion, etc., her action would not be moral. And to the extent that acting courageously out of the desire to be courageous is morally praiseworthy, this is because courage is in aid of the actions characteristic of the substantive moral virtues.

8. Aquinas seems to be aware of the distinction I am pointing to when he says, "By its nature virtue is concerned with the good rather than the difficult," and "A man exposes himself to mortal danger only to preserve justice. Therefore the praise accorded to courage derives in a sense from justice" (Summa Theologiae 2a2ae 123.12). But he is not consistent in this observation that courage and similar virtues do not supply a motive, for he assimilates courage and charity by saying, "Charity does prompt the act of martyrdom as its first and most important moving force by being the virtue commanding it, but courage does so as the directly engaged moving force, being the virtue which brings out the act" (2a2ae 124.2). But unless the martyr is acting not just courageously, but for the sake of courage (which is not the typical case and certainly not necessary for martyrdom), it seems wrong to say that courage "prompts" the act in any sense. In the normal case courage *enables* the act, but only motives *prompt* it.

9. *Republic* 429c–e.

10. Foot, "Virtues and Vices," 9.

11. *The Letters of John Keats*, vol. 2 (Cambridge, Mass.: Harvard University Press, 1958), 101f.

12. *American Philosophical Quarterly* 7 (1970): 23–37.

13. *Virtues and Vices* (Ithaca, N.Y.: Cornell University Press, 1978), 61. Wallace suggests that the "positiveness" of virtues like courage is their capacity to preserve us in the course of practical reason. But as A. O. Rorty has pointed out, the *akrates* need not consider the course which he fails to take to be the more rational of the choices which conflict in him ("Where Does the Akratic Break Take Place?" *Australasian Journal of Philosophy* 58, 94 (1980): 336f). Just as *akrasia* cannot be defined as a form of irrationality, so courage and other virtues which are the opposites of *akrasia* cannot be defined as capacities to preserve rationality. Their "positiveness" lies not here, but in their being capacities.

14. Gilbert Ryle, *Collected Papers*, vol. 2 (London: Hutchinson, 1971), 381ff.

15. See Foot, "Virtues and Vices," 7f.

16. *For Self-Examination and Judge for Yourselves!* trans. Walter Lowrie (Princeton: Princeton University Press, 1968), 69.

17. In a book called *Strength of Will and How to Develop It* discussed in Robert Assagioli, "The Act of Will" (New York: Viking Press, 1973), 39ff.

18. For an explanation of why techniques like this work, see my "Solomon on the Control of Emotions," *Philosophy and Phenomenological Research*, vol. 44 (March 1984), 395–404.

Reading Introduction

Moral Saints
Susan Wolf

There are not only different kinds of *moral* (or "morally significant") virtues, as
Roberts points out, but also many other aspects of the personality that one should
ideally have. There are nonmoral human excellences as well, and Wolf argues
that if somebody went so far as to live out the moral point of view single-
mindedly, it would greatly impoverish him or her as a person and companion. So
the question comes up, What will be the relative weight of these different kinds of
virtues in the constitution of the most perfect personality? Wolf refrains from
offering a rulelike answer to this question, leaving specific cases up to "intuition";
but she argues that the answer will decidedly *not* be that we should cultivate the
moral traits as much as possible. "The moral point of view" is perverse, because it
not only proposes certain values, such as helpfulness, benevolence, and duty, but
also assumes that it is *always better to be morally better*. Thus, given the choice
between honing your philosophical skills at a university and devoting the same
time to liberating some children from prostitution on the streets of Chicago, what
you really *should* do is liberate the children. Or given the choice between
cultivating a taste for $150 French dinners and developing skills for helping
famine victims in Ethiopia, what you really *should* do is work on your famine-
relief skills. Wolf contrasts this with her own proposal, "the point of view of
individual perfection," in which it is left open that "perfection" may mean far
more than "moral perfection."

Moral Saints

SUSAN WOLF

I don't know whether there are any moral saints. But if there are, I am glad that neither I
nor those about whom I care most are among them. By *moral saint* I mean a person whose
every action is as morally good as possible, a person, that is, who is as morally worthy as
can be. Though I shall in a moment acknowledge the variety of types of person that might
be thought to satisfy this description, it seems to me that none of these types serve as
unequivocally compelling personal ideals. In other words, I believe that moral perfection,
in the sense of moral saintliness, does not constitute a model of personal well-being toward
which it would be particularly rational or good or desirable for a human being to strive.

Journal of Philosophy 79, 8 (August 1982): 419–439. Reprinted by permission of the author and the
publisher.

Outside the context of moral discussion, this will strike many as an obvious point. But, within that context, the point, if it be granted, will be granted with some discomfort. For within that context it is generally assumed that one ought to be as morally good as possible and that what limits there are to morality's hold on us are set by features of human nature of which we ought not to be proud. If, as I believe, the ideals that are derivable from common sense and philosophically popular moral theories do not support these assumptions, then something has to change. Either we must change our moral theories in ways that will make them yield more palatable ideals, or, as I shall argue, we must change our conception of what is involved in affirming a moral theory.

In this paper, I wish to examine the notion of a moral saint, first, to understand what a moral saint would be like and why such a being would be unattractive, and, second, to raise some questions about the significance of this paradoxical figure for moral philosophy. I shall look first at the model(s) of moral sainthood that might be extrapolated from the morality or moralities of common sense. Then I shall consider what relations these have to conclusions that can be drawn from utilitarian and Kantian moral theories. Finally, I shall speculate on the implications of these considerations for moral philosophy.

Moral Saints and Common Sense

Consider first what, pretheoretically, would count for us—contemporary members of Western culture—as a moral saint. A necessary condition of moral sainthood would be that one's life be dominated by a commitment to improving the welfare of others or of society as a whole. As to what role this commitment must play in the individual's motivational system, two contrasting accounts suggest themselves to me which might equally be thought to qualify a person for moral sainthood.

First, a moral saint might be someone whose concern for others plays the role that is played in most of our lives by more selfish, or, at any rate, less morally worthy concerns. For the moral saint, the promotion of the welfare of others might play the role that is played for most of us by the enjoyment of material comforts, the opportunity to engage in the intellectual and physical activities of our choice, and the love, respect, and companionship of people whom we love, respect, and enjoy. The happiness of the moral saint, then, would truly lie in the happiness of others, and so he would devote himself to others gladly, and with a whole and open heart.

On the other hand, a moral saint might be someone for whom the basic ingredients of happiness are not unlike those of most of the rest of us. What makes him a moral saint is rather that he pays little or no attention to his own happiness in light of the overriding importance he gives to the wider concerns of morality. In other words, this person sacrifices his own interests to the interests of others, and feels the sacrifice as such.

Roughly, these two models may be distinguished according to whether one thinks of the moral saint as being a saint out of love or one thinks of the moral saint as being a saint out of duty (or some other intellectual appreciation and recognition of moral principles). We may refer to the first model as the model of the Loving Saint; to the second, as the model of the Rational Saint.

The two models differ considerably with respect to the qualities of the motives of the individuals who conform to them. But this difference would have limited effect on the saints' respective public personalities. The shared content of what these individuals are motivated to be—namely, as morally good as possible—would play the dominant role in the determination of their characters. Of course, just as a variety of large-scale projects, from tending the sick to political campaigning, may be equally and maximally morally worthy, so a variety of characters are compatible with the ideal of moral sainthood. One moral saint may be more or less jovial, more or less garrulous, more or less athletic than another. But, above all, a moral saint must have and cultivate those qualities which are apt to allow him to treat others as justly and kindly as possible. He will have the standard moral virtues to a nonstandard degree. He will be patient, considerate, even-tempered, hospitable, charitable in thought as well as in deed. He will be very reluctant to make negative judgments of other people. He will be careful not to favor some people over others on the basis of properties they could not help but have.

Perhaps what I have already said is enough to make some people begin to regard the absence of moral saints in their lives as a blessing. For there comes a point in the listing of virtues that a moral saint is likely to have where one might naturally begin to wonder whether the moral saint isn't, after all, too good—if not too good for his own good, at least too good for his own well-being. For the moral virtues, given that they are, by hypothesis, *all* present in the same individual, and to an extreme degree, are apt to crowd out the nonmoral virtues, as well as many of the interests and personal characteristics that we generally think contribute to a healthy, well-rounded, richly developed character.

In other words, if the moral saint is devoting all his time to feeding the hungry or healing the sick or raising money for Oxfam, then necessarily he is not reading Victorian novels, playing the oboe, or improving his backhand. Although no one of the interests or tastes in the category containing these latter activities could be claimed to be a necessary element in a life well lived, a life in which *none* of these possible aspects of character are developed may seem to be a life strangely barren.

The reasons why a moral saint cannot, in general, encourage the discovery and development of significant nonmoral interests and skills are not logical but practical reasons. There are, in addition, a class of nonmoral characteristics that a moral saint cannot encourage in himself for reasons that are not just practical. There is a more substantial tension between having any of these qualities unashamedly and being a moral saint. These qualities might be described as going against the moral grain. For example, a cynical or sarcastic wit, or a sense of humor that appreciates this kind of wit in others, requires that one take an attitude of resignation and pessimism toward the flaws and vices to be found in the world. A moral saint, on the other hand, has reason to take an attitude in opposition to this—he should try to look for the best in people, give them the benefit of the doubt as long as possible, try to improve regrettable situations as long as there is any hope of success. This suggests that, although a moral saint might well enjoy a good episode of *Father Knows Best*, he may not in good conscience be able to laugh at a Marx Brothers movie or enjoy a play by George Bernard Shaw.

An interest in something like gourmet cooking will be, for different reasons, difficult for a moral saint to rest easy with. For it seems to me that no plausible argument can justify the use of human resources involved in producing a *paté de canard en croute* against possible alternative beneficent ends to which these resources might be put. If there is a justification for the institution of haute cuisine, it is one which rests on the decision *not* to justify every activity against morally beneficial alternatives, and this is a decision a moral saint will never make. Presumably, an interest in high fashion or interior design will fare much the same, as will, very possibly, a cultivation of the finer arts as well.

A moral saint will have to be very, very nice. It is important that he not be offensive. The worry is that, as a result, he will have to be dull-witted or humorless or bland.

This worry is confirmed when we consider what sorts of characters, taken and refined both from life and from fiction, typically form our ideals. One would hope they would be figures who are morally good—and by this I mean more than just not morally bad—but one would hope, too, that they are not just morally good, but talented or accomplished or attractive in nonmoral ways as well. We may make ideals out of athletes, scholars, artists— more frivolously, out of cowboys, private eyes, and rock stars. We may strive for Katharine Hepburn's grace, Paul Newman's "cool"; we are attracted to the high-spirited passionate nature of Natasha Rostov; we admire the keen perceptiveness of Lambert Strether. Though there is certainly nothing immoral about the ideal characters or traits I have in mind, they cannot be superimposed upon the ideal of a moral saint. For although it is a part of many of these ideals that the characters set high, and not merely acceptable, moral standards for themselves, it is also essential to their power and attractiveness that the moral strengths go, so to speak, alongside of specific, independently admirable, nonmoral ground projects and dominant personal traits.

When one does finally turn one's eyes toward lives that are dominated by explicitly moral commitments, moreover, one finds oneself relieved at the discovery of idio-syncrasies or eccentricities not quite in line with the picture of moral perfection. One prefers the blunt, tactless, and opinionated Betsy Trotwood to the unfailingly kind and patient Agnes Copperfield; one prefers the mischievousness and the sense of irony in Chesterton's Father Brown to the innocence and undiscriminating love of St. Francis.

It seems that, as we look in our ideals for people who achieve nonmoral varieties of personal excellence in conjunction with or colored by some version of high moral tone, we look in our paragons of moral excellence for people whose moral achievements occur in conjunction with or colored by some interests or traits that have low moral tone. In other words, there seems to be a limit to how much morality we can stand.

One might suspect that the essence of the problem is simply that there is a limit to how much of *any* single value, or any single type of value, we can stand. Our objection then would not be specific to a life in which one's dominant concern is morality, but would apply to any life that can be so completely characterized by an extraordinarily dominant concern. The objection in that case would reduce to the recognition that such a life is incompatible with well-roundedness. If that were the objection, one could fairly reply that well-roundedness is no more supreme a virtue than the totality of moral virtues embodied by the ideal it is being used to criticize. But I think this misidentifies the objection. For the way in which a concern for morality may dominate a life, or, more to the point, the way in which it may dominate an ideal of life, is not easily imagined by analogy to the dominance an aspiration to become an Olympic swimmer or a concert pianist might have.

A person who is passionately committed to one of these latter concerns might decide that her attachment to it is strong enough to be worth the sacrifice of her ability to maintain and pursue a significant portion of what else life might offer which a proper devotion to her dominant passion would require. But a desire to be as morally good as possible is not likely to take the form of one desire among others which, because of its peculiar psychological strength, requires one to forego the pursuit of other weaker and separately less demanding desires. Rather, the desire to be as morally good as possible is apt to have the character not just of a stronger, but of a higher desire, which does not merely successfully compete with one's other desires but which rather subsumes or demotes them. The sacrifice of other interests for the interest in morality, then, will have the character, not of a choice, but of an imperative.

Moreover, there is something odd about the idea of morality itself, or moral goodness, serving as the object of a dominant passion in the way that a more concrete and specific vision of a goal (even a concrete *moral* goal) might be imagined to serve. Morality itself does not seem to be a suitable object of passion. Thus, when one reflects, for example, on the Loving Saint easily and gladly giving up his fishing trip or his stereo or his hot fudge sundae at the drop of the moral hat, one is apt to wonder not at how much he loves morality, but at how little he loves these other things. One thinks that, if he can give these up so easily, he does not know what it *is* to truly love them. There seems, in other words, to be a kind of joy which the Loving Saint, either by nature or by practice, is incapable of experiencing. The Rational Saint, on the other hand, might retain strong nonmoral and concrete desires—he simply denies himself the opportunity to act on them. But this is no less troubling. The Loving Saint one might suspect of missing a piece of perceptual machinery, of being blind to some of what the world has to offer. The Rational Saint, who sees it but foregoes it, one suspects of having a different problem—a pathological fear of damnation, perhaps, or an extreme form of self-hatred that interferes with his ability to enjoy the enjoyable in life.

In other words, the ideal of a life of moral sainthood disturbs not simply because it is an ideal of a life in which morality unduly dominates. The normal person's direct and specific desires for objects, activities, and events that conflict with the attainment of moral perfection are not simply sacrificed but removed, suppressed, or subsumed. The way in which morality, unlike other possible goals, is apt to dominate is particularly disturbing, for it seems to require either the lack or the denial of the existence of an identifiable, personal self.

This distinctively troubling feature is not, I think, absolutely unique to the ideal of the moral saint, as I have been using that phrase. It is shared by the conception of the pure aesthete, by a certain kind of religious ideal, and, somewhat paradoxically, by the model of the thorough-going, self-conscious egoist. It is not a coincidence that the ways of comprehending the world of which these ideals are the extreme embodiments are sometimes described as "moralities" themselves. At any rate, they compete with what we ordinarily mean by 'morality'. Nor is it a coincidence that these ideals are naturally described as fanatical. But it is easy to see that these other types of perfection cannot serve as satisfactory personal ideals; for the realization of these ideals would be straightforwardly immoral. It may come as a surprise to some that there may in addition be such a thing as a *moral* fanatic.

Some will object that I am being unfair to "common-sense morality"—that it does not really require a moral saint to be either a disgusting goody-goody or an obsessive ascetic. Admittedly, there is no logical inconsistency between having any of the personal characteristics I have mentioned and being a moral saint. It is not morally wrong to notice the faults and shortcomings of others or to recognize and appreciate nonmoral talents and skills. Nor is it immoral to be an avid Celtics fan or to have a passion for caviar or to be an excellent cellist. With enough imagination, we can always contrive a suitable history and set of circumstances that will embrace such characteristics in one or another specific fictional story of a perfect moral saint.

If one turned onto the path of moral sainthood relatively late in life, one may have already developed interests that can be turned to moral purposes. It may be that a good golf game is just what is needed to secure that big donation to Oxfam. Perhaps the cultivation of one's exceptional artistic talent will turn out to be the way one can make one's greatest contribution to society. Furthermore, one might stumble upon joys and skills in the very service of morality. If, because the children are short a ninth player for the team, one's generous offer to serve reveals a natural fielding arm or if one's part in the campaign against nuclear power requires accepting a lobbyist's invitation to lunch at Le Lion d'Or, there is no moral gain in denying the satisfaction one gets from these activities. The moral saint, then, may, by happy accident, find himself with nonmoral virtues on which he can capitalize morally or which make psychological demands to which he has no choice but to attend. The point is that, for a moral saint, the existence of these interests and skills can be given at best the status of happy accidents—they cannot be encouraged for their own sakes as distinct, independent aspects of the realization of human good.

It must be remembered that from the fact that there is a tension between having any of these qualities and being a moral saint it does not follow that having any of these qualities is immoral. For it is not part of common-sense morality that one ought to be a moral saint. Still, if someone just happened to want to be a moral saint, he or she would not have or encourage these qualities, and, on the basis of our common-sense values, this counts as a reason not to want to be a moral saint.

One might still wonder what kind of reason this is, and what kind of conclusion this properly allows us to draw. For the fact that the models of moral saints are unattractive does not necessarily mean that they are unsuitable ideals. Perhaps they are unattractive because they make us feel uncomfortable—they highlight our own weaknesses, vices, and flaws. If so, the fault lies not in the characters of the saints, but in those of our unsaintly selves.

To be sure, some of the reasons behind the disaffection we feel for the model of moral sainthood have to do with a reluctance to criticize ourselves and a reluctance to committing ourselves to trying to give up activities and interests that we heartily enjoy. These considerations might provide an *excuse* for the fact that we are not moral saints, but they do not provide a basis for criticizing sainthood as a possible ideal. Since these considerations rely on an appeal to the egoistic, hedonistic side of our natures, to use them as a basis for criticizing the ideal of the moral saint would be at best to beg the question and at worst to glorify features of ourselves that ought to be condemned.

The fact that the moral saint would be without qualities which we have and which, indeed, we like to have, does not in itself provide reason to condemn the ideal of the moral saint. The fact that some of these qualities are good qualities, however, and that they are qualities we *ought* to like, does provide reason to discourage this ideal and to offer other ideals in its place. In other words, some of the qualities the moral saint necessarily lacks are virtues, albeit nonmoral virtues, in the unsaintly characters who have them. The feats of Groucho Marx, Reggie Jackson, and the head chef at Lutèce are impressive accomplishments that it is not only permissible but positively appropriate to recognize as such. In general, the admiration of and striving toward achieving any of a great variety of forms of personal excellence are character traits it is valuable and desirable for people to have. In advocating the development of these varieties of excellence, we advocate nonmoral reasons for acting, and in thinking that it is good for a person to strive for an ideal that gives a substantial role to the interests and values that correspond to these virtues, we implicitly acknowledge the goodness of ideals incompatible with that of the moral saint. Finally, if we think that it is *as* good, or even better for a person to strive for one of these ideals than it is for him or her to strive for and realize the ideal of the moral saint, we express a conviction that it is good not to be a moral saint.

Moral Saints and Moral Theories

I have tried so far to paint a picture—or, rather, two pictures—of what a moral saint might be like, drawing on what I take to be the attitudes and beliefs about morality prevalent in contemporary, common-sense thought. To my suggestion that common-sense morality generates conceptions of moral saints that are unattractive or otherwise unacceptable, it is open to someone to reply, "so much the worse for common-sense morality." After all, it is often claimed that the goal of moral philosophy is to correct and improve upon common-sense morality, and I have as yet given no attention to the question of what conceptions of moral sainthood, if any, are generated from the leading moral theories of our time.

A quick, breezy reading of utilitarian and Kantian writings will suggest the images, respectively, of the Loving Saint and the Rational Saint. A utilitarian, with his emphasis on happiness, will certainly prefer the Loving Saint to the Rational one, since the Loving Saint will himself be a happier person than the Rational Saint. A Kantian, with his emphasis on reason, on the other hand, will find at least as much to praise in the latter as in the former. Still, both models, drawn as they are from common sense, appeal to an impure mixture of utilitarian and Kantian intuitions. A more careful examination of these moral theories raises questions about whether either model of moral sainthood would really be advocated by a believer in the explicit doctrines associated with either of these views.

Certainly, the utilitarian in no way denies the value of self-realization. He in no way disparages the development of interests, talents, and other personally attractive traits that I have claimed the moral saint would be without. Indeed, since just these features enhance the happiness both of the individuals who possess them and of those with whom they associate, the ability to promote these features both in oneself and in others will have considerable positive weight in utilitarian calculations.

This implies that the utilitarian would not support moral sainthood as a universal ideal. A world in which everyone, or even a large number of people, achieved moral sainthood—even a world in which they *strove* to achieve it—would probably contain less happiness than a world in which people realized a diversity of ideals involving a variety of personal and perfectionist values. More pragmatic considerations also suggest that, if the utilitarian wants to influence more people to achieve more good, then he would do better to encourage them to pursue happiness-producing goals that are more attractive and more within a normal person's reach.

These considerations still leave open, however, the question of what kind of an ideal the committed utilitarian should privately aspire to himself. Utilitarianism requires him to want to achieve the greatest general happiness, and this would seem to commit him to the ideal of the moral saint.

One might try to use the claims I made earlier as a basis for an argument that a utilitarian should choose to give up utilitarianism. If, as I have said, a moral saint would be a less happy person both to be and to be around than many other possible ideals, perhaps one could create more total happiness by not trying too hard to promote the total happiness. But this argument is simply unconvincing in light of the empirical circumstances of our world. The gain in happiness that would accrue to oneself and one's neighbors by a more well-rounded, richer life than that of the moral saint would be pathetically small in comparison to the amount by which one could increase the general happiness if one devoted oneself explicitly to the care of the sick, the downtrodden, the starving, and the homeless. Of course, there may be psychological limits to the extent to which a person can devote himself to such things without going crazy. But the utilitarian's individual limitations would not thereby become a positive feature of his personal ideals.

The unattractiveness of the moral saint, then, ought not rationally convince the utilitarian to abandon his utilitarianism. It may, however, convince him to take efforts not to wear his saintly moral aspirations on his sleeve. If it is not too difficult, the utilitarian will try not to make those around him uncomfortable. He will not want to appear "holier than thou"; he will not want to inhibit others' ability to enjoy themselves. In practice, this might make the perfect utilitarian a less nauseating companion than the moral saint I earlier portrayed. But insofar as this kind of reasoning produces a more bearable public personality, it is at the cost of giving him a personality that must be evaluated as hypocritical and condescending when his private thoughts and attitudes are taken into account.

Still, the criticisms I have raised against the saint of common-sense morality should make some difference to the utilitarian's conception of an ideal which neither requires him to abandon his utilitarian principles nor forces him to fake an interest he does not have or a judgment he does not make. For it may be that a limited and carefully monitored allotment of time and energy to be devoted to the pursuit of some nonmoral interests or to the development of some nonmoral talents would make a person a better contributor to the general welfare than he would be if he allowed himself no indulgences of this sort. The

enjoyment of such activities in no way compromises a commitment to utilitarian principles as long as the involvement with these activities is conditioned by a willingness to give
them up whenever it is recognized that they cease to be in the general interest.

This will go some way in mitigating the picture of the loving saint that an understanding of utilitarianism will on first impression suggest. But I think it will not go very far. For
the limitations on time and energy will have to be rather severe, and the need to monitor
will restrict not only the extent but also the quality of one's attachment to these interests
and traits. They are only weak and somewhat peculiar sorts of passions to which one can
consciously remain so conditionally committed. Moreover, the way in which the utilitarian can enjoy these "extra-curricular" aspects of his life is simply not the way in which
these aspects are to be enjoyed insofar as they figure into our less saintly ideals.

The problem is not exactly that the utilitarian values these aspects of his life only as a
means to an end, for the enjoyment he and others get from these aspects are not a means
to, but a part of, the general happiness. Nonetheless, he values these things only because of
and insofar as they *are* a part of the general happiness. He values them, as it were, under
the description 'a contribution to the general happiness'. This is to be contrasted with the
various ways in which these aspects of life may be valued by nonutilitarians. A person
might love literature because of the insights into human nature literature affords. Another
might love the cultivation of roses because roses are things of great beauty and delicacy. It
may be true that these features of the respective activities also explain why these activities
are happiness-producing. But, to the nonutilitarian, this may not be to the point. For if one
values these activities in these more direct ways, one may not be willing to exchange them
for others that produce an equal, or even a greater amount of happiness. From that point
of view, it is not because they produce happiness that these activities are valuable; it is
because these activities are valuable in more direct and specific ways that they produce
happiness.

To adopt a phrase of Bernard Williams', the utilitarian's manner of valuing the not
explicitly moral aspects of his life "provides (him) with one thought too many."[1] The
requirement that the utilitarian have this thought — periodically, at least — is indicative of
not only a weakness but a shallowness in his appreciation of the aspects in question. Thus,
the ideals toward which a utilitarian could acceptably strive would remain too close to the
model of the common-sense moral saint to escape the criticisms of that model which I
earlier suggested. Whether a Kantian would be similarly committed to so restrictive and
unattractive a range of possible ideals is a somewhat more difficult question.

The Kantian believes that being morally worthy consists in always acting from
maxims that one could will to be universal law, and doing this not out of any pathological
desire but out of reverence for the moral law as such. Or, to take a different formulation of
the categorical imperative, the Kantian believes that moral action consists in treating other
persons always as ends and never as means only. Presumably, and according to Kant
himself, the Kantian thereby commits himself to some degree of benevolence as well as to
the rules of fair play. But we surely would not will that *every* person become a moral saint,
and treating others as ends hardly requires bending over backwards to protect and
promote their interests. On one interpretation of Kantian doctrine, then, moral perfection
would be achieved simply by unerring obedience to a limited set of side-constraints. On

this interpretation, Kantian theory simply does not yield an ideal conception of a person of any fullness comparable to that of the moral saints I have so far been portraying.

On the other hand, Kant does say explicitly that we have a duty of benevolence, a duty not only to allow others to pursue their ends, but to take up their ends as our own. In addition, we have positive duties to ourselves, duties to increase our natural as well as our moral perfection. These duties are unlimited in the degree to which they *may* dominate a life. If action in accordance with and motivated by the thought of these duties is considered virtuous, it is natural to assume that the more one performs such actions, the more virtuous one is. Moreover, of virtue in general Kant says, "it is an ideal which is unattainable while yet our duty is constantly to approximate to it."[2] On this interpretation, then, the Kantian moral saint, like the other moral saints I have been considering, is dominated by the motivation to be moral.

Which of these interpretations of Kant one prefers will depend on the interpretation and the importance one gives to the role of the imperfect duties in Kant's over-all system. Rather than choose between them here, I shall consider each briefly in turn.

On the second interpretation of Kant, the Kantian moral saint is, not surprisingly, subject to many of the same objections I have been raising against other versions of moral sainthood. Though the Kantian saint may differ from the utilitarian saint as to *which* actions he is bound to perform and which he is bound to refrain from performing, I suspect that the range of activities acceptable to the Kantian saint will remain objectionably restrictive. Moreover, the manner in which the Kantian saint must think about and justify the activities he pursues and the character traits he develops will strike us, as it did with the utilitarian saint, as containing "one thought too many." As the utilitarian could value his activities and character traits only insofar as they fell under the description of 'contributions to the general happiness', the Kantian would have to value his activities and character traits insofar as they were manifestations of respect for the moral law. If the development of our powers to achieve physical, intellectual, or artistic excellence, or the activities directed toward making others happy are to have any moral worth, they must arise from a reverence for the dignity that members of our species have as a result of being endowed with pure practical reason. This is a good and noble motivation, to be sure. But it is hardly what one expects to be dominantly behind a person's aspirations to dance as well as Fred Astaire, to paint as well as Picasso, or to solve some outstanding problem in abstract algebra, and it is hardly what one hopes to find lying dominantly behind a father's action on behalf of his son or a lover's on behalf of her beloved.

Since the basic problem with any of the models of moral sainthood we have been considering is that they are dominated by a single, all-important value under which all other possible values must be subsumed, it may seem that the alternative interpretation of Kant, as providing a stringent but finite set of obligations and constraints, might provide a more acceptable morality. According to this interpretation of Kant, one is as morally good as can be so long as one devotes some limited portion of one's energies toward altruism and the maintenance of one's physical and spiritual health, and otherwise pursues one's independently motivated interests and values in such a way as to avoid overstepping certain bounds. Certainly, if it be a requirement of an acceptable moral theory that perfect obedience to its laws and maximal devotion to its interests and concerns be something we can wholeheartedly strive for in ourselves and wish for in those around us, it will count in favor of this brand of Kantianism that its commands can be fulfilled without swallowing up the perfect moral agent's entire personality.

Even this more limited understanding of morality, if its connection to Kant's views is to be taken at all seriously, is not likely to give an unqualified seal of approval to the nonmorally directed ideals I have been advocating. For Kant is explicit about what he calls "duties of apathy and self-mastery" (69/70) — duties to ensure that our passions are never so strong as to interfere with calm, practical deliberation, or so deep as to wrest control from the more disinterested, rational part of ourselves. The tight and self-conscious rein we are thus obliged to keep on our commitments to specific individuals and causes will doubtless restrict our value in these things, assigning them a necessarily attenuated place.

A more interesting objection to this brand of Kantianism, however, comes when we consider the implications of placing the kind of upper bound on moral worthiness which seemed to count in favor of this conception of morality. For to put such a limit on one's capacity to be moral is effectively to deny, not just the moral necessity, but the moral goodness of a devotion to benevolence and the maintenance of justice that passes beyond a certain, required point. It is to deny the possibility of going morally above and beyond the call of a restricted set of duties. Despite my claim that all-consuming moral saintliness is not a particularly healthy and desirable ideal, it seems perverse to insist that, were moral saints to exist, they would not, in their way, be remarkably noble and admirable figures. Despite my conviction that it is as rational and as good for a person to take Katharine Hepburn or Jane Austen as her role model instead of Mother Teresa, it would be absurd to deny that Mother Teresa is a morally better person.

I can think of two ways of viewing morality as having an upper bound. First, we can think that altruism and impartiality are indeed positive moral interests, but that they are moral only if the degree to which these interests are actively pursued remains within certain fixed limits. Second, we can think that these positive interests are only incidentally related to morality and that the essence of morality lies elsewhere, in, say, an implicit social contract or in the recognition of our own dignified rationality. According to the first conception of morality, there is a cut-off line to the amount of altruism or to the extent of devotion to justice and fairness that is worthy of moral praise. But to draw this line earlier than the line that brings the altruist in question into a worse-off position than all those to whom he devotes himself seems unacceptably artificial and gratuitous. According to the second conception, these positive interests are not essentially related to morality at all. But then we are unable to regard a more affectionate and generous expression of good will toward others as a natural and reasonable extension of morality, and we encourage a cold and unduly self-centered approach to the development and evaluation of our motivations and concerns.

A moral theory that does not contain the seeds of an all-consuming ideal of moral sainthood thus seems to place false and unnatural limits on our opportunity to do moral good and our potential to deserve moral praise. Yet the main thrust of the arguments of this paper has been leading to the conclusion that, when such ideals are present, they are not ideals to which it is particularly reasonable or healthy or desirable for human beings to aspire. These claims, taken together, have the appearance of a dilemma from which there is no obvious escape. In a moment, I shall argue that, despite appearances, these claims should not be understood as constituting a dilemma. But, before I do, let me briefly describe another path which those who are convinced by my above remarks may feel inclined to take.

If the above remarks are understood to be implicitly critical of the views on the content of morality which seem most popular today, an alternative that naturally suggests itself is that we revise our views about the content of morality. More specifically, my remarks may be taken to support a more Aristotelian, or even a more Nietzschean, approach to moral philosophy. Such a change in approach involves substantially broadening or replacing our contemporary intuitions about which character traits constitute moral virtues and vices and which interests constitute moral interests. If, for example, we include personal bearing, or creativity, or sense of style, as features that contribute to one's *moral* personality, then we can create moral ideals which are incompatible with and probably more attractive than the Kantian and utilitarian ideals I have discussed. Given such an alteration of our conception of morality, the figures with which I have been concerned above might, far from being considered to be moral saints, be seen as morally inferior to other more appealing or more interesting models of individuals.

This approach seems unlikely to succeed, if for no other reason, because it is doubtful that any single, or even any reasonably small number of substantial personal ideals could capture the full range of possible ways of realizing human potential or achieving human good which deserve encouragement and praise. Even if we could provide a sufficiently broad characterization of the range of positive ways for human beings to live, however, I think there are strong reasons not to want to incorporate such a characterization more centrally into the framework of morality itself. For, in claiming that a character trait or activity is morally good, one claims that there is a certain kind of reason for developing that trait or engaging in that activity. Yet, lying behind our criticism of more conventional conceptions of moral sainthood, there seems to be a recognition that among the immensely valuable traits and activities that a human life might positively embrace are some of which we hope that, if a person does embrace them, he does so *not* for moral reasons. In other words, no matter how flexible we make the guide to conduct which we choose to label "morality," no matter how rich we make the life in which perfect obedience to this guide would result, we will have reason to hope that a person does not wholly rule and direct his life by the abstract and impersonal consideration that such a life would be morally good.

Once it is recognized that morality itself should not serve as a comprehensive guide to conduct, moreover, we can see reasons to retain the admittedly vague contemporary intuitions about what the classification of moral and nonmoral virtues, interests, and the like should be. That is, there seem to be important differences between the aspects of a person's life which are currently considered appropriate objects of moral evaluation and the aspects that might be included under the altered conception of morality we are now considering, which the latter approach would tend wrongly to blur or to neglect. Moral evaluation now is focused primarily on features of a person's life over which that person has control; it is largely restricted to aspects of his life which are likely to have considerable effect on other people. These restrictions seem as they should be. Even if responsible people could reach agreement as to what constituted good taste or a healthy degree of well-roundedness, for example, it seems wrong to insist that everyone try to achieve these things or to blame someone who fails or refuses to conform.

If we are not to respond to the unattractiveness of the moral ideals that contemporary theories yield either by offering alternative theories with more palatable ideals or by understanding these theories in such a way as to prevent them from yielding ideals at all, how, then, are we to respond? Simply, I think, by admitting that moral ideals do not, and need not, make the best personal ideals. Earlier, I mentioned one of the consequences of regarding as a test of an adequate moral theory that perfect obedience to its laws and maximal devotion to its interests be something we can wholeheartedly strive for in ourselves and wish for in those around us. Drawing out the consequences somewhat further should, I think, make us more doubtful of the proposed test than of the theories which, on this test, would fail. Given the empirical circumstances of our world, it seems to be an ethical fact that we have unlimited potential to be morally good, and endless opportunity to promote moral interests. But this is not incompatible with the not-so-ethical fact that we have sound, compelling, and not particularly selfish reasons to choose not to devote ourselves univocally to realizing this potential or to taking up this opportunity.

Thus, in one sense at least, I am not really criticizing either Kantianism or utilitarianism. Insofar as the point of view I am offering bears directly on recent work in moral philosophy, in fact, it bears on critics of these theories who, in a spirit not unlike the spirit of most of this paper, point out that the perfect utilitarian would be flawed in this way or the perfect Kantian flawed in that.[3] The assumption lying behind these claims, implicitly or explicitly, has been that the recognition of these flaws shows us something wrong with utilitarianism as opposed to Kantianism, or something wrong with Kantianism as opposed to utilitarianism, or something wrong with both of these theories as opposed to some nameless third alternative. The claims of this paper suggest, however, that this assumption is unwarranted. The flaws of a perfect master of a moral theory need not reflect flaws in the intramoral content of the theory itself.

Moral Saints and Moral Philosophy

In pointing out the regrettable features and the necessary absence of some desirable features in a moral saint, I have not meant to condemn the moral saint or the person who aspires to become one. Rather, I have meant to insist that the ideal of moral sainthood should not be held as a standard against which any other ideal must be judged or justified, and that the posture we take in response to the recognition that our lives are not as morally good as they might be need not be defensive.[4] It is misleading to insist that one is *permitted* to live a life in which the goals, relationships, activities, and interests that one pursues are not maximally morally good. For our lives are not so comprehensively subject to the requirement that we apply for permission, and our nonmoral reasons for the goals we set ourselves are not excuses, but may rather be positive, good reasons which do not exist *despite* any reasons that might threaten to outweigh them. In other words, a person may be *perfectly wonderful* without being *perfectly moral*.

Recognizing this requires a perspective which contemporary moral philosophy has generally ignored. This perspective yields judgments of a type that is neither moral nor egoistic. Like moral judgments, judgments about what it would be good for a person to be are made from a point of view outside the limits set by the values, interests, and desires that the person might actually have. And, like moral judgments, these judgments claim for themselves a kind of objectivity or a grounding in a perspective which any rational and perceptive being can take up. Unlike moral judgments, however, the good with which these judgments are concerned is not the good of anyone or any group other than the individual himself.

Nonetheless, it would be equally misleading to say that these judgments are made for the sake of the individual himself. For these judgments are not concerned with what kind of life it is in a person's interest to lead, but with what kind of interests it would be good for a person to have, and it need not be in a person's interest that he acquire or maintain objectively good interests. Indeed, the model of the Loving Saint, whose interests are identified with the interests of morality, is a model of a person for whom the dictates of rational self-interest and the dictates of morality coincide. Yet, I have urged that we have reason not to aspire to this ideal and that some of us would have reason to be sorry if our children aspired to and achieved it.

The moral point of view, we might say, is the point of view one takes up insofar as one takes the recognition of the fact that one is just one person among others equally real and deserving of the good things in life as a fact with practical consequences, a fact the recognition of which demands expression in one's actions and in the form of one's practical deliberations. Competing moral theories offer alternative answers to the question of what the most correct or the best way to express this fact is. In doing so, they offer alternative ways to evaluate and to compare the variety of actions, states of affairs, and so on that appear good and bad to agents from other, nonmoral points of view. But it seems that alternative interpretations of the moral point of view do not exhaust the ways in which our actions, characters, and their consequences can be comprehensively and objectively evaluated. Let us call the point of view from which we consider what kinds of lives are good lives, and what kinds of persons it would be good for ourselves and others to be, the *point of view of individual perfection*.

Since either point of view provides a way of comprehensively evaluating a person's life, each point of view takes account of, and, in a sense, subsumes the other. From the moral point of view, the perfection of an individual life will have some, but limited, value—for each individual remains, after all, just one person among others. From the perfectionist point of view, the moral worth of an individual's relation to his world will likewise have some, but limited, value—for, as I have argued, the (perfectionist) goodness of an individual's life does not vary proportionally with the degree to which it exemplifies moral goodness.

It may not be the case that the perfectionist point of view is like the moral point of view in being a point of view we are ever *obliged* to take up and express in our actions. Nonetheless, it provides us with reasons that are independent of moral reasons for wanting ourselves and others to develop our characters and live our lives in certain ways. When we take up this point of view and ask how much it would be good for an individual to act from the moral point of view, we do not find an obvious answer.[5]

The considerations of this paper suggest, at any rate, that the answer is not "as much as possible." This has implications both for the continued development of moral theories and for the development of metamoral views and for our conception of moral philosophy more generally. From the moral point of view, we have reasons to want people to live lives that seem good from outside that point of view. If, as I have argued, this means that we have reason to want people to live lives that are not morally perfect, then any plausible moral theory must make use of some conception of supererogation.[6]

If moral philosophers are to address themselves at the most basic level to the question of how people should live, however, they must do more than adjust the content of their moral theories in ways that leave room for the affirmation of nonmoral values. They must examine explicitly the range and nature of these nonmoral values, and, in light of this examination, they must ask how the acceptance of a moral theory is to be understood and acted upon. For the claims of this paper do not so much conflict with the content of any particular currently popular moral theory as they call into question a metamoral assumption that implicitly surrounds discussions of moral theory more generally. Specifically, they call into question the assumption that it is always better to be morally better.

The role morality plays in the development of our characters and the shape of our practical deliberations need be neither that of a universal medium into which all other values must be translated nor that of an ever-present filter through which all other values must pass. This is not to say that moral value should not be an important, even the most important, kind of value we attend to in evaluating and improving ourselves and our world. It is to say that our values cannot be fully comprehended on the model of a hierarchical system with morality at the top.

The philosophical temperament will naturally incline, at this point, toward asking, "What, then, *is* at the top—or, if there is no top, how *are* we to decide when and how much to be moral?" In other words, there is a temptation to seek a metamoral—though not, in the standard sense, metaethical—theory that will give us principles, or, at least, informal directives on the basis of which we can develop and evaluate more comprehensive personal ideals. Perhaps a theory that distinguishes among the various roles a person is expected to play within a life—as professional, as citizen, as friend, and so on—might give us some rules that would offer us, if nothing else, a better framework in which to think about and discuss these questions. I am pessimistic, however, about the chances of such a theory to yield substantial and satisfying results. For I do not see how a metamoral theory could be constructed which would not be subject to considerations parallel to those which seem inherently to limit the appropriateness of regarding moral theories as ultimate comprehensive guides for action.

This suggests that, at some point, both in our philosophizing and in our lives, we must be willing to raise normative questions from a perspective that is unattached to a commitment to any particular well-ordered system of values. It must be admitted that, in doing so, we run the risk of finding normative answers that diverge from the answers given by whatever moral theory one accepts. This, I take it, is the grain of truth in G. E. Moore's "open question" argument. In the background of this paper, then, there lurks a commitment to what seems to me to be a healthy form of intuitionism. It is a form of intuitionism which is not intended to take the place of more rigorous, systematically developed, moral theories—rather, it is intended to put these more rigorous and systematic moral theories in their place.[7]

Notes

1. "Persons, Character and Morality" in Amelie Rorty, ed., *The Identities of Persons* (Berkeley: University of California Press, 1976), 214.

2. Immanuel Kant, *The Doctrine of Virtue*, trans. Mary J. Gregor (New York: Harper and Row, 1964), 71.

3. See, e.g., Williams, "Persons, Character," and J.J.C. Smart and Bernard Williams, *Utilitarianism: For and Against* (New York: Cambridge, 1973). Also, Michael Stocker, "The Schizophrenia of Modern Ethical Theories," *Journal of Philosophy* 63, 14 (August 12, 1976): 453–66. See reprint of Stocker's article in this volume, pp. 36–45.

4. George Orwell makes a similar point in "Reflections on Gandhi," in *A Collection of Essays by George Orwell* (New York: Harcourt Brace Jovanovich, 1945), 176: "sainthood is . . . a thing that human beings must avoid. . . . It is too readily assumed that . . . the ordinary man only rejects it because it is too difficult; in other words, that the average human being is a failed saint. It is doubtful whether this is true. Many people genuinely do not wish to be saints, and it is probable that some who achieve or aspire to sainthood have never felt much temptation to be human beings."

5. A similar view, which has strongly influenced mine, is expressed by Thomas Nagel in "The Fragmentation of Value," in *Mortal Questions* (New York: Cambridge, 1979), 128–41. Nagel focuses on the difficulties such apparently incommensurable points of view create for specific, isolable practical decisions that must be made both by individuals and by societies. In focusing on the way in which these points of view figure into the development of individual personal ideals, the questions with which I am concerned are more likely to lurk in the background of any individual's life.

6. The variety of forms that a conception of supererogation might take, however, has not generally been noticed. Moral theories that make use of this notion typically do so by identifying some specific set of principles as universal moral requirements and supplement this list with a further set of directives which it is morally praiseworthy but not required for an agent to follow. [See, e.g., Charles Fried, *Right and Wrong* (Cambridge, Mass.: Harvard, 1979).] But it is possible that the ability to live a morally blameless life cannot be so easily or definitely secured as this type of theory would suggest. The fact that there are some situations in which an agent is morally required to do something and other situations in which it would be good but not required for an agent to do something does not imply that there are specific principles such that, in any situation, an agent is required to act in accordance with these principles and other specific principles such that, in any situation, it would be good but not required for an agent to act in accordance with those principles.

7. I have benefited from the comments of many people who have heard or read an earlier draft of this paper. I wish particularly to thank Douglas MacLean, Robert Nozick, Martha Nussbaum, and the Society for Ethics and Legal Philosophy.

Reading Introduction

Saints
Robert M. Adams

Adams undertakes to defend sainthood (though not quite "moral sainthood") against Wolf's attack. There are in fact saints, such as St. Francis of Assisi, Gandhi, and Jesus, and they do not fit Wolf's description. They are not dull, uncreative, unattractive, grim, and lacking in individuality, but are typically the very opposite of these. Wolf's saint is grim (and, one suspects, desperate), because he or she is devoted to an endless, hopeless, and literally exhausting task, the improvement of an exceedingly defective world. The saint is but a tiny power in the face of this overwhelming assignment. But the real saints are not typically grim, because they typically believe that the task is not directly in their hands; *their* task is not to be devoted to the improvement of the world, but to be devoted to *God*, "who's got the whole world in His hands." So real saints do not bear the weight of the world on their shoulders, and this explains the lightheartedness that many of them exemplify. But since God is interested in more things than just morality, it also seems possible that a person maximally devoted to Him (that is, a saint) might "specialize" in some nonmoral endeavor such as painting, music, or philosophy, as long as the products of this endeavor were consistent with God's character.

Adams ends by agreeing with Wolf that something would be missing in "a moral theory that does not contain the seeds of an all-consuming ideal of moral sainthood," but points out that morality as Wolf conceives it (that is, outside the context of devotion to God) is not a suitable object of maximal devotion. So perhaps the likelihood of possessing the moral virtues to a superlative degree is enhanced by religious belief.

Saints

ROBERT M. ADAMS

One of the merits of Susan Wolf's fascinating and disturbing essay on "Moral Saints"[1] is that it brings out very sharply a fundamental problem in modern moral philosophy. On the one hand, we want to say that morality is of supreme value, always taking precedence over other grounds of choice, and that what is normally best must be absolutely best. On the other hand, if we consider what it would be like really to live in accordance with that complete priority of the moral, the ideal of life that emerges is apt to seem dismally grey and unattractive, as Wolf persuasively argues. I want to present a diagnosis of the problem

Journal of Philosophy 81, 7 (July 1984): 392–401. Reprinted by permission of the author and the publisher.

that differs from Wolf's. Replies to Wolf might be offered on behalf of the utilitarian and Kantian moral theories that she discusses, but of them I shall have little to say. My concern here is to see that sainthood, not Kant or utilitarianism, receives its due.

What Are Saints Like?

The first thing to be said is that there *are* saints—people like St. Francis of Assisi and Gandhi and Mother Teresa—and they are quite different from what Wolf thinks a moral saint would be. In the end I will conclude that they are not exactly *moral* saints in Wolf's sense. But she writes about some of them as if they were, and discussions of moral sainthood surely owe to the real saints much of their grip on our attention. So it will be to the point to contrast the actuality of sainthood with Wolf's picture of the moral saint.

Wolf argues that moral saints will be "unattractive" (426, 142) because they will be lacking in individuality and in the "ability to enjoy the enjoyable in life" (424, 141), and will be so "very, very nice" and inoffensive that they "will have to be dull-witted or humorless or bland" (422, 140). But the real saints are not like that. It is easier to think of St. Francis as eccentric than as lacking in individuality. And saints are not bland. Many have been offended at them for being very, very truthful instead of very, very nice. (Think of Gandhi—or Jesus.) Saints may not enjoy all the same things as other people, and perhaps a few of them have been melancholy; but an exceptional capacity for joy is more characteristic of them. (For all his asceticism, one thinks again of St. Francis.) There are joys (and not minor ones) that only saints can know. And as for attractiveness, the people we think of first as saints were plainly people who were intensely interesting to almost everyone who had anything to do with them, and immensely attractive to at least a large proportion of those people. They have sometimes been controversial, but rarely dull; and their charisma has inspired many to leave everything else in order to follow them.

Wolf may have set herself up, to some extent, for such contrasts, by conceiving of moral sainthood purely in terms of commitment or devotion to moral ends or principles. There are other, less voluntary virtues that are essential equipment for a saint—humility, for instance, and perceptiveness, courage, and a mind unswayed by the voices of the crowd. The last of these is part of what keeps saints from being bland or lacking in individuality.

In order to understand how Wolf arrives at her unflattering picture of the moral saint, however, we must examine her stated conception of moral sainthood.

Wolf's Argument

Wolf states three criteria for moral sainthood; and they are not equivalent. (1) In her third sentence she says, "By *moral saint* I mean a person whose every action is as morally good as possible." (2) Immediately she adds: "a person, that is, who is as morally worthy as can be" (419, 137). Her words imply that these two characterizations amount to the same thing, but it seems to me that the first expresses at most a very questionable test for the satisfaction of the second. The idea that only a morally imperfect person would spend half an hour doing something morally indifferent, like taking a nap, when she could have done something morally praiseworthy instead, like spending the time in moral self-examination, is at odds with our usual judgments and ought not to be assumed at the outset. The assumption that the perfection of a person, in at least the moral type of value, depends on the maximization of that type of value in every single action of the person lies behind much that is unattractive in Wolf's picture of moral sainthood; but I believe it is a fundamental error.

(3) On the next page we get a third criterion: "A necessary condition of moral sainthood would be that one's life be dominated by a commitment to improving the welfare of others or of society as a whole" (420, 138). Here again, while it might be claimed that this is a necessary condition of a person's, or her acts', being as morally worthy as possible, the claim is controversial. It has been held as a moral thesis that the pursuit of our own perfection ought sometimes to take precedence for us over the welfare of others. The utilitarian, likewise, will presumably think that many people ought to devote their greatest efforts to their own happiness and perfection, because that is what will maximize utility. Given a utilitarian conception of moral rightness as doing what will maximize utility, why shouldn't a utilitarian say that such people, and their acts, can be as morally worthy as possible (and thus can satisfy Wolf's first two criteria of moral sainthood) when they pursue their own happiness and perfection? Presumably, therefore, Wolf is relying heavily on her third criterion, as an independent test, when she says that such cases imply "that the utilitarian would not support moral sainthood as a universal ideal" (427, 144).

This third criterion is obviously related to Wolf's conception of morality. Later in her paper she contrasts the moral point of view with "the point of view of individual perfection," which is "the point of view from which we consider what kinds of lives are good lives, and what kinds of persons it would be good for ourselves and others to be" (437, 150). "The moral point of view . . . is the point of view one takes up insofar as one takes the recognition of the fact that one is just one person among others equally real and deserving of the good things in life as a fact with practical consequences, a fact the recognition of which demands expression in one's actions and in the form of one's practical deliberations" (436, 150). And moral theories are theories that offer "answers to the question of what the most correct or the best way to express this fact is" (437, 150).

This account of moral theory and the moral point of view is in clear agreement with Wolf's third criterion of moral sainthood on one central issue: morality, for her, has exclusively to do with one's regard for the good (and perhaps she would add, the rights) of other persons. One's own dignity or courage or sexuality pose *moral* issues for Wolf only to the extent that they impinge on the interests of other people. Otherwise they can be evaluated from the point of view of individual perfection (and she obviously takes that evaluation very seriously) but not from the moral point of view. This limitation of the realm of the moral is controversial, but (without wishing to be committed to it in other contexts) I shall use 'moral' and 'morality' here in accordance with Wolf's conception.

It might still be doubted whether her third criterion of moral sainthood follows from her definition of the moral point of view. A utilitarian, for reasons indicated above, might argue that for many people a life not "dominated by a commitment to improving the welfare of others or of society as a whole" could perfectly express "recognition of the fact that one is just one person among others equally real and deserving of the good things of life." Dedication to the good of others is not the same as weighing their good equally with one's own. But if the former is not implied by the latter, it is the altruistic dedication that constitutes Wolf's operative criterion of moral excellence (though I suspect she looks to the equal weighing for a criterion of the morally obligatory). I do not wish to quibble about this; for what interests me most in Wolf's paper is what she says about moral devotion, and weighing one's own good equally with the good of others (demanding as that may be) is something less than devotion.

Thus Wolf's three criteria of moral sainthood seem to me to be separable. The second (maximal moral worthiness of the person, rather than the act) probably comes the closest to expressing an intuitive idea of moral sainthood in its most general form. But the other two seem to be her working criteria. I take all three to be incorporated as necessary conditions in Wolf's conception of moral sainthood.

The center of Wolf's argument can now be stated quite simply. It is that in a life perfectly "dominated by a commitment to improving the welfare of others or of society as a whole" there will not be room for other interests. In particular there will not be time or energy or attention for other good interests, such as the pursuit of aesthetic or athletic excellence. The moral saint will not be able to pursue these interests, or encourage them in others, unless "by happy accident" they have an unusual humanitarian payoff (425, 142). But from the point of view of individual perfection we have to say that some of the qualities that the moral saint is thus prevented from fostering in herself or others are very desirable, and there are commendable ideals in which they have a central place. So "if we think that it is *as* good, or even better for a person to strive for one of these ideals than it is for him or her to strive for and realize the ideal of the moral saint, we express a conviction that it is good not to be a moral saint" (426, 143).

Sainthood and Religion

While those actual saints whom I have mentioned have indeed been exceptionally devoted to improving the lives and circumstances of other people, it would be misleading to say that their lives have been "dominated by a commitment to improving the welfare of others or of society as a whole." For sainthood is an essentially religious phenomenon, and even so political a saint as Gandhi saw his powerful humanitarian concern in the context of a more comprehensive devotion to God. This touches the center of Wolf's argument, and helps to explain why actual saints are so unlike her picture of the moral saint. Wolf's moral saint sees limited resources for satisfying immense human needs and unlimited human desires, and devotes himself wholly to satisfying them as fully (and perhaps as fairly) as possible. This leaves him no time or energy for anything that does not *have* to be done. Not so the saints. The substance of sainthood is not sheer will power striving like Sisyphus (or like Wolf's Rational Saint) to accomplish a boundless task, but goodness overflowing from a boundless source. Or so, at least, the saints perceive it.

They commonly have time for things that do not *have* to be done, because their vision is not of needs that exceed any possible means of satisfying them, but of a divine goodness that is more than adequate to every need. They are not in general even trying to make their *every action* as good as possible, and thus they diverge from Wolf's first criterion of moral sainthood. The humility of the saint may even require that she spend considerable stretches of time doing nothing of any great importance or excellence. Saintliness is not perfectionism, though some saints have been perfectionistic in various ways. There is an unusual moral goodness in the saints, but we shall not grasp it by asking whether any of their actions could have been morally worthier. What makes us think of a Gandhi, for example, as a saint is something more positive, which I would express by saying that goodness was present in him in exceptional power.

Many saints have felt the tensions on which Wolf's argument turns. Albert Schweitzer, whom many have honored as a twentieth-century saint, was one who felt keenly the tension between artistic and intellectual achievement on the one hand and a higher claim of humanitarian commitment on the other. Yet in the midst of his humanitarian activities in Africa, he kept a piano and spent some time playing it—even before he realized that keeping up this skill would help him raise money for his mission. Very likely that time could have been employed in actions that would have been morally worthier, but that fact by itself surely has no tendency to disqualify Schweitzer from sainthood, in the sense in which people are actually counted as saints. We do not demand as a necessary condition of sainthood that the saint's every act be the morally worthiest possible in the circumstances, nor that he try to make it so.

The religious character of sainthood also helps to explain how the saint can be so self-giving without lacking (as Wolf suggests the Loving Saint must) an interest in his own condition as a determinant of his own happiness. In fact saints have typically been intensely and frankly interested in their own condition, their own perfection, and their own happiness. Without this interest they would hardly have been fitted to lead others for whom they desired perfection and happiness. What enables them to give of themselves unstintedly is not a lack of interest in their own persons, but a trust in God to provide for their growth and happiness.

Should Everyone Be a Saint?

Even if it can be shown that the life of a Gandhi or a St. Francis is happier and more attractive than Wolf claims that the life of a moral saint would be, we still face questions analogous to some of those she presses. Would it be good if everyone were a saint? Should we all aspire to be saints?

Not everybody *could* be a Gandhi. He himself thought otherwise. "Whatever is possible for me is possible even for a child," he wrote.[2] This is a point on which we may venture to disagree with him. A life like his involves, in religious terms, a vocation that is not given to everyone. Or to put the matter in more secular terms, not all who set themselves to do it will accomplish as much good by humanitarian endeavor as Wolf seems to assume that any utilitarian can (428, 144). But perhaps some of us assume too easily that we could not be a Gandhi. In all probability there could be more Gandhis than there are, and it would be a very good thing if there were.

Wolf, however, will want to press the question whether there are not human excellences that could not be realized by a Gandhi, or even by someone who seriously aspired to be one, and whether it would not be good for some people to aspire to these excellences instead of aspiring to sainthood. My answer to these questions is affirmative, except for the 'instead of aspiring to sainthood'. Given the limits of human time and energy, it is hard to see how a Gandhi or a Martin Luther King, Jr., could at the same time have been a great painter or a world-class violinist. Such saints may indeed attain and employ great mastery in the arts of speaking and writing. But there are demanding forms of excellence, in the arts and in science, for example, and also in philosophy, which probably are not compatible with their vocation (and even less compatible with the vocation of a St. Francis, for reasons of life-style rather than time and energy). And I agree that it is good that some people aspire to those excellences and attain them.

But if it is right to conclude that not everyone should aspire to be a Gandhi or a Martin Luther King or a St. Francis, it may still be too hasty to infer that not everyone should aspire to sainthood. Perhaps there are other ways of being a saint. That will depend, of course, on what is meant by 'saint'; so it is time to offer a definition.

If sainthood is an essentially religious phenomenon, as I claim, it is reasonable to seek its central feature (at least for theistic religions) in the saint's relation to God. 'Saint' means 'holy' – indeed they are the same word in most European languages. Saints are people in whom the holy or divine can be seen. In a religious view they are people who submit themselves, in faith, to God, not only loving Him but also letting His love possess them, so that it works through them and shines through them to other people. What interests a saint may have will then depend on what interests God has, for sainthood is a participation in God's interests. And God need not be conceived as what Wolf would call a "moral fanatic" (425, 142). He is not so limited that His moral concerns could leave Him without time or attention or energy for other interests. As the author of all things and of all human capacities, He may be regarded as interested in many forms of human excellence, for their own sake and not just for the sake of their connection with what would be classified as *moral* concerns in any narrow sense. This confirms the suggestion that Gandhi and Martin Luther King and St. Francis exemplify only certain types of sainthood, and that other types may be compatible with quite different human excellences – and in particular, with a great variety of demanding artistic and intellectual excellences. I do not see why a Fra Angelico or a Johann Sebastian Bach or a Thomas Aquinas could not have been a saint in this wider sense.

Now I suspect that Wolf will not be satisfied with the conclusion that a saint could be an Angelico or a Bach or an Aquinas. And I do not think that the sticking point here will be that the three figures mentioned all dealt with religious subjects. After all, much of Bach's and Aquinas's work is not explicitly religious, and it would be easy to make a case that a saint could have done most of Cézanne's work. The trouble, I rather expect Wolf to say, is that the forms of artistic and intellectual excellence typified by these figures are too sweet or too nice or too wholesome to be the only ones allowed us. There are darker triumphs of human creativity that we also admire; could a saint have produced them?

Not all of them. I admire the art of Edvard Munch, but I certainly grant that most of his work would not have been produced by a saint. I do not think that is a point against the aspiration to sainthood, however, nor even against a desire for universal sainthood. Who knows? Perhaps Munch would have painted even greater things of another sort if he had been a saint. But that is not the crucial point. Perhaps he would have given up painting and done something entirely different. The crucial point is that although I might aspire to Munch's artistic talent and skill, I certainly would not aspire to be a person who would use it to express what he did, nor would I wish that on anyone I cared about. In view not merely of the intensity of unhappiness, but also of the kind of unhappiness that comes to expression in Munch's art, it would be perverse to aspire to it, nobly as Munch expressed it. The lesson to be learned from such cases is that our ethical or religious view of life ought to allow for some ambivalence, and particularly for the appreciation of some things that we ought not to desire.

Van Gogh provides an interesting example of a different sort. There is much in his life to which one would not aspire, and his canvases sometimes express terror, even madness, rather than peace. Yet I would hesitate to say that a saint could not have painted them. The saints have not been strangers to terror, pain, and sadness; and if in Van Gogh's pictures we often see the finite broken by too close an approach of the transcendent, that is one of the ways in which the holy can show itself in human life. Certainly Van Gogh wanted to be a saint; and perhaps, in an unorthodox and sometimes despairing way, he was one.

Is Morality a Suitable Object of Maximal Devotion?

Wolf's arguments lead her to reject an important received opinion about the nature of morality and about what it means to accept a moral theory — the opinion, namely, that it is "a test of an adequate moral theory that perfect obedience to its laws and maximal devotion to its interests be something we can whole-heartedly strive for in ourselves and wish for in those around us" (435, 149). There are two parts to the received opinion, as it has to do with perfect obedience and with maximal devotion. I cannot see that Wolf's arguments call in question the desirability of perfect obedience to the laws of morality, unless those laws make all good deeds obligatory (as in a rigorous act utilitarianism). Wolf seems on the whole to prefer the view that even nonmoral ideals to which it would be good to aspire ought not to involve the infringement of moral *requirements*; and so she concludes that if (as she has argued) "we have reason to want people to live lives that are not morally perfect, then any plausible moral theory must make use of some conception of supererogation" (438, 151). What she clearly rejects in the received opinion, then, is the desirability of maximal devotion to the interests of morality.

In this I agree with her. We ought not to make a religion of morality. Without proposing, like Kierkegaard and Tillich, to define religion as maximal devotion, I would say that maximal devotion (like sainthood) is essentially religious, or at least that it has its proper place only in religion. Wolf is going too far when she says that "morality itself does not seem to be a suitable object of passion" (424, 141). But maximal devotion is much more than passion. And morality, as Wolf conceives of it, is too narrow to be a suitable object of maximal or religious devotion. Her reason (and one good reason) for thinking this is that a demand for universal maximal devotion to morality excludes too many human excellences.

Religion is richer than morality, because its divine object is so rich. He is not too narrow to be a suitable object of maximal devotion. Since He is lover of beauty, for instance, as well as commander of morals, maximal submission of one's life to Him may in some cases (as I have argued) encompass an intense pursuit of artistic excellence in a way that maximal devotion to the interests of morality, narrowly understood, cannot. Many saints and other religious people, to be sure, have been quite hostile to some of the forms of human endeavor and achievement that I agree with Wolf in prizing. What I have argued is that the breadth of the Creator's interests makes possible a conception of sainthood that does not require this hostility.

There is for many (and not the least admirable) among us a strong temptation to make morality into a substitute for religion, and in so doing to make morality the object of a devotion that is maximal, at least in aspiration, and virtually religious in character. Such a devotion to morality, conceived as narrowly as Wolf conceives of it, would be, from a religious point of view, idolatry. The conclusion to which Wolf's arguments tend is that it would also be, from what she calls "the point of view of individual perfection," oppressive.

On the other hand, the loss of the possibility of sainthood, and of maximal devotion, would be a great loss. Wolf says, "A moral theory that does not contain the seeds of an all-consuming ideal of moral sainthood . . . seems to place false and unnatural limits on our opportunity to do moral good and our potential to deserve moral praise" (433, 147). This seems right, but I do not think it is just our indefinite (not infinite) opportunities and capacities that generate the all-consuming ideal. There are other departments of human life (such as memorization) in which our potential to deserve praise is indefinite but in which it would be bizarre to adopt an all-consuming ideal. The fact is that many of the concepts that we use in morality were developed in a religious tradition; and to tear them loose entirely from a context in which something (distinct perhaps from morality but including it) claims maximal devotion seems to threaten something that is important for the seriousness of morality.

It may not, in other words, be so easy to have a satisfactory conception of morality without religion—that is, without belief in an appropriate object of maximal devotion, an object that is larger than morality but embraces it.[3]

Notes

1. Originally published in *The Journal of Philosophy* 79, 8 (August 1982): 419–439. Numbers in parentheses in the text refer first to pages of Wolf's essay in *The Journal of Philosophy* and then to pages in the reprint in this anthology.

2. M. K. Gandhi, *Gandhi's Autobiography: The Story of My Experiments with Truth*, trans. Mahadev Desai (Washington, D.C.: Public Affairs Press, 1948), 7.

3. I wish to thank the Center of Theological Inquiry for fellowship support during the writing of this paper, and Marilyn McCord Adams, for helpful comments on an earlier version.

❖

Part Three

Some Vices and Virtues

This section contains a very small sampling of the descriptive and analytic work that philosophers are beginning to do on individual virtues and vices. For an ethics of the virtues, it is not enough to delineate the deficiencies of "modern moral philosophy," nor even to sketch the more or less abstract contours of moral psychology. Work on individual virtues and vices and their interrelations is very important to a philosophical ethics of virtue because it begins to sketch in the details of a full portrait. The ethical life has as many facets as there are virtues, and as many false directions as there are vices. (The vices are as important to the picture as the virtues, since they are the negative mirror-image of the virtues, and often reveal features of the virtues that would otherwise not come to light.) It is indeed a rich tapestry, and the challenge of bringing it to clear expression, of filling in its lines and colors, is demanding, requiring the combination of conceptual rigor, psychological insight, and ethical good sense suggested by the word *wisdom*. This challenge has only begun to be addressed, but the essays of the present section are an indication of that beginning.

Reading Introduction

Faces of Envy
Leslie H. Farber

The emotion envy, says Farber, is an unhappy, alienating, and strongly self-deceptive response to seeing that some other person is superior. When you are envious, instead of forthrightly imitating or competing, you engage in passively defensive cognitive behavior designed to put down the superior person and/or to set yourself on center stage. Since envy implies inferiority, passivity, and self-deception, it is a singularly undesirable state of mind. Most people who are envious are not very aware of being so, finding various ways to disguise their envy—for example, as false admiration or false greed.

By contrast with envy, the happy, forthright, and nonalienating way to respond to another person's virtues or other superiority is *admiration*. Farber claims that virtues such as wisdom, humility, and courage can only be admired, not sought. When we enviously fail to admire a courageous or wise person, since it makes no sense to *seek* these virtues, we must turn them into something else, which we *can* seek. And so we lie, telling ourselves that we are just greedy, and really desire something the envied person *possesses*, such as wealth or sex or psychoanalysis. But plain greed has no basis in a negative self-evaluation and thus differs from envy.

Envy is also confused with jealousy. Both the jealous and the envious individual posit a *rival*. But in jealousy the issue of the rivalry is not that of superiority or inferiority, but the loss or retention of a love-object. Thus jealousy is a better subject for drama than envy because the love-object can be lost or retained. By contrast, envy relates entirely to the envier's *view* of the rival. This means also that the envier must *know* (or at least think he or she knows) the rival, whereas the jealous person's rival may be anonymous.

Farber ends with reflections about envy and childhood. Since envy both alienates the child from other persons and discourages frank competition, it fosters inferiority and thus sets the stage for further envy. Parents envious of their child will do two things tending to teach envy: (1) to "put the child down," thus wounding his or her self-esteem, and (2) to model for the child the compensatory cognitive behavior characteristic of envy. Freudian analysis of the childhood origins of envy is likely to provide the envious person with ways to avoid honestly confronting his or her envy.

Faces of Envy

LESLIE H. FARBER

Unlike most words having to do with the human condition, the definitions of envy I have seen are remarkably similar. Unlike other moral terms in the West, whose meanings shift with the temper of the times, the etymology of envy has stayed unusually constant. Envy had the same meaning for Plato that it had for Sullivan. When Horace wrote in the first century that "Sicilian tyrants never invented a greater torment than envy," he was concerned with the sheer and ubiquitous "pain of mind," expressed by Onasander, that caused Richard Sheridan to observe, in the eighteenth century, that "there is not a passion so strongly rooted in the human heart as envy." Dante devised for envy, which he counted as one of the seven deadly sins, a torment chillingly apt: in his Inferno the eyelids of the envious were sewn together. Such punishment would have suited Onasander, who wrote in A.D. 49 that "envy is a pain of mind that successful men cause their neighbors." More recently, it might have seemed equally fitting to Max Beerbohm, when he suggested that "the dullard's envy of brilliant men is always assuaged by the suspicion that they will come to a bad end."

The usual definition of envy, stressing its subjective nature, is "chagrin or discontent at the excellence or good fortune of another."[1] Since such feelings are rarely suffered in silence, some definitions include an objective expression of ill-will, such as disparagement of the envied one (although disparagement is only one of the manifest paths envy may take). For more than two thousand years, this is the meaning envy has borne. My scholarship has perhaps been too casual, but I find it very odd that it is so difficult to discover a systematic treatment for so common and so painful a human experience as envy, whether one looks in the theological, philosophical, or psychological literature. References are scanty and fleeting, and often epigrammatic, suggesting that envy's origins in human history and its manifestations in human sensibility and conduct are not easily discoverable. My guess is that envy, by its very nature, is obstinate in its opposition to investigation.

The protean character of envy and its talent for disguise account, I believe, for the infrequency of studies on the subject. Because of the variety of forms it may take, it is often simply impossible to recognize. This is true, not only for the observer, who by definition must be more gullible about such a subjective state as envy, but also for the envious one himself, whose rational powers may lend almost unholy assistance to the need for self-deception. Therefore, anecdotal examples of envy are usually crude. For instance, I remember with some clarity the first time I heard Harry Stack Sullivan lecture. His subject matter escapes me now as it escaped me then, but how well I recall him fussing with the recording apparatus. As I later explained to a friend, I was appalled that such a respected figure in our profession could so nakedly address himself to posterity. Wanting, of course, to give my friend a wholly objective picture of the occasion, I went on to depict Sullivan's affectations of manner and phraseology, always careful to preface each objective statement with some generous remark such as: "Don't think me envious, because I know this man to be a genius in the field of psychiatry. So it is doubly unfortunate," and so on. The example is as crude as my envy was strong. Inasmuch as envy rendered me impervious to the content of his lecture, the object of my disparagement, it will be noted, was his personal style. What I clearly observed in that style was his egotism, his infatuation with self, his dramatic need to impress that self on both posterity and on his more immediate audience. In brief, I detested his self-assertion, which is not an uncommon focus when envy takes the form of disparagement. But what of my own self-assertion? Certainly, to my friend, I dissembled the degree to which I was at a loss at this particular lecture and concealed the misery and stupidity fostered by my envy, which prevented me from giving him any idea of what Sullivan had said. Instead I asserted myself brashly and authoritatively, if unhappily, representing a confidence in my own abilities that was, at that moment, as necessary as it was undeserved.

Two authors have thought self-assertion to be so crucial in envy that they might have punished the envious in the Inferno by sewing together their lips, instead of their eyelids. Kierkegaard, contrasting envy and admiration, wrote that envy was unhappy self-assertion, while admiration was happy self-surrender. And Alfred Adler, speaking of aggressive children, wrote that "when the desire for self-assertion becomes extraordinarily intense, it will always involve an element of envy." On a prescriptive basis, it would seem that self-assertion was the best way of diminishing another's importance, while at the same time redressing one's own limitations. But, in the more devious forms of envy, self-assertion may not be so apparent, even though it is implicit. Take an example of what could be called "self-assertion by proxy." Using an instance from his own day, Thomas Hobbes wrote that "the praise of ancient authors proceeds not from the reverence of the dead, but from . . . envy of the living." Or, to use our own idiom, we might say to a colleague, more envied than admired, "I thought your paper excellent. Incidentally, didn't you get your central idea from a letter Freud wrote to Ferenczi on his fiftieth birthday?" Seemingly, with such a disheartening compliment, we merely refer to Freud's priority and trust that our demeanor is properly self-effacing. On the other hand, if our colleague is one of those suspicious, thin-skinned fellows, he might very well think we were making a tiny claim for our own scholarship in psychoanalytic matters, while withholding any real praise for his own effort. Indeed, one of envy's favorite stratagems is the attempt to provoke envy in the envied one—in this case, either for Freud's priority and prestige, or for our encyclopedic acquaintance with the field, or for both. There is something about the insistent nature of envy's self-assertion that makes it almost impossible to down. And it is just as hard for the envier to admit his self-assertion as it is to admit envy itself.

Suppose, still envious, we had chosen to chasten our colleague in this manner: "I don't remember when I've been so moved, so impressed. You are simply marvelous on this subject. You have an absolute genius for throwing a new light on difficult questions." As an actor with many faces, envy may try to pass itself off as its exact opposite—namely, admiration. Yet, when envy is the motive, admiration loses its tie both to affection and to the occasion, becoming wholly subject to the will. Unlike true admiration, which, because it is free of conscious will, always has the option of silence, envy's imitation of admiration clamors for public acknowledgment; the more stinging his envy, the more ardently must the envious one dramatize himself as an admirer whose passion overshadows and shames the more reticent responses of others. However, since it is as futile to will admiration as it is to will affection, this attempt at praise, inevitably self-assertive, turns excessive, inappropriate, and even irrelevant. Whereas true admiration keeps its distance, respecting the discrepancy between the admirer and the admired one, envy's assault upon its object with a barrage of compliments serves not only its need to assert itself in the costume of admiration, but also the lust of the envier to possess the very quality that initially incited his envy.

To some extent, envy is always a divisive experience, alienating us not only from our fellows but also from our own rational powers. We tend to forget that praise, just as much as criticism, may become an *ad hominem* venture when envy divorces us from our subject matter. If envy can move us to disparage our colleague's life rather than his subject, so can it move us to exalt his life at the expense of his subject. We tend to assume, mistakenly, that praise of another's character is the highest compliment we can offer him, overlooking how conveniently we may employ such inevitably general and abstract expressions of approval in an effort to avoid making a direct and concrete response to what he has said, done, or produced, this being certainly the most relevant and satisfying praise for the subject himself. Undiscriminating praise may, in fact, have a harsher effect on the envied one than criticism: it may arouse his own envy toward the exalted image we impose on him and, in his awareness of the immense disparity between it and his own image of himself, remind him ever more sharply of his limitations.

The least differentiated, and perhaps most childish, form which envy may assume is that of greed. By ordinary greed I mean merely the craving to possess the world's goods, whether food, drink, flattery, sex, parents, money, or psychoanalysis. In its materialistic and undiscriminating fashion, greed will take little notice of the manner or distinction that permitted their owner to acquire these goods. Greed is not necessarily restricted to those objects I do not have: I can be just as greedy for those goods which I already have in abundance. On the other hand, if I envy you, I begrudge you some quality or qualities of being which I do not possess: your wisdom, your dignity, your courage, your humility. What characterizes such virtues is that, although I may perceive and admire—or envy— them in you, your possession of them lies outside your self-consciousness; they may become a matter of concern to you only insofar as you lack them, or when you, in turn, recognize them in others. Most accomplishments and some virtues do not have this paradoxical nature. Skill or tact or a capacity for honesty, for example, may be pursued directly; to acknowledge and enjoy possession of them does not contradict their nature. But, only the fool proclaims his wisdom, only the proud man, his humility, only the coward, his courage. Not only do these virtues make a liar of the man who claims them, they forever evade any effort to achieve them. I may seek knowledge; I may not seek to be wise. Sharing an essential freedom from self-concern (which also characterizes the capacity for admiration), such virtues are not accomplishments and cannot be learned. They must be deserved, but their possession is a matter of grace, and is given only to him who denies it. If I observe a skill of yours, or some virtue to which imitation *is* appropriate, admiration may move me to emulate you, to work for such skill, to practice that virtue myself. But, when I perceive in you a quality of being such as I have described, my admiration may not move in the direction of emulation: I cannot imitate or learn from you; the attainment of such qualities is as removed from will of the second realm[2] as their possession must be from self-knowledge. I may merely behold your virtue — and acknowledge my own inferiority. This is the most generous, and the most difficult, gesture admiration is called on to make. If my generosity fails, my response turns envious. Posing as greed, my envy will blink the virtues that aroused it and fasten instead on some material possession that has perhaps come to you by virtue of your distinction. Whether I now ridicule or covet this possession is not so important as the seeming advantage I gain by reducing my envy to greed and you to your possession. There is some irony in the circumstance that we have an entire advertising industry deliberately exploiting envy-qua-greed by asserting the proposition that a man is what he owns. The irony is compounded when we remember that we have a sociology of class dedicated to precisely the same proposition. So long as I believe that you are your possessions and that my motive is greed, I can avoid any acknowledgment of the essential inequality between us. However, unless I am especially talented at self-deception, this advantage will reveal itself as illusory; certainly, if I manage to acquire your goods and to satisfy what I imagine to be my greed, the poor comfort this affords me will hasten the exposure of my real motive.

Unlike greed and jealousy, with which it is often confused, envy arises from a person's apprehension of another's superiority, and his consequent critical evaluation of himself. Indeed, it is just this aspect of envy that inspires the envier's zeal and inventiveness in denying it. Greed affords little pleasure, jealousy only pain. Neither, however, requires one to acknowledge a deficiency of quality in himself. Greed admits one's lack of some material object whose acquisition depends not at all on his worthiness of it, but simply on his luck or will in attaining it. Jealousy acknowledges a threat (which may or may not be real) — the possible loss of some possession greatly valued, usually someone's love. Jealousy does not depend, however, on knowledge of the agent of the threat, but merely on knowledge, or suspicion, that a rival exists. If the rival is known, he may invoke envy as well as jealousy in the threatened person. When both emotions are present, they almost inevitably lose their separate identities in the abundance and commotion of feeling; indeed, they often connive at their confusion with one another, each gaining some advantage from concealment and sharing, as they do, fear, resentment, and blindness toward the rival, who ceases to be known in any personal, detached way, becoming merely his effect upon the jealous-envious sufferer. (This reduction of another person is both an aim and an effect of envy and jealousy alike.) However, despite their kinship, their similarities, their attraction for each other, their eagerness to dress up in one another's clothes, jealousy and envy are, in fact, different and separate, notwithstanding the reluctance of committed victims, as well as disinterested students, to concern themselves with a distinction. Jealousy is a monothematic, romantic drama involving three characters, one of whom — the jealous person — doubles variously as author, director, stage-manager, critic, and audience, according to the needs of each plot. Despite the anguished subjectivity of most of the dialogue, the issues of the conflict—loss and gain—are external to character and even to self-esteem (what causes humiliation and the fall of self-esteem in the jealous person is not the wound of his loss, but his jealousy itself), and the three starring figures are required to sacrifice a large measure of individuality to the ritual of their roles. Envy, by contrast, displays itself dramatically only in disguise, and involves two instead of three people, one of whom, by virtue of his self-assertion, is clearly the star; in fact, the scene does not require the actual presence of the other at all (although if played in his company he must be given a line or two for the sake of form). While the envied one cannot be anonymous, as the rival in jealousy can be, he rarely represents any external threat to the person who envies him, so that the central conflict in envy is internal and subjective to the envier. Envy is essentially static rather than dramatic; it has very little movement and no dramatic continuity of its own; and, it shapes its expression to conditions rather than to plot. Jealousy, on the other hand, insists on a relentless continuity; it eats conditions and spews out plot; obsessively, it gathers more and more of the world onto its stage, urging the drama onward toward its feared and assured doom.

Where jealousy has a real cause, and the loss is either imminent or actual, the jealous person is enraged, both at his beloved and at his rival, and craves, or is even greedy for, what has been, or is about to be, taken away. However, unless envy has already entered the picture on its own, the jealous loser is not envious, for he infers no superiority in the winner from the fact of his success. It has always been one of the more mysterious aspects of jealousy that not only is it independent of envy, but that, often, the less respect—or potential envy—the jealous one feels for his rival, the more he is tortured by his jealousy. This oddity may be traceable in part to the unpredictable nature of love, which, unlike other desirable things that we are told life has in store for the deserving, refuses to be earned, discriminates arbitrarily and according to a private standard, and always precedes rather than rewards worthiness. Although jealousy does not provoke envy, envy can easily stimulate jealousy in a susceptible host. And it sometimes happens that envy initially authors the three-cornered drama of jealousy when, out of his envious lust to dispossess and his envious spite to torment his tormenter, the self-appointed rival calculatedly performs the gestures that set the play in motion.

Because of its specific and acutely painful nature and its addiction to homemade theatricals, jealousy is more readily identifiable than its stealthier sister, envy, and has consequently received more attention from both experts and amateurs. It may, as a result, be better understood; it has undoubtedly achieved a more imposing reputation. When Sullivan says, "Jealousy is much more poignant and devastating than envy," I am inclined to agree, insofar as jealousy, which tends toward greater and greater concentration, sucking all things into itself, is thus experienced. Envy, which tends toward diffusion, hiding and effacing itself behind all things, escapes identification and confounds experience. I suspect that envy, because of its talent for disguise, may promote greater mischief, and I am convinced that the envious man is miserable, even though what he knowingly feels is not envy but perplexing pain.

For reasons of space and competence, I shall make only a few general remarks about the beginnings of envy in childhood. In one way or another, as I have tried to indicate, envy is a limp and unhappy response to another's superiority—a response that precludes, by its very nature, such vigorous activities as rivalry, imitation, or emulation. Essentially, it asks something for nothing: by demeaning the envied one and aggrandizing the envier, envy attempts to redress inequality without the risk of intervening effort or development. In this way, envy opposes change, enforces the status quo, and is inimical to learning. Being a painfully estranging experience, envy alienates the envier from the envied one and, in this way, is inimical to what might be called mutuality, or relation. In childhood, even more than in adult life, learning and relation are—ideally, at least—reciprocal movements; neither can flourish very long without the other. (While life begins for the infant almost wholly in relation, the intrusions of self-consciousness soon bring the other pole of this dualism into being.) Learning the most ordinary physical skills in childhood occurs only in the context of relation. On the other hand, relation between a child and his parents cannot long exist of itself: inevitably, it requires learning for its perpetuation.

Envy, in its inhibition of both relation and learning, invariably feeds on itself. Out of envy, the child may abandon the acquisition of a given skill that might repair the imbalance between him and the envied person—whether it be a parent or another child— resorting instead to some uncomfortable display of self-assertion. The more skills envy forces him to relinquish, the harsher grows the discrepancy between himself and others, providing him, of course, with greater opportunity for envy.

In addition to feeding on itself, envy breeds itself. To some extent, envy in the parents will provide the conditions for envy in the child. I do not mean by this that envy itself is a learned response, although to some degree a child may learn the policy of derogation where superiority is involved, and certainly may learn that even the capacity for admiration can provoke his parents' envy. But where envy is habitual to the parents, it is more than likely to direct itself sooner or later toward the child, and, strangely enough, to fasten on those qualities and capacities of his that the parents most admire. The child will probably at first find the invidious comparisons to which his parents' envy subjects him bewildering, arbitrary, and jolting to his own wavering experience of himself. In a house where envy is in the air, however, the child need but look, listen, and breathe to be instructed in consolation and counterattack. If he submits to such instruction he will respond in kind to the envy that is aimed at him, by imitating its self-assertive gestures; in embracing that which is inimical to relation, he conspires with his parents to substitute a style, dramatizing and posing as relation, for relation; in imitating that which is inimical to learning he learns to substitute a style, impersonating competence and authority, for learning. If he accepts the conditions offered him and agrees to be instructed by the example of his elders, thus will their envy breed his own. There is always, of course, the possibility that by finding, or imagining, other teachers, he will undertake to choose in a different direction.

Since childhood is a time of vast and manifold inequalities, the opportunities for envy or admiration are myriad. If the qualities of being, mentioned earlier, are beyond the perceptual reach of the child, certainly the privileges and possessions and appearances of adulthood are not. Given his intellectual limitations at this stage in life, his apprehension— whether admiring or envious—of superiority in the adults around him will be remarkably literal, concrete, and physical, reminding us of the manifestations of envy-qua-greed. Such states as penis-envy or breast-envy, which have occupied much of the psychoanalytic literature on this subject, are of this literal variety, mistaking possession of the physical attribute for the various prerogatives of adulthood. I suspect, also, that whatever its aggregation, whatever its disguise, envy, which by nature is nourished on self-consciousness, can take root in the mind only when considerable differentiation has been achieved, making its appearance in early childhood unlikely. It is my guess, however, that because of its dependence on self-awareness and its imperious claims on the will, envy's origins, although of interest, are less crucial than its manifestations and effects. In fact, the attempt to expose and explain present envy by means of propositions concerning its earliest forms may render a service, not to the patient who seeks relief from the oppression of his envy, but to the very envy itself. Such propositions offer the envier a double temptation. Rather than contend, painfully, with his present envious feelings, which would require acknowledgment of another's excellence and his own limitation, he may fall to scrutinizing the history of his envy, contenting his conscience with an "acknowledgment" of some ancient state of mind, possibly fictional and certainly irrelevant to his immediate discomfort. Second, in his absorption with historical origins, he may find it all too easy to locate a "first cause" for his envy somewhere outside himself; this established, a few simple operations of logic can lead him to a deterministic reconstruction of the whole development of envy in him, guaranteeing his escape from the responsibility with which possible freedom of choice, past and present, would burden him. It seems to me that the most pressing concern, for the patient or for ourselves, in regard to so damaging and disturbing an affliction as envy, is not so much to ponder when, or even why, it may originally come into being, as to discover it now where it is, to outwit its distractions and disguises, to measure its fear of being called by name.

Notes

1. *Webster's International Dictionary*, 2d ed., s.v. "envy."
2. [Editors' note: By "will of the second realm" Farber means conscious choosing. It is opposed to "will of the first realm," the self-direction of one's life by one's needs, hopes and emotions, which is not consciously experienced, but only inferred after it occurs. For example, a self-centered talker might promise herself (will of the second realm) not to dominate the conversation at the party tonight, but once there 'discover' that she's done it again (will of the first realm), because all she thinks about is herself. The virtue of sensitivity in conversation is not available to her will of the second realm. See Leslie H. Farber, "Introduction: The Two Realms of Will," *The Ways of the Will: Essays Toward a Psychology and Psychopathology of Will* (New York: Basic Books, 1966), 1–25.]

Reading Introduction

Servility and Self-Respect
Thomas E. Hill, Jr.

The vice of servility is an attitude of disrespect for oneself. A servile person views himself or herself as basically inferior and as not having the same rights as other people. The attitude may be based on such things as one's race, failures in life, or one's sex. Hill's question is, What makes servility a moral vice?

Servility cannot be condemned because it takes away from happiness, as utilitarians may argue. Servile people are often happy, and they can bring happiness to others. Nor is servility bad because the person deserves better treatment than he or she demands. It is not wrong to demand less than you deserve; besides, some servile people *don't* deserve any more than they demand. That servility is nevertheless wrong suggests that some rights are not based on *earning* them. There is a distinction "between saying that someone deserves respect for his merits and saying that he is owed respect as a person."

Servility is a moral defect, according to Hill, because the servile person fails to understand and acknowledge his or her own moral rights. Just as the "arrogant" person denies the rights of others, so the servile person denies his or her own. Thus a racial minority member may believe he has fewer rights than his oppressors; someone may think that by his failure as a parent he has forfeited his claim to decent treatment; a deferential wife may be ignorant of her right not to defer to her husband. These are cases in which someone does not *understand* his or her rights. If people do understand their rights, and have a strong reason for not claiming them, then not claiming the rights does not make them servile. But if they fail to claim them merely out of laziness, inertia, or mild fear, they exemplify the vice of servility.

But while a person would certainly be submoral not to respect somebody *else's* rights, isn't what the person does with his or her *own* rights the person's own business? What puts a person under a moral obligation to press his or her own rights? Hill says that to waive one's basic rights for no morally good reason, as the servile person does, is to *disrespect the moral law*. That law bears on everybody, and it includes some rights provisions that cannot be waived, at least not in the offhand way the servile person attempts to waive them. Morality requires each person to respect himself or herself, and servility is a violation of this requirement.

Servility and Self-Respect

THOMAS E. HILL, JR.

Several motives underlie this paper.[1] In the first place, I am curious to see if there is a legitimate source for the increasingly common feeling that servility can be as much a vice as arrogance. There seems to be something morally defective about the Uncle Tom and the submissive housewife; and yet, on the other hand, if the only interests they sacrifice are their own, it seems that we should have no right to complain. Secondly, I have some sympathy for the now unfashionable view that each person has duties to himself as well as to others. It does seem absurd to say that a person could literally violate his own rights or owe himself a debt of gratitude, but I suspect that the classic defenders of duties to oneself had something different in mind. If there are duties to oneself, it is natural to expect that a duty to avoid being servile would have a prominent place among them. Thirdly, I am interested in making sense of Kant's puzzling, but suggestive, remarks about respect for persons and respect for the moral law. On the usual reading, these remarks seem unduly moralistic; but, viewed in another way, they suggest an argument for a kind of self-respect which is incompatible with a servile attitude.

My procedure will not be to explicate Kant directly. Instead I shall try to isolate the defect of servility and sketch an argument to show why it is objectionable, noting only in passing how this relates to Kant and the controversy about duties to oneself. What I say about self-respect is far from the whole story. In particular, it is not concerned with esteem for one's special abilities and achievements or with the self-confidence which characterizes the especially autonomous person. Nor is my concern with the psychological antecedents and effects of self-respect. Nevertheless, my conclusions, if correct, should be of interest; for they imply that, given a common view of morality, there are nonutilitarian moral reasons for each person, regardless of his merits, to respect himself. To avoid servility to the extent that one can is not simply a right but a duty, not simply a duty to others but a duty to oneself.

I

Three examples may give a preliminary idea of what I mean by *servility*. Consider, first, an extremely deferential black, whom I shall call the *Uncle Tom*. He always steps aside for white men; he does not complain when less qualified whites take over his job; he gratefully accepts whatever benefits his all-white government and employers allot him, and he would not think of protesting its insufficiency. He displays the symbols of deference to whites, and of contempt towards blacks: he faces the former with bowed stance and a ready 'sir' and 'Ma'am'; he reserves his strongest obscenities for the latter. Imagine, too, that he is not

From *The Monist* 62 (January 1979): 87–104. Reprinted by permission of the publisher, The Hegeler Institute.

playing a game. He is not the shrewdly prudent calculator, who knows how to make the best of a bad lot and mocks his masters behind their backs. He accepts without question the idea that, as a black, he is owed less than whites. He may believe that blacks are mentally inferior and of less social utility, but that is not the crucial point. The attitude which he displays is that what he values, aspires for, and can demand is of less importance than what whites value, aspire for, and can demand. He is far from the picture book's carefree, happy servant, but he does not feel that he has a right to expect anything better.

Another pattern of servility is illustrated by a person I shall call the *Self-Deprecator*. Like the Uncle Tom, he is reluctant to make demands. He says nothing when others take unfair advantage of him. When asked for his preferences or opinions, he tends to shrink away as if what he said should make no difference. His problem, however, is not a sense of racial inferiority but rather an acute awareness of his own inadequacies and failures as an individual. These defects are not imaginary: he has in fact done poorly by his own standards and others'. But, unlike many of us in the same situation, he acts as if his failings warrant quite unrelated maltreatment even by strangers. His sense of shame and self-contempt make him content to be the instrument of others. He feels that nothing is owed him until he has earned it and that he has earned very little. He is not simply playing a masochist's game of winning sympathy by disparaging himself. On the contrary, he assesses his individual merits with painful accuracy.

A rather different case is that of the *Deferential Wife*. This is a woman who is utterly devoted to serving her husband. She buys the clothes *he* prefers, invites the guests *he* wants to entertain, and makes love whenever *he* is in the mood. She willingly moves to a new city in order for him to have a more attractive job, counting her own friendships and geographical preferences insignificant by comparison. She loves her husband, but her conduct is not simply an expression of love. She is happy, but she does not subordinate herself as a means to happiness. She does not simply defer to her husband in certain spheres as a trade-off for his deference in other spheres. On the contrary, she tends not to form her own interests, values, and ideals; and, when she does, she counts them as less important than her husband's. She readily responds to appeals from Women's Liberation that she agrees that women are mentally and physically equal, if not superior, to men. She just believes that the proper role for a woman is to serve her family. As a matter of fact, much of her happiness derives from her belief that she fulfills this role very well. No one is trampling on her rights, she says; for she is quite glad, and proud, to serve her husband as she does.

Each one of these cases reflects the attitude which I call servility.[2] It betrays the absence of a certain kind of self-respect. What I take this attitude to be, more specifically, will become clearer later on. It is important at the outset, however, not to confuse the three cases sketched above with other, superficially similar cases. In particular, the cases I have sketched are not simply cases in which someone refuses to press his rights, speaks disparagingly of himself, or devotes himself to another. A black, for example, is not necessarily servile because he does not demand a just wage; for, seeing that such a demand would result in his being fired, he might forbear for the sake of his children. A self-critical person is not necessarily servile by virtue of bemoaning his faults in public; for his behavior may be merely a complex way of satisfying his own inner needs quite independent of a willingness to accept abuse from others. A woman need not be servile whenever she works to make her husband happy and prosperous; for she might freely and knowingly choose to do so from love or from a desire to share the rewards of his success. If the effort did not require her to submit to humiliation or maltreatment, her choice would not mark her as servile. There may, of course, be grounds for objecting to the attitudes in these cases; but the defect is not servility of the sort I want to consider. It should also be noted that my cases of servility are not simply instances of deference to superior knowledge or judgment. To defer to an expert's judgment on matters of fact is not to be servile; to defer to his every wish and whim is. Similarly, the belief that one's talents and achievements are comparatively low does not, by itself, make one servile. It is no vice to acknowledge the truth, and one may in fact have achieved less, and have less ability, than others. To be servile is not simply to hold certain empirical beliefs but to have a certain attitude concerning one's rightful place in a moral community.

II

Are there grounds for regarding the attitudes of the Uncle Tom, the Self-Deprecator, and the Deferential Wife as morally objectionable? Are there moral arguments we could give them to show that they ought to have more self-respect? None of the more obvious replies is entirely satisfactory.

One might, in the first place, adduce utilitarian considerations. Typically the servile person will be less happy than he might be. Moreover, he may be less prone to make the best of his own socially useful abilities. He may become a nuisance to others by being overly dependent. He will, in any case, lose the special contentment that comes from standing up for one's rights. A submissive attitude encourages exploitation, and exploitation spreads misery in a variety of ways. These considerations provide a prima facie case against the attitudes of the Uncle Tom, the Deferential Wife, and the Self-Deprecator, but they are hardly conclusive. Other utilities tend to counterbalance the ones just mentioned. When people refuse to press their rights, there are usually others who profit. There are undeniable pleasures in associating with those who are devoted, understanding, and grateful for whatever we see fit to give them—as our fondness for dogs attests. Even the servile person may find his attitude a source of happiness, as the case of the Deferential Wife illustrates. There may be comfort and security in thinking that the hard choices must be made by others, that what I would say has little to do with what ought to be done. Self-condemnation may bring relief from the pangs of guilt even if it is not deliberately used for that purpose. On balance, then, utilitarian considerations may turn out to favor servility as much as they oppose it.

For those who share my moral intuitions, there is another sort of reason for not trying to rest a case against servility on utilitarian considerations. Certain utilities seem irrelevant to the issue. The utilitarian must weigh them along with others, but to do so seems morally inappropriate. Suppose, for example, that the submissive attitudes of the Uncle Tom and the Deferential Wife result in positive utilities for those who dominate and exploit them. Do we need to tabulate *these* utilities before conceding that servility is objectionable? The Uncle Tom, it seems, is making an error, a moral error, quite apart from consideration of how much others in fact profit from his attitude. The Deferential Wife may be quite happy; but if her happiness turns out to be contingent on her distorted view of her own rights and worth as a person, then it carries little moral weight against the contention that she ought to change that view. Suppose I could cause a woman to find her happiness in denying all her rights and serving my every wish. No doubt I could do so only by nonrational manipulative techniques, which I ought not to use. But is this the only objection? My efforts would be wrong, it seems, not only because of the techniques they require but also because the resultant attitude is itself objectionable. When a person's happiness stems from a morally objectionable attitude, it ought to be discounted. That a sadist gets pleasure from seeing others suffer should not count even as a partial justification for his attitude. That a servile person derives pleasure from denying her moral status, for similar reasons, cannot make her attitude acceptable. These brief intuitive remarks are not intended as a refutation of utilitarianism, with all its many varieties; but they do suggest that it is well to look elsewhere for adequate grounds for rejecting the attitudes of the Uncle Tom, the Self-Deprecator, and the Deferential Wife.

One might try to appeal to meritarian considerations. That is, one might argue that the servile person *deserves* more than he allows himself. This line of argument, however, is no more adequate than the utilitarian one. It may be wrong to deny others what they deserve, but it is not so obviously wrong to demand less for oneself than one deserves. In any case, the Self-Deprecator's problem is not that he underestimates his merits. By hypothesis, he assesses his merits quite accurately. We cannot reasonably tell him to have more respect for himself because he *deserves* more respect; he knows that he has not *earned* better treatment. His problem, in fact, is that he thinks of his moral status with regard to others as entirely dependent upon his merits. His interests and choices are important, he feels, only if he has earned the right to make demands; or if he had rights by birth, they were forfeited by his subsequent failures and misdeeds. My Self-Deprecator is no doubt an atypical person, but nevertheless he illustrates an important point. Normally when we find a self-contemptuous person, we can plausibly argue that he is not so bad as he thinks, that his self-contempt is an overreaction prompted more by inner needs than by objective assessment of his merits. Because this argument cannot work with the Self-Deprecator, his case draws attention to a distinction, applicable in other cases as well, between saying that someone deserves respect for his merits and saying that he is owed respect as a person. On meritarian grounds we can only say 'You deserve better than this', but the defect of the servile person is not merely failure to recognize his merits.

Other common arguments against the Uncle Tom, et al., may have some force but seem not to strike to the heart of the problem. For example, philosophers sometimes appeal to the value of human potentialities. As a human being, it is said, one at least has a capacity for rationality, morality, excellence, or autonomy, and this capacity is worthy of respect. Although such arguments have the merit of making respect independent of a person's actual deserts, they seem quite misplaced in some cases. There comes a time when we have sufficient evidence that a person is not ever going to *be* rational, moral, excellent, or autonomous even if he still has a capacity, in some sense, for being so. As a person approaches death with an atrocious record so far, the chances of his realizing his diminishing capacities become increasingly slim. To make these capacities the basis of his self-respect is to rest it on a shifting and unstable ground. We do, of course, respect persons for capacities which they are not exercising at the moment; for example, I might respect a person as a good philosopher even though he is just now blundering into gross confusion. In these cases, however, we respect the person for an active capacity, a ready disposition, which he has displayed on many occasions. On this analogy, a person should have respect for himself only when his capacities are developed and ready, needing only to be triggered by an appropriate occasion or the removal of some temporary obstacle. The Uncle Tom and the Deferential Wife, however, may in fact have quite limited capacities of this sort, and, since the Self-Deprecator is already overly concerned with his own inadequacies, drawing attention to his capacities seems a poor way to increase his self-respect. In any case, setting aside the Kantian nonempirical capacity for autonomy, the capacities of different persons vary widely; but what the servile person seems to overlook is something by virtue of which he is equal with every other person.

III

Why, then, is servility a moral defect? There is, I think, another sort of answer which is worth exploring. The first part of this answer must be an attempt to isolate the objectionable features of the servile person; later we can ask why these features are objectionable. As a step in this direction, let us examine again our three paradigm cases. The moral defect in each case, I suggest, is a failure to understand and acknowledge one's own moral rights. I assume, without argument here, that each person has moral rights.[3] Some of these rights may be basic human rights; that is, rights for which a person needs only to be human to qualify. Other rights will be derivative and contingent upon his special commitments, institutional affiliations, etc. Most rights will be prima facie ones; some may be absolute. Most can be waived under appropriate conditions; perhaps some cannot. Many rights can be forfeited; but some, presumably, cannot. The servile person does not, strictly speaking, violate his own rights. At least in our paradigm cases he fails to acknowledge fully his own moral status because he does not fully understand what his rights are, how they can be waived, and when they can be forfeited.

The defect of the Uncle Tom, for example, is that he displays an attitude that denies his moral equality with whites. He does not realize, or apprehend in an effective way, that he has as much right to a decent wage and a share of political power as any comparable white. His gratitude is misplaced; he accepts benefits which are his by right as if they were gifts. The Self-Deprecator is servile in a more complex way. He acts as if he has forfeited many important rights which in fact he has not. He does not understand, or fully realize in his own case, that certain rights to fair and decent treatment do not have to be earned. He sees his merits clearly enough, but he fails to see that what he can expect from others is not merely a function of his merits. The Deferential Wife *says* that she understands her rights vis-à-vis her husband, but what she fails to appreciate is that her consent to serve him is a valid waiver of her rights only under certain conditions. If her consent is coerced, say, by the lack of viable options for women in her society, then her consent is worth little. If socially fostered ignorance of her own talents and alternatives is responsible for her consent, then her consent should not count as a fully legitimate waiver of her right to equal consideration within the marriage. All the more, her consent to defer constantly to her husband is not a legitimate setting aside of her rights if it results from her mistaken belief that she has a moral duty to do so. (Recall: "The *proper* role for a woman is to serve her family.") If she believes that she has a *duty* to defer to her husband, then, whatever she may say, she cannot fully understand that she has a *right* not to defer to him. When she says that she freely gives up such a right, she is confused. Her confusion is rather like that of a person who has been persuaded by an unscrupulous lawyer that it is legally incumbent on him to refuse a jury trial but who nevertheless tells the judge that he understands that he has a right to a jury trial and freely waives it. He does not really understand what it is to have and freely give up the right if he thinks that it would be an offense for him to exercise it.

Insofar as servility results from moral ignorance or confusion, it need not be something for which a person is to blame. Even self-reproach may be inappropriate; for at the time a person is in ignorance he cannot feel guilty about his servility, and later he may conclude that his ignorance was unavoidable. In some cases, however, a person might reasonably believe that he should have known better. If, for example, the Deferential Wife's confusion about her rights resulted from a motivated resistance to drawing the implications of her own basic moral principles, then later she might find some ground for self-reproach. Whether blameworthy or not, servility could still be morally objectionable at least in the sense that it ought to be discouraged, that social conditions which nourish it should be reformed, and the like. Not all morally undesirable features of a person are ones for which he is responsible, but that does not mean that they are defects merely from an esthetic or prudential point of view.

In our paradigm cases, I have suggested, servility is a kind of deferential attitude towards others resulting from ignorance or misunderstanding of one's moral rights. A sufficient remedy, one might think, would be moral enlightenment. Suppose, however, that our servile persons come to know their rights but do not substantially alter their behavior. Are they not still servile in an objectionable way? One might even think that reproach is more appropriate now because they know what they are doing.

The problem, unfortunately, is not as simple as it may appear. Much depends on what they tolerate and why. Let us set aside cases in which a person merely refuses to *fight* for his rights, chooses not to exercise certain rights, or freely waives many rights which he might have insisted upon. Our problem concerns the previously servile person who continues to display the same marks of deference even after he fully knows his rights. Imagine, for example, that even after enlightenment our Uncle Tom persists in his old pattern of behavior, giving all the typical signs of believing that the injustices done to him are not really wrong. Suppose, too, that the newly enlightened Deferential Wife continues to defer to her husband, refusing to disturb the old way of life by introducing her new ideas. She acts as if she accepts the idea that she is merely doing her duty though actually she no longer believes it. Let us suppose, further, that the Uncle Tom and the Deferential Wife are not merely generous with their time and property; they also accept without protest, and even appear to sanction, treatment which is humiliating and degrading. That is, they do not simply consent to waive mutually acknowledged rights; they tolerate violations of their rights with apparent approval. They pretend to give their permission for subtle humiliations which they really believe no permission can make legitimate. Are such persons still servile despite their moral knowledge?

The answer, I think, should depend upon why the deferential role is played. If the motive is a morally commendable one, or a desire to avert dire consequences to oneself, or even an ambition to set an oppressor up for a later fall, then I would not count the role player as servile. The Uncle Tom, for instance, is not servile in my sense if he shuffles and bows to keep the Klan from killing his children, to save his own skin, or even to buy time while he plans the revolution. Similarly, the Deferential Wife is not servile if she tolerates an abusive husband because he is so ill that further strain would kill him, because protesting would deprive her of her only means of survival, or because she is collecting atrocity stories for her book against marriage. If there is fault in these situations, it seems inappropriate to call it *servility*. The story is quite different, however, if a person continues in his deferential role just from laziness, timidity, or a desire for some minor advantage. He shows too little concern for his moral status as a person, one is tempted to say, if he is willing to deny it for a small profit or simply because it requires some effort and courage to affirm it openly. A black who plays the Uncle Tom merely to gain an advantage over other blacks is harming them, of course; but he is also displaying disregard for his own moral position as an equal among human beings. Similarly, a woman throws away her rights too lightly if she continues to play the subservient role because she is used to it or is too timid to risk a change. A Self-Deprecator who readily accepts what he knows are violations of his rights may be indulging his peculiar need for punishment at the expense of denying something more valuable. In these cases, I suggest, we have a kind of servility independent of any ignorance or confusion about one's rights. The person who has it may or may not be blameworthy, depending on many factors; and the line between servile and nonservile role playing will often be hard to draw. Nevertheless, the objectionable feature is perhaps clear enough for present purposes: it is a willingness to disavow one's moral status, publicly and systematically, in the absence of any strong reason to do so.

My proposal, then, is that there are at least two types of servility: one resulting from misunderstanding of one's rights and the other from placing a comparatively low value on them. In either case, servility manifests the absence of a certain kind of self-respect. The respect which is missing is not respect for one's merits but respect for one's rights. The servile person displays this absence of respect not directly by acting contrary to his own rights but indirectly by acting as if his rights were nonexistent or insignificant. An arrogant person ignores the rights of others, thereby arrogating for himself a higher status than he is entitled to; a servile person denies his own rights, thereby assuming a lower position than he is entitled to. Whether rooted in ignorance or simply lack of concern for moral rights, the attitudes in both cases may be incompatible with a proper regard for morality. That this is so is obvious in the case of arrogance; but to see it in the case of servility requires some further argument.

IV

The objectionable feature of the servile person, as I have described him, is his tendency to disavow his own moral rights either because he misunderstands them or because he cares little for them. The question remains: why should anyone regard this as a moral defect?

After all, the rights which he denies are his own. He may be unfortunate, foolish, or even distasteful; but why *morally* deficient? One sort of answer, quite different from those reviewed earlier, is suggested by some of Kant's remarks. Kant held that servility is contrary to a perfect nonjuridical duty to oneself.[4] To say that the duty is perfect is roughly to say that it is stringent, never overridden by other considerations (e.g., beneficence). To say that the duty is nonjuridical is to say that a person cannot legitimately be coerced to comply. Although Kant did not develop an explicit argument for this view, an argument can easily be constructed from materials which reflect the spirit, if not the letter, of his moral theory. The argument which I have in mind is prompted by Kant's contention that respect for persons, strictly speaking, is respect for moral law.[5] If taken as a claim about all sorts of respect, this seems quite implausible. If it means that we respect persons only for their moral character, their capacity for moral conduct, or their status as "authors" of the moral law, then it seems unduly moralistic. My strategy is to construe the remark as saying that at least one sort of respect for persons is respect for the rights which the moral law accords them. If one respects the moral law, then one must respect one's own moral rights; and this amounts to having a kind of self-respect incompatible with servility.

The premises for the Kantian argument, which are all admittedly vague, can be sketched as follows:

First, let us assume, as Kant did, that all human beings have equal basic human rights. Specific rights vary with different conditions, but all must be justified from a point of view under which all are equal. Not all rights need to be earned, and some cannot be forfeited. Many rights can be waived but only under certain conditions of knowledge and freedom. These conditions are complex and difficult to state; but they include something like the condition that a person's consent releases others from obligation only if it is autonomously given, and consent resulting from underestimation of one's moral status is not autonomously given. Rights can be objects of knowledge, but also of ignorance, misunderstanding, deception, and the like.

Second, let us assume that my account of servility is correct; or, if one prefers, we can take it as a definition. That is, in brief, a servile person is one who tends to deny or disavow his own moral rights because he does not understand them or has little concern for the status they give him.

Third, we need one formal premise concerning moral duty, namely, that each person ought, as far as possible, to respect the moral law. In less Kantian language, the point is that everyone should approximate, to the extent that he can, the ideal of a person who fully adopts the moral point of view. Roughly, this means not only that each person ought to do what is morally required and refrain from what is morally wrong but also that each person should treat all the provisions of morality as valuable—worth preserving and prizing as well as obeying. One must, so to speak, take up the spirit of morality as well as meet the letter of its requirements. To keep one's promises, avoid hurting others, and the like, is not sufficient; one should also take an attitude of respect towards the principles, ideals, and goals of morality. A respectful attitude towards a system of rights and duties consists of more than a disposition to conform to its definite rules of behavior; it also involves holding the system in esteem, being unwilling to ridicule it, and being reluctant to give up one's place in it. The essentially Kantian idea here is that morality, as a system of equal fundamental rights and duties, is worthy of respect, and hence a completely moral person would respect it in word and manner as well as in deed. And what a completely moral person would do, in Kant's view, is our duty to do so far as we can.

The assumptions here are, of course, strong ones, and I make no attempt to justify them. They are, I suspect, widely held though rarely articulated. In any case, my present purpose is not to evaluate them but to see how, if granted, they constitute a case against servility. The objection to the servile person, given our premises, is that he does not satisfy the basic requirement to respect morality. A person who fully respected a system of moral rights would be disposed to learn his proper place in it, to affirm it proudly, and not to tolerate abuses of it lightly. This is just the sort of disposition that the servile person lacks. If he does not understand the system, he is in no position to respect it adequately. This lack of respect may be no fault of his own, but it is still a way in which he falls short of a moral ideal. If, on the other hand, the servile person knowingly disavows his moral rights by pretending to approve of violations of them, then, barring special explanations, he shows an indifference to whether the provisions of morality are honored and publicly acknowledged. This avoidable display of indifference, by our Kantian premises, is contrary to the duty to respect morality. The disrespect in this second case is somewhat like the disrespect a religious believer might show towards his religion if, to avoid embarrassment, he laughed congenially while nonbelievers were mocking the beliefs which he secretly held. In any case, the servile person, as such, does not express disrespect for the system of moral rights in the obvious way by violating the rights of others. His lack of respect is more subtly manifested by his acting before others as if he did not know or care about his position of equality under that system.

The central idea here may be illustrated by an analogy. Imagine a club, say, an old German dueling fraternity. By the rules of the club, each member has certain rights and responsibilities. These are the same for each member regardless of what titles he may hold outside the club. Each has, for example, a right to be heard at meetings, a right not to be shouted down by the others. Some rights cannot be forfeited: for example, each may vote regardless of whether he has paid his dues and satisfied other rules. Some rights cannot be waived: for example, the right to be defended when attacked by several members of the rival fraternity. The members show respect for each other by respecting the status which the rules confer on each member. Now one new member is careful always to allow the others to speak at meetings; but when they shout him down, he does nothing. He just shrugs as if to say, 'Who am I to complain?' When he fails to stand up in defense of a fellow member, he feels ashamed and refuses to vote. He does not deserve to vote, he says. As the only commoner among illustrious barons, he feels that it is his place to serve them and defer to their decisions. When attackers from the rival fraternity come at him with swords drawn, he tells his companions to run and save themselves. When they defend him, he expresses immense gratitude—as if they had done him a gratuitous favor. Now one might argue that our new member fails to show respect for the fraternity and its rules. He does not actually violate any of the rules by refusing to vote, asking others not to defend him, and deferring to the barons, but he symbolically disavows the equal status which the rules confer on him. If he ought to have respect for the fraternity, he ought to change his attitude. Our servile person, then, is like the new member of the dueling fraternity in having insufficient respect for a system of rules and ideals. The difference is that everyone ought to respect morality whereas there is no comparable moral requirement to respect the fraternity.

The conclusion here is, of course, a limited one. Self-sacrifice is not always a sign of servility. It is not a duty always to press one's rights. Whether a given act is evidence of servility will depend not only on the attitude of the agent but also on the specific nature of his moral rights, a matter not considered here. Moreover, the extent to which a person is responsible, or blameworthy, for his defect remains an open question. Nevertheless, the conclusion should not be minimized. In order to avoid servility, a person who gives up his rights must do so with a full appreciation for what they are. A woman, for example, may devote herself to her husband if she is uncoerced, knows what she is doing, and does not pretend that she has no decent alternative. A self-contemptuous person may decide not to press various unforfeited rights but only if he does not take the attitude that he is too rotten to deserve them. A black may demand less than is due to him provided he is prepared to acknowledge that no one has a right to expect this of him. Sacrifices of this sort, I suspect, are extremely rare. Most people, if they fully acknowledged their rights, would not autonomously refuse to press them.

An even stronger conclusion would emerge if we could assume that some basic rights cannot be waived. That is, if there are some rights that others are bound to respect regardless of what we say, then, barring special explanation, we would be obliged not only to acknowledge these rights but also to avoid any appearance of consenting to give them up. To act as if we could release others from their obligation to grant these rights, apart from special circumstances, would be to fail to respect morality. Rousseau held, for example, that at least a minimal right to liberty cannot be waived. A man who consents to be enslaved, giving up liberty without *quid pro quo*, thereby displays a conditioned slavish mentality that renders his consent worthless. Similarly, a Kantian might argue that a person cannot release others from the obligation to refrain from killing him: consent is no defense against the charge of murder. To accept principles of this sort is to hold that rights to life and liberty are, as Kant believed, rather like a trustee's rights to preserve something valuable entrusted to him: he has not only a right but a duty to preserve it.

Even if there are no specific rights which cannot be waived, there might be at least one formal right of this sort. This is the right to some minimum degree of respect from others. No matter how willing a person is to submit to humiliation by others, they ought to show him some respect as a person. By analogy with self-respect, as presented here, this respect owed by others would consist of a willingness to acknowledge fully, in word as well as action, the person's basically equal moral status as defined by his other rights. To the extent that a person gives even tacit consent to humiliations incompatible with this respect, he will be acting as if he waives a right which he cannot in fact give up. To do this, barring special explanations, would mark one as servile.

V

Kant held that the avoidance of servility is a duty to oneself rather than a duty to others. Recent philosophers, however, tend to discard the idea of a duty to oneself as a conceptual confusion. Although admittedly the analogy between a duty to oneself and a duty to others is not perfect, I suggest that something important is reflected in Kant's contention.

Let us consider briefly the function of saying that a duty is *to* someone. *First*, to say that a duty is *to* a given person sometimes merely indicates who is the object of that duty. That is, it tells us that the duty is concerned with how that person is to be treated, how his interests and wishes are to be taken into account, and the like. Here we might as well say that we have a duty *towards*, or *regarding* that person. Typically the person in question is the beneficiary of the fulfillment of the duty. For example, in this sense I have a duty to my children and even a duty to a distant stranger if I promised a third party that I would help that stranger. Clearly a duty to avoid servility would be a duty to oneself at least in this minimal sense, for it is a duty to avoid, so far as possible, the denial of one's own moral status. The duty is concerned with understanding and affirming one's rights, which are, at least as a rule, for one's own benefit.

Second, when we say that a duty is *to* a certain person, we often indicate thereby the person especially entitled to complain in case the duty is not fulfilled. For example, if I fail in my duty to my colleagues, then it is they who can most appropriately reproach me. Others may sometimes speak up on their behalf, but, for the most part, it is not the business of strangers to set me straight. Analogously, to say that the duty to avoid servility is a duty to oneself would indicate that, though sometimes a person may justifiably reproach himself for being servile, others are not generally in the appropriate position to complain. Outside encouragement is sometimes necessary, but, if any blame is called for, it is primarily self-recrimination and not the censure of others.

Third, mention of the person to whom a duty is owed often tells us something about the source of that duty. For example, to say that I have a duty to another person may indicate that the argument to show that I have such a duty turns upon a promise to that person, his authority over me, my having accepted special benefits from him, or, more generally, his rights. Accordingly, to say that the duty to avoid servility is a duty to oneself would at least imply that it is not entirely based upon promises to others, their authority, their beneficence, or an obligation to respect their rights. More positively, the assertion might serve to indicate that the source of the duty is one's own rights rather than the rights of others, etc. That is, one ought not to be servile because, in some broad sense, one ought to respect one's own rights as a person. There is, to be sure, an asymmetry: one has certain duties to others because one ought not to violate their rights, and one has a duty to oneself because one ought to affirm one's own rights. Nevertheless, to dismiss duties to oneself out of hand is to overlook significant similarities.

Some familiar objections to duties to oneself, moreover, seem irrelevant in the case of servility. For example, some place much stock in the idea that a person would have no duties if alone on a desert island. This can be doubted, but in any case is irrelevant here. The duty to avoid servility is a duty to take a certain stance towards others and hence would be inapplicable if one were isolated on a desert island. Again, some suggest that if there were duties to oneself then one could make promises to oneself or owe oneself a debt of gratitude. Their paradigms are familiar ones. Someone remarks, "I promised myself a vacation this year" or "I have been such a good boy I owe myself a treat." Concentration on these facetious cases tends to confuse the issue. In any case the duty to avoid servility, as presented here, does not presuppose promises to oneself or debts of gratitude to oneself. Other objections stem from the intuition that a person has no duty to promote his own happiness. A duty to oneself, it is sometimes assumed, must be a duty to promote one's own happiness. From a utilitarian point of view, in fact, this is what a duty to oneself would most likely be. The problems with such alleged duties, however, are irrelevant to the duty to avoid servility. This is a duty to understand and affirm one's rights, not to promote one's own welfare. While it is usually in the interest of a person to affirm his rights, our Kantian argument against servility was not based upon this premise. Finally, a more subtle line of objection turns on the idea that, given that rights and duties are correlative, a person who acted contrary to a duty to oneself would have to be violating his own rights, which seems absurd.[6] This objection raises issues too complex to examine here. One should note, however, that I have tried to give a sense to saying that servility is contrary to a duty to oneself without presupposing that the servile person violates his own rights. If acts contrary to duties to others are always violations of their rights, then duties to oneself are not parallel with duties to others to that extent. But this does not mean that it is empty or pointless to say that a duty is to oneself.

My argument against servility may prompt some to say that the duty is "to morality" rather than "to oneself." All this means, however, is that the duty is derived from a basic requirement to respect the provisions of morality; and in this sense every duty is a duty "to morality." My duties to my children are also derivative from a general requirement to respect moral principles, but they are still duties *to* them.

Kant suggests that duties to oneself are a precondition of duties to others. On our account of servility, there is at least one sense in which this is so. Insofar as the servile person is ignorant of his own rights, he is not in an adequate position to appreciate the rights of others. Misunderstanding the moral basis for his equal status with others, he is necessarily liable to underestimate the rights of those with whom he classifies himself. On the other hand, if he plays the servile role knowingly, then, barring special explanation, he displays a lack of concern to see the principles of morality acknowledged and respected and thus the absence of one motive which can move a moral person to respect the rights of others. In either case, the servile person's lack of self-respect necessarily puts him in a less than ideal position to respect others. Failure to fulfill one duty to oneself, then, renders a person liable to violate duties to others. This, however, is a consequence of our argument against servility, not a presupposition of it.

Notes

1. An earlier version of this paper was presented at the meetings of the American Philosophical Association, Pacific Division. A number of revisions have been made as a result of the helpful comments of others, especially Norman Dahl, Sharon Hill, Herbert Morris, and Mary Mothersill.

2. Each of the cases is intended to represent only one possible pattern of servility. I make no claims about how often these patterns are exemplified nor do I mean to imply that only these patterns could warrant the labels "Deferential Wife," "Uncle Tom," etc. All the more, I do not mean to imply any comparative judgments about the causes or relative magnitude of the problems of racial and sexual discrimination. One person, e.g., a self-contemptuous woman with a sense of racial inferiority, might exemplify features of several patterns at once; and, of course, a person might view her being a woman the way an Uncle Tom views his being black, etc.

3. As will become evident, I am also presupposing some form of cognitive or "naturalistic" interpretation of rights. If, to accommodate an emotivist or prescriptivist, we set aside talk of moral

knowledge and ignorance, we might construct a somewhat analogous case against servility from the point of view of those who adopt principles ascribing rights to all; but the argument, I suspect, would be more complex and less persuasive.

4. See Immanuel Kant, *The Doctrine of Virtue*, pt. 2 of *The Metaphysics of Morals*, ed. M. J. Gregor (New York: Harper and Row, 1964), 99–103; Prussian Academy edition, vol. 6, 434–37.

5. Immanuel Kant, *Groundwork of the Metaphysics of Morals*, ed. H. J. Paton (New York: Harper and Row, 1964), 69; Prussian Academy edition, vol. 4, 401; *The Critique of Practical Reason*, ed. Lewis W. Beck (New York: Bobbs-Merrill, 1956), 81, 84; Prussian Academy edition, vol. 5, 78, 81. My purpose here is not to interpret what Kant meant but to give a sense to his remark.

6. This, I take it, is part of M. G. Singer's objection to duties to oneself in *Generalization in Ethics* (New York: Alfred A. Knopf, 1961), 311–18. I have attempted to examine Singer's arguments in detail elsewhere.

Reading Introduction

What Is Wrong With Sentimentality?
Mark Jefferson

Most people would agree that sentimentality is a character defect, but it is difficult to say what is wrong with it—or for that matter, to say precisely what the trait is. Jefferson criticizes two recent attempts to do so and offers his own account.

The word *sentimentality* does not, as Michael Tanner thinks, sometimes name a defective "intrinsic quality" of an emotion, much less a range of such qualities. Sentimentality has to do not with the way an emotion *feels*, but with the *relation* of some emotions to their "objects"—their "intentionality" or "aboutness." Mary Midgley, who says that being sentimental is "misrepresenting the world in order to indulge our feelings," is right in making sentimentality a kind of *dishonesty*. We like to feel warm and sympathetic toward certain things, such as our nation or some injured person of our acquaintance, and so we choose to distort our perception so as to see in the object only those qualities that tend to support such feelings.

But Midgley's theory is also wrong on two counts: First, it is not the immorality of dishonesty or self-deception that makes sentimentality bad. There are countless ways in which we fictionalize or even distort reality for ourselves, and this is not always wrong. Second, Midgley's account of what is wrong with sentimentality is not sufficiently focused: sentimentality is just one of a *variety* of character traits that warp reality for the sake of emotional indulgence. Jefferson lists five other character traits besides sentimentalism that fit Midgley's description: thrill seeking, love of melodrama, disdainfulness, self-righteousness, and "wondrousness." A sentimentalist is *one* kind of person who warps reality for the sake of feelings—namely, one who "misrepresent[s] the world in order to feel unconditionally warm-hearted about bits of it."

The evil of choosing to see some things exclusively in their aspects of "sweetness, dearness, littleness, blamelessness, and vulnerability" is not so much its distortion of *this* reality. Sentimentality derives its evil from a corresponding distortion with which it tends to be associated. This corresponding distortion is *brutality*, which sees some things exclusively in their aspects of treachery, lust, malice, cruelty, savagery, and fiendishness. (Widespread sentimentality is perhaps a predisposing condition for a successful war.) Sentimentalism and brutality tend to be two sides of the same distortion.

What Is Wrong With Sentimentality?

MARK JEFFERSON

It is generally agreed that there is something unwholesome about sentimentality: it would certainly be a mistake to think it a virtue. But just what sentimentality is and why it is objectionable is something of a mystery. Of course we know that it is an emotional quality or range of qualities, and that it is expressive of (or in itself) an ethical or aesthetic defect; but we don't know quite what it is that makes certain emotions sentimental or why it is that certain emotion types are more likely hosts for it than others. Nor is it clear what sort of objection we are making when we call something sentimental. Sometimes the charge seems to impart nothing more than mild ridicule: on other occasions it has more sinister implications. And between these range usages expressing more or less serious rebuke.

What we ordinarily say is, in this case, a peculiarly poor source of illumination. Our intuitions about what counts as sentimentality and why we find it, in varying degrees, objectionable seem very frail. There are some very general reasons why this should be true within the context of the Anglo-American ethical tradition. The influence of Kant towards the theoretical denigration and neglect of the role of emotion in moral life is part of the story. The empiricist tradition of Mill and Moore has been equally neglectful and equally influential. But there are special reasons in addition to these why sentimentality should be obscure to us. For a start, it is a relative newcomer to the vocabulary of critical abuse. 'Sentimentality' has undergone a rapid evolution since it first appeared, in the eighteenth century, as a term of commendation. It was then a fine thing to be sentimental — it set one apart from the coarser types. One had refined feelings, not brute passions. It could be said without a sneer that 'your squires are an agreeable race of people, refined, sentimental, formed for the belle passion'. By the first quarter of the nineteenth century there were signs of disaffection. In 1823 the poet Southey wrote of Rousseau that he 'addressed himself to the sentimental classes, persons of ardent and morbid sensibility, who believe themselves to be composed of finer elements than the gross multitude'. Despite the mocking tone, 'sentimental' still fits best here as a compliment. But from this time its descent into ridicule and odium proceeded apace. By the mid-century it seemed to signify a brand of culpable naivity. A contributor to the 1839 *Quarterly Review* wrote accusingly of someone that his 'implied negation of the inevitable results of evil training has a tendency to countenance their studied sentimentalization of the genus scamp'. By the turn of the century 'sentimentality' standardly functioned as an insult. Witness Oscar Wilde tirading against Lord Alfred Douglas as a 'sentimentalist' and against sentimentality as a 'contemptible affair'. It was denounced in the Futurist Manifestos as a demeaning relic of romanticism. D. H. Lawrence derided it as emotional failure and dissemblance. Sentimentality had truly fallen from favor.[1]

In the light of such a rapid transformation it is perhaps small wonder that there is some confusion about sentimentality. But there is another, connected reason for the elusiveness

From *Mind* 92 (October 1983): 519–29. Reprinted by permission of Oxford University Press.

of the notion. That is the markedly apparent divergence between demotic and literary usage. At street level there is an insistence that sentimentality is the near exclusive preserve of those who buy Christmas presents for their dogs. With this goes the view that sentimentality is just a sort of silliness, not particularly damning and not worth much serious attention. This would be fine were it not for a persistent and highly literate minority who tell us that sentimentality is a dangerous corruption and who tend, as a mark of their seriousness, to cite cases involving Nazis.[2] A favorite but mystifying example is that of Hoess, weeping over music played for him by a Jewish orchestra that he was about to have murdered. I myself hesitate to call *this* a case of sentimentality. It seems instead to be a rather good example of the baffling discordance some people exhibit between the sensitivity of their emotional responses to music and the emotional crassness of their interpersonal affairs. But I won't dwell on the point, for I agree with the fundamental insight that sentimentality can be more than just a brand of silliness and can have sinister implications. In the remainder of this piece I shall try to show how this might be so.

A good place to begin the investigation is with a hint from one of the few philosophical contributions to the question, Mary Midgley's short piece, 'Brutality and Sentimentality'.[3] Her chief purpose in this was to undermine the wantonly perverse suggestion that it is sentimental to attribute feelings to animals. I cannot see that this is a particularly worthy target thesis for her but, that aside, in the course of her demolition job she does make some promising remarks about sentimentality. In particular, she claims that being sentimental is 'misrepresenting the world in order to indulge our feelings'.[4] Now I think that this is partially correct. It does at least identify the genus of which sentimentality is a species. My complaint, though, is that it is much too broad; it fails to bring out what, amongst the range of possible emotional indulgences, is peculiar to sentimentality. Correspondingly, it fails to explain why sentimentality is especially singled out as an objectionable indulgence. But in speaking of sentimentality as the product of misrepresentation of the world two useful conjectures can be seen close beneath the surface. Firstly there is the implication that sentimentality should be located in the context of a broadly cognitivistic theory of emotion. And this is importantly connected with a second hint which is that sentimental emotion is in some sense an expression of choice. The truth of this would, of course, greatly enlarge the potential moral significance of sentimentality. But I want to put these matters aside for a time and look firstly at an objection to the idea that sentimentality is a property of the intentional constituents and causal antecedents of emotion. For this objection provides the chief ground for another claim to the effect that sentimentality is 'the name of several kinds of disease of the feelings'[5] and not, as I contend, the name of a very specific emotional abuse. The objection occurs in the only other recent and sustained attempt to explain sentimentality, i.e. that of Michael Tanner.

Rather discouragingly, Tanner claims that 'sentimentality is an intrinsic quality of some emotions, though it may be tempting when one thinks of situations where there are objects to claim that the sentimentality resides in the relationship between the feelings and what they are feelings about, or towards'.[6] If Tanner is right about this, then in pursuing the idea that sentimentality involves misrepresentation, I am bound to be telling, at best, only part of the story. For this idea seems to have no application to those emotions whose sentimentality is 'an intrinsic quality'. Now it would help here if we could have some clue as to what is meant by 'intrinsic quality'. I think the answer Tanner would approve is that an intrinsic quality of an emotion is one that inheres to the purely sensational aspect of emotion and not to any of its intentional causes or constituents. For his chief ground for saying that some emotion is intrinsically sentimental involves an appeal to the sentimentality of certain pieces of instrumental music. He notes that 'for most instrumental music it seems simply mistaken to say that it is concerned with a situation or has an object'.[7] The argument then seems to go like this. Instrumental music can be sentimental but is not, in any precise sense, ever about anything. So sentimentality need not be a feature of the 'aboutness' of emotion. Therefore it must sometimes be an intrinsic quality of emotion. Rather than directly confront the idea of the purely sensational qualities of emotions it would, I think, be more fruitful to examine the move from the sentimentality of some music to the sentimentality of some people. Music may be expressive of emotion in at least two ways. It can be the vehicle by which a player or writer expresses what he or she feels and, apart from this, it may somehow represent or embody certain emotions. The distinction here is sometimes put as the difference between the expression of emotion *through* music and its expression *in* music. The last of these is surprisingly underexplored and this in itself is good reason for hesitancy about the sort of move Tanner makes. While there are striking similarities there are also some very fundamental differences between the expression of emotion in music and its manifestations in people. Not least among these differences is the fact that music, unlike us, doesn't *feel* anything. Certainly such differences are enough to suggest that when terms like 'angry' and 'sentimental' are applied to music they are functioning in a parasitic relation to their usage in respect of people. In the present context, then, there is no obvious need to worry about the secondary use of 'sentimental' as an occasional description of the sensational aspect of emotion: we will keep our attention focused on the primary application of the term to people. In this last context Tanner gives us no good reason to suppose that 'sentimentality' loosely refers to many kinds of emotional corruption.

We go back then to Mrs. Midgley's claim that to be sentimental is to misrepresent the world in order to indulge our feelings. To this claim she adds another. She says that the notion of sentimentality is ill-formed. By this I think she means that its limited application to the indulgence of 'softer' feelings embodies an objection that applies equally to indulgence of *any* feeling, so long as that indulgence is secured by misrepresenting reality. Since the alleged offence in sentimentality is the dishonest distortion of reality, for Mrs. Midgley it makes no difference what sort of emotion is being secured as a result. I think she is mistaken about this. It is true that we misrepresent the world in order to indulge in many types of emotion — 'soft' and 'hard' — but it is not true that every sort of emotional indulgence is equally objectionable. There are significant differences in the sorts of misrepresentation required for different kinds of indulgence. What gives sentimentality its claim to be properly formed is the peculiar nature of the misrepresentation it involves; and this is also what makes it more objectionable than many other sorts of emotional indulgence.

To aid the descent from general to particular I want to introduce a group of Theophrastic-style characters. The group is not supposed to be comprehensive or entirely serious; its members serve only to gesture towards some commonly recognized phenomena. Each of the characters relates to a disposition across a range of emotion types and each such disposition is found by some to be attractive, sometimes addictively so. In each case the pleasure may be secured by dishonest or self-deceptive appraisals of the world or bits thereof.

The first character is a thrill seeker. He takes pleasure in certain emotions though typically, in fear. The nature of his pleasure is a sort of exhilaration. His type climbs mountains or become mercenaries or, generally, find fearful situations to put themselves in. Since dangerous situations abound in the world, they rarely have need to selectively misrepresent things in order to, as it were, indulge their passion; though no doubt someone, somewhere, is doing just this. Of course one can be less discriminating about the source of one's emotional thrills. One might, for example, thrill to jealousy, anger or any emotion so long as it is strong and followed quickly by another. This brings us to our second type, the melodramatic man. He seeks out intense emotional involvement; he exercises his entire emotional repertoire frequently and at as high a volume as possible. He likes, in short, to emulate the sort of emotional chaos that American television drama would have us accept as the norm. Such a man could stage manage his life to accommodate his tastes (i.e. he could choose his friends, location and vocation accordingly) but if his emotions were to match the world he would need to seek out an enclave of it that was populated with affectionate, adulterous psychopaths. More likely though, he will misrepresent things. He will need to overstate and over-attend to the dramatic quality of experience and to neglect his and its mundanity. The third character, the disdainful man takes pleasure in an emotional attitude towards things, particularly people and by extension their works, which is characterized by derision or contempt. Pouring scorn is his forte. To sustain this he must see people as motivationally transparent and shabby. He must systematically neglect acknowledgement of anything resembling or akin to nobility of motive in his fellows. In short, he must play the cynic. Another well-known and much abused type is the self-righteous man. He takes pleasure in a range of emotion from indignation to outrage, always other directed and always made pleasurable by the backhanded contribution to his moral self-esteem. Self-righteousness involves concentration upon the failures of others and thrives at the expense of acknowledgement of one's own capacity for moral failure. The wondrous man has a rather more specialized indulgence. He delights in the mysterious. He seeks out remarkable correlations and the like but, in order to preserve their sparkle, he may take to declining any sort of account of them that isn't equally provocative of wonder. Finally there is the man who takes his pleasure in untrammelled, unequivocal feelings of the sympathetic variety. He can arrange his world to suit by concentrating on the likeable, the endearing qualities of people, animals and things and by neglecting aspects of them that would adversely qualify these features. He may embellish his picture of the object of his sentimentality by attributing wholly fictional qualities to that object. He is a sentimentalist and his trick is to misrepresent the world in order to feel unconditionally warm-hearted about bits of it.

The point I have been overworking is this. Sentimentality looks like one of a family of emotional habits some of which I have caricatured above. Each of these habits may be sustained by the misrepresentation of things. But the nature of the misrepresentation differs according to the sort of indulgence desired. Each indulgence type requires the projection upon the world of a different kind of unreality. My contention is that sentimentality is objectionable because of the nature of its sustaining fantasy and not simply because it must employ one. Indeed I am not convinced that there is a good moral case to be made against any sort of emotional indulgence that involves misrepresenting the world. That there is such a case is the ground to Mrs. Midgley's objection to sentimentality. The sentimentalist is objectionable for her because in being sentimental he is partaking of 'the central offence . . . self deception, in distorting reality to get a pretext for indulging in any emotion'. The reasons given for supposing that this practice is morally objectionable appeal to two of its likely consequences. Firstly it is said that sentimentality 'distorts expectations; it can make people unable to deal with the real world'. And the second complaint is that sentimental pity 'can so absorb [people] that they cannot react to what is genuinely pitiful in the world around them'.[8] These are, apparently, perils attaching to any emotional indulgence and not just to the indulgence of 'softer' feelings. In fact the first point has an even broader scope than this. When it was said that emotional indulgence 'distorts expectations' the particular reference was to one of Dickens' syrupy creations, Little Nell. To be overly moved by Little Nell is to risk inability to deal 'with the real world, and particularly with real girls'.[9] Now this might be true. Being overly impressed by Dan Dare may make us unable to cope with real spacemen but this is a very general, quasi-Platonic point about the perils of fiction. It is also an argument that seems likely to lead to some very illiberal prescriptions. For there are a great many activities that in some sense tempt us to involvement in a fiction. Without any of them life would be unendurably drab. We cannot spurn sentimentality merely because it involves us in an expectation warping fiction. At least we cannot do so without explaining why it remains acceptable to indulge in other pursuits like daydreaming, filmgoing and the like. The second point may take us further. If we do allow ourselves to wallow in our sympathies for Little Nell we may cease to be alive to the genuinely pitiable. If this is true then most probably it is so in virtue of there being, for most of us, something that might be called an emotional economy. I suspect that most of us have limits to our emotional expenditure. We cannot afford to be emotionally spendthrift – to squander too much emotional energy on the likes of Little Nell. There is, as it were, barely enough of the sympathetic in us to allow for such wastage. There are those who have such an emotional abundance that they may effuse in all directions without deadening themselves to the genuinely pitiable, admirable or contemptible but they are rare creatures. The rest of us must be a little sparing. None of this, of course, singles out sentimentality. It would provide grounds for a very general injunction, in Aristotelian vein, about feeling the right thing towards the right people, for the right reasons and to the right degree. More specifically it constitutes an objection to any sort of emotional overplaying whether it be self-indulgent or simply wrong-headed. But it does not seem to explain our particular suspicions about sentimentality.

Let me try then to connect, as I earlier claimed was possible, some thoughts about the influence of choice on emotion with a cognitive theory of emotion. The combination of these can then be applied to sentimentality. The cognitivism will provide a background legitimizing talk of 'misrepresentations' and the attendant implication of a certain passional voluntariness will sanction the suggestion of moral significance attaching to sentimentality.

Emotional episodes are typically expressive of a concatenation of beliefs and desires. Some of these are actually type-differentiating constituents of emotions. They are grounded in a further causal-rational infrastructure of beliefs and desires which give the constituent ones their rationale and, together with these, provide a rationale for the emotion itself. This is, I think, a widely accepted picture of the nature of emotion. It suggests that one's emotional responses to the world are typically determined by how one sees the world. And how we see the world – our beliefs and the desires they inform – is not something that the world entirely imposes upon us. There is a degree of choice in the vision one adopts of things. The nature of the choice we can exercise over our beliefs need be no more than that we may or may not employ certain truth-orienting procedures. But that is enough to secure responsibility for at least some, a good many, of our beliefs. And to the extent that emotion is a product of belief, through our responsibility for our beliefs, we may also be responsible for our emotions. Now I think that this line of thought has very general implications for our thinking about the role of emotion in moral life; but this is not the time or place to develop these. I want only to point out its relevance to sentimentality. I have earlier accepted that sentimentality involves attachment to a distorted series of beliefs and I have now suggested that this attachment is not something that simply befalls people. I am therefore suggesting that sentimentality is not something that simply befalls us either.

What distinguishes the fictions that sustain sentimentality from those that occur in other forms of emotional indulgence? Well, chiefly it is their emphasis upon such things as the sweetness, dearness, littleness, blamelessness, and vulnerability of the emotions' objects. The qualities that sentimentality imposes on its objects are the qualities of innocence. But this almost inevitably involves a gross simplification of the nature of the object. And it is a simplification of an overtly moral significance. The simplistic appraisal necessary to sentimentality is also a direct impairment to the moral vision taken of its objects. This may in itself be harmless. Often enough it is. Though the sentimentalists in the poodle parlors may have a morally warped view of their little darlings no one need be too alarmed by it. But sentimentality does have its moral dangers and these are rather more apparent when its objects are people or countries. For the moral distortions of sentimentality are very difficult to contain just to its objects. Frequently these objects interrelate with other things and sentimentality may impair one's moral vision of these things too. The parody of moral appraisal that begins in sentimental response to something, naturally extends itself elsewhere. The unlikely creature and moral caricature that is someone unambiguously worthy of sympathetic response has its natural counterpart in a moral caricature of something unambiguously worthy of hatred.

An extraordinary example of how sentimentality corrupts one's moral vision of its objects and of how this corruption naturally extends itself occurs in E. M. Forster's *A Passage to India*. Miss Quested, the fiancée of a colonial official, returns in disarray from an outing and claims to have narrowly escaped indecent assault by a young Indian doctor. The effect of this claim upon the British community is revealing. On the one hand Miss

Quested is transformed into a semi-mythical figure. She comes to symbolize the purity, bravery and vulnerability of English womanhood. Her alleged attacker, Dr. Aziz, comes to symbolize a lust-ridden and perfidious people. In fact Miss Quested was hardly known to the British community before the incident. And what was known of her was not particularly liked. But as innocence assailed, 'an English girl fresh from England', she becomes the focus of a lavish compassion. Amongst her compatriots is felt 'a not unpleasing glow, in which the chilly and half-known features of Miss Quested vanished, and were replaced by all that is sweetest and warmest in the private life'.[10] And they want revenge. Even the leading official, who recognizes his duty to fairness and 'the old weary business of compromise and moderation' wishes that he could 'flog every native that he saw' and longs, too, for the moral simplicity of 'the good old days when an Englishman could satisfy his own honour and no questions asked afterwards'.

The community's sentimentalized portrayal of Miss Quested is strengthened and sustained by its corollary, a vilification of her supposed attacker. The distorted picture of Miss Quested as an ingénue is matched by an equal and opposite distortion of Aziz. He becomes a treacherous monster — a man whose attack upon Miss Quested, though foul enough itself, is made trebly so by its having been carefully planned. It is said that servants were bribed and circumstances arranged well in advance. The moral fantasy, with sentimentality at its source, develops a life of its own which ends, finally, in the humiliation of those who partook of it. But such fervors may have other sorts of result. Sentimentality has often been associated with brutality though the nature of that association has remained obscure. Perhaps we are now in a better position to understand it. For the simple-minded sympathies bestowed upon Miss Quested generate an equally simple-minded antipathy to Dr. Aziz. Crude hatreds tend to have crude expression. This connection has not been lost upon propagandists. Early cartoons of the First World War regularly portrayed Belgium as a simpering maiden, beset by leering, sub-human molesters. And later, British audiences were treated to ludicrous film 're-enactments' of spike-hatted Huns, ugly to a man, bayoneting Belgian babies. The purpose of these untruths was simply to set a moral scene in which the death of Germans was something to be applauded, something worth doing. Sentimentality is rightly connected with brutality because it is a principal component of the sort of moral climate that will sanction crude antipathy and its active expression.

So, we began by registering some slight precariousness in our understanding of sentimentality. We had no precise grip either upon what sentimentality is, or why it is objectionable. At the very broadest level I have set my attempt to clarify the notion against a background which has emotions as importantly cognitive phenomena. This enables us to see emotion generally and sentimentality in particular as something integral to the moral self. That is, a cognitive theory of emotion introduces the possibility that there is a degree of choice involved in the sort of emotional repertoire a man may have. I went on to suggest that sentimentality is a rather more precise notion than has been supposed. Particular attention was paid to two suggestions that would have it otherwise. The first of these sought to establish that sentimentality is sometimes a property of the purely sensational aspect of emotion; and more broadly, that it picks out several sorts of emotional malaise. The second suggestion was that sentimentality is distinguished and objectionable simply because it is a form of emotional indulgence that depends upon a distortion of the way things are. I have suggested that there is no general moral objection to emotional indulgence but that there is a moral objection peculiar to sentimentality. And this objection arises from the special character of the fiction that sentimentality employs. We located this fiction as, roughly speaking, a fiction of innocence. It then became clear why sentimentality had come to be associated with brutality. For to maintain the innocence one has projected upon a favored object it is often necessary to construct other, dangerous fictions about the things that object interacts with.[11]

Notes

1. See *The Letters of Oscar Wilde*, ed. R. Hart-Davis, 501; Valentine de Saint-Point in *Futurist Manifestos*, ed. Umbro Apollonio, 70-74; and D. H. Lawrence, *Phoenix*.

2. See Michael Tanner, "Sentimentality," *Proceedings of the Aristotelian Society* (1976–77), 144; and Anthony Burgess, *Earthly Powers* (Harmondsworth, England: Penguin, 1980), 451.

3. Mary Midgley, "Brutality and Sentimentality," *Philosophy* 54 (July 1979), 385–89.

4. Midgley, 385.

5. Tanner, 140.

6. Tanner, 137.

7. Tanner, 129.

8. Midgley, 385.

9. Midgley, 385.

10. *A Passage to India* (Harmondsworth, England: Penguin, 1961), 180.

11. I would like to thank Peter Smith, George Botterill and Clive Meachen, all from University College of Wales, Aberystwyth, for their assistance in writing this paper.

Reading Introduction

Justice as a Virtue: Changing Conceptions
Alasdair MacIntyre

Conservatives argue that it's unfair to tax the wealthy to support the poor if the wealthy have *justly acquired* what they have—by working for it, inheriting it, and so on. Liberals argue that it's unfair to let some people starve, freeze in the dark, or go without an education, while others have far more than they need for a comfortable life, because *all human beings are equal with respect to these basic needs.* Contemporary debates over justice can never end in rational agreement, says MacIntyre, since the concepts of justice guiding these debates come from different and rival moral traditions. If *just acquisition of property* is one person's most basic principle, and *equal distribution of the necessities of life* is another person's most basic principle, then in debates over issues in which one of these principles must override the other, these two persons can never settle their dispute in a rational and mutually satisfying way.

MacIntyre shows how philosophers' debates about justice recapitulate such "political" debates. John Rawls and Robert Nozick seek to provide principles for resolving such justice disputes, but they succeed only in mirroring them—along with their unsettleable quality. However, nonphilosophers tend to appeal to yet another justice concept that Rawls and Nozick rule out—desert. An ordinary liberal is likely to say that poor people *deserve* to have their basic needs provided for; an ordinary conservative is likely to say that people who have justly acquired their goods *deserve* to keep them. But the idea of somebody deserving something comes from *the tradition of the virtues* and makes no sense apart from a social setting in which the relationships between persons establish the propriety of claiming that someone deserves this or that.

But it is precisely this tradition that Rawls and Nozick implicitly agree to reject. For behind both their theories is a social philosophy of individualism. They both think justice is a set of rules for protecting *individuals* against dangers presented by other *individuals*. They have no notion of persons initially *bound together* in their pursuit of a *common* good. But another way of thinking about justice, characteristic of the tradition of the virtues, is surely possible. The way to avoid the unsettleable dispute between the conservative and the liberal is for them both to break loose from their individualistic orientation and see themselves as members of a *community* whose good they both seek, a community that gives them their identities and the basis for a different concept of justice than can occur to them given their individualism. (This concept will no doubt have a feature relating to just acquisition of goods, as well as one providing for fair distribution of life's necessities; but both of these will be set in the context of a larger conception of *the common human good*.) This "resolution" of the conflict between Rawls and Nozick—and of countless daily social conflicts in our own experience—

will result only from abandoning the individualism characteristic of our culture
and our philosophies, and recovering, for our own day, the tradition of the virtues.

Justice as a Virtue:
Changing Conceptions

ALASDAIR MacINTYRE

When Aristotle praised justice as the first virtue of political life, he did so in such a way as
to suggest that a community which lacks practical agreement on a conception of justice
must also lack the necessary basis for political community. But the lack of such a basis must
therefore threaten our own society. For the outcome of that history . . .[1] has not only
been an inability to agree upon a catalogue of the virtues and an even more fundamental
inability to agree upon the relative importance of the virtue concepts within a moral
scheme in which notions of rights and of utility also have a key place. It has also been an
inability to agree upon the content and character of particular virtues. For since a virtue is
now generally understood as a disposition or sentiment which will produce in us
obedience to certain rules, agreement on what the relevant rules are to be is always a
prerequisite for agreement upon the nature and content of a particular virtue. But this
prior agreement in rules is . . . something which our individualist culture is unable to
secure. Nowhere is this more marked and nowhere are the consequences more threatening than in the case of justice. Everyday life is pervaded by them and basic controversies
cannot therefore be rationally resolved. Consider one such controversy, endemic in the
politics of the United States today — I present it in the form of a debate between two ideal-
typical characters unimaginatively named 'A' and 'B'.

A, who may own a store or be a police officer or a construction worker, has struggled
to save enough from his earnings to buy a small house, to send his children to the local
college, to pay for some special type of medical care for his parents. He now finds all of his
projects threatened by rising taxes. He regards this threat to his projects as *unjust*; he claims
to have a right to what he has earned and that nobody else has a right to take away what he
acquired legitimately and to which he has a just title. He intends to vote for candidates for
political office who will defend his property, his projects *and* his conception of justice.

B, who may be a member of one of the liberal professions, or a social worker, or
someone with inherited wealth, is impressed with the arbitrariness of the inequalities in
the distribution of wealth, income and opportunity. He is, if anything, even more
impressed with the inability of the poor and the deprived to do very much about their own
condition as a result of inequalities in the distribution of power. He regards both these
types of inequality as *unjust* and as constantly engendering further injustice. He believes

From *After Virtue*, 2d ed. (Notre Dame: University of Notre Dame Press, 1984), 244–55. Reprinted by
permission of the publisher, University of Notre Dame Press.

more generally that all inequality stands in need of justification and that the only possible justification for inequality is to improve the condition of the poor and the deprived – by, for example, fostering economic growth. He draws the conclusion that in present circumstances redistributive taxation which will finance welfare and the social services is what justice demands. He intends to vote for candidates for political office who will defend redistributive taxation *and* his conception of justice.

It is clear that in the actual circumstances of our social and political order A and B are going to disagree about policies and politicians. But *must* they so disagree? The answer seems to be that under certain types of economic condition their disagreement need not manifest itself at the level of political conflict. If A and B belong to a society where economic resources are such, or are at least believed to be such, that B's public redistributive projects can be carried through at least to a certain point without threatening A's private life-plan projects, A and B might for some time vote for the same politicians and policies. Indeed they might on occasion be one and the same person. But if it is, or comes to be, the case that economic circumstances are such that either A's projects must be sacrificed to B's or *vice versa*, it at once becomes clear that A and B have views of justice which are not only logically incompatible with each other but which . . . invoke considerations which are incommensurable with those advanced by the adversary party.

The logical incompatibility is not difficult to identify. A holds that principles of just acquisition and entitlement set limits to redistributive possibilities. If the outcome of the application of the principles of just acquisition and entitlement is gross inequality, the toleration of such inequality is a price that has to be paid for justice. B holds that principles of just distribution set limits to legitimate acquisition and entitlement. If the outcome of the application of the principles of just distribution is interference – by means of taxation or such devices as eminent domain – with what has up till now been regarded in this social order as legitimate acquisition and entitlement, the toleration of such interference is a price that has to be paid for justice. We may note in passing – it will not be unimportant later – that in the case of both A's principle and B's principle the price for one person or group of persons receiving justice is always paid by someone else. Thus different identifiable social groups have an interest in the acceptance of one of the principles and the rejection of the other. Neither principle is socially or politically neutral.

Moreover it is not simply that A and B advance principles which produce incompatible practical conclusions. The type of concept in terms of which each frames his claim is so different from that of the other that the question of how and whether the dispute between them may be rationally settled begins to pose difficulties. For A aspires to ground the notion of justice in some account of what and how a given person is entitled to in virtue of what he has acquired and earned; B aspires to ground the notion of justice in some account of the equality of the claims of each person in respect of basic needs and of the means to meet such needs. Confronted by a given piece of property or resource, A will be apt to claim that it is justly his because he owns it – he acquired it legitimately, he earned it; B will be apt to claim that it justly ought to be someone else's, because they need it much more, and if they do not have it, their basic needs will not be met. But our pluralist culture possesses no method of weighing, no rational criterion for deciding between claims based on legitimate entitlement against claims based on need. Thus these two types of claim are indeed, as I suggested, incommensurable, and the metaphor of 'weighing' moral claims is not just inappropriate but misleading.

It is at this point that recent analytical moral philosophy makes important claims. For it aspires to provide rational principles to which appeal may be made by contending parties with conflicting interests. And the two most distinguished recent attempts to carry through this project have a special relevance for the argument between A and B. For Robert Nozick's account of justice[2] is at least to some large degree a rational articulation of key elements in A's position, while John Rawls's account[3] is in the same way a rational articulation of key elements in B's position. Thus if the philosophical considerations which either Rawls or Nozick urge upon us turn out to be rationally compelling, the argument between A and B will have been rationally settled one way or another and my own characterization of the dispute will in consequence turn out to be quite false.

I begin with Rawls's account. Rawls argues that the principles of justice are those which would be chosen by a rational agent 'situated behind a veil of ignorance' (136) such that he does not know what place in society he will occupy—that is, what his class or status will be, what talents and ability he will possess, what his conception of the good or his aims in life will be, what his temperament will be or what kind of economic, political, cultural or social order he will inhabit. Rawls argues that any rational agent so situated will define a just distribution of goods in *any* social order in terms of two principles and a rule for allocating priorities when the two principles conflict.

The first principle is: 'Each person is to have an equal right to the most extensive total system of equal basic liberties compatible with a similar system of liberty for all'. The second principle is: 'Social and economic inequalities are to be arranged so that they are both (a) to the greatest benefit of the least advantaged, consistent with the joint savings principle [the joint savings principle provides for fair investment in the interests of future generations], and (b) attached to offices and parties open to all under conditions of fair equality of opportunity' (302). The first principle has priority over the second; liberty is to be restricted only for the sake of liberty. And justice generally has priority over efficiency. So Rawls arrives at his general conception: 'All social primary goods—liberty and opportunity, income and wealth, and the bases of self-respect—are to be distributed equally unless an unequal distribution of any or all of these goods is to the advantage of the least favored' (303).

Many critics of Rawls have focussed their attention on the ways in which Rawls derives his principles of justice from his statement of the initial position of the rational agent 'situated behind a veil of ignorance'. Such critics have made a number of telling points, but I do not intend to dwell on them, if only because I take it not only that a rational agent in *some such* situation as that of the veil of ignorance would indeed choose *some such* principles of justice as Rawls claims, but also that it is *only* a rational agent in such a situation who would choose such principles. Later in my argument this point will become important. For the moment however I shall put it on one side in order to turn to a characterization of Nozick's view.

Nozick claims that 'if the world were wholly just' (151) the only people entitled to hold anything, that is to appropriate it for use as they and they alone wished, would be those who had justly acquired what they held by some just act of original acquisition and those who had justly acquired what they held by some just act of transfer from someone else who had either acquired it by some just act of original acquisition or by some just transfer . . . and so on. In other words, the justifiable answer to the question 'Why are you entitled to use that seashell as you wish?' will either be 'I picked it up on the seashore, where it belonged to no one and where there were plenty left for everyone else' (a just act of original acquisition), *or* 'Someone else picked it up at the seashore and freely sold or gave it to someone . . . to someone . . . who freely sold or gave it to me' (a series of just acts of transfer). It follows from Nozick's view as he himself immediately notes that: 'The complete principle of distributive justice would say simply that a distribution is just if everyone is entitled to the holdings that they possess under the distribution' (153).

Nozick derives these conclusions from premises about the inalienable rights of each individual, premises for which he does not himself offer arguments. As in the case of Rawls, I do not want to quarrel with Nozick's derivation of his principles from his premises; once again I shall want to stress instead that it is *only* from some such premises that such principles could be rationally derived. That is to say, in the case of both Nozick's account of justice and Rawls's account of justice the problems that I want to raise do not concern the coherence of the internal structure of their arguments. Indeed my own argument requires that their accounts do not lack such coherence.

What I want to argue is threefold: first, that the incompatibility of Rawls's and Nozick's accounts does up to a point genuinely mirror the incompatibility of A's position with B's, and that to this extent at least Rawls and Nozick successfully articulate at the level of moral philosophy the disagreement between such ordinary non-philosophical citizens as A and B; but that Rawls and Nozick also reproduce the very same type of incompatibility and incommensurability at the level of philosophical argument that made A's and B's debate unsettlable at the level of social conflict; and secondly, that there is nonetheless an element in the position of both A and B which neither Rawls's account nor Nozick's captures, an element which survives from that older classical tradition in which the virtues were central. When we reflect on both these points, a third emerges: namely, that in their conjunction we have an important clue to the social presuppositions which Rawls and Nozick to some degree share.

Rawls makes primary what is in effect a principle of equality with respect to needs. His conception of 'the worst off' sector of the community is a conception of those whose needs are gravest in respect of income, wealth and other goods. Nozick makes primary what is a principle of equality with respect to entitlement. For Rawls how those who are now in grave need come to be in grave need is irrelevant; justice is made into a matter of present patterns of distribution to which the past is irrelevant. For Nozick only evidence about what has been legitimately acquired in the past is relevant; present patterns of distribution in themselves must be irrelevant to *justice* (although not perhaps to kindness or generosity). To say even this much makes it clear how close Rawls is to B and how close Nozick is to A. For A appealed against distributive canons to a justice of entitlement, and B appealed against canons of entitlement to a justice which regards needs. Yet it is also at once clear not only that Rawls's priorities are incompatible with Nozick's in a way parallel to that in which B's position is incompatible with A's, but also that Rawls's position is incommensurable with Nozick's in a way similarly parallel to that in which B's is incommensurable with A's. For how can a claim that gives priority to equality of needs be rationally weighed against one which gives priority to entitlements? If Rawls were to argue that anyone *behind the veil of ignorance*, who knew neither whether and how his needs would be met nor what his entitlements would be, ought rationally to prefer a principle which respects needs to one which respects entitlements, invoking perhaps principles of rational decision theory to do so, the immediate answer must be not only that *we* are *never* behind such a veil of ignorance, but also that this leaves unimpugned Nozick's premise about inalienable rights. And if Nozick were to argue that any distributive principle, if enforced, could violate a freedom to which everyone of us is entitled—as he does indeed argue—the immediate answer must be that in so interpreting the inviolability of basic rights he begs the question in favor of his own argument and leaves unimpugned Rawls's premises.

Nonetheless there is something important, if negative, which Rawls's account shares with Nozick's. Neither of them make any reference to *desert* in their account of justice, nor could they consistently do so. And yet both A and B did make such a reference—and it is imperative here to notice that 'A' and 'B' are not the names of mere arbitrary constructions of my own; their arguments faithfully reproduce, for example, a good deal of what was actually said in recent fiscal debates in California, New Jersey and elsewhere. What A complains of on his own behalf is not merely that he is entitled to what he has earned, but that he *deserves* it in virtue of his life of hard work; what B complains of on behalf of the poor and deprived is that their poverty and deprivation is *undeserved* and therefore unwarranted. And it seems clear that in the case of the real-life counterparts of A and B it is the reference to desert which makes them feel strongly that what they are complaining about is injustice, rather than some other kind of wrong or harm.

Neither Rawls's account nor Nozick's allows this central place, or indeed any kind of place, for desert in claims about justice and injustice. Rawls (310) allows that common sense views of justice connect it with desert, but argues first that we do not know what anyone deserves until we have already formulated the rules of justice (and hence we cannot base our understanding of justice upon desert), and secondly that when we have formulated the rules of justice it turns out that it is not desert that is in question anyway, but only legitimate expectations. He also argues that to attempt to apply notions of desert would be impracticable—the ghost of Hume walks in his pages at this point.

Nozick is less explicit, but his scheme of justice being based exclusively on entitlements can allow no place for desert. He does at one point discuss the possibility of a principle for the rectification of injustice, but what he writes on that point is so tentative and cryptic that it affords no guidance for amending his general viewpoint. It is in any case clear that for both Nozick and Rawls a society is composed of individuals, each with his or her own interest, who then have to come together and formulate common rules of life. In Nozick's case there is the additional negative constraint of a set of basic rights. In Rawls's case the only constraints are those that a prudent rationality would impose. Individuals are thus in both accounts primary and society secondary, and the identification of individual interests is prior to, and independent of, the construction of any moral or social bonds between them. But we have already seen that the notion of desert is at home only in the context of a community whose primary bond is a shared understanding both of the good for man and of the good of that community and where individuals identify their primary interests with reference to those goods. Rawls explicitly makes it a presupposition of his view that we must expect to disagree with others about what the good life for man is and must therefore exclude any understanding of it that we may have from our formulation of the principles of justice. Only those goods in which everyone, whatever their view of the good life, takes an interest are to be admitted to consideration. In Nozick's argument too, the concept of community required for the notion of desert to have application is simply absent. To understand this is to clarify two further points.

The first concerns the shared social presuppositions of Rawls and Nozick. It is, from both standpoints, as though we had been shipwrecked on an uninhabited island with a group of other individuals, each of whom is a stranger to me and to all the others. What have to be worked out are rules which will safeguard each one of us maximally in such a situation. Nozick's premise concerning rights introduces a strong set of constraints; we do know that certain types of interference with each other are absolutely prohibited. But there is a limit to the bonds between us, a limit set by our private and competing interests. This individualistic view has of course . . . a distinguished ancestry: Hobbes, Locke (whose views Nozick treats with great respect), Machiavelli and others. And it contains within itself a certain note of realism about modern society; modern society is indeed often, at least in surface appearance, nothing but a collection of strangers, each pursuing his or her own interests under minimal constraints. We still of course, even in modern society, find it difficult to think of families, colleges and other genuine communities in this way; but even our thinking about those is now invaded to an increasing degree by individualist conceptions, especially in the law courts. Thus Rawls and Nozick articulate with great power a shared view which envisages entry into social life as—at least ideally—the voluntary act of at least potentially rational individuals with prior interests who have to ask the question 'What kind of social contract with others is it reasonable for me to enter into?' Not surprisingly it is a consequence of this that their views exclude any account of human community in which the notion of desert in relation to contributions to the common tasks of that community in pursuing shared goods could provide the basis for judgments about virtue and injustice.

Desert is ruled out too in another way. I have remarked upon how Rawls's distributive principles exclude reference to the past and so to claims to desert based on past actions and sufferings. Nozick too excludes that of the past on which such claims might be based, by making a concern for the legitimacy of entitlements the sole ground for taking an interest in the past in connection with justice. What makes this important is that Nozick's account serves the interest of a particular mythology about the past precisely by what it excludes from view. For central to Nozick's account is the thesis that all legitimate entitlements can be traced to legitimate acts of original acquisition. But, if that is so, there are in fact very few, and in some large areas of the world *no*, legitimate entitlements. The property-owners of the modern world are not the legitimate heirs of Lockean individuals who performed quasi-Lockean ('quasi' to allow for Nozick's emendations of Locke) acts of original acquisition; they are the inheritors of those who, for example, stole, and used violence to steal the common lands of England from the common people, vast tracts of North America from the American Indian, much of Ireland from the Irish, and Prussia from the original non-German Prussians. This is the historical reality ideologically concealed behind any Lockean thesis. The lack of any principle of rectification is thus not a small side issue for a thesis such as Nozick's; it tends to vitiate the theory as a whole—even if we were to suppress the overwhelming objections to any belief in inalienable human rights.

A and B differ from Rawls and Nozick at the price of inconsistency. Each of them in conjoining either Rawls's principles or Nozick's with an appeal to desert exhibits an adherence to an older, more traditional, more Aristotelian and Christian view of justice. This inconsistency is thus a tribute to the residual power and influence of the tradition, a power and influence with two distinct sources. In the conceptual *mélange* of moral thought and practice today fragments from the tradition—virtue concepts for the most part—are still found alongside characteristically modern and individualist concepts such as those of rights or utility. But the tradition also survives in a much less fragmented, much less distorted form in the lives of certain communities whose historical ties with their past remain strong. So the older moral tradition is discernible in the United States and elsewhere among, for example, some Catholic Irish, some Orthodox Greeks and some Jews of an Orthodox persuasion, all of them communities that inherit their moral tradition not only through their religion, but also from the structure of the peasant villages and households which their immediate ancestors inhabited on the margins of modern Europe. Moreover it would be wrong to conclude . . . that Protestantism did not in some areas become the bearer of this very same moral tradition; in Scotland for example, Aristotle's *Nicomachean Ethics* and *Politics* were the secular moral texts in the universities, coexisting happily with a Calvinist theology which was often elsewhere hostile to them, until 1690 and after. And there are today both black and white Protestant communities in the United States, especially perhaps those in or from the South, who will recognize in the tradition of the virtues a key part of their own cultural inheritance.

Even however in such communities the need to enter into public debate enforces participation in the cultural *mélange* in the search for a common stock of concepts and norms which all may employ and to which all may appeal. Consequently the allegiance of such marginal communities to the tradition is constantly in danger of being eroded, and this in search of what, if my argument is correct, is a chimaera. For what analysis of A's and B's position reveals once again is that we have all too many disparate and rival moral concepts, in this case rival and disparate concepts of justice, and that the moral resources of the culture allow us no way of settling the issue between them rationally. Moral philosophy, as it is dominantly understood, reflects the debates and disagreements of the culture so faithfully that its controversies turn out to be unsettlable in just the way that the political and moral debates themselves are.

It follows that our society cannot hope to achieve moral consensus. For quite non-Marxist reasons Marx was in the right when he argued against the English trade unionists of the 1860s that appeals to justice were pointless, since there are rival conceptions of justice formed by and informing the life of rival groups. Marx was of course mistaken in supposing that such disagreements over justice are merely secondary phenomena, that they merely reflect the interests of rival economic classes. Conceptions of justice and allegiance to such conceptions are partly constitutive of the lives of social groups, and economic interests are often partially defined in terms of such conceptions and not *vice versa*. Nonetheless Marx was fundamentally right in seeing conflict and not consensus at the heart of modern social structure. It is not just that we live too much by a variety and multiplicity of fragmented concepts; it is that these are used at one and the same time to express rival and incompatible social ideals and policies *and* to furnish us with a pluralist political rhetoric whose function is to conceal the depth of our conflicts.

Important conclusions follow for constitutional theory. Liberal writers such as Ronald Dworkin invite us to see the Supreme Court's function as that of invoking a set of consistent principles, most and perhaps all of them of moral import, in the light of which particular laws and particular decisions are to be evaluated. Those who hold such a view are bound to consider certain decisions of the Supreme Court inadequate in the light of these supposed principles. The type of decision which I have in mind is exemplified by the Bakke case, where two, at first sight strongly incompatible, views were held by members of the court, and Mr. Justice Powell who wrote the decision was the one justice to hold both views. But, if my argument is correct, one function of the Supreme Court must be to keep the peace between rival social groups adhering to rival and incompatible principles of justice by displaying a fairness which consists in even-handedness in its adjudications. So the Supreme Court in *Bakke* both forbade precise ethnic quotas for admission to colleges and universities, but allowed discrimination in favor of previously deprived minority groups. Try to conjure up a set of consistent principles behind such a decision and ingenuity may or may not allow you to find the court not guilty of formal inconsistency. But even to make such an attempt is to miss the point. The Supreme Court in *Bakke*, as on occasion in other cases, played the role of a peacemaking or truce-keeping body by negotiating its way through an impasse of conflict, not by invoking our shared moral first principles. For our society as a whole has none.

What this brings out is that modern politics cannot be a matter of genuine moral consensus. And it is not. Modern politics is civil war carried on by other means, and *Bakke* was an engagement whose antecedents were at Gettysburg and Shiloh. The truth on this matter was set out by Adam Ferguson: 'We are not to expect that the laws of any country are to be framed as so many lessons of morality. . . . Laws, whether civil or political, are expedients of policy to adjust the pretensions of parties, and to secure the peace of society. The expedient is accommodated to special circumstances. . . .'[4] The nature of any society therefore is not to be deciphered from its laws alone, but from those understood as an index of its conflicts. What our laws show is the extent and degree to which conflict has to be suppressed.

Yet if this is so, another virtue too has been displaced. Patriotism cannot be what it was because we lack in the fullest sense a *patria*. The point that I am making must not be confused with the commonplace liberal rejection of patriotism. Liberals have often—not always—taken a negative or even hostile attitude towards patriotism, partly because their allegiance is to values which they take to be universal and not local and particular, and partly because of a well-justified suspicion that in the modern world patriotism is often a façade behind which chauvinism and imperialism are fostered. But my present point is not that patriotism is good or bad as a sentiment, but that the practice of patriotism as a virtue is in advanced societies no longer possible in the way that it once was. In any society where government does not express or represent the moral community of the citizens, but is instead a set of institutional arrangements for imposing a bureaucratized unity on a society which lacks genuine moral consensus, the nature of political obligation becomes systematically unclear. Patriotism is or was a virtue founded on attachment primarily to a political and moral community and only secondarily to the government of that community; but it is characteristically exercised in discharging responsibility to and in such government. When however the relationship of government to the moral community is put in question both by the changed nature of government and the lack of moral consensus in the society, it becomes difficult any longer to have any clear, simple and teachable conception of patriotism. Loyalty to my country, to my community—which remains unalterably a central virtue—becomes detached from obedience to the government which happens to rule me.

Just as this understanding of the displacement of patriotism must not be confused with the liberal critique of moral particularity, so this necessary distancing of the moral self from the governments of modern states must not be confused with any anarchist critique of the state. Nothing in my argument suggests, let alone implies, any good grounds for rejecting certain forms of government as necessary and legitimate; what the argument does entail is that the modern state is not such a form of government. . . . The tradition of the virtues is at variance with central features of the modern economic order and more especially its individualism, its acquisitiveness and its elevation of the values of the market to a central social place. It now becomes clear that it also involves a rejection of the modern political order. This does not mean that there are not many tasks only to be performed in and through government which still require performing: the rule of law, so far as it is possible in a modern state, has to be vindicated, injustice and unwarranted suffering have to be dealt with, generosity has to be exercised, and liberty has to be defended, in ways that are sometimes only possible through the use of governmental institutions. But each particular task, each particular responsibility has to be evaluated on its own merits. Modern systematic politics, whether liberal, conservative, radical or socialist, simply has to be rejected from a standpoint that owes genuine allegiance to the tradition of the virtues; for modern politics itself expresses in its institutional forms a systematic rejection of that tradition.

Notes

1. For a brief summary of the history to which MacIntyre refers, see the introduction to this volume.
2. Robert Nozick, *Anarchy, State and Utopia* (New York: Basic Books, 1974). References to this work will be indicated in the text.
3. John Rawls, *A Theory of Justice* (Cambridge, Mass.: Belknap Press of Harvard University Press, 1971). References to this work will be indicated in the text.
4. Adam Ferguson, *Principles of Moral and Political Science* (1792) (New York: AMS Press, 1973): ii, 144.

Reading Introduction

Who Is the Autonomous Man?
John Benson

The origins of the word *autonomous* suggest a person who is a "law to himself or herself," or is "his or her own lawgiver," and some recent ethicists—both existentialists and analytic philosophers—have regarded autonomy in this way. But if Benson is right, this suggestion is misleading. Following Aristotle, he proposes that autonomy is a "mean," or middle point, between two extreme character traits—that of relying too much, and that of relying too little, "on one's own powers of acting, choosing, and forming opinions."

Autonomy of theoretical judgment is not just a matter of always finding out the truth for oneself; often it is most reasonable to accept truth claims on authority. The autonomous person accepts authority when appropriate and investigates for himself or herself when *that* is appropriate. Both are cases of being "in charge of one's epistemic life."

But it is primarily autonomy of moral judgment that Benson wants to clarify, and he argues for a close parallel with intellectual autonomy. There are appropriate ways to take over moral judgments from other people. It is not wrong to get your morality from your parents, and membership in a solid moral tradition is an important basis for autonomy. But this should not obscure the differences between intellectual and moral autonomy. It is morally defective to believe that racism is evil just because somebody whose moral judgment you respect believes it is evil. The reason for this is not that, since there is no moral truth, you have to invent right and wrong for yourself. It is rather because to assent to a moral truth requires *feeling its force*, and this means making that truth your *own*.

Benson ends by noting that a certain kind of rigidity is an important background to thinking morally for oneself. Being open and supple in one's judgments, as any person must be who really thinks for oneself, has to be backed up with strength of will. It was not the intellectuals, but the Jehovah's Witnesses, who best retained their independence of judgment under the pressures of Hitler's concentration camps.

Who Is the Autonomous Man?

JOHN BENSON

> Who is the happy warrior? Who is he
> That every man in arms would wish to be?

Anyone who recalls the description of the exemplary figure in Wordsworth's poem will probably agree that it can rarely have been adequately imitated. In some recent philosophical discussions the autonomous man has seemed an equally distant and intimidating ideal. But whereas the happy warrior, were he to exist, would be a splendid, if humbling, character to have around, I doubt if the autonomous man would be very nice to know. The portrait at times has a positively Faustian cast. We are expected to admire 'the person who is his own cause, his own handiwork' because he 'has realized the potentialities of his autarchic status to a higher degree than someone who merely falls in with the projects of others and assesses his performance by standards thrust on him by his environment'.[1] The rather extreme nature of this contrast fails to suggest that there are humbler relations of this exalted ideal which Everyman might find fit for imitation. Even accounts which manage not to put one in mind of W. E. Henley's *Invictus* seem to me to put too much emphasis on autonomy conceived as a highly conscious, explicitly critical attitude to one's own beliefs and principles. The ideas of self-creation and of persistent radical self-questioning go together in the picture of the autonomous man as captain of his soul. This needs not obliteration but some re-painting to make the lineaments more homely.

I

The virtue of autonomy is a mean state of character with regard to reliance on one's own powers in acting, choosing and forming opinions. The deficiency is termed heteronomy, and there are many terms which may be used to describe the heteronomous person, some of which suggest specific forms of the vice: credulous, gullible, compliant, passive, submissive, over-dependent, servile. For the vice of excess there is no name in common use, but solipsism might do, or arrogant self-sufficiency. To be deficient in autonomy is to be too dependent on the support, prompting and advice of others. The opposite extreme is to rely on oneself when it would be more judicious to accept the counsel or testimony of others.

It has become common to speak of autonomy in connection with both the will and the intellect.[2] Given its etymology the word is already metaphorical as applied to the individual agent, but that is a sleeping metaphor. It is by a further metaphorical stretching that it is applied to the thinker, but that use too has become natural, at least in the philosophy of education. The autonomous man has a mind of his own and a will of his own. He exercises independence in his thinking and in his decisions about practical affairs.

From *Philosophy* 58 (1983): 5–17. Reprinted by permission of Cambridge University Press.

These are of course not watertight compartments. Practical decisions must normally be based on factual information. If one's decision is to be one's own one may have to make an independent assessment of the relevant factual information. Still, this does not obliterate the distinction. There are theoretical tasks whose upshot is the acquisition of knowledge, not action; and there is more to practical thinking than acquiring information.

The first question I want to ask is what we take thinking for oneself to consist in, and why we take it for a virtue. For many, and perhaps for most, of our beliefs we have no reasons at all. We have picked them up from a variety of sources, but this does not mean that we have reasons for them, only that there are reasons why we hold them. To believe a proposition because someone has told it to you is not necessarily, or even normally, to be in a position to cite as your reason for the belief the fact that that person told you it was so. The first step in thinking for yourself is to realize that you may raise a question about the truth of a proposition, even though it comes from a trusted source. If you support the belief by appeal to the fact that you were told it by so-and-so then you go a step beyond merely accepting it from him, you cite *his* acceptance of it as a reason why you should accept it. This invites a further question. What is being claimed is that the source would be unlikely to hold this belief unless it were true. To entertain such a claim is not a mark of an uncritical person. The government issues the warning that smoking can damage your health. There is good reason to think that the government would not have issued the warning without good reasons for its belief. There have been investigations by competent people, whose reports are publicly available and have been assessed by other competent people who advise the government. To remind yourself of these points is itself to think for yourself about the matter.

But there are, of course, more ambitious moves that you can make. You can study the reports of the various investigations, looking at the statistics, the sampling techniques and so on. If you do this you are moving a step nearer to a direct confrontation with the truth. You are no longer dependent on the competence and veracity of government advisers assessing the medical evidence, but are in as good a position as they are (subject to the important proviso that you have acquired sufficient skill in appraising this kind of evidence—which in practice is unlikely to be the case).

You may still feel that you have not removed all the veils that hide the naked truth from direct gaze. You may be as well off as the government's advisers, but they are not as well off as they could be, for they rely on the competence and veracity of the original investigators, clinicians, pathologists, etc. Only by repeating their first-hand investigations could you put yourself in as good a position as they are. Short of that you are dependent on their competence and veracity, and no one can be in a better position than they, for the chain of testimony can only be as strong as the first-hand knowledge to which it is anchored.

To be able to think for oneself about some such matter involves an awareness of the way in which beliefs about it derive from first-hand investigations. But it is obviously too extreme to suppose that to have any rationally grounded beliefs one must decline to accept anything that one has not checked by one's own observation. It may well be the case that one's chance of possessing a justified true belief is greater if one makes no attempt to investigate the matter at first hand. This will obviously be true if one lacks expertise in the appropriate field, say anatomy, skill in diagnosis, experience in using a microscope, etc.

If one considers a simple observational statement it seems a truism to say that there is an epistemologically most favored position for forming a belief about it. But with regard to a complex empirical matter such as the link between cancer and smoking no one is in the most favored position with regard to all the propositions on which the final generalizations rest. The clinicians, pathologists and so on have neither the time nor all the different competencies necessary to making all the first-hand observations. If they are in the most favored position it is collectively, not individually.

The point of thinking about a matter for oneself is to maximize one's chance of having a justified true belief, and so, in view of the limitations of first-hand investigations, a large part must be played in the thought of the critical thinker by the assessment of testimony. To insist on using one's own eyes instead of the botanist's is as irrational as to insist on using the naked eye instead of a microscope. My account escapes the anxiety expressed by Elizabeth Telfer that intellectual autonomy as an ideal might 'permit an arrogantly solipsistic approach' which excluded careful consideration 'of the views and criteria of others in the field'.[3] This could happen only as a result of identifying intellectual autonomy with a commitment to first-hand investigation, as such, rather than truth-directed enquiry, which only sometimes coincides with first-hand investigation. The danger to which Miss Telfer points is the danger of veering from the mean towards the extreme of excessive self-reliance. (I thank her for suggesting solipsism as its name.)

With whom is the intellectually autonomous man to be contrasted, if not with the person who accepts what he has good reason to regard as reliable testimony? He is to be contrasted with the person who accepts what he is told without any reason, or with too little reason to think that the testimony is reliable.

Autonomy, then, is compatible with the acceptance of testimony. But it must be emphasized equally that such acceptance, not less than first-hand investigation, presupposes that there is truth to be enquired after. One accepts testimony because one has good reason to believe that its author has access to the truth, either through more testimony, or through his own direct knowledge. (By direct knowledge here I do not only mean observational knowledge: one may accept the result of a calculation from someone on the ground that he is good at such calculations and has worked it out himself.)

To be autonomous in this sphere is to put oneself in the best position to answer for the reliability of one's beliefs. It is to be in charge of one's epistemic life.

While it is true, I believe, that this autonomy is consistent with making much use of the evidence of testimony, it does also require willingness to buckle down to first-hand investigation when that is the only way of being in the best position. A variety of circumstances may demand this. One is when a matter is open to view, and only idleness or extreme lack of self-confidence could prevent someone from using his own powers of observation or thought. Another is when the experts, so-called, are clearly unreliable, either because they are working in a field in which nothing is very well-founded, or because they cannot be trusted to be impartial. Should one eat butter? The experts who say 'No' are funded by margarine manufacturers; those who say 'Yes' are funded by the

Milk Marketing Board. The man of sense will ignore both. His own simple inductions may not be very reliable but they are the best guide available.

II

In speaking of autonomy in the practical sphere I shall be chiefly concerned again with independence in making judgments. But I should not like to neglect entirely a kind of autonomy which is a much more basic virtue, namely the ability and willingness to undertake for oneself the ordinary tasks of daily life. It is lack of this kind of autonomy that provides social workers with many of their clients. Many of us manage without social workers because we have wives or husbands who see that the bills are paid and the income tax returns made. There was once a long-married man whose wife had to desert him for a day. So she arranged for a neighbor to come in and prepare his tea. The neighbor cooked it and set the table, and before leaving poured him his first cup. Within minutes he was round at her door. 'What about the sugar?' he asked. 'I put it on the table', she said. 'But I don't know how much she puts in'. This minor tragedy illustrates a general point: that there is a relation of interdependence between volitional and cognitive aspects of basic autonomy. One may be unable to act for oneself because one lacks a bit of knowledge-how, but that lack itself arises from a habit of dependence. Knowing how to perform various tasks is necessary if one is to act for oneself, but one may fail to acquire the knowledge unless one has the desire to try out one's own powers. A common symptom of a lack of basic autonomy is undue anxiety about a slightly unfamiliar task. One often meets the student who shows anxiety about how long an essay should be, exactly what he is expected to do. A natural enough desire to know where he stands, one may think. But others just go ahead and find some way of tackling the job, being willing to venture their powers without instructions.

To be autonomous is to trust one's own powers and to have a disposition to use them, to be able to resist the fear of failure, ridicule or disapproval that threatens to drive one into reliance on the guidance of others. This holds good both for basic everyday tasks and for the higher level tasks of moral thinking. But it is perhaps especially clear with regard to the former that autonomy, like courage—to which it is closely allied—is an essential virtue that everyone needs. It is not the virtue of a reflective aristocracy. It is essential quite simply because without it one cannot live effectively the life of a member of society. But it is not merely of instrumental value. To be able to take charge of one's own life is an important element of a person's self-respect.

III

In discussing autonomy in practical thinking I shall concentrate on moral thinking. Autonomy is important in prudential thinking too, but is perhaps less problematical there. Moral autonomy has attracted a lot of attention because it is very problematical. I shall argue that autonomous moral thinking is closely parallel to autonomous theoretical thinking, the one being concerned with what should be done, the other with what is the case.

I have defined autonomy as correctness in the avoidance and acceptance of the testimony and guidance of others. Autonomy is a proper degree and kind of reliance on others, what is proper being determined by the end of the activity in which one is engaging. In considering how that general account applies to moral autonomy it is convenient to make a classification of modes of reliance on or submission to the word of another person.

First there is the unreflective acceptance of authority which does not say 'This is right because so-and-so, or everyone, says so', but accepts what others say without reflecting that their saying so is a reason for accepting that it *is* so. The authority may be an impersonal one. Each recipient may be aware that the particular person from whom he receives his teaching is not merely speaking for himself, but is passing on what has always been known. To be an acceptor of authority in this sense is not the same as being a gull, one who has a disposition to believe anything he is told.

Secondly, there is another kind of unreflective acceptance which could be named after the paradigm described by Tolstoy in the person of Oblonsky in *Anna Karenina*:

Oblonsky never chose his tendencies and opinions any more than he chose the style of his hat or frock-coat. He always wore those which happened to be in fashion. Moving in a certain circle where a desire for some form of mental activity was part of maturity, he was obliged to hold views in the same way as he was obliged to wear a hat. If he had a reason for preferring Liberalism to the Conservatism of many in his set, it was not that he considered the liberal outlook more rational but because it corresponded better with his mode of life. The Liberal Party maintained that everything in Russia was bad; and in truth Oblonsky had many debts and decidedly too little money. The Liberal Party said that marriage was an obsolete institution which ought to be reformed; and indeed family life gave Oblonsky very little pleasure, forcing him to tell lies and dissemble, which was quite contrary to his nature. The Liberal Party said, or rather assumed, that religion was only a curb on the illiterate; and indeed Oblonsky could not stand through even the shortest church service without aching feet, or understand the point of all that dreadful, high-flown talk about the other world, when life in this world was really very pleasant. . . . Thus Liberalism had become a habit with Oblonsky and he enjoyed his newspaper, as he did his afterdinner cigar, for the slight haze it produced in his brain.[4]

The two key features of the Oblonsky syndrome are first the reliance on what is already accepted by at least a sub-set of one's circle (who are of course the right people) without having reason to think it true, and secondly the choice between alternative fashionable opinions on the basis of personal convenience.

Thirdly, there is the My Lai syndrome, the acceptance of an order as authoritative because it is issued by the appropriate source. The officer says 'shoot anything that moves', so it must be OK. The authority's having spoken not only explains why the subordinate accepts, it is the reason he would give for accepting. To that extent this is not an entirely unreflective kind of acceptance.

Fourthly, there is the reliance on authority of one who says, 'It is right because he says so, and he has good reason to know'.

IV

These modes of acceptance of the word of others are related in importantly different ways to autonomy. It is facile to think that the virtue of autonomy requires emancipation from all of them, and failure to distinguish them with enough care may be responsible for some of the romantic inflation of autonomy.

The difference between the first two kinds of dependence is important in two ways. The first is compatible with the transmission from generation to generation of values which are essential to a properly human way of life, whereas the second mode is a recipe for the dissipation of truth: it ensures that genuine values will be hit upon by accident if at all, and soon lost again. Then, secondly, someone who has the second relation to the source of his opinions has very shallow-rooted opinions to which he will adhere only for so long as to do so remains a condition of his having an agreeable life; they are not his own in the sense of being necessary to the sense he has of being a distinct self. To receive opinions in the first way involves their becoming related to a person's sense of identity in a much deeper way.

The third mode is one that can be ignored in connection with the forming of opinions concerning truth and matter of fact. This is because, in this sphere, saying cannot make it so. Whether a proposition is true depends on whether things are as the proposition says they are. Thus it is manifestly irrational to say, in defence of an opinion, that Smith says that things are thus and so, unless one is prepared to offer reasons for supposing that Smith would not say that things were thus and so unless, independently of what he says, that is how things were. But to defend a moral opinion in this way is not manifestly irrational in the same way, although it is certainly mistaken. There are some commands, and some rules, which come into force simply by being issued by the right person in the right way, and it is possible to treat moral precepts as originating in this way. Theories which give quasi-legal status to moral precepts, and societies or sects in which they are regarded for practical purposes as having that status do exist. Regarded in this way questions about right and wrong are objective, in the sense that there are correct answers to them which are independent of the minds of those trying to discover them. If this account were correct there would be no criticism to be made of someone who relies on authority for his moral principles.

It was on the basis of a rejection of this quasi-legal model that the rationalist moralists argued against both divine law and social contract theories of morality.[5] Neither a single will, nor many wills agreeing together, can be the source of moral laws because that would involve the absurdity of supposing that murder can be made wrong by an act of will. That makes no more sense than supposing that an act of will might determine whether or not $2 + 2 = 4$. Moral laws are 'natural and eternal' truths. Since God is perfectly wise he necessarily knows what the moral laws are and enjoins them on his creatures. But that God has forbidden murder, though a good reason for believing that murder must be wrong, is not what it is for murder to be wrong. No person, not even a democratically elected committee, can introduce a new moral law, nor decide to modify an old one. We can only discover what morality *is*, not decide what it shall be.

Such a view gives a decisive reason against treating any authoritative source of moral precepts as ultimately safe. And it makes intelligible the claim that autonomy requires us to think for ourselves about morality. Just as God, though with greater certainty, sees by his understanding that murder is wrong, so, it may be argued, we can independently by the use of our own understanding see the same. Someone who thinks that an authority's word is a reason for accepting a moral judgment without more ado is mistaken about what the truth of moral judgments depends on. He may hold correct opinions, but he is not entitled to them, cannot defend them and has no reason to be confident that he will not acquire false ones from the same source. The person who thinks for himself, who in short *thinks*, may also make mistakes, but has also adopted the method by which he may detect and correct them.

V

So if there is such a thing as objective truth to be had about right and wrong there is good reason to commend the person who applies his mind to its discovery. But it does not follow that this will preclude the fourth kind of reliance on other people: 'It is right because he says so, and he has good reasons for his opinion'. Yet I suspect that many people will be inclined to say that although autonomy in speculative matters is compatible with the fourth kind of reliance, things are otherwise in practical, and most certainly in moral, matters. It may be consistent with the role of critical enquirer to ask a competent authority whether smoking will damage my health, but it is not consistent with the role of critical moral agent to ask anyone whether I ought to be a conscientious objector, practice contraceptive intercourse, or approve of abortion. It is often said that there are no moral experts, and that one's moral conclusions must be one's own. To be autonomous in morality involves a greater degree of self-sufficiency than to be intellectually autonomous.

Of course this is sometimes said by people who are sceptical about moral truth, and who think that the special importance of autonomy in moral reflection is a consequence of the lack of an objective way of establishing moral conclusions. The objectivist might simply reply that as this scepticism is unfounded the alleged difference between intellectual and moral autonomy is in reality no difference. I do not believe that there is a difference of the sort that the sceptic claims. But there surely is a difference. One can make some show of explaining it without supposing any fundamental difference between the two kinds of enquiry. If I am normally sighted I do not consult experts about whether it is raining. There is no place for experts when the question to be decided calls for normal senses and wits. Kant, it will be remembered, believed that even quite subtle moral distinctions are made with sureness by the common moral consciousness. People who befuddled their minds with sophisticated theories were much more likely, he thought, to allow sophisms to corrupt their clarity of understanding. Then there is the consideration, an important one on any view, that everyone needs his own moral first-aid kit because he is bound to have to deal with emergencies. If he has to call in a specialist every time it will often be too late to save the patient. And after all the ability to make moral decisions is part of the equipment needed if one is to function effectively as a member of society.

These considerations seem to miss something important however. If someone whose practical wisdom I respect says that the torture of prisoners to obtain information is wicked, it would be odd to say, 'Well I don't know about these things, but I know you generally have good reasons for what you say, so I'll take your word for it'. The belief that whales are viviparous is none the worse for being taken from a reliable textbook. I may not know what the reasons are for this proposition; but it is enough that I know that there are some. But it is doubtful whether I know what I am saying if I say that torture is wicked, if my only reason is that I am confident that someone else has good reasons, though I do not know what they are. The evil of torture lies partly in the physical and mental suffering that the victim undergoes, partly in the more permanent damage inflicted on his personality. If I am not myself aware of these features, and if my judgment does not represent a response evoked by them, then it is not the judgment that torture is wicked.

Hume said 'Morality is more properly felt than judged of'. He thought that to judge an action to be virtuous was nothing else than to feel a sentiment of approval or esteem towards it. He may have been wrong in thinking that it was nothing else but he was surely right in thinking that some kind of feeling is a necessary part of a moral judgment. Judging torture to be wicked and loathing it, hating to think that it is going on, feeling impelled to protest about it—these are not readily detachable from one another. To feel appropriately however it is necessary to be exposed to the character of the action, if not through experience then through highly explicit and circumstantial description, so that I really know what it is like.

None of the reasons that I have reviewed would justify the conclusion that there is no such thing as arriving at a mistaken conclusion in thinking about a moral question. Indeed to accept the conclusion of someone more experienced, more imaginative or better at drawing together the implications of a complex array of considerations may mean that one is more likely to have the right opinion. What is at stake however is not only the truth of the opinion but the character of the assent. It must be not notional but real assent.[6] This requires that one should not just take over the conclusions of the practically wise man but try to follow through the process of deliberation that he has followed, so that by appreciating the force and relevance of his reasons one makes the conclusion one's own.

It is fair to ask: What if one does that and still disagrees? Can it ever be consistent with rational autonomy, when faced with such disagreement, to accept the view of the wise man and set one's own on one side? I cannot see anything in the reasons for autonomy that I have considered that would justify one in saying 'No' to this question.

This brings me into direct conflict with a theory which I have up to now ignored, whose main contention is that the moral agent is autonomous in such a sense that he has no alternative, without giving up that status, to arriving at his own moral beliefs. This would be impossible if it were possible to present a person with facts which he could not deny to be facts and from which he could not fail, on pain of irrationality, to draw a unique moral conclusion. This is the view set out by Hare at the beginning of *Freedom and Reason*. It is supported in a more recent book, *Moral Reasoning and Truth*, by Thomas D. Perry. Perry appeals to the presumption that each person has the right to decide general and particular moral issues as an argument against the possibility of giving moral reasoning an objective basis. For if it had one 'then it would be possible to prove to a person, by a moral argument, that his own most careful and sincere moral opinion about something was wrong'. And he says, 'Such a result seems offensive and incorrect'.[7] He concedes that such an argument begs the question against theological or naturalistic ethics, but believes that autonomy in his sense is presupposed by the kind of evaluation that philosophers since Kant and Rousseau have been interested in.

The account of autonomy that I have tried to present could be taken as an attempt to answer this position indirectly. I have tried to explicate a notion of autonomy which is compatible with an objective account of moral reasoning. The suggestion that it is is made plausible by the close parallel with a notion of autonomy that applies to theoretical enquiry. The idea that in enquiries which can yield truth there is no scope for an individual to exercise a right to arrive at his own conclusions will not bear examination. There is an ambiguity which may lend it some color of truth. For 'a right to form one's own opinions' may mean a right to look at the evidence and make inferences for oneself, rather than accept the results of someone else doing it; or it may mean a right to cry up one's own conclusion as 'correct' whatever objections are made against it. The latter is an absurd right to claim in theoretical matters. Whether it makes more sense in practical matters must depend upon the prior question whether there is practical truth.

It cannot be denied that moral arguments even when pursued with patience often end without one party being able to convict the other of error. But can it be denied that they often do not end this way, or that theoretical arguments often do end this way? Moral issues are complex and people can be stubborn.

VI

I remarked earlier that autonomy is closely allied to courage, and that there is a close connection between cognitive and volitional processes in the autonomous person. This applies I think not only to autonomy in the management of daily affairs, but equally to autonomy in thinking, theoretical and practical. To be autonomous in one's thinking calls for intellectual skills, including the ability to judge when someone else knows better than oneself. But it calls also for the ability to control the emotions that prevent those skills from being properly exercised. This is a complex matter. Courage and self-control enter into the *forming* of judgments as well as into acting upon them. That is one complication. A second is that certain emotions, e.g. fear or impatience, may prevent one from thinking clearly, or thinking at all; as, equally, intense emotions may prevent one from acting as judgment would dictate. But there is a more insidious and intimate way in which emotions may subvert thought. The fear of getting the wrong answer, of being thought unorthodox, may actually prevent a person from trusting himself to accept the truth of his own observations or the safety of his own inferences. This is a more fundamental relation between thought and emotion because whereas intense emotions may temporarily make thinking ineffective the fear of being wrong corrupts the faculty itself. A person who cannot take the next step in a process of deliberation without seeing whether the last one is applauded cannot really be said to possess the ability to deliberate. Intellectual skills cannot exist without qualities of character. The fear and anxiety that subvert the mind in forming judgments also subvert the will in standing by them and translating them into action. If others can, by their nods and winks, make up your mind for you, they can also change it for you.

If autonomy calls for a supple mind it also calls for a stiff neck. And from this a problem arises, for the right balance between stiffness and suppleness is hard to strike, and the same balance may not be right for all circumstances. The person who is ever-willing to revise his opinions in the light of criticism, to entertain the thought that even his criteria may need revision, will need to have more than usual confidence in his ability to sort out conflicting considerations and estimate the force of arguments. He will require great strength of character.

There are circumstances in which to maintain control over one's life it may be a definite advantage to have a rigidity of mind that in other circumstances might not be admired. The psycho-analyst Bruno Bettelheim has written a study,[8] based largely on his own observations when an inmate of Hitler's concentration camps, of the response made by different types of personality to the pressures of life in the camps. People from a social class in which external badges of status were important, who depended on the respect and approval of their fellows, were quick to succumb when deprived of these props, 'which had served them in place of self-respect and inner strength'. They tried to copy the life-patterns of other prisoners. Some adopted the outlook of the SS and tried to get accepted as their loyal subordinates. These people conform to a recognizable type of heteronomy.

But who were the people who were best able to make an inner stand against the Nazis and to maintain some standards of decent behavior? They were not intellectuals. Bettelheim distinguishes two groups. There were political prisoners, many of them old Communists, who expected persecution and were not overturned by it. And there were Jehovah's Witnesses, imprisoned as conscientious objectors, who stood out as exceptionally capable of preserving their integrity and helping their fellow-prisoners. Although they were, Bettelheim says, generally narrow in outlook and experience they were 'exemplary comrades, helpful, correct, dependable'. Their conscientious work-habits meant that often they were made foremen of working-parties, a position which gave them much power over other prisoners, but alone of all groups they 'never abused or mistreated other prisoners'.

What should we make of this? There are two main lessons to be drawn. First, much more careful thought needs to be given to the relation between autonomy and tradition. It is easy, but quite mistaken surely, to regard as unimportant the difference between a person who accepts his beliefs and standards of behavior because they are the ones that are for the time approved by his set, and the person who has internalized, whose mind and will have come to embody, beliefs and standards which belong to his tradition. I think that some writers have looked on these as simply two ways of failing to be one's own man. But the second is actually a way of being one's own man; at least it does not preclude it.

The second lesson is this. It may be true that there is a kind of autonomy which is exemplified only by the person who is aware of and can articulate his principles, and is also aware that there are others against which he must be prepared to defend his own. And the Jehovah's Witnesses described by Bettelheim do not have autonomy in that sense. But the kind of autonomy they do have should prevent us from agreeing too easily that the articulate and critical ideal represents a more perfect development of the human personality. Perhaps there can be no single ideal of autonomy.[9]

Notes

1. S. I. Benn, "Freedom, Autonomy and the Concept of a Person," *Proceedings of the Aristotelian Society* 76 (1975–76): 109–131.
2. Cf. R. F. Dearden and Elizabeth Telfer in their symposium, "Autonomy as an Educational Ideal," in *Philosophers Discuss Education*, ed. S. C. Brown (London: Macmillan, 1975).
3. Telfer, 34.
4. L. Tolstoy, *Anna Karenina*, trans. Rosemary Edmonds (Harmondsworth: Penguin Classics, 1954), 19.
5. See, e.g., Ralph Cudworth, *A Treatise Concerning Eternal and Immutable Morality* (1731); extracts from bk. 1 in *British Moralists 1650–1800*, vol. 1, ed. D. D. Raphael (Oxford University Press, 1969), 105f.
6. In the sense of these terms introduced by J. H. Newman, *An Essay in Aid of a Grammar of Assent* (New York: Image Books, 1955), ch. 4.
7. Thomas D. Perry, *Moral Reasoning and Truth: An Essay in Philosophy and Jurisprudence* (Oxford University Press, 1976), 31f.
8. Bruno Bettelheim, *The Informed Heart* (London: Free Press, 1970). Benn ("Freedom, Autonomy," 130, n. 12) refers to this study of "what happens to heteronomous and anomic personalities under conditions of stress." Those who survived best under these circumstances were almost certainly heteronomous on Benn's criteria.
9. I have profited in writing this paper from comments made on an earlier one on the same topic by my colleague Professor F. N. Sibley and my former colleague Mrs. Dorothy Mitchell. They will have forgotten, I have not, and wish to thank them.

Reading Introduction

Generosity and the Diversity of the Virtues
Lester H. Hunt

This essay has two purposes: (1) to point out some features of generosity that
distinguish it from other virtues, and (2) to argue that there are not only many
different virtues, but that virtues can be distinguished into *kinds*, according to the
different kinds of principles they embody.

A *principle*, as Hunt uses the word, is an evaluative belief that some individual
holds in such a way that this belief motivates him or her to act in accordance with
it. Thus a principle is not just an idling opinion about what is good or what ought
to be done. Hunt distinguishes three kinds of principles: (1) *act-necessitating*
principles, such as "I ought to pay my debts," (2) *axiological* principles, such as
"the well-being of other people is, in itself, worth promoting," and (3) *limiting*
principles, such as "my own safety has no more than a certain measure of
importance." Act-necessitating principles are embodied in such virtues as justice
and being a person of one's word. Axiological principles are contained in virtues
like industriousness and generosity. And limiting principles are embedded in such
virtues as courage and temperance.

According to Hunt, because generosity is based on an axiological principle
rather than an act-necessitating one, it has certain special features: (1) It is not
possible to act generously to fulfill an obligation or duty, or because someone
deserves something. (2) If a person omits to do acts of justice and promise-keeping
when they are appropriate, he or she is at fault; no one who omits to do acts of
generosity when the opportunity arises is at fault. (3) When we benefit somebody
through honest or just treatment, we do so "because" this is required in some way;
but with generous actions there is no such further aim beyond that of benefiting
somebody. This explains why generous acts are "spontaneous" and often are (or
seem to be) "impulsive." This last fact seems to imply that generous acts are
"irrational" in a way that acts of justice and honesty are not. Hunt's answer is that
generous acts are, indeed, not rational in the *same way* as acts of justice and
honesty. But this does not mean that they are irrational, for they are done on the
axiological principle of generosity—namely, the principle that the good of other
people is, in itself, worth bringing about.

Generosity and the Diversity of the Virtues

LESTER H. HUNT

I

Thinking about the virtues has often brought out the Eleatic tendencies of philosophers. Socrates, the Sophists, Plato, Aristotle, and Kant all believed in some form of "the unity of the virtues," the idea that the virtues are all one thing, either because they are really the same trait or because they are somehow inseparable from one another. But reflecting on virtue can also lead one to believe in the diversity of the virtues. This is the notion that they are not only distinct and separable traits, but differ from one another in important ways.

In what follows I will use generosity as evidence for the diversity of virtue. I will try to show that, interestingly enough, one can provide evidence for this idea by adopting a thesis which is typically also used in monistic theories of virtue: the idea that virtue rests on the agent's understanding of the right and the good. This can be done because, as it will turn out, what the agent must understand in order to possess different virtues is different. I will begin, in sections II through IV, by contrasting generosity with four other ways of acting which are generally thought to have ethical merit. Our first clue concerning the nature of generosity will be found in the fact that the other four have a certain characteristic in common, one which generous conduct lacks.[1]

II

It is very natural to want to say that, whatever else might be true of them, ethically meritorious acts are always done "in order to fulfill our obligations" or "for the sake of duty." Such remarks can mean various things. For philosophers, "obligation" and "duty" are often synonymous, and simply refer to anything we are morally required to do. But it is possible, by simplifying somewhat, to see these two words as bearing two different meanings as they are ordinarily used by non-philosophers. I will suppose that obligations in the ordinary use of the word, are typically incurred by previous committing actions (such as signing one's name) while a person is generally said to have duties in virtue of one's special status or position relative to other people (for instance, one's profession).[2] It is easy to see that in this sense it is not true that generous acts are done in order to fulfill one's duties or obligations. In itself, this fact is perhaps not very interesting, but when it is understood it will suggest why, in the more traditionally philosophical sense of those words, this statement is still not true.

Consider an example of an obligation in the ordinary sense of the word. If I were to take a bottle of wine next door and give it to my neighbor my act would not be generous if, for instance, I borrowed a similar one from him last week and am giving him one today in

Lester H. Hunt, "Generosity and the Diversity of the Virtues." Printed by permission of the author.

order to set matters straight. That is not a generous act but an attempt to pay a debt. (I say "attempt" because it is not in virtue of the fact that it *is* the payment of a debt but rather because it is intended to be, that an act fails to be generous.) For example, suppose that I have forgotten that I had borrowed the wine from my neighbor and give him some today as a friendly favor: afterwards he reminds me of the debt and we agree that it is settled. In that case the act would be both a generous deed and the payment of a debt. But if I do it *in order to* pay the debt what I do will not ordinarily be generous at all. In general, to the extent that acts are done to fulfill one's obligations—to pay one's bills, keep one's promises, and live up to one's contracts, for instance—they cannot be generous.

The same is also true of acting to fulfill the duties of one's station in life: father, janitor, citizen, and so forth. Peter is not being generous in sweeping Paul's floor, if he is Paul's janitor and is supposed to sweep his floor, and does it for that reason. The point is sufficiently obvious without adding more examples.

The actions that are interesting for ethics are not often done for a single reason. But we can see, by considering such reasons in isolation from one another, that some reasons fail to distinguish an act as generous and make it some other sort of act instead. Early in Thucydides' *History* a group of representatives from the city of Corcyra come to Athens to ask the Athenians to fight with them in their present conflict with Corinth. At the beginning of their plea they make a frank admission:

> We have come to ask for help, but cannot claim that this is due us because of any
> great services we have done you in the past or on the basis of any existing alliance.[3]

That is, Athens neither has an obligation to help in virtue of favors it has accepted in the past, nor does it have a duty to do so as a member of a league. But the Corcyrean embassy goes on to say that their request is actually "an extraordinary stroke of good luck" for Athens because under the circumstances helping them would be a noble thing to do: "the world in general will admire you for your generosity."[4] It would be a generous thing for them to do *because* it is not due them in these ways. On the basis of what we have seen so far it is at least plausible to say that if the Corcyreans had argued for assistance on the grounds that it was owed them, they would be recommending it as something other than a generous act. I will return to this point in section IV.

III

There is another sort of act, similar to the two just considered, which can easily be distinguished from generosity. It includes those actions in which something is given to someone because the recipient is thought to deserve it. It is just, and not generous, to give a student an "A" for having done excellent work, or to give a soldier a medal for unusual bravery. To say that it was generous to give a certain student an "A", or a certain soldier a medal, is to say that they did *not* deserve it, or that it is not clear whether they did—at least in the giver's estimation. Generosity—as, perhaps, tolerance and mercy as well—includes a certain disregard for desert, and it should be helpful in understanding the ways in which the virtues are related to one another to notice that it is a sort of disregard that can be liable to criticism at times. For instance: Imagine a person who believes that an essay by Peter is obviously superior to one by Paul which is on the same subject and discovers that Peter has included Paul's essay in an anthology he has edited, but not his own. Such a person could either criticize Peter for being unfair to himself and for giving Paul more than he deserves—or he could praise him for his generosity.

From these facts we can see that there is a sort of tension between generosity on the one hand and justice in the form of recognizing and rewarding personal desert on the other, in that (a) those actions which can be generous—ones in which something is given to someone—are precisely those which can be just, (b) in some types of transactions—grading, for instance—the same act cannot be both at once, and (c) acts which are liable to praise for being generous can easily also be liable to criticism for failing to be just. This does not mean that such actions are *un*just, provided that we accept the view, apparently held by Aristotle,[5] that it is not unjust to benefit someone else more than they deserve, nor to benefit oneself less than one deserves, but only the reverse. In that case, some actions which fail to be just—which could be just but are not—are not unjust acts, and this would be the sort of failure to be just that is connected with generosity. But this way of failing to be just *is* liable to criticism.

IV

Each of these three sorts of action—those I have associated with obligation, duty, and desert—are actions in which something is given to someone, and in each one the recipient of the act has some characteristic (this person has loaned me a certain thing, this person is my employer, this person is a student who has done outstanding work) in virtue of which the giving is *called for*, and the thing given is *the person's due*. In the case of duties and obligations this means that the person who has the duty or obligation *must* do the giving (unless there are counteracting considerations involved), that it is a fault to omit it (a failure to do one's duties, etc.). The case of desert is somewhat different, in that the fact that someone deserves something, such as praise, does not by itself mean that any particular person should give it to them; that would depend on further facts about the particular person (if the deserving individual is a film maker and I am a film reviewer discussing his film, then it would be a fault of mine if I were to fail to praise him). But still, the fact that someone deserves a certain thing means that it would be bad if they were not to get it, that someone (if not anyone in particular) should give it to them; so there is a sort of necessity in this case too.

The contrast between generosity and these other ways of acting re-enforces the suggestion I have made in section II that in generous acts what is given is not given because it is owed to the recipient in *any* way. It is obvious, though, that this suggestion is too broad to be adequately supported by the evidence I have given so far. A philosopher who believes that the intention to fulfill one's obligations or duties is what makes an act ethically meritorious might well want to object to it as it stands:

"We are sure to be misled here," someone might say to me, "unless we make an important distinction which you referred to earlier. When the ambassadors in the incident from Thucydides say that it would be morally praiseworthy for the Athenians to help their city, they are not saying that Athens owes them assistance in the sense that I owe money to the telephone company—that they have an 'obligation' in virtue of having entered into some sort of agreement. But this is not quite what 'obligation' means when the word occurs in philosophical theories which say that a praiseworthy act is one which is done to fulfill one's obligations. There it is used to convey a *philosophical* concept. The philosophical concept of obligation has an application in this case which might be explained as follows: In arguing for assistance the Corcyreans must be appealing to some principle which they and their audience hold in common. This principle would be a rule which they think enjoins help in these circumstances. To obey such a rule is to do the right thing, to disobey it is a fault—just as, if I owe money to the phone company it would be wrong for me not to pay it, other things being equal. In this sense they are saying that assistance is their due and Athens 'owes' it to them, and this sense is what the philosopher's concept of obligation amounts to. If the Athenians respond in a morally meritorious way they will act because they think the Corcyreans' claim is true."

This interpretation of the facts derives from a view of what all ethically meritorious action must be like, which in turn rests on a theory of what all principles must be like. Here, principles are seen as rules which enjoin actions and which do so by declaring which act must be done in the circumstances to which the rule applies. I will call such rules "act-necessitating rules." The rules of etiquette, and perhaps those of grammar, are act-necessitating rules.

My imaginary interlocutor is saying that whenever one acts generously one is following an act-necessitating rule. Is this true? It should be noticed that his description of the incident from Thucydides merely assumes that this is so; the example does not support this point by itself. The Corcyreans neither say nor suggest that the Athenians would be at fault if they didn't come to their aid and it is not obvious that they must think so. They appear to be requesting help, not demanding it. Whether generous acts are ones which follow act-necessitating rules is still an open question, unless some good reason can be found for answering it one way or the other.

There is actually a rather simple reason why generous acts cannot be observances of act-necessitating rules. As the interlocutor has suggested, failure to act as an act-necessitating rule enjoins is (assuming the soundness of the rule and the absence of a valid excuse) a fault—conduct worthy of criticism or censure. For instance, the omission of an act enjoined by a rule of etiquette is generally an impropriety: a slip, a blunder, or a piece of rude or crude behavior. But there does not seem to be any generous act the omission of which would be a fault. Admittedly, it might be wrong of me to omit helping someone who I know is in serious need and whom I can easily help, but in that case—to introduce what seems to me a useful and natural distinction—the act which I would be omitting would be an act of charity rather than generosity. In this sense[6] a charitable act is a response to conditions of need, such as poverty, in virtue of which the act is called for, while a generous act is not. Charitable acts appear to be observances of act-necessitating rules, but that would not mean that generous acts are. Again, it is natural to suppose that, since stinginess is the opposite of generosity, the omission of any generous act is stingy and therefore worthy of censure. But this will not do. Stinginess is never simply the omission of a generous act; stinginess is a trait of character and must include its own underlying motivational source just as generosity does, which means that a stingy act (or omission) is one which is done for certain reasons and is not the mere omission of some other sort of act. Generosity and stinginess are contraries, and not contradictories, as observances and breaches of etiquette are.

I will soon give another reason why generous acts cannot be observances of act-necessitating rules, but first I must press the analysis of generosity a bit further.

V

So far, I have distinguished generosity from other ways of acting by indicating reasons for action which do not produce generous action. I will eventually try to show what generosity itself is by showing what reasons do lie behind it. As a first step toward this end, I will focus on a somewhat simpler and easier task: that of showing with what intention generous acts are done. "The generous intention," as it might be called, is crucial for understanding what it is to act generously. By saying what sort of intention it is, I will have distinguished generosity from nearly every other way of acting. I can then distinguish it from the rest by making a small addition to my account of the reasons for which generous things are done. When this is done, we will have an account of what generosity is.

One fact about the generous intention is quite obvious. In acting generously, one always intends to benefit someone other than oneself. But this fact does not distinguish generous acts from ones done to fulfill one's duties or obligations, or to give someone what he deserves. Sometimes the duties of a person's station in life include not only specific actions, like the janitor's sweeping the floor, but also a requirement to benefit someone in some general way, to protect and advance their real interests. A father stands in such a relation toward his children, and the same is true of what the law calls a trustee and the person in whose behalf the trust is managed. In such cases, an action may be done in order to benefit someone and by that fact be an action done in fulfillment of duty. And, in similar ways, acts in which something is given because one has an obligation to do so or because the recipient deserves it can be done with the intention of benefiting him.

But in generous acts the *way* the benefit is intended is different from the way it is intended in the other cases. If we ask a man with a worthless son why he persists in helping him out of trouble, the answer will be something like "Because he's my son," insofar as he is doing it because it is his paternal duty. That is, so far he is benefiting him in order to fulfill the requirements of being a father, and what he does is to that extent not generous. The same result obtains with acts in which we benefit someone in order to give them what they deserve or in order to return a favor. In the case of generous acts there is no such "because" or "in order to" beyond the intention of benefiting someone: we do not do *that* in order to do something else. In this way, the intention in such acts is gratuitous.[7]

This provides us with an explanation of some facts mentioned in sections II and III: that it is sometimes impossible for an act to be done in order to fulfill a duty or an obligation, or in order to give someone what they deserve, and also be generous; in fact we can see that these phenomena have something necessary about them. The contrast between generosity and these other ways of acting is not a matter of having two different sorts of intention in doing what one does; it is a contrast between having certain intentions and *not* having them. There are cases in which an act can be characterized as generous and also as belonging to one of the types I discussed in sections II and III, but such cases don't seem to be the sort that show this principle to be false. An act can be both generous and done in order to fulfill a duty if the duty is one that the agent does not find clearly binding (a "duty" to give gifts to relatives at Christmas could be like this). Just as a vague statement can be said to be both true and false, so an intention that is vague in this way can be said to be in a way dutiful and a way not. We find something similar in the cases of some supererogatory acts, as when I repay cheap wine with excellent wine. Here part of what I do is something required of me (giving back what I have borrowed) and part of it is not (giving more than I received). In both sorts of cases a person may be said both to have and not to have the sort of intention that cancels the generosity of the act.

VI

For many generous acts, if we ask the agent why it was done—"Why did you give your neighbor a bottle of wine?"—we are liable to get an answer like "I just thought I would" or "It was an impulse." At any rate, such answers to such questions would always make perfect sense. Answers like these, however, do not make sense with many other transactions in which something is given to someone. If you ask a man why he gave a dollar bill to his grocer and he replies, "I just thought I would," that means he was not trying to buy something. If a teacher is asked why he or she gave certain students high grades and the teacher responds, "It was an impulse," it means that the teacher was not trying to give the students what they deserve. If I told you that I sent ten dollars to the telephone company "on impulse," you would probably suppose that, whatever I was doing, I was not trying to pay my bill. If a person gives something and then claims that it was given on impulse, he or she thereby excludes the act from these three classes: attempts to purchase something, attempts to reward personal desert, and attempts to pay one's debts. And, what is most important, such claims have the same significance in relation to observances of act-necessitating rules. If a man at a dinner party truthfully claims that he has just eaten his mashed potatoes with his spoon (rather than his hands) "on impulse" it means that he is not doing so because he believes that this is what one should do in these circumstances—because, that is, he subscribes to a rule of etiquette. Generous acts are different in kind from such observances because such claims do not exclude an act from being generous.

This suggests, at least with the aid of some reflection, that there is a problem about the connection between generosity and human rationality. The problem is that the connection can be made to seem rather loose. In one sense of "rational," an act can be said to be rational only if the agent had some reason (perhaps a bad one) for what he or she did. A clue to the nature of the problem can be found in a remark Elizabeth Anscombe has made, to the effect that such claims as "It was an impulse" and "I just thought I would" signify that the speaker *had no reason* for what he or she did.[8] In other words, it looks as if the generosity of an act is always compatible with a claim which would indicate that the act was not rational. This would mean that generous acts are not necessarily rational ones. However, this somewhat exaggerates the nature of the problem. While many acts that are done "on impulse" are done for no reason at all, this is not true, without qualification, of all of them. If someone generously gives a book to someone else and we ask them why, there are *some* things they might truthfully say which could be called "giving a reason": they might say, "Because it's an interesting one," for instance, or "I thought he would enjoy it," or "It explains some things very well." And it seems that, even if someone had acted for "reasons" like these, they might instead have truthfully said "It was an impulse" or "I just thought I would." However, although acting on impulse and the like is compatible with acting for such reasons, it is not compatible with acting on the basis of certain types of *principles*:

a. Many kinds of acts have what might be called a "constitutive aim": that is, there is some state of affairs which must be mentioned in the definition of that kind of act as the one which the agent intends, by the act, to bring about. Every generous act is an attempt to bring it about that someone other than the agent possesses some good. All other effects of the act might be called its "consequences." In this sense, although an act which is done on impulse may have a constitutive aim, such acts are never done for their consequences. Every one who opens a window on impulse intends to get the window open, but if I open the window on impulse, I do not do *that* in order to cool the room down, signal someone across the street, etc. The same thing is true of impulsively generous acts and, indeed, of generous acts in general. This implies that impulsive acts and generous ones as well are not done because they are required by rules which cite some consequence of the act as a reason for doing it. In this sense, they are not done on the basis of a "hypothetical imperative."
b. As I have said, impulsive acts and generous acts are not done on the basis of act-necessitating rules.[9]

Together, (a) and (b) suggest that Miss Anscombe's remark about acting on impulse may be substantially correct, and that it might with the same force apply to generous acts as such. The fact that generous acts — to concentrate on the case that concerns us directly — have a constitutive aim makes possible such answers to the question "Why did you do that?" as "Because it's an interesting one," "I thought he would like it," and so forth. Such claims simply assert the efficiency of the act as a route to its constitutive aim. But (a) and (b) cut off two classic ways of giving one's reason for *doing the act at all*. In fact, it rather looks as though all ways have been cut off. The answers in my example all make sense as answers to the question "Why give this person this book (instead of something else)?" But suppose we were to ask the person who has given the book, "Why give him something (anything)?" The answers given are not answers to *this* question, and indeed it seems as if any answer that might be given to this one would signify that the act was so far not generous — for instance, "I owe him a favor," "I promised I would," "It's his reward for being a good boy," "He's in a position to help me out later on." It looks as though, to put the point another way, the *way* a generous act is done can have a reason, but *that* it is done cannot.

Kant seems to have believed, at least when he wrote the *Groundwork*, that actions which do not proceed from either hypothetical imperatives or act-necessitating rules do not proceed from reason at all but merely from the blind stirrings of inclination or impulse. Given what I have said about generosity so far, this idea would seem to impose a dilemma on me: I seem to have to choose between rejecting the notion that generosity is a virtue and accepting the notion that one of the virtues arises from an utterly irrational source. In what follows I will try to show that generosity does, in a sense, proceed "from reason." In doing so, though, I must do justice to the antinomian physiognomy of generosity, which gives it at least a superficial similarity to things done on blind impulse. This can be done if one realizes that hypothetical imperatives and act-necessitating rules are not the only sorts of principles which move human beings to act.

VII

In the preceding section of this paper I distinguished generosity from many other ways of acting by referring solely to the agent's intention to bring about a certain state of affairs. But different intentions relate to the agent's beliefs and desires in radically different ways. It is apparently possible to intend to bring about a state of affairs which one does not believe is really worthwhile. An alcoholic can buy a bottle of whiskey with the intention of drinking it in spite of the fact that he believes on religious and hygienic grounds that drinking, as he does it, is bad, and in spite of the fact that he has in good faith made promises to his wife and his clergyman never to drink again. Of course, there is pleasure in his drinking as there would be pain in his abstaining — that is why he intends to drink — but he regards the pleasure as worthless and the pain as salubrious. There is evidently a difference between believing that something is good, on the one hand, and such things as finding it pleasant or liking it, on the other; and just as the *akratic* behavior of this alcoholic is possible, so is it possible to attempt to bring some state of affairs about because one believes it is important or worthwhile. Generous acts are plainly of the latter sort. That is, such acts are done at least partly because one believes *that the good of others is important or worthwhile*. But we have seen that insofar as acts are generous, those who do them do not benefit someone else in order to accomplish some further result. Consequently, if they were to believe that the good of others is only worth pursuing when one thereby accomplishes something else, they would believe that the end they seek is not worth pursuing in the way they pursue it. If we call ends which do not need this further support ones which are "important or worthwhile in themselves," we must add that one who acts generously believes that the good of others is important or worthwhile *in itself*.

At this point it should be helpful to use a bit of terminology which I have introduced elsewhere.[10] Normative and evaluative beliefs have implications about how one should act. Such implications may be quite vague, but there are always ways of behaving which are appropriate, given that one holds a particular belief of this sort. I will call a normative or evaluative belief a principle when one acts in the way that is appropriate to it and does so because one holds that belief.[11] In spite of the similarity which generosity bears to acting on blind impulse, it does proceed from principle in this sense of the word. It arises from some part of the agent's understanding of the right and the good.

However, the way in which it is generated by principle is different from the way my interlocutor had in mind, since the principle I have just formulated is quite different from an act-necessitating rule: although to hold the principle of generosity, as I will call it, is to act in certain ways, the principle itself does not require that any *particular* act be done. For instance, at this moment I know that I would be benefiting my neighbor if I went next door and gave a certain book to him. But even though I know this, and would lose nothing of importance by doing so, I am not at all inclined to do it. Such a consideration does not ordinarily function as a reason to do something, all by itself. There are further considerations, however, which could *make* it a reason: if my neighbor had recently done me a favor and I believed that favors should always be returned, that could make the fact that doing this would benefit my neighbor a reason for going out and doing it (perhaps not a sufficient reason, but a reason all the same); the belief that I could advance some particular interest of mine by doing it would have the same sort of significance. But the notion that the good of others is a worthwhile end of action does not have this significance; it does not imply (even vaguely) that one should (now, in these circumstances) give something to a certain person; it does not answer the question "Why give this man something?" Granting that this notion is true, the question of whether I should now give my neighbor a certain book is still wide open. To answer a question like this, one needs other kinds of principles. This principle can move me to act, but it would not do so by implying what I should do. It can only do so by enabling me to see certain possible courses of action as *opportunities*.

VIII

This last point can easily be generalized. Generous behavior is not done because circumstances require it, but because the agent *seeks* to do such things. In this sense, generosity is spontaneous. It has this characteristic because of the type of principle on which it is based. The principle of generosity is what I will call an "axiological principle," one which identifies some good as a worthwhile end of action in itself. Such principles have a definite function in the life of the individual who holds them. They do not enable us to solve problems or do what is appropriate to our circumstances, they simply turn us and direct us toward the good. We should expect other traits which are based on principles of this kind to be spontaneous in the same way that generosity is. For instance, this is true of industriousness, which is apparently generated by an axiological principle—namely, the principle that effort is worthwhile as such. Although one's effort can be required by one's circumstances, an act is never industrious if it is done simply for that reason: industriousness is not a dutiful willingness to do what must be done. In fact, the most distinctive sign of an industrious person is precisely his or her aptness to look for opportunities for effort, and to press activity further than circumstance requires—even, sometimes, further than it properly allows. These two traits suit very well the view of virtue expressed in Ferdinand Galiani's ambivalent aphorism, "Virtue is enthusiasm."

Traits which arise from principles which are relevantly different from those of generosity and industriousness are not characterized by spontaneity. It does not belong to the nature of courage as such to spontaneously seek to do courageous things. If brave people do sometimes seek to do such things, it is not simply because they are courageous, but because (for instance) they are aggressive or love adventure or honor. Nor is temperance spontaneous. The very idea that temperance leads people to seek out pleasures of the flesh in order to exercise their iron wills in resisting them has something absurd about it. These facts are not hard to explain if we suppose, as I have argued elsewhere,[12] that courage and temperance are based on what I call "limiting principles." These are principles which consist in the agent's recognizing a limit on the importance of some end of action. In the case of courage and temperance, the relevant ends are safety and physical pleasure, respectively. While axiological principles commit the agent to seek certain goods, limiting principles do not. They commit the agent to *letting go* of certain goods in certain circumstances. Traits like courage and temperance are revealed, not in what the agent seeks, but in what the agent can do without or put up with. Such traits are illustrations of the Stoic maxim "Bear and forbear."

IX

Perhaps a disclaimer is needed here. I have argued that generous acts are not irrational, in that they do not proceed from a blind stirring of the will, but rather from the agent's beliefs about what is good. This does not by any means imply that such acts are essentially intelligent, as we ordinarily use that word. The belief which makes an act generous is general in nature; it is not a belief about the agent, the recipient, or their circumstances. Consequently, the fact that someone did not think rightly about such things does not mean that what they did failed to be generous. There is no contradiction at all in saying something like "He shouldn't have given that much money away because he can't afford to, but you can't doubt his generosity," or "She shouldn't have given him that money because he will only use it to harm himself, but you can't fault her for her generosity." An act can only be intelligent because of what the agent thinks about the particulars involved, such as the appropriateness of the act to its recipient or to the agent's own circumstances. And this means that a generous act is not necessarily intelligent, for, as Aristotle would say, one may possess the universal and lack the particular. Of course, if an action shows a gross sort of negligence, that would lead us quite rightly to doubt that it was a generous one,[13] but only because it would lead us to doubt the genuineness of the agent's intention to benefit someone — not because intelligence in the ordinary sense is part of the concept of generosity. The fact remains that a fully generous act may be utterly misguided and miscarried.

This indicates a radical disanalogy between generosity and the virtue of justice, in addition to the ones which are more or less obvious from my previous discussion. To say that an act is just is to say that it brings about a situation in which someone has what is their due. This would seem to mean that in acting justly one follows an act-necessitating rule, or something very much like one (see section IV). In addition, an act is only said to be just if it would *actually* bring about such a state of affairs, unless something extraneous to the agent prevents it (as when a judge renders a just decision and the police fail to enforce it). Justice, unlike generosity, is not a matter of good intentions. It requires accurate perception and good judgement concerning the recipient and the recipient's circumstances. Consequently, justice by nature requires a certain measure of intelligence.

The same sort of contrast can be found between generosity and prudence. It is clear that no one would call an act prudent if it would fail to serve the agent's interest in the absence of external interference. In ordering the murder of Banquo and Fleance, Macbeth intended to ensure that his interests would prevail, but his action was imprudent (among other things) nonetheless. This was so because, through his own fault, he actually put himself in danger needlessly, whatever he may have intended. Actions are called just and prudent at least partly in virtue of their relation to things other than the agent, in such a way that they require that the agent know something about the world, but they are called generous only in relation to the agent's own thoughts and intentions.

X

The case of generosity should be rather intimidating to anyone who is trying to formulate an interesting thesis about the characteristics which all the virtues have in common. It prevents us from saying, as Kant did, that virtue is the subjection of our natural inclinations to the commands of the moral law. It also stands in our way if we wish to say, as Aristotle did, that it consists in the fact that our actions and passions consistently find a mean between too much and too little. It also implies that we cannot say that virtue consists in doing what one ought to do, or that it always involves accurate perceptions and good judgement about the world around us. Of course, the data I have collected here are not incompatible with all possible characterizations of virtue in general. It allows us to say, for instance, that a virtue is a trait of character in which one acts on some principle which is true. But, considering that principles in this sense of the word form a rather wide and heterogeneous class of beliefs, this characterization seems impoverished in comparison with the traditional definitions of virtue. The others say more, and consequently are more interesting.

This indicates an important truth about how the virtues ought to be studied. If we thought that there is a characterization of virtue in general which is both interesting and true, we might well have relatively little reason—other than a scrupulous concern for small details—for looking at the differences between individual virtues. The truth seems to be, though, that it is in investigating these differences that the interesting results are to be found. If what I have said here is true, it is by investigating them that we will understand what kinds of traits the various virtues are and how they work in forming a good life.[14]

Notes

1. Much of the following discussion is adapted from portions of a paper I wrote twelve years ago on the same subject: "Generosity," *American Philosophical Quarterly* 12 (1975): 235–44. The view of generosity I present here, however, is markedly different from the one I presented in the earlier paper. This difference is entirely due to the fact that I now have at my disposal a general theory of

traits of character which I set forth in two later papers: "Character and Thought," *American Philosophical Quarterly* 15 (1978): 177–86; and "Courage and Principle," *Canadian Journal of Philosophy* 10 (1980): 281–93. This theory of character has enabled me to avoid certain vaguely irrationalist connotations of my earlier account of generosity.

2. Here I am following a precedent set by E. J. Lemmon in "Moral Dilemmas," *The Philosophical Review* 71 (1962): 140–42.

3. Thucydides, *The Peloponnesian War*, trans. Rex Warner (Baltimore: Penguin Books, 1954), 30.

4. Thucydides, 31.

5. *Nicomachean Ethics*, 1134a 1–7 and 1138a 4–28.

6. In Christian literature, "charity" is often used to signify (something like) benevolence in general; here I am using it in the narrower sense in which it means almsgiving.

7. This fact distinguishes generous acts from otherwise similar acts which are done out of guilt. If I give a bottle of wine to my friend today because I feel guilty about having insulted him yesterday, I benefit him in order to expiate for what I have done.

8. G.E.M. Anscombe, *Intention* (Ithaca, N.Y.: Cornell University Press, 1963), §17–18.

9. I will avoid trying to settle the issue of whether hypothetical imperatives and act-necessitating rules are mutually exclusive classes. Kant would say that no hypothetical imperative can necessitate an act because any such principle only applies to agents with certain desires, and those desires *could be otherwise*. This seems to confuse two kinds of necessity: practical necessity (which is simply the fact that the omission of a certain act would be a fault) and what can be called metaphysical necessity (which is the fact that something could not be otherwise).

10. See "Character and Thought" and "Courage and Principle," passim.

11. Note that I do not assume that the agent is aware of holding the belief or acting on it. As far as what I am saying here is concerned, all of this may be quite unconscious (as it probably usually is). See "Character and Thought," 183.

12. "Courage and Principle," 284–93.

13. There is one sort of negligence which is definitely incompatible with generosity. Generous actions are intended to promote someone's good, and what is good for people is not necessarily what they want or what pleases them. Acts which are done in order to give people such things, and *not* what is good for them, are not generous. No one would call it generous if Peter gives ten dollars to Paul when he believes that, because Paul is an alcoholic, he will only use the money to harm himself. "If that's what he wants, let him have it!" is not the sort of reason for acting which reveals a generous intention.

14. I would like to thank Robert C. Roberts for his useful comments on an earlier draft of this paper.

Reading Introduction

Compassion
Lawrence Blum

Blum's discussion of compassion is a sample of the descriptive work that philosophers are beginning to do on individual virtues and vices. From such work we can hope that a larger picture of the life of virtue will emerge, both comprehensive and rich in detail. But beyond the particular insights into compassion that this essay yields, it is interesting for a number of reasons. It shows one of the ways emotion figures in the life of virtue—for this virtue *is* a disposition to a certain emotional state. It illustrates also that emotions are not just "irrational" internal happenings—the psychological equivalent of hunger pangs, orgasms, or the passing of gas. Instead, an emotion like compassion can be a full participant in the moral life because it is internally connected in certain definite ways with such things as recognizing and caring about another person's suffering, the conceptualization of the person as a member of the human community, and the performance of actions (in particular, ones aimed at relieving the sufferer's distress). A consideration of compassion also shows that virtues can be valuable in themselves, not just because of the actions that they cause people to do.

Compassion

LAWRENCE BLUM

This paper offers an account of compassion as a moral phenomenon. I regard compassion as a kind of emotion or emotional attitude; though it differs from paradigmatic emotions such as fear, anger, distress, love, it has, I will argue, an irreducible affective dimension.

Compassion is one among a number of attitudes, emotions, or virtues which can be called "altruistic" in that they involve a regard for the good of other persons. Some others are pity, helpfulness, well-wishing. Such phenomena and the distinctions between them have been given insufficient attention in current moral philosophy. By distinguishing compassion from some of these other altruistic phenomena I want to bring out compassion's particular moral value, as well as some of its limitations.[1]

My context for this inquiry is an interest in developing an alternative to Kantianism, in particular to its minimization of the role of emotion in morality and its exclusive emphasis on duty and rationality. I am influenced here by Schopenhauer's critique of Kant's ethics

From *Explaining Emotions*, ed. Amelie O. Rorty (Berkeley: University of California Press, 1980): 507–18. Reprinted by permission of the publisher, University of California Press.

and by his view of compassion as central to morality.[2] But discussion of the specific views of these two philosophers will be peripheral to my task here.

The Objects of Compassion

How must a compassionate person view someone in order to have compassion for him?[3] Compassion seems restricted to beings capable of feeling or being harmed. Bypassing the question of compassion for plants, animals, institutions, I will focus on persons as objects of compassion. A person in a negative condition, suffering some harm, difficulty, danger (past, present, or future) is the appropriate object of compassion. But there are many negative conditions and not all are possible objects of compassion. The inconvenience and irritation of a short detour for a driver on his way to a casual visit are not compassion-grounding conditions.[4] The negative condition must be relatively central to a person's life and well-being, describable as pain, misery, hardship, suffering, affliction, and the like. Although it is the person and not merely the negative condition which is the object of compassion, the focus of compassion is the condition.

Compassion can be part of a complex attitude toward its object; it is possible to have compassion for someone in a difficult or miserable situation without judging his overall condition to be difficult or miserable. It is therefore necessary to distinguish the conditions for someone being an appropriate object of compassion from the conditions for compassion being the appropriate dominant response to the person. One might predominantly admire and take pleasure in the happiness of a blind person who has gotten through college, found a rewarding job, made close friends—someone whose life is generally happy and who does not dwell on what he misses by being blind. Nevertheless one can also feel compassion for him because his life is deficient and damaged by his blindness.

It is not necessary that the object of compassion be aware of his condition; he might be deceiving himself with regard to it. Nor, as in the case of the happy blind man, need he think of it as a substantial affliction, even if he is aware of it as a deficiency.

That compassion is limited to grave or serious negative conditions does not exclude other altruistic emotions from being entirely appropriate to less serious states. One can feel sorry for, commiserate with, or feel sympathy for a person's irritation, discomfort, inconvenience, displeasure. Nor are all altruistic attitudes primarily directed to particular persons: they can be directed to classes of persons (the blind) or to general conditions (poverty). In addition, there are altruistic virtues not so clearly involving emotions, which come into play in regard to less serious negative conditions: considerateness, thoughtfulness, helpfulness. It would be considerate or thoughtful to warn an acquaintance of an unexpected detour so that he could avoid needless inconvenience and irritation. Such virtues as these, while not necessarily involving emotion or feeling, do involve attention to another's situation and a genuine regard for the other's good, even when more self-regarding attitudes are conjointly brought into play.

Not all altruistic emotions are focused on negative states. Someone might take delight in giving pleasure to others. Though this altruistic attitude shares with compassion a regard for the good of others, compassion focuses on pain, suffering, and damage, whereas this other attitude focuses on pleasure. The capacity for one altruistic attitude is no assurance of the capacity for others. It is quite possible for a compassionate person to be insensitive to the pleasures of others. A focus on misery and suffering in the absence of regard for others' joys and pleasures constitutes a limitation in the moral consciousness of the merely compassionate person.[5]

The Emotional Attitude of Compassion

The compassionate person does not merely believe that the object suffers some serious harm or injury; such a belief is compatible with indifference, malicious delight in his suffering, or intense intellectual interest, for example of a novelist or psychologist for whom the suffering is primarily material for contemplation or investigation. Even a genuine interest in relieving someone's suffering can stem from meeting an intellectual or professional challenge rather than from compassion.

Compassion is not a simple feeling-state but a complex emotional attitude toward another, characteristically involving imaginative dwelling on the condition of the other person, an active regard for his good, a view of him as a fellow human being, and emotional responses of a certain degree of intensity.

Imaginatively reconstructing someone's condition is distinct from several sorts of "identification" with the other person. For instance, it does not involve an identity confusion in which the compassionate person fails to distinguish his feelings and situation from the other person's.[6] Such a pathological condition actually precludes genuine compassion because it blurs the distinction between subject and object.

In a second type of identification the subject "identifies" with the object because of having had an experience similar to his, the memory of which his experience evokes. ("I can identify with what you are going through, since I've suffered from the same problem myself.") Here no identity confusion is involved. While such identification can promote compassion and imaginative understanding it is not required for it. For compassion does not require even that its subject have experienced the sort of suffering that occasions it. We can commiserate with someone who has lost a child in a fire, even if we do not have a child or have never lost someone we love. The reason for this is that the imaginative reconstruction involved in compassion consists in imagining what the other person, given his character, beliefs, and values is undergoing, rather than what we ourselves would feel in his situation. For example I might regard my son's decision to work for the CIA with distress, while someone with different beliefs and values might regard such a decision with pride; yet this other person may well be able to understand my reaction and to feel compassion for me in regard to it.

The degree of imaginative reconstruction need not be great. The friend in the previous example might find it difficult to reconstruct for herself the outlook and set of values within which my son's decision is viewed with distress. But to have compassion she must at least dwell in her imagination on the fact that I am distressed. So some imaginative representation is a necessary condition for compassion, though the degree can be minimal. Certainly a detailed and rich understanding of another person's outlook and consciousness, of the sort available only to persons of exceptional powers of imagination, is not required for compassion.

Nevertheless, as a matter of empirical fact, we often do come to understand someone's condition by imagining what our own reactions would be. So expanding our powers of imagination expands our capacity for compassion. And conversely the limits of a person's capacities for imaginative reconstruction set limits on her capacity for compassion. Finding another person's experience opaque may well get in the way of compassion. Persons who are in general quite poor at imagining the experiences of others who are different from themselves, may well be less likely to have compassion for them. Yet this failure of imagination is typically not a purely intellectual or cognitive failure; for it can itself be part of a more general failure to regard the other as fully human, or to take that humanity sufficiently seriously. That a white colonialist in Africa does not imagine to himself the cares and sufferings of the blacks whom he rules cannot be separated from the fact that he does not see them as fully human.

A second constituent of compassion is concern for or regard for the object's good. It is not enough that we imaginatively reconstruct someone's suffering; for, like belief, such imagining is compatible with malice and mere intellectual curiosity. (In fact it is likely to be a component of them.) In addition we must care about that suffering and desire its alleviation. Suppose a neighbor's house burns down, though no one is hurt. Compassion would involve not only imagining what it is like for the neighbor to be homeless but also concerned responses such as the following: being upset, distressed, regretting the different aspects of his plight (his homelessness, his loss of prized possessions, his terror when inside the burning house, etc.); wishing the tragedy had not happened; giving thought to what might be done to alleviate the neighbor's situation; worrying whether he will be able to find another place to live; hoping that he will obtain a decent settlement from the insurance company; hoping and desiring that, in general, his suffering will be no greater than necessary.

The relation between concern for another person's good and these thoughts, feelings, hopes, desires is a necessary or conceptual one; compassionate concern would not be attributed to someone who lacked them (or at least most of them). This concern is not merely tacked on to the imaginative reconstruction as a totally independent component of compassion. Rather the manner in which we dwell on the other's plight expresses the concern for his good.

These concerned reactions must be directed toward the other's plight and not merely caused by it. The distress that is part of compassion cannot take as its focus the vivid realization that I might be afflicted with a like misfortune; for it would then be self-regarding rather than altruistic.

Compassion also involves viewing the other person and his suffering in a certain way. I can put this by saying that compassion involves a sense of shared humanity, of regarding the other as a fellow human being. This means that the other person's suffering (though not necessarily their particular afflicting condition) is seen as the kind of thing that could happen to anyone, including oneself insofar as one is a human being.[7]

This way of viewing the other person contrasts with the attitude characteristic of pity, in which one holds oneself apart from the afflicted person and from their suffering thinking of it as something that defines that person as fundamentally different from oneself. In this way the other person's condition is taken as given whereas in compassion the person's affliction is seen as deviating from the general conditions of human flourishing. That is why pity (unlike compassion) involves a kind of condescension, and why compassion is morally superior to pity.

Because compassion involves a sense of shared humanity, it promotes the *experience* of equality, even when accompanied by an acknowledgment of actual social inequality. Compassion forbids regarding social inequality as establishing human inequality. This is part of the moral force of compassion: by transcending the recognition of social inequality, it promotes the sensed experience of equality in common humanity.

Sometimes the reason we feel pity rather than compassion is that we feel that the object has in some way brought the suffering on himself or deserved it, or in any case that he has allowed himself to be humiliated or degraded by it. But such ways of regarding the object do not necessarily undermine compassion, and they are not incompatible with it. It would be a mistake to see the essential difference between pity and compassion in such differing beliefs about the object's condition. No matter how pitiful or self-degraded one regards another human being, it is possible (and not necessarily unwarranted) to feel compassion and concern for him, simply because he is suffering.

Nietzsche's use of the term *Mitleid* does not distinguish between compassion and pity. Because Mitleid is focused on the negative states of others, Nietzsche saw it as life-denying and without positive value. But insofar as compassion involves a genuine concern for the good of others and a "living sense of another's worth,"[8] it is, unlike pity, fundamentally life-affirming and positive.

A fourth aspect of compassion is its strength and duration. If the distress, sorrow, hopes, and desires of an altruistic attitude were merely passing reactions or twinges of feeling, they would be insufficient for the level of concern, the imaginative reconstruction, and the disposition to beneficent action required for compassion. Though there are degrees of compassion, the threshold of emotional strength required from compassion (in contrast with other altruistic attitudes) is relatively high and enduring. Because well-wishing and pity can be more episodic and less action-guiding, they are morally inferior to compassion. As the etymology of the word suggests, compassion involves "feeling with" the other person, sharing his feelings. In one sense this means that the subject and the object have the same feeling-type: distress, sorrow, desire for relief. But in a more important sense the feelings are not the same; for the relation between their subjects and their objects are different. The focus of my neighbor's distress is *his own* homelessness; the focus of my distress in having compassion for him is *my neighbor's* homelessness (or his distress at his homelessness). This can partly be expressed as a matter of degree. My neighbor suffers; in "suffering with" him there is a sense in which I suffer too, but my suffering is much less than his.

Compassion and Beneficent Action

When it is possible for her to relieve another person's suffering without undue demands on her time, energy, and priorities, the compassionate person is disposed to attempt to help. We would hardly attribute compassion to X if she were to saunter by on a spring day and, seeing an elderly man fall on the sidewalk, walk right by, perhaps with a sad shudder of dismay, leaving the old man lying alone.

Characteristically, then, compassion requires the disposition to perform beneficent actions, and to perform them because the agent has had a certain sort of imaginative reconstruction of someone's condition and has a concern for his good. The steps that the person takes to ameliorate the condition are guided by and prompted by that imaginative reconstruction and concern. So the beneficent action of a compassionate person has a specific sort of causal history, which distinguishes it from an equally beneficent action that might be prompted by other sorts of attitudes and emotions.

We saw that concern exists at different degrees of strength in different altruistic emotions and attitudes. Hence its corresponding disposition to beneficence exists at different levels of strength also. The stronger the disposition the more one is willing to go out of one's way, to act contrary to inclination and interest, in order to help the other person.[9] That compassion as a motive can and often does withstand contrary inclination begins to address the Kantian charge that emotions, including compassion, are unreliable as motives to beneficent action.[10] As a motive to beneficence, compassion can have the strength, stability, and reliability that Kant thought only the sense of duty could have. As a trait of character compassion can be as stable and consistent in its prompting of appropriate beneficent action as a conscientious adherence to principles of beneficence.

Though compassion is a type of emotion or emotional attitude, it is not like a Kantian "inclination." Acting from compassion does not typically involve doing what one is in the mood to do, or feels like doing. On the contrary the regard for the other's good which compassion implies means that one's compassionate acts often involve acting very much contrary to one's moods and inclinations. Compassion is fundamentally other-regarding rather than self-regarding; its affective nature in no way detracts from this.

Compassionate action may extinguish or diminish compassion itself, most obviously when its object is relieved of the negative condition by the action. But even merely *engaging* in action may involve a shift in the subject's consciousness from the imaginative reconstruction of the object's condition to a focus on the expected relief of that condition, thereby diminishing the compassion (though not the regard for the other's good and hence not the moral value of the attitude or state of mind).

Compassion, however, is not always linked so directly to the prompting of beneficent actions. For in many situations it is impossible (without extraordinary disruption of one's life and priorities) for the compassionate person herself to improve the sufferer's condition (for instance, when one is concerned for the welfare of distant flood victims). In other situations the beneficence might be inappropriate, as when intervention might jeopardize the sufferer's autonomy. Compassionate concern, in such cases, involves hope and desire for the relief of the condition by those in a position to provide it. It does not involve an active setting oneself in readiness to perform beneficent acts, once one firmly believes such acts to be impossible or inappropriate.

In the cases so far discussed a link exists between compassion and beneficent action, through the desire that action be taken by someone to relieve the sufferer's condition. But compassion is also appropriate in situations in which nothing whatever can be done to alleviate the affliction, as for instance when someone is suffering from incurable blindness or painful terminal cancer. In such situations compassionate concern involves sorrowing for the person, hoping that the condition might — all expectations to the contrary — be mitigated or compensated, being pleased or grateful if this occurs, and similar responses.

Because being compassionate involves actively giving thought to the relief of the sufferer's condition, a compassionate person may discover the possibility of beneficent action when it seemed unclear whether any existed. Compassion often involves resisting regarding situations as absolutely irremediable. On the other hand the compassionate person may for this reason fail to see and hence to face up to the hopelessness of the sufferer's situation.

That compassion is often appropriate when there is little or no scope for the subject's disposition to beneficence indicates that compassion's sole significance does not lie in its role as motive to beneficence. Even when nothing can be done by the compassionate person to improve the sufferer's condition, simply being aware that one is an object or recipient of compassion can be an important human good. The compassionate person's expression of concern and shared sorrow can be valuable to the sufferer for its own sake, independently of its instrumental value in improving his condition. Nor does the good of recognizing oneself to be an object of compassion depend on the compassionate person wanting to convey his attitude, though the recipient can in addition value the intention to communicate.

The compassionate attitude is a good to the recipient, not only because it signifies that the subject would help if she could but because we are glad to receive the concern of others, glad of the sense of equality that it promotes. Yet it is morally good to be compassionate even when — as often happens — the object of compassion is unaware of it. For any concern for the welfare of others, especially when it promotes the sense of equality, is (ceteris paribus) morally good. In this, compassion contrasts with attitudes and feelings such as infatuation or admiration which may convey goods to their recipients but which are without moral value because they do not essentially involve a regard for their recipient's good. The moral significance of compassion is not exhausted by the various types of goods it confers on its recipients.

Compassion can hurt its recipient. It may, for instance, cause him to concentrate too much on his plight, or to think that people around him see him primarily in terms of that plight. But these dangers and burdens of compassion can be mitigated to the extent that a person recognizes that compassion is not the sole or the dominant attitude with which one is regarded.

Compassion can also be misguided, grounded in superficial understanding of a situation. Compassion is not necessarily wise or appropriate. The compassionate person may even end up doing more harm than good. True compassion must be allied with knowledge and understanding if it is to serve adequately as a guide to action: there is nothing inherent in the character of compassion that would prevent — and much that would encourage — its alliance with rational calculation. Because compassion involves an active and objective interest in another person's welfare, it is characteristically a spur to a deeper understanding of a situation than rationality alone could ensure. A person who is compassionate by character is in principle committed to as rational and as intelligent a course of action as possible.

Notes

1. Compassion has a particular cultural history: its sources are Christian, it was further developed by Romanticism, especially by the German Romantics. Though I do not focus on this history explicitly, my emphasis on compassion as a particular moral emotion among others should leave room for the results of such a historical account.

2. Arthur Schopenhauer, *On the Basis of Morality* (New York: Bobbs-Merrill, 1965).

3. In general I will use feminine pronouns to refer to the person having compassion (the "subject") and masculine pronouns to refer to the person for whom she has compassion (the "object").

4. I am making a conceptual rather than a moral point. The compassionate person cannot regard the object of her compassion as merely irritated or discomforted; but of course a genuinely compassionate person might mistakenly take an inconvenience to be a serious harm. To say that compassion is "appropriate" in this context is, then, simply to say that the object actually possesses the compassion-grounding feature which the subject takes him to possess. I do not discuss the further issue of when compassion is *morally* appropriate or inappropriate.

5. Nietzsche saw this focus on misery and suffering as a kind of morbidity in the compassionate consciousness; this view formed part of his critique of compassion.

6. Philip Mercer, *Sympathy and Ethics* (Oxford: Clarendon Press, 1972), and Max Scheler, *The Nature of Sympathy*, trans. Werner Stark (London: Routledge & Kegan Paul, 1965).

7. This way of viewing the other's plight differs from fundamentally self-regarding sentiment in which the person's plight is regarded as a symbol of what could happen to oneself. It is not actually necessary that one believe that the afflicting condition *could* happen to oneself: one might have compassion for someone suffering napalm burns without believing that there is any possibility of oneself being in that condition.

8. Nicolai Hartmann, *Ethics* (London: George Allen and Unwin, 1932), II, 273.

9. Aristotle recognizes differences in the strength of the disposition to beneficence in his discussion of *eunoia* ("well-wishing" or "good will" in Thompson's translation). Of persons who have eunoia toward others, Aristotle says, "All they wish is the good of those for whom they have a kindness; they would not actively help them to attain it, nor would they put themselves out for their sake." Aristotle, *Nichomachean Ethics*, b. IX (Baltimore: Penguin Books, 1955), 269.

10. For this Kantian view, see Kant, *Fundamental Principles of the Metaphysics of Morals*, trans. Beck (New York: Bobbs-Merrill, 1960), 6, 14, 28; and *Critique of Practical Reason*, trans. Beck (New York: Bobbs-Merrill, 1956), 75, 122.

Selected Bibliography

Two difficulties attend the choice of items for this bibliography. First, the boundaries of "virtue ethics" are not clearly defined; contributions to action theory, philosophical psychology, moral education theory, philosophical and theological anthropology, spirituality, etc., are included when their focus is on character or the virtues. Second, the amount of research on the virtue tradition is vast; essays on the history of ethics are included only when the approach is not primarily expository.

1. General Studies

Baier, Annette C. *Postures of the Mind: Essays on Mind and Morals*. Minneapolis: University of Minnesota Press, 1985.

————. "What Do Women Want in a Moral Theory?" *Nous* 19 (March 1985): 53–64.

Burnyeat, Myles. "Virtues in Action." In *The Philosophy of Socrates*, edited by Gregory Vlastos, 209–34. Garden City, N.Y.: Doubleday, 1971.

Crossin, John W. *What Are They Saying About Virtue?* New York: Paulist Press, 1985.

Ewin, R. E. *Co-operation and Human Values: A Study in Moral Reasoning*. New York: St. Martin's Press, 1981.

Flemming, Arthur. "Reviving the Virtues." *Ethics* 40 (July 1980):587–95.

Foot, Philippa R. *Virtues and Vices*. Berkeley: University of California Press, 1978.

Geach, Peter. *The Virtues*. Cambridge, England: Cambridge University Press, 1977.

Guardini, Romano. *The Virtues: On Forms of Moral Life*. Translated by Stella Lange. Chicago: Henry Regnery, 1967.

Hauerwas, Stanley, and Alasdair MacIntyre, eds. *Revisions*. Notre Dame, Ind.: University of Notre Dame Press, 1983.

Klubertanz, George P. *Habits and Virtues: A Philosophical Analysis*. New York: Appleton-Century-Crofts, 1965.

MacIntyre, Alasdair. *After Virtue*, 2d ed. Notre Dame, Ind.: University of Notre Dame Press, 1984.

Mackie, J. L. *Ethics: Inventing Right and Wrong*. Harmondsworth, Middlesex, England: Penguin Books, 1977.

Meilaender, Gilbert C. *The Theory and Practice of Virtue*. Notre Dame, Ind.: University of Notre Dame Press, 1984.

Murdoch, Iris. *The Sovereignty of Good*. New York: Schocken Books, 1971.

Noddings, Nel. *Caring: A Feminine Approach to Ethics and Moral Education*. Berkeley: University of California Press, 1984.

Pence, Gregory E. "Recent Work on Virtues." *American Philosophical Quarterly* 21 (1984):281–96.

Pieper, Josef. *The Four Cardinal Virtues*. Notre Dame, Ind.: University of Notre Dame Press, 1966.

Rescher, Nicholas. *Unselfishness*. Pittsburgh: University of Pittsburgh Press, 1975.

Sabini, John, and Maury Silver. *Moralities of Everyday Life*. Oxford, England: Oxford University Press, 1982.

Slote, Michael. *Goods and Virtues*. Oxford, England: Oxford University Press, 1983.

Sommers, Christina Hoff. *Vice and Virtue in Everyday Life: Introductory Readings in Ethics*. New York: Harcourt Brace Jovanovich, 1985.

Taylor, Richard. *Good and Evil: A New Direction*. New York: Macmillan, 1970.

Trilling, Lionel. *Sincerity and Authenticity*. Cambridge, Mass.: Harvard University Press, 1971.

Von Wright, George Henrik. *The Varieties of Goodness*. London: Routledge and Kegan Paul, 1963.

Wallace, James D. *Virtues and Vices*. Ithaca, N.Y.: Cornell University Press, 1978.

Williams, Bernard. *Moral Luck*. Cambridge, England: Cambridge University Press, 1981.

Wong, David B. *Moral Relativity*. Berkeley: University of California Press, 1984.

2. Applied Philosophy and Virtue Ethics

Bogen, James. "Suicide and Virtue." In *Suicide: The Philosophical Issues*, edited by David J. Mayo, 286–92. New York: St. Martin's Press, 1980.

Frankena, William K. "Beneficence in an Ethics of Virtue." In *Philosophy and Medicine: Beneficence and Health Care*, edited by Earl E. Shelp, 63–82. The Hague: D. Reidel, 1982.

Hill, Thomas E., Jr. "Ideals of Human Excellence and Preserving Natural Environments." *Environmental Ethics* 5 (Fall 1983):211–24.

Kupfer, Joseph. "Sexual Perversion and the Good." *The Personalist* 59 (January 1978): 70–7.

MacIntyre, Alasdair. "How Virtues Become Vices: Values, Medicine and Social Context." In *Evaluation and Explanation in the Biomedical Sciences*, edited by H. T. Engelhardt, Jr. and S. F. Spicker, 97–111. The Hague: D. Reidel, 1975.

May, William F. "Care of the Aging: A Clue to the American Character." *Cross Currents* 32 (Summer 1982):193–209.

————. "The Virtues in a Professional Setting." *Soundings* 67 (Fall 1984):245–66.

Pence, Gregory E. "Can Compassion Be Taught?" *Journal of Medical Ethics* 9 (December 1983):189–91.

————. *Ethical Options in Medicine*. Oradell, N.J.: Medical Economics Co., 1980.

Pincoffs, Edmund L. "Virtue, the Quality of Life, and Punishment." *The Monist* 63 (April 1980):38–50.

Richards, Norvin. "Double Effect and Moral Character." *Mind* 93 (July 1984):381–97.

Shelp, Earl E. "Courage and Tragedy in Clinical Medicine." *Journal of Medicine and Philosophy* 8 (November 1983):417–30.

———. "Courage: A Neglected Virtue in the Patient-Physician Relationship." *Social Science and Medicine* 18 (1984):351–60.

Wren, Thomas E. "Whistle Blowing and Loyalty to One's Friends." In *Police Ethics*, edited by W. Heffernan and T. Stroup. New York: John Jay Press, 1985.

3.   Criticisms of Virtue Ethics

Baron, Marcia. "The Alleged Moral Repugnance of Acting From Duty." *Journal of Philosophy* 81 (April 1984):197–220.

———. "Varieties of Ethics of Virtue." *American Philosophical Quarterly* 22 (January 1985):47–53.

Beauchamp, Tom L. "What's So Special About the Virtues?" In *Virtue and Medicine: Explorations in the Character of Medicine*, edited by Earl E. Shelp, 307–28. The Hague: D. Reidel, 1985.

Brandt, Richard B. "W. K. Frankena and Ethics of Virtue." *The Monist* 64 (July 1981): 271–92.

Fletcher, Joseph. "Virtue Is a Predicate." *The Monist* 54 (January 1970):66–85.

Frankena, William K. "Prichard and the Ethics of Virtue: Notes on a Footnote." *The Monist* 54 (January 1970):1–17.

Herman, Barbara. "Rules, Motives and Helping Actions." *Philosophical Studies* 45 (May 1984):367–77.

Nielsen, Kai. "Critique of Pure Virtue: Animadversions on a Virtue-Based Ethics." In *Virtue and Medicine: Explorations in the Character of Medicine*, edited by Earl E. Shelp, 133–50. The Hague: D. Reidel, 1985.

Ogletree, Thomas. "Value, Obligation, and Virtues: Approaches to Bio-Medical Ethics." *Journal of Religious Ethics* 4 (Spring 1976):105–30.

Veatch, Robert M. "Against Virtue: A Deontological Critique of Virtue Theory in Medical Ethics." In *Virtue and Medicine: Explorations in the Character of Medicine*, edited by Earl E. Shelp, 329–46. The Hague: D. Reidel, 1985.

4.   Immoral Character

Beehler, Rodger. "Moral Delusion." *Philosophy* 56 (July 1981):313–31.

Benn, S. I. "Wickedness." *Ethics* 95 (July 1985):795–810.

Gilbert, Margaret. "Vices and Self-Knowledge." *Journal of Philosophy* 15 (August 5, 1971):443–53.

Midgley, Mary. *Wickedness: A Philosophical Essay*. Boston: Routledge and Kegan Paul, 1984.

Milo, Ronald D. "Amorality." *Mind* 92 (October 1983):481–98.

———. *Immorality*. Princeton: Princeton University Press, 1984.

———. "Moral Indifference." *The Monist* 64 (July 1981):373–93.

———. "Wickedness." *American Philosophical Quarterly* 20 (January 1983):69–80.

5. Alasdair MacIntyre and the Virtue Ethic Tradition

Barbour, John D. "The Virtues in a Pluralistic Context." *Journal of Religion* 63 (April 1983):175–82.

Bernstein, Richard J. "Nietzsche or Aristotle: Reflections on Alasdair MacIntyre's *After Virtue*." *Soundings* 67 (Spring 1984):6–29.

Casey, John. "*After Virtue* [review article]." *Philosophical Quarterly* 33 (July 1983): 296–300.

Edel, Abraham. "*After Virtue* [review article]." *Zygon* 18 (September 1983):343–49.

Edel, Abraham, and Elizabeth Flowers. "*After Virtue* [review article]." *Journal of the History of Philosophy* 21 (July 1983):426–29.

Feinberg, Walter. "On *After Virtue*." *Theory and Society* 13 (1984):249–62.

Frankena, William K. "MacIntyre and Modern Morality." *Ethics* 93 (April 1983): 579–87.

Gaita, Raimond. "Virtues, Human Good, and the Unity of Life." *Inquiry* 26 (December 1983):407–24.

Gewirth, Alan. "Rights and Virtues." *Review of Metaphysics* 38 (June 1985):739–62.

Hauerwas, Stanley, and Paul Wadell. "*After Virtue* [review article]." *Thomist* 46 (April 1982):313–22.

MacIntyre, Alasdair. "*After Virtue* and Marxism: A Response to Wartofsky." *Inquiry* 27 (July 1984):251–54.

———. "Intelligibility, Goods, and Rules." *Journal of Philosophy* 79 (November 1982):663–65.

———. "Moral Rationality, Tradition, and Aristotle: A Reply to O'Neill, Gaita, and Clark." *Inquiry* 26 (December 1983):447–66.

Madigan, Arthur S. J. "Plato, Aristotle and Professor MacIntyre." *Ancient Philosophy* 3 (Fall 1983):171–83.

O'Neill, Onora. "Kant After Virtue." *Inquiry* 26 (December 1983):387–406.

Phillips, D. Z. "Critical Notice: A. MacIntyre, *After Virtue*." *Mind* 93 (January 1984): 111–24.

Ross, Steven L. "Practice (+ Narrative Unity + Moral Tradition) Makes Perfect: Alistair [sic] MacIntyre's *After Virtue*." *Journal of Value Inquiry* 19 (1985):13–26.

Schneewind, Jerome B. "Moral Crisis and the History of Ethics." *Midwest Studies in Philosophy* 8 (1983):525–42.

————. "Virtue, Narrative, and Community: MacIntyre and Morality." *Journal of Philosophy* 79 (November 1982):653–63.

Sheffler, Samuel. "*After Virtue* [review article]." *Philosophical Review* 92 (July 1983): 443–47.

Stout, Jeffrey. "Virtue Among the Ruins: An Essay on MacIntyre." *Neue Zeitschrift für systematische Theologie und Religionsphilosophie* 26 (1984):256–73.

Wartofsky, Marx W. "Virtue Lost or Understanding MacIntyre." *Inquiry* 27 (1984): 235–50.

6.   Modern Ethical Theory and Virtue Ethics

Adams, Robert Merrihew. "Motive Utilitarianism." *Journal of Philosophy* 73 (August 12, 1976):467–81.

Allen, Glen O. "Coordination in Moral Theory: Comment on Lawrence Becker." *Journal of Value Inquiry* 10 (Summer 1976):140–48.

Anscombe, G.E.M. "Authority in Morals." In *The Collected Papers of G.E.M. Anscombe, Volume I: Ethics, Religion and Politics*. Minneapolis: University of Minnesota Press, 1981:43–50.

————. "Modern Moral Philosophy." *Philosophy* 33 (January 1958):1–19. Reprinted in *The Collected Papers of G.E.M. Anscombe, Volume I: Ethics, Religion and Politics*. Minneapolis: University of Minnesota Press, 1981:26–42.

Baier, Kurt. "Moral Value and Moral Worth." *The Monist* 54 (January 1970):18–30.

————. "Virtue Ethics." *Philosophy Exchange* 3 (Summer 1982):57–70.

Becker, Lawrence C. "Axiology, Deontology, and Agent Morality: The Need for Coordination." *Journal of Value Inquiry* 4 (Fall 1972):213–20.

————. "The Neglect of Virtue." *Ethics* 85 (January 1975):110–22.

Brandt, Richard B. "The Psychology of Benevolence and Its Implications for Philosophy." *Journal of Philosophy* 73 (August 12, 1976):429–53.

Brown, James M. "Right and Virtue." *Proceedings of the Aristotelian Society* 82 (1981–82): 143–58.

Conly, Sarah. "The Objectivity of Morals and the Subjectivity of Agents." *American Philosophical Quarterly* 22 (October 1985):275–86.

————. "Utilitarianism and Integrity." *The Monist* 66 (April 1983):298–311.

Cua, A. S. "Morality and Human Nature." *Philosophy East and West* 32 (July 1982): 279–94.

Cunningham, Stanley B. "Does 'Does Moral Philosophy Rest on a Mistake?' Make an Even Greater Mistake?" *The Monist* 54 (January 1970):86–99.

Davie, William E. "Does Morality Focus on Action?" *Southwestern Journal of Philosophy* 8 (Winter 1977):33–47.

Dent, N.J.H. "Duty and Inclination." *Mind* 83 (October 1974):552–70.

Duff, Antony. "Desire, Duty and Moral Absolutes." *Philosophy* 55 (April 1980):223–38.

Dunbar, Scott. "On Art, Morals and Religion: Some Reflections on the Work of Iris Murdoch." *Religious Studies* 14 (December 1978):515–24.

Foot, Philippa R. "Morality as a System of Hypothetical Imperatives." *Philosophical Review* 81 (July 1972):305–16. Reprinted in Foot, Philippa R. *Virtues and Vices*. Berkeley: University of California Press, 1978.

————. "Utilitarianism and the Virtues." *Mind* 94 (April 1985):196–209.

Hauerwas, Stanley. "Obligation and Virtue Once More." *Journal of Religious Ethics* 3 (Spring 1975):27–44.

Heil, John. "Thoughts on the Virtues." *Journal of Value Inquiry* 19 (1985):27–34.

Hepburn, R. W. "Vision and Choice in Morality." In *Christian Ethics and Contemporary Philosophy*, edited by Ian Ramsey, 181–95. London: SCM Press, 1966.

Herman, Barbara. "Integrity and Impartiality." *The Monist* 66 (April 1983):233–50.

Herms, Eilert. "Virtue: A Neglected Concept in Protestant Ethics." *Scottish Journal of Theology* 35 (1982):481–95.

Heyd, David. "Ethical Universalism, Justice, and Favoritism." *Australasian Journal of Philosophy* 56 (May 1978):25–31.

Hinman, Lawrence M. "On the Purity of Our Moral Motives: A Critique of Kant's Account of the Emotions and Acting for the Sake of Duty." *The Monist* 66 (April 1983):251–67.

Hudson, Stephen D. "Taking Virtues Seriously." *Australasian Journal of Philosophy* 59 (June 1981):189–202.

Kalin, Jesse. "Lies, Secrets, and Love: The Inadequacy of Contemporary Moral Philosophy." *Journal of Value Inquiry* 4 (Winter 1976):253–65.

Kekes, John. "Moral Sensitivity." *Philosophy* 59 (January 1984):3–19.

————. "'Ought Implies Can' and Two Kinds of Morality." *The Personalist* 34 (October 1984):460–67.

Kilcullen, John. "Utilitarianism and Virtue." *Ethics* 93 (April 1983):451–66.

Koehn, Donald R. "Normative Ethics That Are Neither Teleological nor Deontological." *Metaphilosophy* 5 (July 1974):173–80.

Laird, J. "Act-Ethics and Agent-Ethics." *Mind* 55 (April 1946):113–32.

Laney, James T. "Characterization and Moral Judgments." *Journal of Religion* 55 (October 1975):405–14.

Murdoch, Iris. "Against Dryness: A Polemical Sketch." In *Revisions*, edited by Stanley Hauerwas and Alasdair MacIntyre, 43–50. Notre Dame, Ind.: University of Notre Dame Press, 1983.

————. "Metaphysics and Ethics." In *The Nature of Metaphysics*, edited by D. T. Pears, 99–123. London: Macmillan, 1957.

————. "Vision and Choice in Morality." In *Christian Ethics and Contemporary Philosophy*, edited by Ian Ramsey, 195–218. London: SCM Press, 1966.

Nussbaum, Martha. "'Finely Aware and Richly Responsible': Moral Attention and the Moral Task of Literature." *Journal of Philosophy* 82 (October 1985): 516–29.

Oesterle, John A. "Morally Good and Morally Right." *The Monist* 54 (January 1970): 31–39.

Pincoffs, Edmund L. "Quandary Ethics." *Mind* 80 (October 1971):552–71. Reprinted in *Revisions*, edited by Stanley Hauerwas and Alasdair MacIntyre, 92–112. Notre Dame, Ind.: University of Notre Dame Press, 1983.

Richards, Norvin. "Moral Symptoms." *Mind* 89 (January 1980):49–66.

Robbins, J. Wesley. "Frankena on the Difference Between an Ethic of Virtue and an Ethic of Duty." *Journal of Religious Ethics* 4 (Spring 1976):57–62.

Rogerson, Kenneth F. "Williams and Kant on Integrity." *Dialogue* (Canada) 22 (September 1983):461–78.

Ryle, Gilbert. "Jane Austen and the Moralists." In *Collected Papers*, Volume I. New York: Barnes and Noble, 1971:276–91.

Schenck, David, Jr. "Recasting the 'Ethics of Virtue/Ethics of Duty Debate'." *Journal of Religious Ethics* 4 (Fall 1976):269–86.

Slote, Michael A. "Morality Not a System of Imperatives." *American Philosophical Quarterly* 19 (October 1982):331–40.

Stocker, Michael. "Act and Agent Evaluations." *Review of Metaphysics* 27 (September 1973):42–61.

————. "Good Intentions in Greek and Modern Moral Virtue." *Australasian Journal of Philosophy* 57 (September 1979):220–24.

————. "Morally Good Intentions." *The Monist* 54 (January 1970):124–41.

————. "Rightness and Goodness: Is There a Difference?" *American Philosophical Quarterly* 10 (April 1973):87–98.

Sullivan, Roger J. "The Kantian Critique of Aristotle's Moral Philosophy: An Appraisal." *Review of Metaphysics* 28 (September 1974):24–53.

Trianosky, Gregory W. "Supererogation, Wrongdoing, and Vice: On the Autonomy of the Ethics of Virtue." *Journal of Philosophy* 83 (January 1986):26–40.

Wilkerson, T. E. "Duty, Inclination and Morals." *Philosophical Quarterly* 23 (January 1973):28–40.

Williams, Bernard. "Utilitarianism and Moral Self-Indulgence." In *Contemporary British Philosophy*, 4th Series, edited by H. D. Lewis. London: Allen and Unwin, 1976.

Wolf, Susan. "Above and Below the Line of Duty." *Philosophical Topics* 14 (Fall 1986).

7.   Modern Society and Virtue Ethics

Baier, Annette C. "Secular Faith." *Canadian Journal of Philosophy* 10 (March 1980): 131–48. Reprinted in *Postures of the Mind: Essays on Mind and Morals*. Minneapolis: University of Minnesota Press, 1985:93–108. Reprinted in *Revisions*, edited by Stanley Hauerwas and Alasdair MacIntyre, 203–21. Notre Dame, Ind.: University of Notre Dame Press, 1983.

Den Uyl, Douglas J. "Freedom and Virtue." *Reason Papers* (Winter 1979):1–12. Reprinted in *The Libertarian Reader*, edited by Tibor R. Machan. Totowa, N.J.: Rowan and Littlefield, 1982.

Hawkesworth, M. E. "Freedom and Virtue: The Covert Connection." *Cogito* 2 (March 1984):73–106.

Hunt, Lester H. "On Improving Mankind by Political Means." *Reason Papers* 10 (Spring 1985):61–76.

———. "The Politics of Envy." *Original Papers*, 2 (1983). Bowling Green, Ohio: Social Philosophy and Policy Center.

———. "Punishment, Revenge, and the Minimal Functions of the State." *Bowling Green Studies in Applied Philosophy* 1 (1979):79–88.

Neuhaus, Richard John, ed. *Virtue: Public and Private*. Grand Rapids, Mich.: William B. Eerdmans, 1986.

Wilson, James Q. "The Rediscovery of Character: Private Virtue and Public Policy." *The Public Interest* 81 (Fall 1985):3–16.

8.   Moral Education

Baron, Marcia. "The Ethics of Duty/Ethics of Virtue Debate and Its Relevance to Educational Theory." *Educational Theory* 35 (Spring 1985):135–49.

Blum, Lawrence. "Particularity and Responsiveness." In *The Emergence of Morality in Children*, edited by J. Kagan. Chicago: University of Chicago Press, 1986.

Capitan, William H. "Can Virtue Be Taught?" *Diotima* 1 (1973):101–24.

Carr, David. "Moral Philosophy and Psychology in Progressive and Traditional Educational Thought." *Journal of Philosophy of Education* 18 (1984):41–54.

———. "Three Approaches to Moral Education." *Educational Philosophy and Theory* 15 (October 1983):39–52.

DeNicola, Daniel R. "The Education of the Emotions." *Proceedings of the Philosophy of Education Society* 35 (1979).

Duska, Ronald. "Philosophy, Literature and Views of the Good Life." *Proceedings of the American Catholic Philosophical Society* 54 (1980):181–88.

Dykstra, Craig. "Moral Virtue or Social Reasoning." *Religious Education* 75 (March–April, 1980):115–28.

———. *Vision and Character*. New York: Paulist Press, 1981.

Engeman, T. S. "Practical Possibilities in American Moral Education: A Comparison of Values Clarification and the Character Education Curriculum." *Journal of Moral Education* 4 (October 1974):53–59.

Flanagan, Owen J., Jr. "Virtue, Sex, and Gender: Some Philosophical Reflections on the Moral Psychology Debate." *Ethics* 92 (April 1982):499–512.

Gilligan, Carol. *In a Different Voice*. Cambridge, Mass.: Harvard University Press, 1982.

Joy, Donald M. *Moral Development Foundations*. Nashville: Abingdon Press, 1983.

Kohlberg, Lawrence. *Essays on Moral Development*. Volumes I and II. San Francisco: Harper and Row, 1981, 1984.

Locke, Don. "Doing What Comes Morally: The Relation Between Behavior and Stages of Moral Reasoning." *Human Development* 26 (1983):11–25.

Munsey, Brenda, ed. *Moral Development, Moral Education, and Kohlberg*. Birmingham: Religious Education Press, 1980.

Peters, R. S. "Moral Development and Moral Learning." *The Monist* 58 (October 1974):541–67.

———. "The Place of Kohlberg's Theory in Moral Education." *Journal of Moral Education* 7 (May 1978):147–57.

Philibert, Paul J. "Lawrence Kohlberg's Use of Virtue in His Theory of Moral Development." *International Philosophical Quarterly* 15 (December 1975):455–79.

Ryle, Gilbert. "Teaching and Training." In *Collected Papers*, Volume II. London: Hutchinson, 1971.

Schleifer, Michael. "Moral Education and Indoctrination." *Ethics* 86 (January 1976): 154–63.

Smith, Joanmarie. "The Need for 'Rule' Ethics and the Practice of Virtue." *Religious Education* 80 (Spring 1985):255–64.

Sommers, Christina Hoff. "Ethics Without Virtue: Moral Education in America." *American Scholar* 53 (Summer 1984):381–89.

9.   Psychology of the Virtues

9.1   Akrasia

Audi, Robert. "Weakness of the Will and Practical Judgment." *Nous* 13 (May 1979): 173–96.

Bratman, Michael. "Practical Reasoning and Weakness of the Will." *Nous* 13 (May 1979):153–72.

Corder, Christopher. "Jackson on Weakness of Will." *Mind* 94 (April 1985):273–80.

Davidson, Donald. "How Is Weakness of the Will Possible?" In *Essays on Actions and Events*. Oxford, England: Clarendon Press, 1980, 21–43.

Heil, John. "Doxastic Incontinence." *Mind* 93 (January 1984):56–70.

Jackson, Frank. "Weakness of Will." *Mind* 93 (January 1983):1–18.

King-Farlow, John. "Akrasia, Self-Mastery and the Master Self." *Pacific Philosophical Quarterly* 62 (January 1981):47–60.

Matthews, Gareth. "Weakness of Will." *Mind* 75 (July 1966):405–19.

Mele, Alfred R. "Akrasia, Reasons and Causes." *Philosophical Studies* 44 (November 1983):345–68.

―――. "Pears on Akrasia, and Defeated Intentions." *Philosophia* 14 (August 1984): 145–52.

Pears, David. "How Easy Is Akrasia?" *Philosophia* 11 (February 1982):33–50.

―――. *Motivated Irrationality*. Oxford, England: Oxford University Press, 1984.

Rapaport, Elizabeth. "Describing Moral Weakness." *Philosophical Studies* 28 (October 1975):273–80.

―――. "Explaining Moral Weakness." *Philosophical Studies* 24 (May 1973):174–82.

Reilly, Richard. "Moral Weakness." *International Philosophical Quarterly* 17 (June 1977):167–78.

Richman, Robert J. "Acrasia and Practical Reasoning." *Pacific Philosophical Quarterly* 61 (July 1980):245–57.

Rorty, Amelie O. "Akrasia and Conflict." *Inquiry* 23 (June 1980):193–212.

―――. "Akratic Believers." *American Philosophical Quarterly* 20 (April 1983):175–83.

―――. "Where Does the Akratic Break Take Place?" *Australasian Journal of Philosophy* 58 (December 1980):333–46.

Schueler, G. F. "Akrasia Revisited." *Mind* 92 (October 1983):580–84.

Stocker, Michael. "Desiring the Bad: An Essay in Moral Psychology." *Journal of Philosophy* 76 (December 1979):738–53.

Taylor, C.C.W. "Plato, Hare and Davidson on Akrasia." *Mind* 89 (October 1980): 499–518.

―――. "Reply to Schueler on Akrasia." *Mind* 93 (October 1984):584–86.

Vinci, Tom. "Comment on 'Doxastic Incontinence'." *Mind* 94 (January 1985):116–19.

Watson, Gary. "Scepticism about Weakness of Will." *Philosophical Review* 86 (July 1977):316–39.

Wiggins, David. "Weakness of Will, Commensurability, and the Objects of Deliberation and Desire." *Proceedings of the Aristotelian Society* 79 (1978–79):251–77. Reprinted in *Essays on Aristotle's Ethics* edited by Amelie Oksenberg Rorty, 241–66. Berkeley: University of California Press, 1980.

9.2   Freedom, Responsibility, and Character

Adams, Robert Merrihew. "Involuntary Sins." *Philosophical Review* 94 (January 1985): 3–32.

Eshete, Andreas. "Character, Virtue and Freedom." *Philosophy* 57 (October 1982): 495–513.

Frankfurt, H. G. "Freedom of the Will and the Concept of a Person." *Journal of Philosophy* 68 (January 14, 1971):5–20.

———. "Necessity and Desire." *Philosophy and Phenomenological Research* 45 (September 1984):1–14.

Frey, R. G. "What a Good Man Can Bring Himself to Do." *Journal of Value Inquiry* 12 (1978):134–41.

Haydon, Graham. "On Being Responsible." *Philosophical Quarterly* 28 (January 1978): 46–57.

Henderson, G. P. "Habit and Reflection in Morality." *Dialogue* (Canada) 9 (January 1970):20–34.

Mew, Peter. "Compulsive Behavior and Sympathetic Concern." *Mind* 89 (April 1980):256–60.

Neely, Wright. "Freedom and Desire." *Philosophical Review* 83 (January 1974):32–54.

Sankowski, Edward. "Freedom, Determinism and Character." *Mind* 89 (January 1980):106–13.

———. "Responsibility of Persons for Their Emotions." *Canadian Journal of Philosophy* 7 (December 1977): 829–40.

Slote, Michael A. "Understanding Free Will." *Journal of Philosophy* 77 (March 1980): 136–50.

Strawson, P. F. "Freedom and Resentment." *Proceedings of the British Academy* 48 (1962):187–211. Reprinted in *Studies in the Philosophy of Thought and Action*, edited by P. F. Strawson, 71–96. Oxford, England: Oxford University Press, 1968.

Taylor, Charles. "Responsibility for Self." In *The Identities of Persons*, edited by Amelie Oksenberg Rorty, 281–300. Berkeley: University of California Press, 1976.

Taylor, Paul W. "Moral Virtue and Responsibility for Character." *Analysis* 25 (October 1964):17–23.

Watson, Gary. "Free Agency." *Journal of Philosophy* 72 (April 24, 1975):205–20.

Wolf, Susan. "Asymmetrical Freedom." *Journal of Philosophy* 77 (March 1980):151–65.

Zimmerman, David. "Hierarchical Motivation and Freedom of the Will." *Pacific Philosophical Quarterly* 62 (October 1981): 354–68.

9.3　Happiness, Eudaimonism

Attfield, Robin. "On Being Human." *Inquiry* 17 (Summer 1974):175–92.

Austin, Jean. "Pleasure and Happiness." *Philosophy* 43 (January 1968):51–62.

Benditt, Theodore M. "Happiness." *Philosophical Studies* 25 (January 1974):1–20.

———. "Happiness and Satisfaction—A Rejoinder to Carson." *The Personalist* 59 (January 1978):108–9.

Campbell, Richmond. "The Pursuit of Happiness." *The Personalist* 53 (Autumn 1973): 325–39.

Carson, Thomas. "Happiness and Contentment: A Reply to Benditt." *The Personalist* 59 (January 1978):101–7.

———. "Happiness and the Good Life." *Southwestern Journal of Philosophy* 9 (Fall 1978):73–88.

———. "Happiness and the Good Life: A Rejoinder to Mele." *Southwestern Journal of Philosophy* 10 (Summer 1979):189–92.

———. "Happiness, Contentment and the Good Life." *Pacific Philosophical Quarterly* 62 (October 1981):378–92.

Davis, Wayne. "Pleasure and Happiness." *Philosophical Studies* 39 (April 1981):305–17.

———. "A Theory of Happiness." *American Philosophical Quarterly* 18 (April 1981): 111–20.

Den Uyl, Douglas J., and Tibor R. Machan. "Recent Work on the Concept of Happiness." *American Philosophical Quarterly* 20 (April 1983):115–34.

Friedman, R. Z. "Virtue and Happiness: Kant and Three Critics." *Canadian Journal of Philosophy* 11 (March 1981):95–110.

Goldstein, Irwin. "Happiness: The Role of Non-Hedonic Criteria in Its Evaluation." *International Philosophical Quarterly* 13 (1973):523–34.

Green, T. M. "Life, Value, Happiness." *Journal of Philosophy* 53 (1956):317–30.

Hagberg, Garry. "Understanding Happiness." *Mind* 93 (October 1984):589–91.

Kekes, John. "Happiness." *Mind* 91 (July 1982):358–76.

———. "Human Nature and Moral Theories." *Inquiry* 28 (June 1985):231–45.

Kraut, Richard. "Two Conceptions of Happiness." *Philosophical Review* 88 (April 1979):167–97.

McDonald, R. C. "Pursuing Happiness." *The Personalist* 58 (April 1977):179–81.

McFall, Lynne. "Happiness, Rationality, and Individual Ideals." *Review of Metaphysics* 38 (March 1984):595–613.

McShea, Robert J. "Human Nature Ethical Theory." *Philosophy and Phenomenological Research* 39 (March 1979):386–401.

Mele, Alfred R. "On 'Happiness and the Good Life'." *Southwestern Journal of Philosophy* 10 (Summer 1979):181–87.

Meynell, H. "Human Flourishing." *Religious Studies* 5 (1969):147–54.

Midgley, Mary. "Human Ideals and Human Needs." *Philosophy* 58 (January 1983): 89–94.

Montague, Roger. "Happiness." *Proceedings of the Aristotelian Society* 67 (1967):87–102.

Moravcsik, J.M.E. "On What We Aim At and How We Live." In *The Greeks and the Good Life*, edited by David Depew, 198–235. Indianapolis: Hackett, 1981.

Norton, David L. *Personal Destinies: A Philosophy of Ethical Individualism*. Princeton: Princeton University Press, 1976.

————. "Social Entailments of the Theory of Self-Actualization." *Journal of Value Inquiry* 7 (Summer 1973):106–20.

————, and Mary K. Norton. "From Law to Love: Social Order as Self-Realization." *Journal of Value Inquiry* 6 (Summer 1972):91–101.

Scruton, Roger. "Reason and Happiness." In *Nature and Conduct*, edited by R. S. Peters, 139–61. New York: Macmillan, 1975.

Simpson, R. W. "Happiness." *American Philosophical Quarterly* 12 (April 1975):169–76.

Slote, Michael A. "Goods and Lives." *Pacific Philosophical Quarterly* 63 (October 1982): 311–26.

Tatarkiewicz, Wladyslaw. *Analysis of Happiness*. Amsterdam: Martinus Nijhoff, 1976.

————. "Happiness and Time." *Philosophy and Phenomenological Research* 27 (January 1966):1–10.

Theron, Stephen. "Happiness and Eternal Happiness." *Religious Studies* 21 (September 1985):349–67.

Thomas, D.A.L. "Happiness." *Philosophical Quarterly* 18 (1968):97–113.

Walhout, Donald. "Human Nature and Value Theory." *Thomist* 44 (April 1980):278–97.

White, David. "Human Perfection in the Bhagavadgita." *Philosophy East and West* 21 (January 1971):43–53.

Wilson, John. "Happiness." *Analysis* 29 (January 1968):13–21.

9.4 Motivational Structures

Benson, John. "The Characterization of Actions and the Virtuous Agent." *Proceedings of the Aristotelian Society* 63 (1963):251–66.

————. "Varieties of Desires." *Proceedings of the Aristotelian Society, Supplementary Volume* 50 (1976):177–92.

Dent, N.J.H. *The Moral Psychology of the Virtues*. Cambridge, England: Cambridge University Press, 1984.

————. "Varieties of Desires." *Proceedings of the Aristotelian Society, Supplementary Volume* 50 (1976):153–75.

de Sousa, Ronald B. "The Rationality of Emotions." *Dialogue* (Canada) 18 (March 1979):41–63.

Fisher, Mark. "Reason, Emotion, and Love." *Inquiry* 20 (Summer 1977):189–203.

Frankfurt, H. G. "Identification and Externality." In *The Identities of Persons*, edited by Amelie Oksenberg Rorty, 239–52. Berkeley: University of California Press, 1976.

Green, O. H. "Obligations Regarding Passions." *The Personalist* 60 (April 1979):134–38.

Kamler, Howard. "Strong Feelings." *Journal of Value Inquiry* 19 (1985):3–12.

Kelly, Jack. "Virtue and Pleasure." *Mind* 82 (July 1973):401–8.

Leighton, Stephen R. "A New View of Emotion." *American Philosophical Quarterly* 22 (April 1985):133–42.

Locke, Don. "Beliefs, Desires and Reasons for Action." *American Philosophical Quarterly* 19 (July 1982):241–50.

MacIntyre, Alasdair. "How Moral Agents Became Ghosts, or Why the History of Ethics Diverged From That of the Philosophy of Mind." *Synthese* 53 (November 1982): 295–312.

Morton, Adam. "Character and the Emotions." In *Explaining Emotions*, edited by Amelie Oksenberg Rorty, 153–62. Berkeley: University of California Press, 1980.

Neblett, William R. "The Ethics of Guilt." *Journal of Philosophy* 71 (October 24, 1974):652–62.

Neu, Jerome. *Emotion, Thought and Therapy*. Boston: Routledge and Kegan Paul, 1977.

Roberts, Robert C. "Solomon On the Control of the Emotions." *Philosophy and Phenomenological Research* 44 (March 1984):395–404.

Robinson, Jenefer. "Emotion, Judgment, and Desire." *Journal of Philosophy* 80 (November 1983):731–40.

Rorty, Amelie O. "Explaining Emotions." *Journal of Philosophy* 75 (March 1978):139–61. Reprinted in *Explaining Emotions*, edited by Amelie Oksenberg Rorty, 103–26. Berkeley: University of California Press, 1980.

————. "From Passions to Emotions and Sentiments." *Philosophy* 57 (April 1982): 159–72.

Scheffler, Israel. "In Praise of the Cognitive Emotions." In *Science and Subjectivity*. 2d ed. Indianapolis: Hackett Publishing Company, 1982, 139–57.

Solomon, Robert C. "Emotions and Choice." *Review of Metaphysics* 27 (September 1973):20–41. Expanded version in *Explaining Emotions*, edited by Amelie Oksenberg Rorty, 251–82. Berkeley: University of California Press, 1980.

————. *The Passions: The Myth and Nature of Human Emotions*. New York: Anchor Press, 1976.

Stocker, Michael. "Psychic Feelings: Their Importance and Irreducibility." *Australasian Journal of Philosophy* 61 (March 1983):5–26.

Taylor, Gabriele. "Justifying the Emotions." *Mind* 84 (July 1975):390–402.

Taylor, Gabriele, and Sybil Wolfram. "Virtues and Passions." *Analysis* 31 (January 1971):76–83.

Walsh, W. H. "Pride, Shame and Responsibility." *Philosophical Quarterly* 20 (January 1970):1–13.

Whiteley, C. H. "Love, Hate and Emotion." *Philosophy* 54 (April 1979):235.

Wick, Warner. "The Rat and the Squirrel, or The Rewards of Virtue." *Ethics* 82 (October 1971):21–32.

Williams, Bernard. "Internal and External Reasons." In *Rational Action*, edited by Ross Harrison, 17–28. Cambridge, England: Cambridge University Press, 1979.

————. "Morality and Emotions." In *Problems of the Self*. Cambridge, England: Cambridge University Press, 1973:207–29.

————. "Persons, Character, and Morality." In *The Identities of Persons*, edited by Amelie Oksenberg Rorty, 197–216. Berkeley: University of California Press, 1976.

Wollheim, Richard. "On Persons and Their Lives." In *Explaining Emotions*, edited by Amelie Oksenberg Rorty, 299–322. Berkeley: University of California Press, 1980.

————. "The Moral Psychology of British Idealism and the English School of Psychoanalysis Compared." *Proceedings of the British Academy* 61 (1975):373–98.

9.5   Practical Reasoning

Barbour, John D. *Tragedy as a Critique of Virtue: The Novel and Ethical Reflection*. Chico, Cal.: Scholars Press, 1984.

————. "Tragedy and Ethical Reflection." *Journal of Religion* 63 (January 1983):1–25.

Brown, Harold I. "On Being Rational." *American Philosophical Quarterly* 15 (October 1978):241–48.

Burrell, David, and Stanley Hauerwas. "From System to Story: An Alternative Pattern for Rationality in Ethics." In *The Roots of Ethics*, edited by Daniel Callahan and H. Tristram Engelhardt, Jr., 75–116. New York: Plenum, 1976.

Cooper, John M. *Reason and the Human Good in Aristotle*. Cambridge, Mass.: Harvard University Press, 1975.

Gibbs, Benjamin. "Virtue and Reason." *Proceedings of the Aristotelian Society, Supplementary Volume* 48 (1974):23–41.

Harman, Gilbert. "Practical Reasoning." *Review of Metaphysics* 29 (March 1976):431–63.

Jackson, Jennifer. "Virtues With Reason." *Philosophy* 53 (April 1978):229–46.

McDowell, John. "Virtue and Reason." *The Monist* 62 (July 1979):331–50.

Nussbaum, Martha. "Aeschylus and Practical Conflict." *Ethics* 95 (January 1985):233–67.

Raz, J. "Reasons for Action, Decisions and Norms." *Mind* 84 (October 1975):431–99.

Sapontzis, S. F. "Moral Value and Reason." *The Monist* 66 (January 1983):146–59.

Weston, Michael. *Morality and the Self*. New York: New York University Press, 1975.

9.6   Self-Deception

Audi, Robert. "Self-Deception, Action and Will." *Erkenntnis* 18 (September 1982):133–58.

————. "Self-Deception and Rationality." In *Self-Deception and Self-Understanding*, edited by Mike W. Martin, 169–94. Lawrence, Kan.: University Press of Kansas, 1985.

Bach, Kent. "An Analysis of Self-Deception." *Philosophy and Phenomenological Research* 41 (March 1981):351–70.

————. "More on Self-Deception." *Philosophy and Phenomenological Research* 45 (June 1985):611–14.

Bok, Sissela. "The Self Deceived." *Social Science Information* 19 (Summer 1980):923–35.

Champlin, T. S. "Self-Deception: A Reflexive Dilemma." *Philosophy* 52 (1977):281–99.

Demos, Raphael. "Lying to Oneself." *Journal of Philosophy* 57 (1960):588–95.

de Sousa, Ronald B. "Self-Deceptive Emotions." *Journal of Philosophy* 75 (November 1978):684–96.

Factor, R. Lance. "Self-Deception and the Functionalist Theory of Mental Processes." *The Personalist* 58 (April 1977):115–23.

Fingarette, Herbert. *Self-Deception*. New York: Humanities Press, 1969.

Gardiner, Patrick. "Error, Faith, and Self-Deception." *Proceedings of the Aristotelian Society* 70 (1969–70):197–220.

Haight, M. R. *A Study of Self-Deception*. Sussex, England: Harvester Press, 1980.

Hamlyn, D. W. "Self-Deception." *Proceedings of the Aristotelian Society* 45 (1971):45–60.

Hauerwas, Stanley, and David Burrell. "Self-Deception and Autobiography: Reflections on Speer's *Inside the Third Reich*." *Journal of Religious Ethics* 2 (Spring 1974):99–118. Reprinted in *Truthfulness and Tragedy: Further Investigations into Christian Ethics*, edited by Stanley Hauerwas, Richard Bondi, and David Burrell, 82–98. Notre Dame, Ind.: University of Notre Dame Press, 1977.

Hellman, Nathan. "Bach on Self-Deception." *Philosophy and Phenomenological Research* 44 (September 1983):113–20.

King-Farlow, John, and Richard Bosley. "Self-Formation and the Mean (Programmatic Remarks on Self-Deception." In *Self-Deception and Self Understanding*, edited by Mike W. Martin, 195–220. Lawrence, Kan.: University Press of Kansas, 1985.

Kipp, David. "On Self-Deception." *Philosophical Quarterly* 30 (October 1980):305–17.

————. "Self-Deception, Inauthenticity, and Weakness of Will." In *Self-Deception and Self Understanding*, edited by Mike W. Martin, 261–84. Lawrence, Kan.: University Press of Kansas, 1985.

Linehan, Elizabeth A. "Ignorance, Self-Deception and Moral Accountability." *Journal of Value Inquiry* 16 (1982):101–15.

Martin, Michael W. "Immorality and Self-Deception: A Reply to Bela Szabados." *Dialogue* (Canada) 16 (June 1977):274–80.

————. "Morality and Self-Deception: Paradox, Ambiguity, or Vagueness?" *Man and World* 12 (1979):47–60.

————. "Self-Deception, Self-Pretence, and Emotional Detachment." *Mind* 88 (July 1979):441–46.

————, ed. *Self-Deception and Self Understanding*. Lawrence, Kan.: University Press of Kansas, 1985.

Mele, Alfred R. "Self-Deception, Action and Will: Comments." *Erkenntnis* 18 (September 1982):159–64.

Miri, M. "Self-Deception." *Philosophy and Phenomenological Research* 34 (1974):576–85.

Mounce, H. O. "Self-Deception." *Proceedings of the Aristotelian Society, Supplementary Volume* 45 (1971):61–72.

Palmer, Anthony. "Characterizing Self-Deception." *Mind* 88 (January 1979):45–58.

Paluch, Stanley. "Self-Deception." *Inquiry* 10 (1967):268–78.

Paskow, Alan. "Toward a Theory of Self-Deception." *Man and World* 12 (1979):178–91.

Peterman, James. "Self-Deception and the Problem of Avoidance." *Southern Journal of Philosophy* 21 (Winter 1983):565–74.

Pugmire, David. "'Strong' Self-Deception." *Inquiry* 12 (1969):339–46.

Reilly, Richard. "Self-Deception: Resolving the Epistemological Paradox." *The Personalist* 57 (Fall 1976):391–94.

Rorty, Amelie O. "Belief and Self-Deception." *Inquiry* 15 (Winter 1972):387–410.

———. "Self-Deception, Akrasia, and Irrationality." *Social Science Information* 19 (Summer 1980):905–22.

Ross, Jeffrey. "Rethinking Self-Deception." *American Philosophical Quarterly* 17 (July 1980):237–44.

Saunders, John Turk. "The Paradox of Self-Deception." *Philosophy and Phenomenological Research* 35 (June 1975):559–70.

Siegler, F. A. "Demos on Lying to Oneself." *Journal of Philosophy* 59 (1962):469–75.

Snyder, C. R. "Collaborative Companions: The Relationship of Self-Deception and Excuse Making." In *Self-Deception and Self Understanding*, edited by Mike W. Martin, 35–51. Lawrence, Kan.: University Press of Kansas, 1985.

Sorensen, Roy A. "Self-Deception and Scattered Events." *Mind* 94 (January 1985): 64–69.

Szabados, Bela. "The Morality of Self-Deception." *Dialogue* (Canada) 13 (March 1974): 25–34.

———. "Rorty on Belief and Self-Deception." *Inquiry* 17 (Winter 1974):464–74.

———. "Self-Deception." *Canadian Journal of Philosophy* 4 (September 1974):51–68.

———. "The Self, Its Passions and Self-Deception." In *Self-Deception and Self Understanding*, edited by Mike W. Martin, 143–68. Lawrence, Kan.: University Press of Kansas, 1985.

9.7 Self-Respect, Self-Esteem

Baron, Marcia. "Servility, Critical Deference and the Deferential Wife." *Philosophical Studies* 48 (November 1985):393–400.

Boxill, Bernard R. "Self-Respect and Protest." *Philosophy and Public Affairs* 6 (Fall 1976): 58–69.

Deigh, John. "Shame and Self-Esteem: A Critique." *Ethics* 93 (January 1983):225–45.

Friedman, Marylin A. "Moral Integrity and the Deferential Wife." *Philosophical Studies* 47 (January 1985):141–51.

Kolnai, Aurel. "Dignity." *Philosophy* 51 (July 1976):251–71.

Massey, Stephen J. "Is Self-Respect a Moral or a Psychological Concept?" *Ethics* 93 (January 1983):246–61.

Penelhum, Terence. "Human Nature and External Desires." *The Monist* 62 (July 1979):304–19.

———. "Self-Identity and Self-Regard." In *The Identities of Persons*, edited by Amelie Oksenberg Rorty, 253–80. Berkeley: University of California Press, 1976.

Sachs, David. "How to Distinguish Self-Respect from Self-Esteem." *Philosophy and Public Affairs* 10 (Fall 1981):346–60.

10.   Saints, Moral Perfection

Baron, Marcia. "On De-Kantianizing the Perfect Moral Person." *Journal of Value Inquiry* 17 (1983):281–93.

Conn, Walter E. "Morality, Religion, and Kohlberg's 'Stage 7'." *International Philosophical Quarterly* 21 (December 1981):379–90.

Cua, A. S. "The Concept of Paradigmatic Individuals in the Ethics of Confucius." *Inquiry* 14 (Summer 1971):41–55.

———. *Dimensions of Moral Creativity*. University Park: The Pennsylvania State University Press, 1978.

Duff, Antony. "Must a Good Man Be Invulnerable?" *Ethics* 86 (July 1976):294–311.

Flanagan, Owen J., Jr. "Admirable Immorality and Admirable Imperfection." *Journal of Philosophy* 83 (January 1986):41–60.

Garside, Christine. "Can a Woman Be Good in the Same Way as a Man?" *Dialogue* (Canada) 10 (September 1971):534–44.

Neville, Robert C. *Soldier, Sage, Saint*. New York: Fordham University Press, 1978.

Pybus, Elizabeth M. "Saints and Heroes." *Philosophy* 57 (April 1982):193–99.

Urmson, J. O. "Saints and Heroes." In *Essays in Moral Philosophy*, edited by A. I. Melden, 198–216. Seattle: University of Washington Press, 1958.

11.   Vices

Barnes, M. W. "Vulgarity." *Ethics* 91 (October 1980):72–83.

Carrier, L. S. "Perversity." *Philosophical Quarterly* 26 (July 1976):229–42.

Dyke, C. "The Vices of Altruism." *Ethics* 81 (April 1971):241–52.

Farber, Leslie. "On Jealousy." *Commentary* 56 (October 1973):50–58.

Farrell, Daniel M. "Jealousy." *The Philosophical Review* 89 (October 1980):527–59.

Isenberg, Arnold. "Natural Pride and Natural Shame." *Philosophy and Phenomenological Research* 10 (September 1949). Reprinted in *Explaining Emotions*, edited by Amelie Oksenberg Rorty, 355–84. Berkeley: University of California Press, 1980.

Kittay, Eva Feder. "On Hypocrisy." *Metaphilosophy* 13 (July/October 1982):277–89.

Koutsouvilis, A. "On Benevolence." *Mind* 85 (July 1976):428–31.

Neu, Jerome. "Jealous Thoughts." In *Explaining Emotions*, edited by Amelie Oksenberg Rorty, 425–64. Berkeley: University of California Press, 1980.

Newman, Jay. "Prejudice as Prejudgment." *Ethics* 90 (October 1979):47–57.

Shklar, Judith N. *Ordinary Vices*. Cambridge, Mass.: Harvard University Press, 1984.

Szabodos, Bela. "Hypocrisy." *Canadian Journal of Philosophy* 9 (June 1979):195–210.

Tanner, Michael. "Sentimentality." *Proceedings of the Aristotelian Society* 77 (1977): 127–47.

12. Definition of Virtue

Attfield, Robin. "Talents, Abilities and Virtues." *Philosophy* 46 (July 1971):255–58.

Bondi, Richard. "The Elements of Character." *Journal of Religious Ethics* 12 (Fall 1984):201–18.

Brandt, Richard B. "Traits of Character: A Conceptual Analysis." *American Philosophical Quarterly* 7 (January 1970):23–37.

Dent, N.J.H. "Virtues and Actions." *Philosophical Quarterly* 25 (October 1975):318–35.

Gert, Bernard. "Virtue and Vice." In *Virtue and Medicine: Explorations in the Character of Medicine*, edited by Earl E. Shelp, 95–109. The Hague: D. Reidel, 1985.

———. "Virtue and Vices." In *The Moral Rules*. New York: Harper and Row, 1970, 150–71.

Hudson, Stephen D. "Character Traits and Desires." *Ethics* 90 (July 1980):539–49.

Hunt, Lester H. "Character and Thought." *American Philosophical Quarterly* 15 (July 1978):177–86.

Hursthouse, Rosalind. "A False Doctrine of the Mean." *Proceedings of the Aristotelian Society* 81 (1980–81):57–72.

Pincoffs, Edmund L. "Two Cheers for Meno: The Definition of the Virtues." In *Virtue and Medicine: Explorations in the Character of Medicine*, edited by Earl E. Shelp, 111–32. The Hague: D. Reidel, 1985.

Taylor, Gabriele, and Sybil Wolfram. "The Self-Regarding and Other-Regarding Virtues." *Philosophical Quarterly* 18 (July 1968):238–48.

Urmson, J. O. "Aristotle's Doctrine of the Mean." *American Philosophical Quarterly* 10 (July 1973):223–30. Reprinted in *Essays on Aristotle's Ethics*, edited by Amelie Oksenberg Rorty, 157–70. Berkeley: University of California Press, 1980.

Vorobej, Mark. "Relative Virtue." *Southern Journal of Philosophy* 22 (Winter 1984): 535–41.

Wallace, James D. "Excellences and Merit." *Philosophical Review* 83 (April 1974):182–99.

Watson, Gary. "Virtues in Excess." *Philosophical Studies* 46 (July 1984):57–74.

13.   Virtues

13.1   Autonomy

Adams, Robert Merrihew. "Autonomy and Theological Ethics." *Religious Studies* 15 (June 1979):191–94.

Bernstein, Mark. "Socialization and Autonomy." *Mind* 92 (January 1983):120–23.

Husak, Douglas N. "Paternalism and Autonomy." *Philosophy and Public Affairs* 10 (Winter 1981):27–46.

Kuflik, Arthur. "The Inalienability of Autonomy." *Philosophy and Public Affairs* 13 (Fall 1984):271–98.

Ladenson, Robert F. "A Theory of Personal Autonomy." *Ethics* 86 (October 1975): 30–48.

Quinn, Philip L. "Religious Obedience and Moral Autonomy." *Religious Studies* 11 (September 1975):265–81.

Young, Robert. "Autonomy and Socialization." *Mind* 89 (October 1980):565–76.

—. "Autonomy and the 'Inner Self.'" *American Philosophical Quarterly* 17 (January 1980):35–44.

—. "The Value of Autonomy." *Philosophical Quarterly* 32 (January 1982):35–44.

13.2   Intellectual

Bell, D. R. "Impartiality and Intellectual Virtue." *Philosophical Quarterly* 15 (July 1965):229–39.

Drengson, Alan R. "The Virtue of Socratic Ignorance." *American Philosophical Quarterly* 18 (July 1981):237–42.

Houlgate, Laurence D. "Virtue Is Knowledge." *The Monist* 54 (January 1970):142–53.

Kekes, John. "Wisdom." *American Philosophical Quarterly* 20 (July 1983):277–86.

Porreco, Rocco E. "Virtue Really Is Knowledge." *Proceedings of the American Catholic Philosophical Society* 54 (1980):189–96.

Roberts, Robert C. "Passion and Reflection." In *International Kierkegaard Commentary: Two Ages*, edited by Robert Perkins, 87–106. Macon, Georgia: Mercer University Press, 1984.

—. "Thinking Subjectively." *International Journal for Philosophy of Religion* 11 (1980):71–92.

Sosa, Ernest. "Knowledge and Intellectual Virtue." *The Monist* 68 (April 1985):226–45.

Stocker, Michael. "Intellectual Desire, Emotion, and Action." In *Explaining Emotions*, edited by Amelie Oksenberg Rorty, 323–38. Berkeley: University of California Press, 1980.

13.3   Substantive and Motivational

Berger, Fred R. "Gratitude." *Ethics* 85 (July 1975):298–309.

Berger, Peter. "On the Obsolescence of the Concept of Honor." *Archives Europeennes de Sociologie* 11 (1970):339–47. Reprinted in *Revisions*, edited by Stanley Hauerwas and Alasdair MacIntyre, 172–81. Notre Dame, Ind.: University of Notre Dame Press, 1983.

Boden, Margaret A. "Optimism." *Philosophy* 41 (October 1966):291–303.

Day, J. P. "Hope." *American Philosophical Quarterly* 6 (April 1969):89–102.

Hunt, Lester H. "Generosity." *American Philosophical Quarterly* 12 (July 1975):235–44.

Kekes, John. "Constancy and Purity." *Mind* 92 (October 1983):499–518.

Nagel, Thomas. *The Possibility of Altruism*. Oxford, England: Oxford University Press, 1970.

Newman, Jay. "Humility and Self-Realization." *Journal of Value Inquiry* 16 (1982): 275–85.

———. "The Idea of Religious Tolerance." *American Philosophical Quarterly* 15 (July 1978):187–95.

Pugmire, David. "Altruism and Ethics." *American Philosophical Quarterly* 15 (January 1978):75–80.

Quinn, Michael Sean. "Hoping." *Southwestern Journal of Philosophy* 7 (Winter 1976): 53–65.

Ross, Angus. "The Status of Altruism." *Mind* 92 (April 1983):204–18.

Weiss, Roslyn. "The Moral and Social Dimensions of Gratitude." *Southern Journal of Philosophy* 23 (Winter 1985):491–502.

13.3.1 Justice

Benditt, Theodore M. "The Demands of Justice." *Ethics* 95 (January 1985):224–32.

Deigh, John. "Love, Guilt, and the Sense of Justice." *Inquiry* 25 (December 1982): 391–416.

Galston, William A. "Moral Personality and Liberal Theory: John Rawls's 'Dewey Lectures.'" *Political Theory* 10 (November 1982):492–519.

Gauthier, David. "Three Against Justice: The Foole, the Sensible Knave, and the Lydian Sheperd." *Midwest Studies in Philosophy* 7 (1982):11–29.

Gibbard, Allan. "Human Evolution and the Sense of Justice." *Midwest Studies in Philosophy* 7 (1982):31–46.

Gutman, Amy. "Communitarian Critics of Liberalism." *Philosophy and Public Policy* 14 (Summer 1985):308–22.

Hestevold, H. Scott. "Disjunctive Desert." *American Philosophical Quarterly* 19 (October 1983):357–63.

———. "Justice to Mercy." *Philosophy and Phenomenological Review* 46 (December 1985):281–91.

Lucas, J. R. "Justice." *Philosophy* 47 (July 1972):229–48.

Norton, David L. "Rawls' Theory of Justice: A 'Perfectionist' Rejoinder." *Ethics* 85 (October 1974):50–57.

Prichard, Michael S. "Rawls' Moral Psychology." *Southwestern Journal of Philosophy* 8 (Winter 1977):59–72.

Rawls, John. *A Theory of Justice*. Cambridge, Mass.: Belknap Press of the Harvard University Press, 1971.

Sandel, Michael J. *Liberalism and the Limits of Justice*. Cambridge, England: Cambridge University Press, 1982.

———. "The Procedural Republic and the Unencumbered Self." *Political Theory* 12 (February 1984):81–96.

Thomas, Laurence. "Beliefs and the Motivation to Be Just." *American Philosophical Quarterly* 22 (October 1985):347–52.

Williams, Bernard. "Justice as a Virtue." In *Essays on Aristotle's Ethics*, edited by Amelie Oksenberg Rorty, 189–200. Berkeley: University of California Press, 1980.

13.3.2   Love

Ashmore, Robert B. "Friendship and the Problem of Egoism." *Thomist* 41 (January 1977):105–30.

Badhwar, Neera K. "Friendship, Justice, and Supererogation." *American Philosophical Quarterly* 22 (April 1985):123–32.

Baier, Annette C. "Caring About Caring: A Reply to Frankfurt." *Synthese* 53 (November 1982):273–90. Reprinted in *Postures of the Mind: Essays on Mind and Morals*. Minneapolis: University of Minnesota Press, 1985, 93–108.

———. "Trust and Antitrust." *Ethics* 96 (January 1986):231–60.

Betz, Joseph. "The Relation Between Love and Justice: A Survey of Five Possible Positions." *Journal of Value Inquiry* 4 (Fall 1970):191–203.

Blum, Lawrence C. *Friendship, Altruism, and Morality*. Boston: Routledge and Kegan Paul, 1980.

Cooper, John M. "Aristotle on Friendship." In *Essays on Aristotle's Ethics*, edited by Amelie Oksenberg Rorty, 301–40. Berkeley: University of California Press, 1980.

Dalcourt, Gerard. "Agape as a Cardinal Virtue." *Proceedings of the American Catholic Philosophical Association* 43 (1969):165–70.

Ehman, Robert R. "Personal Love and Individual Value." *Journal of Value Inquiry* 10 (Summer 1976):91–105.

Eshete, Andreas. "Fraternity." *Review of Metaphysics* 35 (September 1981):27–44.

Frankena, William K. "The Ethics of Love Conceived as an Ethics of Virtue." *Journal of Religious Ethics* 1 (Fall 1973):21–36.

———. "Conversations with Carney and Hauerwas." *Journal of Religious Ethics* 3 (Spring 1975):45–62.

Frankfurt, H. G. "The Importance of What We Care About." *Synthese* 53 (November 1982):257–72.

Homiak, Marcia L. "Virtue and Self-Love in Aristotle's Ethics." *Canadian Journal of Philosophy* 11 (December 1981):633–51.

Lewis, C. S. *The Four Loves*. New York: Harcourt Brace Jovanovich, 1960.

MacIntyre, Alasdair. "Comments on Frankfurt's 'The Importance of What We Care About.'" *Synthese* 53 (November 1982):291–94.

Mayeroff, Milton. *On Caring*. New York: Perennial Library, 1971.

Meilaender, Gilbert C. *Friendship: A Study in Theological Ethics*. Notre Dame, Ind.: University of Notre Dame Press, 1981.

Nakhnikian, George. "Love in Human Reason." *Midwest Studies in Philosophy* 3 (1980):286–317.

Oldenquist, Andrew. "Loyalties." *Journal of Philosophy* 79 (April 1982):173–93.

Reeder, John P. "Assenting to Agape." *Journal of Religion* 60 (January 1980):17–31.

Ryle, Gilbert. "On Forgetting the Difference Between Right and Wrong." In *Collected Papers*, Volume II. London: Hutchinson, 1971.

Scheman, Naomi. "On Sympathy." *The Monist* 62 (July 1979):320–30.

Schoeman, Ferdinand. "Aristotle on the Good of Friendship." *Australasian Journal of Philosophy* 63 (September 1985):269–82.

Stafford, J. Martin. "On Distinguishing Between Love and Lust." *Journal of Value Inquiry* 11 (Winter 1977):292–303.

Stocker, Michael. "Values and Purposes: The Limits of Teleology and the Ends of Friendship." *Journal of Philosophy* 78 (December 1981):747–65.

Warner, Martin. "Love, Self and Plato's *Symposium*." *Philosophical Quarterly* 29 (October 1979):329–39.

Whittaker, John H. "Selfishness, Self-Concern and Happiness." *Journal of Religious Ethics* 8 (Spring 1980):149–59.

13.3.3 Prudence

Bricker, Phillip. "Prudence." *Journal of Philosophy* 77 (July 1980):381–400.

Broughton, Janet. "The Possibility of Prudence." *Philosophical Studies* 43 (March 1983):253–66.

Davie, William E. "Being Prudent and Acting Prudently." *American Philosophical Quarterly* 10 (January 1973):57–60.

Foley, Richard. "Prudence and the Desire Theory of Reasons." *Journal of Value Inquiry* 12 (1978):68–73.

Horsbrugh, H.J.N. "Prudence." *Proceedings of the Aristotelian Society, Supplementary Volume* 36 (1962):65–76.

Hubin, D. Clayton. "Prudential Reasons." *Canadian Journal of Philosophy* 10 (March 1980):63–81.

Kraut, Richard. "The Rationality of Prudence." *Philosophical Review* 81 (July 1972): 351–59.

Mabbott, J. D. "Prudence." *Proceedings of the Aristotelian Society, Supplementary Volume* 36 (1962):51–64.

McInerny, Ralph. "Prudence and Conscience." *Thomist* 38 (April 1974):291–305.

Rotenstreich, Nathan. "Prudence and Folly." *American Philosophical Quarterly* 22 (April 1985):93–104.

13.4   Theological

Adams, Robert M. "Pure Love." *Journal of Religious Ethics* 8 (Spring 1980):83–99.

———. "The Virtue of Faith." *Faith and Philosophy* 1 (January 1984):3–15.

Barbour, John D. "Religious 'Ressentiment' and Public Virtues." *Journal of Religious Ethics* 11 (Fall 1983):264–79.

Camenisch, Paul. "Gift and Gratitude in Ethics." *Journal of Religious Ethics* 9 (1981):1–34.

Cua, A. S. "Reflections on the Structure of Confucian Ethics." *Philosophy East and West* 21 (April 1971):189–94.

Dunbar, Scott. "On God and Virtue." *Religious Studies* 18 (December 1982):489–502.

Evans, Donald. *Faith, Authenticity, and Morality*. Toronto: University of Toronto Press, 1980.

———. *Struggle and Fulfillment: The Inner Dynamics of Religion and Morality*. Philadelphia: Fortress Press, 1979.

Gardner, E. Clinton. "Character, Virtue, and Responsibility in Theological Ethics." *Encounter* 44 (Autumn 1983):315–39.

Green, Ronald. "Jewish Ethics and the Virtue of Humility." *Journal of Religious Ethics* 1 (Fall 1973):53–64.

Gustafson, James M. *Christ and the Moral Life*. Chicago: University of Chicago Press, 1968.

———. *Christian Ethics and the Community*. Philadelphia: Pilgrim Press, 1971.

Harned, David Baily. *Faith and Virtue*. Philadelphia: United Church Press, 1973.

Harrison, Jonathan. "Be Ye Therefore Perfect or The Ineradicability of Sin." *Religious Studies* 21 (March 1985):1–19.

———. "Christian Virtues." *Proceedings of the Aristotelian Society, Supplementary Volume* 37 (1963):69–82.

Hauerwas, Stanley. *Character and the Christian Life: A Study in Theological Ethics*. San Antonio: Trinity University Press, 1975.

———. *A Community of Character*. Notre Dame, Ind.: University of Notre Dame Press, 1981.

————. *Vision and Virtue*. Notre Dame, Ind.: University of Notre Dame Press, 1981.

Hauerwas, Stanley, Richard Bondi, and David B. Burrell. *Truthfulness and Tragedy: Further Investigations into Christian Ethics*. Notre Dame, Ind.: University of Notre Dame Press, 1977.

Kruschwitz, Robert B. "Christian Virtues and the Mean." *Faith and Philosophy* 3 (October 1986).

Kupperman, Joel J. "Confucious and the Nature of Religious Ethics." *Philosophy East and West* 21 (April 1971):189–94.

Lewis, C. S. *Mere Christianity*. New York: Macmillan, 1943.

McPherson, T. H. "Christian Virtues." *Proceedings of the Aristotelian Society, Supplementary Volume* 37 (1963):51–68.

Meilaender, Gilbert C. "Josef Pieper: Explorations in the Thought of a Philosopher of Virtue." *Journal of Religious Ethics* 11 (Spring 1983):114–34.

————. "The Virtues: A Theological Analysis." In *Virtue and Medicine: Explorations in the Character of Medicine*, edited by Earl E. Shelp, 151–74. The Hague: D. Reidel, 1985.

Mitchell, Donald W. "Faith in Zen Buddhism." *International Philosophical Quarterly* 20 (June 1980):183–98.

Muyskens, James. "What Is Virtuous About Faith?" *Faith and Philosophy* 2 (January 1985):43–52.

Niebuhr, H. Richard. "Reflections on Faith, Hope and Love." *Journal of Religious Ethics* 2 (Spring 1974):151–56.

Outka, Gene. *Agape: An Ethical Analysis*. New Haven: Yale University Press, 1972.

Roberts, Robert C. "Carl Rogers and the Christian Virtues." *Journal of Psychology and Theology* 13 (1985):263–73.

————. *Spirituality and Human Emotion*. Grand Rapids, Michigan: William B. Eerdmans, 1982.

————. *The Strengths of a Christian*. Philadelphia: Westminster Press, 1984.

Sokolowski, Robert. "Natural Virtue" and "Theological Virtue." In *The God of Faith and Reason*. Notre Dame, Ind.: University of Notre Dame Press, 1982.

Streng, Frederick J. "Three Approaches to Authentic Existence: Christian, Confucian, and Buddhist." *Philosophy East and West* 32 (October 1982):371–92.

Taylor, Richard. *Ethics, Faith, and Reason*. Englewood Cliffs, N.J.: Prentice-Hall, 1985.

Yearley, Lee H. "The Nature-Grace Question in the Context of Fortitude." *Thomist* 35 (October 1971):557–80.

13.4.1   Forgiveness, Mercy

Beatty, Joseph. "Forgiveness." *American Philosophical Quarterly* 7 (July 1970):246–52.

Card, Claudia. "On Mercy." *Philosophical Review* 81 (April 1972):182–207.

Downie, R. S. "Forgiveness." *Philosophical Quarterly* 15 (April 1965):128–34.

Hauerwas, Stanley. "Constancy and Forgiveness: The Novel as a School for Virtue [A Trollope]." *Notre Dame English Journal* 15 (1983):23–54.

Horsbrugh, H.J.N. "Forgiveness." *Canadian Journal of Philosophy* 4 (December 1974): 269–82.

Kolnai, Aurel. "Forgiveness." *Proceedings of the Aristotelian Society* 74 (1973–74):91–106. Reprinted in *Ethics, Value, and Reality: Selected Papers of Aurel Kolnai*, edited by Bernard Williams and David Wiggins, 211–24. Indianapolis: Hackett, 1978.

Lewis, Meirlys. "On Forgiveness." *Philosophical Quarterly* 30 (July 1980):236–45.

Minas, Anne C. "God and Forgiveness." *Philosophical Quarterly* 25 (April 1975):138–50.

Murphy, Jeffrie G. "Forgiveness and Resentment." *Midwest Studies in Philosophy* 7 (1982):503–16.

Neblett, William R. "Forgiveness and Ideals." *Mind* 83 (April 1974):269–75.

O'Driscoll, Lyla H. "The Quality of Mercy." *Southern Journal of Philosophy* 21 (Summer 1983):229–52.

Smart, Alwynne. "Mercy." *Philosophy* 43 (October 1968):345–59.

Twambley, P. "Mercy and Forgiveness." *Analysis* 36 (January 1976):84–90.

13.5   Will Power

Arras, John D. "A Critique of Sartrean Authenticity." *The Personalist* 57 (Spring 1976):171–80.

Botros, Sophie. "Acceptance and Morality." *Philosophy* 58 (October 1983):433–53.

Campbell, Keith. "Self-Mastery and Stoic Ethics." *Philosophy* 60 (July 1985):327–40.

Dent, N.J.H. "The Ideal of Sincerity: Notes on a Footnote." *Mind* 89 (July 1980): 418–19.

———. "The Value of Courage." *Philosophy* 56 (October 1981):574–77.

Gaita, Raimond. "Integrity." *Proceedings of the Aristotelian Society* 55 (1981):160–76.

Hunt, Lester H. "Courage and Principle." *Canadian Journal of Philosophy* 10 (June 1980):281–93.

Mayo, Bernard. "Moral Integrity." In *Human Values*, edited by Godfrey Vesey, 27–43. Atlantic Highlands, N.J.: Humanities Press, 1978.

Pears, David. "Aristotle's Analysis of Courage." *Midwest Studies in Philosophy* 3 (1980): 274–85.

———. "Courage as a Mean." In *Essays on Aristotle's Ethics*, edited by Amelie Oksenberg Rorty, 171–88. Berkeley: University of California Press, 1980.

Quinton, Anthony. "Character and Culture." *The New Republic* 189 (October 17, 1983):26–30.

———. "Character in Real Life." In *Thoughts and Thinkers*. New York: Holmes and Meier, 1982:21–26.

Taylor, Gabriele. "Integrity." *Proceedings of the Aristotelian Society, Supplementary Volume* 55 (1981):143–59.

Walker, A.D.M. "The Ideal of Sincerity." *Mind* 87 (October 1978):481–97.

Winch, Peter. "Moral Integrity." In *Ethics and Action*, edited by Peter Winch. London: Routledge and Kegan Paul, 1972.

13.5.1   Conscience

Bennett, Jonathan. "The Conscience of Huckleberry Finn." *Philosophy* 49 (April 1974):323–33.

Goldstick, D. "Immorality with a Clear Conscience." *American Philosophical Quarterly* 17 (July 1981):245–50.

Govier, Trudy R. "Is Conscientiousness Always—or Ever—a Virtue?" *Dialogue* (Canada) 11 (June 1972):241–51.

Harris, John. "Principles, Sympathy and Doing What's Right." *Philosophy* 52 (January 1977):96–99.

May, Larry. "On Conscience." *American Philosophical Quarterly* 20 (January 1983): 57–68.

Montague, Phillip. "Re-examining Huck Finn's Conscience." *Philosophy* 55 (October 1980):542–46.

Ryle, Gilbert. "Conscience and Moral Convictions." In *Collected Papers*, Volume II. London: Hutchinson, 1971.

Szabodos, Bela. "Butler on a Corrupt Conscience." *Journal of the History of Philosophy* 14 (October 1976):462–9.

Teichman, Jenny. "Mr. Bennett on Huckleberry Finn." *Philosophy* 50 (July 1975): 358–59.

Ward, Keith. "Moral Seriousness." *Philosophy* 45 (April 1970):128–40.